On-Premise Catering

HOTELS,

CONVENTION &
CONFERENCE CENTERS,

and

CLUBS

Patti J. Shock
John M. Stefanelli
University of Nevada, Las Vegas

JOHN WILEY & SONS, INC.

New York   Chichester   Weinheim   Brisbane   Singapore   Toronto

This book is printed on acid-free paper. ∞

This publication is designed to provide accurate and authoritative information in regard to the subject matter covered. It is sold with the understanding that the publisher is not engaged in rendering professional services. If professional advice or other expert assistance is required, the services of a competent professional person should be sought.

Library of Congress Cataloging-in-Publication Data

Shock, Patti J.
  On-premise catering / by Patti J. Shock and John M. Stefanelli.
     p. cm.
  ISBN 0-471-38908-0 (cloth: alk. paper)
  1. Caterers and catering—Handbooks, manuals, etc.   I. Stefanelli, John M.   II. Title.

TX921 .S48 2001
642'.4—dc21

                                                                        00-036820

Printed in the United States of America

10 9 8 7 6 5 4 3 2 1

Contents

Foreword   vii
Preface   ix

Chapter 1   Overview of On-Premise Catering   **1**
Types of Catering   3
Types of Caterers   3
Catering Department Management Functions   6
Catering Department Objectives   6
Catering Department Organization   7
Catering Department Policies   19
Major Challenges Faced by a Catering Department   23

Chapter 2   Markets and Marketing   **27**
Business Market   28
Business Market Events   30
Special Events—Social Market   34
Client Decision Makers   38
The Marketing Plan   41
The Marketing Budget   44

iii

Marketing Research   47

The Four P's of Marketing   51

Sales Procedures   79

Identifying Your Markets and How to Reach Them   96

Marketing Tools   96

Client Relations   98

Relationship Marketing   99

Telephone Marketing   100

Value   102

Up$elling   103

Space Utilization   104

Chapter 3   Theme Parties, Weddings, Outdoor Parties, and Other Special Events   **109**

Theme Parties   110

Weddings   119

Outdoor Parties   138

Bar and Bat Mitzvahs   142

Chapter 4   Meal Functions   **143**

Purpose of a Meal Function   144

Menu Planning   144

Truth-in-Menu Guidelines   158

Menu Pricing   162

Tips and Gratuities   162

Types of Meal Functions   165

Off-Premise Catering   176

Chapter 5   Beverage Functions   **181**

Purpose of the Beverage Function   181

Menu Planning   183

Menu Pricing   186

Types of Beverage Functions   194
Liquor Laws   200

Chapter 6   Function Room Selection and Setup   **209**

Appearance   209
Location   212
Utilities   212
Space Requirements   213
Planning the Function Room Setup   222

Chapter 7   Production and Service Planning   **249**

Production Planning   249
Service Planning   267
Catering Safety and Sanitation   280

Chapter 8   Intermediaries and Suppliers   **287**

Providing Other Client Services   288
Audiovisual Services   294
Entertainment   310
Lighting   312
Intermediaries   313

Chapter 9   Staffing   **321**

Employee Recruitment   322
Orientation   331
Training   331
Compensation   337

Chapter 10   Financial Controls and Reports   **339**

Control Documents   341
Credit Management   348
Postevent Management   352
Food and Beverage-Cost Control   352

Payroll-Cost Control   367

Control of Other Expenses   372

Computerized Control Procedures   373

Chapter 11   Working with Other Departments   **377**

Kitchen   378

Beverage   379

Purchasing   379

Receiving and Storeroom   380

Housekeeping   381

Convention Service   382

Maintenance   386

Engineering   387

Property Manager   388

Steward   388

Print Shop   389

Room Service   390

Human Resources   390

Controller   392

Security   393

Sales   394

Front Office   395

Audiovisual   397

Recreation   398

Entertainment   398

Business Services   399

Glossary   *401*

Appendix   *415*

Index   *429*

Foreword

Throughout human history, no festive event or gathering has happened without the serving of food and beverages and providing some kind of entertainment. Someone was needed to pull all of the details together and ensure that the guests left happy and the host was pleased with the results. This "someone" has evolved into today's catering executive, an accomplished individual who must be able to coordinate and translate wishes into reality. The mental picture he or she draws for the client must be transformed into reality. He or she must be able to coordinate the timing of florists, entertainers, decorators, setup crews, electricians, culinary and service staffs, and many others to a fine-tuned precision that culminates in a perfect event for the host or hostess.

Until the early 1990s, formal studies in the catering field were rather difficult to come by, inasmuch as few, if any, colleges offered classes related to this exciting career field. Fortunately, the situation is changing and this book is an excellent vehicle to assist students to develop into competent catering executives. It is my sincere hope, wish, and even dream, to someday see a university offering a bachelor's degree in Catering/Convention Services. This profession has become extremely versatile and demands not only technical expertise and superb human relations capabilities, but also a healthy dose of strong work ethics, creativity, and imagination.

The authors have researched the subject matter thoroughly and addressed the many different aspects of catering, combining their experiences in catering and as educators on the university level. Leading members of the National Association of Catering Executives (NACE) have generously contributed their time and talents, providing input from their day-to-day experiences to make this book as authentic as possible. Therefore, this book dispels the notion that a caterer is someone who cooks food in his or her kitchen, loads it into the trunk of a car, and drops it off at a client's house. Today's catering executive must be educated not only in the culinary arts, but also in accounting procedures, logistical planning, the properties and use of wine and other beverages, etiquette and protocol, various computer software programs, religious dietary laws, salesmanship, customer service, and a number of other essentials. The word *no* is not part of a catering executive's vocabulary. Above all, we must remember that this is a "people" business, and with the kaleidoscope of personalities, races, and religions in our society, the successful catering executive is the one who recognizes, honors, and values the vast diversity of the public and strives to meet its needs and wishes.

Business practices, computer programs, and trends change in our business, just as in any other. The fundamentals discussed in this book, however, do not change. People want and need to get together for a plethora of reasons. There will always be conventions, weddings, fund-raisers and simply joyous celebrations of various kinds—and there will always be a need for a catering executive.

Nothing is more exciting for a catering executive than to see all of the planning, negotiating, and advance work come together, to stand in the midst of "organized chaos" while supervising the setting up of an event for hundreds or even thousands of guests, and then experience the magic of finally seeing everything in place, to see the doors open and, as the guests enter, to witness the delight and wonder on their faces as they discover a magnificent event unlike any other they have seen. May this book assist you in discovering and pursuing a journey in the catering business. It is a rewarding career, demanding dedication, the pursuit of excellence, and implementation of creativity and imagination.

Peter E. Günther, CMP, CPCE
Director of Convention Catering Sales
Marriott Hotel, Anaheim, California
Past President, National Association of Catering Executives
Founder and Past President, Educational Foundation of NACE

Preface

The catering business continues to grow at an accelerated rate. Statistics show that catering is one of the fastest growing segments of the food and beverage industry and that all sorts of foodservices, from mega-hotels to local restaurant operators, are reaping the rewards.

On-premise catering is especially popular. Patrons are enjoying the advantages and pleasures of catered events and are engaging professional caterers at an ever increasing rate. In fact, in some parts of the country, guests have to book their events well in advance in order to guarantee space.

The objective of this book is to provide all levels of on-premise catering and banquet professionals, as well as aspiring professionals, with an in-depth, one-stop source of generally accepted catering principles and procedures. Armed with this knowledge, it is hoped that readers will be able to increase their opportunities in this exciting and dynamic field.

The book includes several major topics. Readers wishing to gain a perspective of the on-premise catering business will be especially interested in Chapters 1 and 2. Those who want specific information that can be used to plan, develop, implement, supervise, and follow up on a catering function should read and study the remaining chapters.

Chapters 3 through 11 contain an extensive discussion of on-premise catering procedures as well as a considerable amount of col-

reference. This book will assist the reader who needs to know, for example, how many servers to schedule for a particular function, how to price meal and beverage functions, how to develop catering proposals, and how to set up function space. With the incorporation of a companion web site <http://www.wiley.com/college/shock> for this book, the authors hope to give readers the most up-to-date material available.

No one book can claim to be the last word on any subject. Much of the information in the book is open to opinion and interpretation. We believe that the material presented in this volume provides a thorough view of on-premise catering. However, because a book is a living document, subject to revision as our industry changes, we welcome your ideas and suggestions. We are particularly eager to incorporate reader input into our web site.

We want to thank the following reviewers of the manuscript for their important contributions:

Tracey Amernick
Catering Director
Bahia Resort
San Diego, California

Rich Benninger, CMP
Executive Director of
    Catering Sales
MGM Grand Hotel and Casino
Las Vegas, Nevada

Jennifer Fyllingness
Catering Sales Manager
Sunriver, Oregon

Peter E. Günther, CPCE, CMP
Director of Convention
    Catering Sales
Marriott Hotel
Anaheim, California

Elizabeth Kitzman, CMP
Catering Sales Manager
Holiday Inn Town Lake
Austin, Texas

Becky Morgan
Director of Catering and
    Conference Services
Omni Jacksonville Hotel
Jacksonville, Florida

Jane Jaeger Nipps
Vice-President Sales, Marketing &
    Human Resources
MGR Food Services
Atlanta, Georgia

Shelley Pedersen, CPCE
Beyond Cuisine, Inc.
Atlanta, Georgia

Rod Westmaas, CPCE
Rusty Pelican Restaurant
Miami, Florida

Patti J. Shock
John M. Stefanelli
Las Vegas, Nevada
October 2000

Overview of On-Premise Catering

On-premise catering is catering for any function—banquet, reception, or event—that is held on the physical premises of the establishment or facility that is producing the function. On-premise catering differs from off-premise catering, whereby the function takes place in a remote location, such as a client's home, a park, an art gallery, or even a parking lot, and the staff, food, and decor must be transported to that location. Off-premise catering often involves producing food at a central kitchen, with delivery to and service provided at the client's location. Part or all of the production of food may be executed or finished at the event location. At times, off-premise caterers must rely on generators for electricity, truck in potable water, devise a trash system, and otherwise "rough it."

Although some hotels and restaurants offer off-premise catering, most do not "cater-out." A few of them, however, have entered the off-premise catering market and are capable of providing off-site production and service. Exact statistics are not kept for these two functions, but it is estimated that on-premise catering accounts for about two thirds of all catering sales in the United States, with off-premise catering accounting for the remaining third.

Catering, both on-premise and off-premise, is one of the fastest growing segments of the U.S. foodservice industry and has enjoyed success and expansion over the years. The National Restaurant Association (NRA) notes that catering and take-out sales will generate considerable growth in U.S. foodservice sales throughout the foreseeable future.

Every day thousands of business and social groups get together for their members to enjoy each other's company and the variety of refreshments that are usually found at these gatherings. Groups generally prefer professionally prepared and served food and beverages. This allows hosts to concentrate on their personal, social, and business activities, simultaneously enjoying the events. And, as a bonus, they can leave the cleanup to someone else.

On-premise caterers—such as hotels, convention centers, and restaurants—usually have the advantage of offering many services under one roof. They can also provide sufficient space to house an entire event and plenty of parking. In general, each catered event has one host and one bill.

Many localities have independent banquet halls, civic auditoriums, stadiums, arenas, ethnic social clubs, fraternal organizations, women's clubs, private city or country clubs, athletic clubs, hospitals, universities, libraries, executive dining rooms in office buildings or corporate headquarters, churches, recreation rooms in large apartment or condominium complexes, parks, museums, aquariums, and restaurants with banquet rooms. Some of these facilities are often more competitive than hotels, as they have more flexible price structures because of their lower overhead expenses. Some are public facilities and are tax-exempt. A number of these facilities provide their own catering in-house, others are leased to and operated by contract foodservice companies that have exclusive contracts. Still others will rent their facilities to off-premise caterers.

Another recent competitor for catering business has been the proliferation of take-out services. Some supermarkets and department stores have developed gourmet take-out, deli, and bakery facilities, and many can produce beautiful, reasonably priced buffet platters. More and more restaurants are heavily engaged in take-out business, particularly around the holidays. However, if not properly monitored, a "cater-out" can disrupt the normal work flow and efficiency of a restaurant, damage morale, and skew ordering and purchasing routines.

Off-premise functions can be a significant source of additional sales revenue and profits for those hotels and restaurants that have the necessary equipment and personnel to handle large off-site catered affairs. However, unless the facility is set up to do this correctly, the work can be too distracting and the added expense may wipe out any incremental profits. For example, transporting perishable food requires proper trucking for food safety. A refrigerated truck or a great amount of ice must be used to maintain safe temperatures.

Staffing is also an issue. Hotel servers are accustomed to a division of labor and often are not pleased when they are asked to perform tasks off-site that are not required when they are working within the facility. In a hotel, servers do not set up equipment or do the cleaning, hauling, and other duties that are required at an off-premise site. There may also be union implications if job descriptions are violated.

TYPES OF CATERING

Catering can also be classified as social catering and corporate (or business) catering. Social catering includes such events as weddings, bar and bat mitzvahs, high school reunions, birthday parties, and charity events. The National Association of Catering Executives (NACE) estimates that social catering accounts for about 25 percent of all catering sales.

Business catering includes such events as association conventions and meetings, civic meetings, corporate sales or stockholder meetings, recognition banquets, product launches, educational training sessions, seller-buyer entertaining, service awards banquets, and entertaining in hospitality suites. The estimated 75 percent of all catering sales generated by business catering is due to the sheer volume of people served daily at meetings in hotels and convention centers, where meals for thousands are produced regularly.

TYPES OF CATERERS

The hotel caterer is only one of many types of caterers that seek to satisfy the public's catering needs. A hotel usually has the advantage in this competitive field because it can normally offer many services under one roof as well as sufficient space to house an entire event, thereby enticing the customer with a one-stop-shopping opportunity. An upscale hotel often provides a more glamorous and exciting location. The hotel must realize, however, that other caterers abound in the industry, and even though they may be much smaller and unable to offer a smorgasbord of choices, they nevertheless eagerly court many of the same customers sought by hotel caterers.

For instance, in some parts of the country there are independent banquet halls, convention facilities, and conference centers. Some of these properties are able to compete with hotels for the same customers because they have more flexible price structures owing to lower overhead expenses. A hotel may have the advantage in some instances: If a client is able to buy out the entire facility, the hotel can offer a generous price reduction because of the sleeping room revenue derived from the group.

Some restaurant operations have attached banquet rooms that can be used for several types of catered events. It is expensive to maintain a room that may be empty three or four nights per week, so the banquet room is often used as overflow restaurant dining space on busy nights. A restaurant can book many small functions if it takes time to court this business. However, before going after this business, the catering executive must be careful to avoid those catered events that cannot be charged enough to cover all variable and fixed overhead costs associated with opening a function room. For instance, a restaurant that uses a section of its regular dining room to house a catered event will not incur significantly greater heating and cooling expenses; the dining room must be heated or cooled regardless of the number of guests expected. A hotel, however, must consider the feasibility of opening a function room; if the room is opened, incremental heating and cooling expenses will be incurred, whereas if the room remains closed, these expenses are avoidable. In some cases, although a particular group may turn a profit for the average restaurant, a hotel property may be less fortunate.

Private clubs do a great deal of catering for their members. Country clubs concentrate on social events, such as weddings and dances. City clubs specialize in business catering, such as for corporate meetings, board luncheons, and civic events.

Resorts often have outdoor functions at remote locations on the property. For example, The Pointe at Tapatio Cliffs in Phoenix, Arizona, has a special hayride party. Guests are transported via horse-drawn wagon to a hilltop where they enjoy a mountainside steak-fry barbecue with all the trimmings.

Profit-oriented hospitals do a good amount of catering business for medical meetings and staff functions. In most cases, they compete directly with hotels for these functions.

There are several types of tax-exempt organizations that offer catering services to anyone willing to pay for them. For instance, universities, colleges, hospitals, libraries, churches, museums, and military clubs vigorously compete for catering events because they help subsidize their major nonprofit activities. Many tax-paying catering businesses are especially unhappy with these so-called nonprofit competitors; however, nonprofit groups consistently fight any type of government restraints on these activities.

Contract foodservice companies operate many facilities that are capable of supporting catering events. For instance, many of these firms operate foodservices in large office buildings, where executive dining rooms can be used to house special parties and meetings. Some contract foodservice companies are also capable of handling off-premise catering functions.

Most convention centers are public institutions that use in-house contract services typically operated by national catering companies (such as ARAMARK or Fine Host). A few use smaller, privately owned companies (such as the Levy Corporation at McCormick Place in Chicago). These companies function as an internal catering department and enjoy all of the amenities and unique environments offered by the facility. They tend to focus on conventions and trade shows and often have the opportunity to cater mega-events because of the large amount of exhibit space, as well as attached areas (such as public arenas or public parks), available.

Take-out and delivery business accounts for an ever increasing proportion of total U.S. foodservice sales. It is unlikely that a hotel caterer would want to compete in these business segments. However, we have noticed that some hotel properties have done this quite successfully. For example, at Marriott's Camelback Inn in Scottsdale, Arizona, people living next to its golf courses can dial the hotel's room service department. A room service server hops on a catering "golf cart" and delivers the finished products. The hotel also takes orders for box lunches.

Some mobile caterers, with the proper equipment, provide complete meal production and service on location. For instance, a few companies specialize in feeding forest fire fighters, disaster relief workers, movie and television production crews in the field, people taking extended camping trips or fishing/rafting excursions, construction site workers, or other such groups.

CATERING DEPARTMENT MANAGEMENT FUNCTIONS

The person in charge of the catering department must perform the normal management functions. Whether working in a one-person department in a restaurant or in a convention center with a staff of 30, he or she has the following responsibilities:

1 *Planning.*   The catering department must accomplish both financial and nonfinancial objectives. To do so, it must develop appropriate marketing, production, and service procedures. It must also ensure that the department's operating budgets and action plans are consistent with the facility's overall company objectives.

2 *Organizing.*   The catering department must organize the human and other resources needed to follow the plan. Staff members must be recruited and trained. Work schedules must be prepared. And performance evaluations must be administered.

3 *Directing.*   Employee supervision is an integral part of every supervisor's job. The supervisory style will emanate from top management. The catering department's supervisory procedures must be consistent with company policies.

4 *Controlling.*   The catering department manager must ensure that actual performance corresponds with planned performance. Effective financial controls ensure that actual profit and loss statements are consistent with pro forma budgets, and effective quality controls ensure that production and service meet company standards.

CATERING DEPARTMENT OBJECTIVES

Catering departments have a variety of objectives. The weight and priority given to each will depend on company policy. The following are among the most common objectives:

1 *Earn a fair profit on assets invested in the catering business.*
2 *Generate sufficient catering sales volume, enough to defray all expenses and leave a fair profit.*   Caterers must be careful not to generate a lot of business that will not pay for itself. They must practice selective sales strategies in order to maximize profits. Usually, the only time a catering executive should consider booking a marginally profitable

event is if it is a party designed to show off the catering facilities, such as a charity event. It may also be contemplated if the property wants to host VIPs who may indirectly generate future catering revenues, or during the slow season, to keep staff employed.

3   *Deliver customer satisfaction.*   Meeting this objective will lead to repeat patronage as well as positive referrals. All foodservice operations, including the catering segment, thrive on repeat patronage.

4   *Provide consistent quality and service.*   Customers are happy when the actual quality and service received parallel those that were promised. Punctuality and consistency are hallmarks of a well-run catering department.

5   *Convey a particular image.*   Caterers often want to be known as specializing in certain types of products and services, such as weddings or unusual themed events. They strive to be unique because they want customers to think of them whenever a specific atmosphere or ambiance is required. Catering is often a facility's most visible characteristic on the local and national levels. It alone has the greatest potential to become a facility's "signature"—its major claim to fame.

6   *Develop a reputation for dependability.*   Regardless of the pressure that any event places on the staff, catering departments want clients to have confidence that their needs will be met. The catering department must adequately fill the role of liaison between clients and all of the property's services.

7   *Develop a reputation for flexibility.*   To be dependable, the caterer must be flexible. The catering department must be able to react on a moment's notice. Clients will remember fondly the facility that bailed them out at the last minute.

8   *Stay on budget.*   To meet this objective, the caterer must be on guard against adding "surprise" charges that go over budget.

CATERING DEPARTMENT ORGANIZATION

Catering departments are organized according to the needs of the particular facility. For example, a hotel's primary profit center is its sleeping rooms division, with the catering department usually being the second most profitable department. Consequently, all hotel departments are generally organized and administered to maximize the sales and profits of sleeping rooms and catered functions.

There are two general types of catering department organizations. In one form, the department is organized in such a way that all catering personnel are under the supervision of the property's food and beverage director (see Figures 1.1 and 1.2). The food and beverage director is responsible for the kitchens, restaurant outlets, and banquet operations, as well as for client solicitation and service. Within this structure, catering must secure the right to sell function space from the sales department, which controls meeting space. Sales managers are often reluctant to call their clients and ask them to release space they are holding as part of a meeting they have booked. Meetings are often booked years in advance, and savvy meeting planners, not knowing all of their space needs that far ahead, will institute a "hold all space" clause in their contracts. In such an organizational structure, convention service managers are primarily responsible for room setup, but not for food or beverages.

Alternatively, the catering department may be organized so that catering personnel are under the supervision of the sales and marketing director, with other employees, especially banquet servers, still reporting to the food and beverage director (see Figure 1.3). In this situation there is generally a director of catering and convention services, who must work closely with the director of sales and marketing as well as with the food and beverage director.

Within this structure, catering managers and convention service are in the same department, both taking care of the food, beverage, and room setup needs of clients. The convention service managers do not sell the event, but take over client business booked by sales and marketing. They handle the planning and logistics of any meals or receptions and develop the appropriate service procedures needed to plan and implement successful and profitable catered events. In this scenario, most selling is "up$elling," or trying to get the client to purchase a more expensive meal, wine, or service. Catering managers then sell short-term food and beverage events to the local market or to functions without sleeping rooms, such as weddings, local banquets, and the like. With the revenue of catering being the responsibility of the marketing director, rather than the food and beverage director, sales managers are more likely to call clients to have rooms released for local banquets.

In the second type of organizational pattern, the sales and marketing and food and beverage directors split the workload and coordinate catering sales and service. In some properties, convention services personnel handle room setup and any food function that uses more than 20 sleeping rooms, and the catering department handles all local functions. In other facilities, the catering department handles all

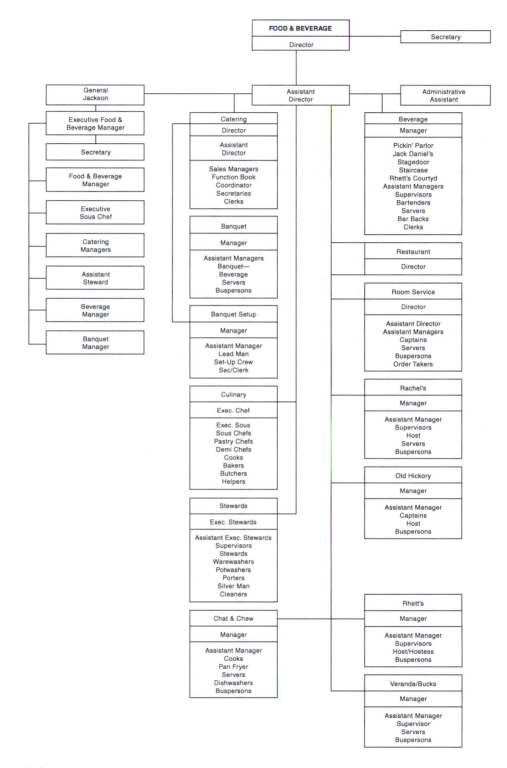

FIGURE 1.1 Food and beverage department organization chart. (Courtesy Opryland Hotel, Nashville, Tenn.)

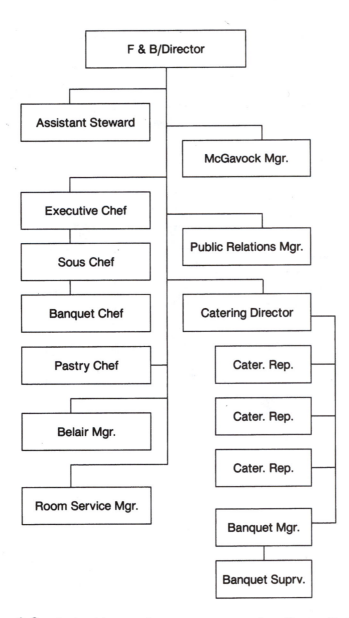

 FIGURE 1.2   Food and beverage department organization chart. (Courtesy Music City Sheraton Corporation.)

food and beverage service, and convention services personnel take care of all nonfood logistics, such as function room setups and teardowns, sleeping room arrangements, and so forth.

There are advantages and disadvantages with each organizational form. The major advantages associated with the organizational forms depicted in Figures 1.1 and 1.2 are as follows:

1   *Increased efficiency.*   Clients work with one designated person who has authority to oversee the event from inception to completion. Last-minute requests and changes can be implemented quickly.

2   *Isolated responsibility.*   Responsibility is assigned to one person. Management and clients know exactly whom to contact if questions arise. This is a very critical position, in that the contact person is responsible for translating a client's needs and wishes into reality.

3   *Job enrichment.*   A person in charge of an event enjoys more variety than does a person involved with only one or two aspects.

4   *Repeat patronage.*   When clients deal with one person, there are additional opportunities to solicit repeat patronage and referrals.

5   *Improved communications.*   Because there are fewer persons on the communications chain, ambiguities and misinterpretations should be minimal.

The following are the major disadvantages of the organizational forms depicted in Figures 1.1 and 1.2:

1   *Excessive workload.*   One person may not have enough hours in the day to perform all the necessary tasks.

2   *Too many bosses.*   The food and beverage department cannot be totally isolated; it must interact to some degree with the sales and marketing department. Unfortunately, this overlap may violate established chain-of-command policies unless the relationships are spelled out clearly.

3   *Lack of specialization.*   It is difficult to train one person to be expert in so many areas. However, if the catering manager is only the information point of exchange between clients and all other facility services, this potential problem can be minimized.

4   *Excessive delegation.*   If one person is not expert in all areas, the odds are that he or she will delegate responsibility freely. This can defeat the positive aspects of including all tasks under one person's direction. It also can confuse catering staff members.

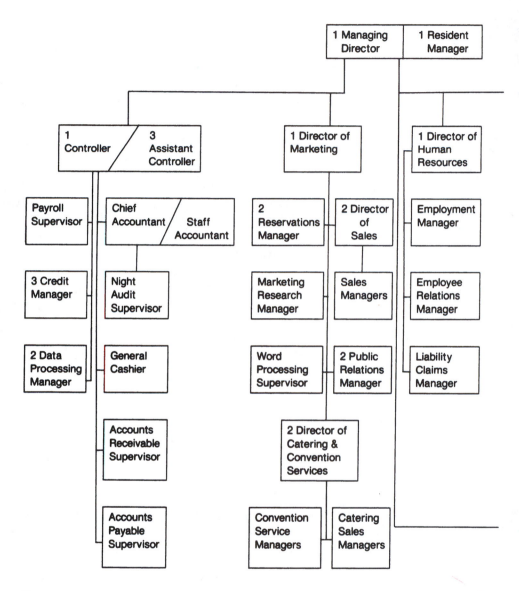

Key:
1 - Executive Committee/Operations Committee and Department Head
2 - Operations Committee and Department Head
3 - Department Head

 FIGURE 1.3 Hotel organization chart. (Courtesy Westin Peachtree Plaza Hotel, Atlanta, Ga.)

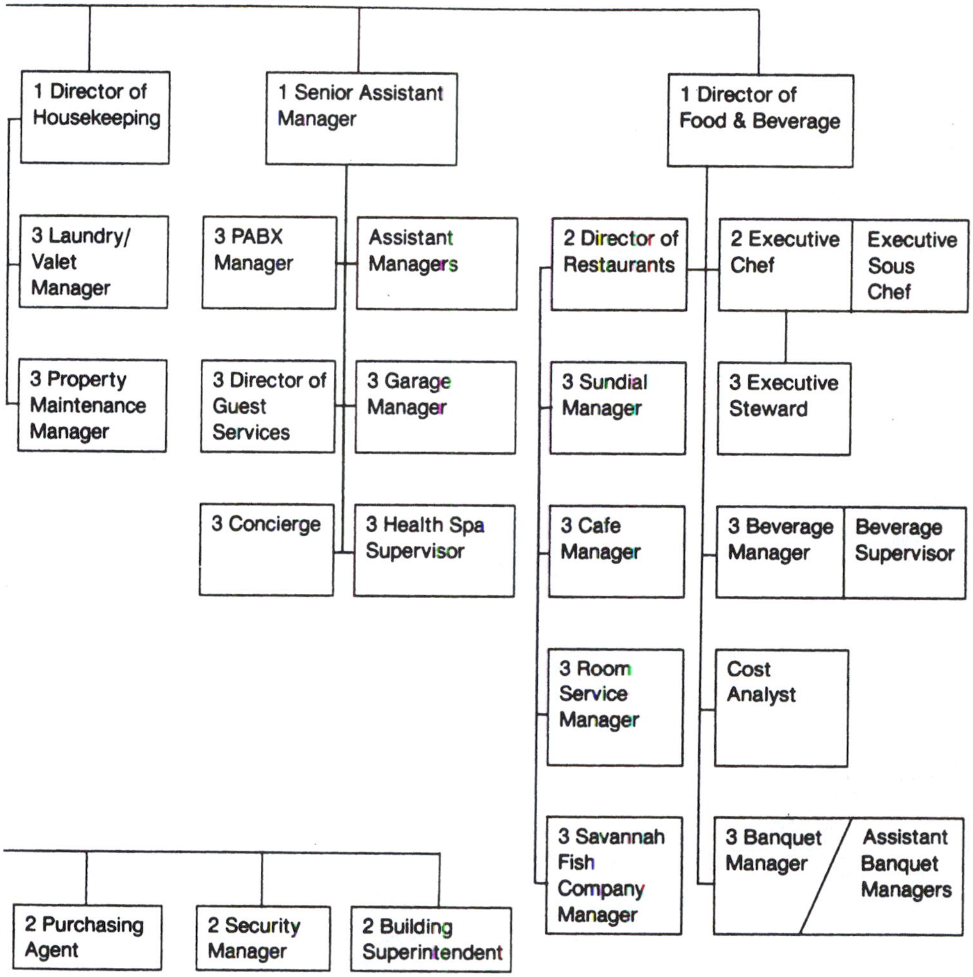

FIGURE 1.3 (Continued)

The advantages and disadvantages associated with the organizational form depicted in Figure 1.3 are the opposites of those associated with the organizational form depicted in Figures 1.1 and 1.2.

Which organizational form is appropriate? As a general rule, catering department organization will be influenced by the support of upper management and (1) the size of the facility, (2) the types of functions catered, (3) corporate policy, and (4) the overall level of service offered by the facility.

Although there is no single organizational form suitable for all facilities, it appears that the most typical organizational pattern is that

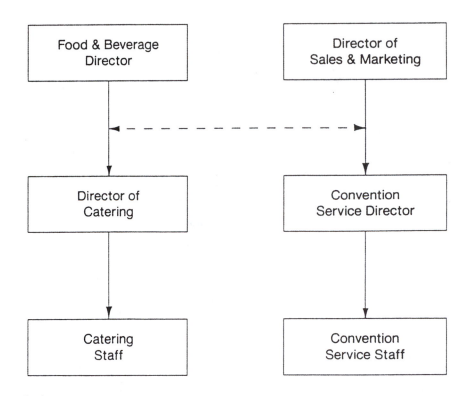

FIGURE 1.4   Typical catering organizational pattern.

depicted in Figure 1.4. In this case, the catering and convention service staffs work together, each handling specific activities. Catering typically handles all food and beverage requirements, and convention service handles all nonfood arrangements.

Catering Staff Positions

All types of catering departments require a variety of staff positions in order to operate effectively and efficiently. Depending on the type of catered event, they also depend on other departments' employees to handle meal and beverage functions. In a large facility, the typical positions needed to service clients are as follows:

1   Director of Catering (DOC)
2   Assistant Catering Director
3   Catering Manager
4   Catering Sales Manager

5   Catering Sales Representative
6   Director of Convention/Conference Service
7   Convention/Conference Service Managers
8   Banquet Manager
9   Banquet Setup Manager
10 Assistant Banquet Manager
11 Scheduler
12 Maître d' Hôtel
13 Captain
14 Server
15 Bartender and Bar Back
16 Sommelier
17 Houseman
18 Attendant
19 Clerical Person
20 Engineer
21 Cashier
22 Ticket Taker
23 Steward/Food Handler

Job Specifications

A job specification contains the qualities sought in a job candidate. Before hiring a catering department employee, a manager generally looks for at least five major qualities:

1 *Technical skills.*   Ideally, catering employees will have knowledge and skills in food and beverage preparation and service. At the very least, they must have an aptitude to learn and become familiar with the items on your menus and your services so that they can respond adequately to client inquiries.

It is required that most, if not all, catering employees have excellent sales skills. For some job positions, the primary qualification is the ability to sell. For instance, a sales representative's major asset is his or her ability to sell. However, even those employees primarily involved with guest service should have the ability to up$ell clients. They should be able to encourage clients to purchase additional, or higher-quality, products and services, thereby increasing catering profits.

Communications skills are absolutely essential for catering staff members. Each function is a unique undertaking. There is no standard pattern or event template. Consequently, open and intelligible communications are critical to the success of a catered event. It is important for staff to be sufficiently articulate to communicate effectively with the host, the guests, and other staff members.

2 *Conceptual skills.* As much as possible, catering department employees must be able to view the entire catering function and not see things exclusively from the perspective of their particular jobs. For instance, a banquet chef must appreciate the ceremonies involved with a wedding function and not ignore them when preparing and coordinating food courses.

Catering staff members must be able to take a client's "vision" of the function (including needs, wishes, purpose of the function, and budgetary constraints) and develop an event (through negotiations) consistent with this vision that can be delivered effectively and efficiently by the catering department. The planned catered event must meet the client's requirements.

3 *Human (interpersonal) skills.* Customer-contact skills are extremely important in the hospitality industry. Getting along with people, and satisfying them while simultaneously making a profit, is a challenge that must be met and overcome by all catering staff members. Unlike technical and conceptual skills, these skills generally cannot be taught—they are inherent. As Ellsworth Statler, founder of Statler Hotels, said once in the late 1800s, "Hire only good-natured people."

4 *Honesty and integrity.* Most staff members will be handling a considerable amount of catering property and equipment. They will also be making promises to clients, other customers, and several intermediaries (such as entertainers and florists). They must be aboveboard in all their dealings. Accepting kickbacks is not an acceptable practice.

5 *Other qualities.* Other characteristics that managers look for in job candidates depend on the type of position and company policies. For instance, if the facility has a promotion-from-within policy, a manager will seek a job candidate who has the ability and desire to advance and grow with the company.

Job Descriptions

A job description contains a list of duties an employee must perform. It also includes the name of the job candidate's manager, job performance evaluation criteria, the job objectives, and a career path.

The following are examples of abbreviated typical job descriptions for staff positions involved directly or indirectly with catering:

Director of Catering (DOC).   Assigns and oversees all functions; oversees all marketing efforts; interacts with clients and catering managers; coordinates with sales staff; creates menus (in cooperation with the chef).

Assistant Catering Director.   Services accounts; helps with marketing.

Catering Manager.   Maintains client contacts; services accounts.

Catering Sales Manager.   Oversees sales efforts; administers the sales office.

Catering Sales Representative.   Involved only in selling; handles outside sales and/or inside sales.

In some smaller facilities, the preceding three jobs are one and the same. The rule of thumb in such instances seems to be, "If you book it, you work it!"

Convention/Conference Service Manager.   Handles room setup in hotels, conference centers, and/or convention centers; sometimes handles catering for meetings and conventions.

Banquet Manager.   Implements requests of the Director of Catering; oversees room captains; supervises all functions in progress; staffs and schedules servers and bartenders; coordinates all support departments. He or she is the operations director, as opposed to a catering executive, who handles primarily the selling and planning chores.

Banquet Setup Manager.   Supervises the banquet setup crew (housemen); orders tables, chairs, and other room equipment from storage; supervises teardown of event.

Assistant Banquet Manager.   Reports to Banquet Manager; supervises table settings and decor. There may be two (or more) assistants, one for the day shift and one for the evening shift.

Scheduler.   Sometimes referred to as a diary clerk. Enters bookings in master log; oversees the timing of all functions and provides adequate turnover time; responsible for scheduling meeting rooms, reception areas, poolside areas, other areas, meal functions, beverage functions, other functions, and equipment requirements; keeps appropriate records to ensure against overbooking and double booking; responsible for communicating this information to all relevant departments. In larger facilities this function is computerized. There are a number of excellent software programs on the market, many of which are linked to the companion Web site for this book.

Maître d' Hôtel.   Floor manager; in charge of all service personnel; oversees all aspects of guest service during meal and beverage functions.

Captain.   In charge of service at meal functions; typically oversees all activity in the entire function room, or a portion of it, during a meal; supervises servers.

Server.   There are two types: food servers and cocktail servers. Food servers deliver foods, wine, nonalcoholic beverages, and utensils to tables; clear tables; attend to guest needs. Cocktail servers perform similar duties, but concentrate on serving alcoholic beverages, usually at receptions. Servers are sometimes backed up by buspersons, whose primary responsibilities are to clear tables, restock side stands, and serve ice water, rolls, butter, and condiments.

Food Handler.   Sometimes referred to as a food steward. Prepares finished food products noted on banquet event orders (BEO). Responsible for having them ready according to schedule.

Bartender.   Concentrates on alcoholic beverage production and service. Bartenders are often assisted by bar backs, whose primary responsibilities are to stock initially and replenish the bars with liquor, ice, glassware, and operating supplies.

Sommelier.   Wine steward; usually used only at fancy, upscale events.

Houseman.   Sometimes referred to as a porter or convention porter. Physically sets up rooms with risers, hardware, tables, chairs, and other necessary equipment; reports to Assistant Banquet Manager.

Attendant.   Refreshes meeting rooms; that is, does spot cleaning and trash removal during break periods and replenishes supplies—such as notepads, pencils, and ice water; responds to requests for service by meeting function hosts. Some catered functions may require rest room attendants, and some may require cloakroom attendants.

Clerical Person.   Handles routine correspondence; types contracts; types banquet event orders (BEO); handles and routes telephone messages; distributes documents to relevant staff members and other departments.

Engineer.   Provides necessary utilities service, such as setting up electrical panels for major exhibits; hangs banners; prepares special platforms and displays; sets up exhibits; maintains catering furniture, fixtures, and equipment (FFE). He or she may also handle audiovisual (AV) and lighting installation, teardown, and service.

Cashier.   Collects cash at cash bars; sells drink tickets; may also sell meal or concession tickets.

Ticket Taker. Responsible for collecting tickets from guests before they are allowed to enter a function.

Steward. Delivers requisitioned china, glass, flatware, salt and pepper shakers, and other similar items to function rooms, kitchens, and bar areas.

CATERING DEPARTMENT POLICIES

The facility must establish policies to guide the catering department's relations with clients. Typical policies include the following considerations.

Food and beverage prices. These must be clearly listed. It is a good idea to note that any listed prices are subject to change; in other words, the caterer should not assume responsibility if potential clients are viewing outdated menus. Caterers usually note that published menu prices are subject to change unless firm price guarantees are negotiated and included in a catering contract. If competitive bids are being prepared, all prices must be computed according to standard company pricing procedures. All printed menus should be dated to ensure that the client is not looking at an outdated version.

Taxes. Clients must be informed that all relevant state and local consumption taxes, such as sales tax and entertainment tax, will be added to the catering prices. It is helpful to the client to have applicable taxes stated on the menu. Tax-exempt clients must usually furnish an exemption certificate to the caterer prior to the event.

Gratuities or service charges. These are automatic charges added to the catering prices. Most properties add a 15 to 19 percent gratuity to the bill. You cannot assume that all clients are aware of these traditional charges: They must be informed about them up front.

Tips. These are voluntary gifts. Some clients will want to tip some or all employees if they receive exceptional service. If you have a no-tipping policy, however, clients must know about it. Most government-owned facilities do not allow tipping.

Deposits. The deposit procedures must be spelled out clearly. Clients must be informed of the amount that must be paid, when it must be tendered, and how it will be applied to the final billing.

Refunds. Although no one likes to broach a negative subject, it is important to detail your refund policies and procedures in advance.

Guarantees. A client must usually give a firm guarantee (guest count) two or three days in advance of the event. The facility will prepare food for that number of guests, plus a stipulated percentage over the guarantee to accommodate any guests who decide to attend at the last minute. For instance, most facilities will agree to handle the guaranteed number of guests and to overset about 3 to 5 percent, up to a maximum number—for example, 5 percent over or up to 100 persons maximum.

If the function is very large, a facility generally uses a sliding scale guarantee. For instance, although it may agree to a 5 percent overset for parties up to 500 persons, it may agree to accommodate only a 3 percent overage for parties in excess of 500.

Negotiating guarantees is a very tricky undertaking. The wise catering executive ensures that clients understand clearly the facility's position.

Guarantees, as well as deposits, refund policies, miscellaneous charges, menu prices, and so forth, should always be spelled out very clearly in the catering contract. Some caterers require a client to initial each line item to indicate understanding.

Minimum purchase. This policy requires a client to purchase a minimum amount of catering services if he or she wants to book one or more events. For example, some big hotels in Las Vegas will not allow a convention to block out meeting room space unless there is a corresponding minimum amount of food and beverage business guaranteed. This food and beverage minimum is based on a set amount per guest room night. For example, a convention may have to agree to purchase a minimum of $100 worth of services per room night in order to obtain the room block and meeting room space it needs. The food and beverage minimum must be agreed to when the contract is signed so that there are no surprises. Both parties then know what space is being provided and the total amount of food and beverage revenue required.

Setup charges. If they are not included in the food and beverage menu prices, clients must be told in advance about these extra charges. A large function does not ordinarily incur additional setup charges; however, small groups may be subject to them. Extra charges can accrue if a room needs a fast turnover and extra labor must be called in to accomplish the job.

Room rental rates. Most facilities will charge clients rent for the use of function rooms if they are used for meetings and other events that do not include significant food and beverage sales. For instance, there may be a charge for a room if the event does not generate at least $35 per person for food and/or beverage. The rental rate is usually calculated to cover the fixed overhead and provide a fair profit for the caterer. Some facilities have a sliding scale, with the charge depending on the dollar amount being generated.

Other extra charges.   Depending on the size of the function, a facility may add on extra charges for bartenders, cashiers, valet parking, coat-checking facilities, and directional displays. If clients require additional labor because their functions are scheduled to last longer than normal, they will usually be assessed a service charge to cover the extra payroll cost (sometimes calculated as man-hour overtime).

Credit terms.   Clients who have established credit ratings are usually allowed to put up a minimum deposit and pay the remaining balance within an allotted time, generally 30 days. Clients without credit approval usually must put up a large deposit and pay the remaining balance at least 2 days prior to the event or immediately after the function ends. Clients who are somewhere between having an established credit rating and no credit rating normally must provide a deposit and pay the remaining balance at the end of the catered event.

Outside food and beverage.   Most, if not all, facilities will not allow clients to bring in their own food and beverage supplies. In most situations, the facility's liquor license, liability insurance, health permit, and/or business license forbids the use of personal products.

Setup service charge.   If the law and the facility allow clients to bring in their own products, there is usually a charge for setup service. For instance, if a client is allowed to bring in his or her own liquor, there may be a standard, one-time corkage fee for the service, or the facility may charge a standard fee for each drink prepared and served.

Underage or visibly intoxicated guests.   The facility must ensure that clients realize that the pertinent liquor laws will not be suspended during their catered events. For instance, wedding hosts may not see anything wrong with serving wine to an underage guest at a private party. However, the law does not make this distinction. The same is true for service to visibly intoxicated guests; they cannot legally be served by the banquet staff.

If clients request self-service bars, some caterers will require them to sign a waiver of liquor liability so that they are not held responsible for the actions of the guests. This type of waiver is necessary because, in the case of self-service, the facility does not have bartenders and cocktail servers on-site to monitor underage drinking and service to visibly intoxicated guests. Because of this potential liability, many caterers do not permit self-service bars.

Display restrictions. Many clients need to use their own signs, displays, decorations, and/or demonstrations at booked events. The facility usually reserves the right to approve these items and to control their placement and location. If clients are allowed to have displays, the facility usually expects the clients to be responsible for any damage done and any extraordinary cleanup that may result. The removal of confetti (especially Mylar confetti), rice, and birdseed can pose a challenge. Similar restrictions may apply to other materials, such as paper products, decorations, and equipment. Tape and tacks can damage walls, and some items can be fire hazards.

Responsibility for loss and/or damage. Personal property brought into the facility by guests are not usually covered by the facility's insurance policies. Consequently, clients and their guests must be informed of this policy, and agree to it, before receiving permission to use their own property.

Indemnification. A facility usually expects clients to agree to indemnify it against any claims, losses, and/or damages, except those due solely to the negligence and/or willful misconduct of the facility staff. The facility also wants protection from claims made by outside service contractors, such as florists, decorators, or audiovisual (AV) firms engaged by clients. Furthermore, clients are expected to stipulate that by paying the final bill, they agree that there are no disputes with the products and services received.

Uncontrollable acts. There are times when a facility will be unable to perform through no fault of its own. For instance, bad weather, a strike, a labor dispute, or another circumstance may hamper the facility's ability to service its clients. Consequently, clients must agree to hold harmless the facility under uncontrollable conditions of this type.

Substitutions. A policy regarding substitutions is similar to the policy on uncontrollable acts. Occasionally, supply problems may force a caterer to substitute menu products, or it may be necessary to move a function from one meeting room to another. For instance, an outdoor event may have to be moved indoors at the last minute because of inclement weather. Or a contractor's strike may force the facility to substitute other space of comparable size and quality. Although few of us want to think about these potential problems, clients must be advised in advance that they could occur. Always provide proper advance communication with clients so surprises do not anger them.

Security. A facility may require a client to provide additional security for his or her event. For instance, a meeting of diamond dealers would be expected to schedule a great deal of personal security that is provided by or approved by the facility. Alternatively, the facility may reserve the right to hire additional security guards and bill the event host. If you outsource valet parking, always check references to ensure the security of your patron's automobiles.

Licenses and permits. Some functions may need to be approved and/or licensed by the local government licensing agency. For instance, a function that has a cover charge may need a temporary admission license. The facility should reserve the right to refuse service to any client who does not hold the appropriate licenses and permits prior to the event.

MAJOR CHALLENGES FACED BY A CATERING DEPARTMENT

Some of the major challenges encountered by the catering department while working to attain its objectives are discussed in the following paragraphs.

Marketing the catering department's services. A great deal of time must be spent in this effort to distinguish your facility in the minds of potential clients. Too many caterers can seem exactly alike. Clients tend to perceive caterers as interchangeable as buses: There is always another one available who can handle their needs. You will need to battle this perception constantly.

Excessive amount of time spent with clients. Unfortunately, only a small number of persons and groups contacted will end up purchasing catered events. Moreover, once business is booked, a great deal of time must be spent planning and coordinating the events. Although some clients need more hand-holding than others, the wise catering executive will expect to devote much time to these tasks.

To maximize available catering sales time, savvy caterers learn to determine how much time is necessary and/or appropriate to spend with a prospective client, who may be a serious buyer or merely a casual shopper for catering services.

Unique demands. All functions have unique demands. For instance, refreshment breaks are sometimes permanently set, but clients may not have a particular schedule in mind and merely wish to visit the refreshment area when time permits. This is especially true in conference centers, where attendees can break at will. Consequently, setups must to be freshened periodically, which requires an employee to be constantly alert to fluctuating needs.

Difficulty in costing out and pricing certain functions.   Special requests and last-minute needs will cost more because of the special circumstances. The aforementioned refreshment breaks fall into this category. Because the demands these events present cannot always be predicted in advance, function hosts usually must wait until a final accounting is made by the catering department. This can cause ill will among clients, especially those who are on a tight budget and would appreciate price guarantees.

Ethical traps.   Sometimes a catering department may encounter conflict-of-interest dilemmas. For example, clients who need outside contractors, such as tour buses, entertainers, and decorators, may ask the caterer for a recommendation. The facility, always mindful of its image and reputation, will tend to recommend only a few outside contractors that can fill the bill adequately. However, such favoritism may be perceived by some as shady dealing.

Responsibility greater than authority.   It is very important to determine in advance who is responsible for each part of an event. For instance, a convention may want to hire its own band but simultaneously expect the facility to coordinate the details. This can easily lead to misunderstandings and client dissatisfaction unless everything is spelled out clearly.

Time pressures.   The catering department is a pressure cooker. It seems as if everything must be ready "yesterday." Catering personnel must learn to work well within time constraints.

Working with and coordinating with other departments and outside agencies.   Proper advance planning is necessary to avoid service glitches that could cause guest dissatisfaction. Caterers must cultivate the ability to communicate effectively.

Maintaining qualified staff members.   Many catering departments experience severe volume swings. For instance, convention centers pose a unique challenge in terms of volume and staffing. One day you may have a breakfast for 5,000, which requires a lot of labor. But you may not have another similar function for two weeks; as a result, it is very difficult to keep qualified employees, many of whom prefer more predictable work schedules.

In addition to full-time management and hourly employees, many facilities maintain two lists of service staff (i.e., banquet staff) employees: an A-list and a B-list. A-list personnel are the steady extras;

they are the first ones called by the manager when help is needed. If a sufficient number of people on the A-list are not available, the manager will call those on the B-list.

The B-list personnel are casual labor. They are used to fill in the gaps. They present more problems than do A-list people, because the typical B-list worker is probably on the B-list of every caterer in town. As a result, major functions can go begging for adequate staff. The catering executive must be a creative personnel recruiter and a superb planner in order to overcome these obstacles.

A unionized facility is usually required to go through the local union hiring hall for its steady and casual servers. A union generally keeps lists of steadies and extras, similar to the A-list and B-list kept by nonunionized facilities. If the union has enough advance notice of all of your labor requirements, chances are it can plan for them and satisfy the catering department's needs. The Christmas season and New Year's Eve are a challenge everywhere.

The lack of technical foodservice skills. Many caterers today, both men and women, have less knowledge about food than ever before. They are increasingly reliant on chefs and food and beverage directors for advice. This would not be a major problem if standardized menus were used consistently; however, things are more trendy these days, there is more competition, and many clients want custom menus and something special. This can make it difficult to respond quickly to unusual customer requests.

A potential client may become restless with the catering executive who needs to confer constantly with other food and beverage people in the organization. However, an executive's confidence and poise can transcend the bonds of ignorance. Instead of dismay, a potential client may be quite pleased with the executive who may not have the answer at the very moment, but who promises to get it quickly.

In this day and age, no one is expected to know everything. The catering executive does, however, need to know where to get the expertise and information to handle client needs. In a well-run facility there is a tremendous network of specialized professionals available, as well as a sophisticated communications system that can be used to tap into this bundle of resources. The web is also an excellent source of information. Organizations such as the National Association of Catering Executives (NACE, *http://www.nace.net*) provide education on a national level via conferences and through 47 local chapters that hold monthly meetings. There are excellent trade journals, such as *Event Solutions, Special Event, CaterSource* (http://www.catersource.

com), *Food Arts,* and *Food & Wine,* that provide excellent articles to educate the neophyte or aspiring caterer. As catering clients become more sophisticated and/or jaded, the caterer cannot remain competitive without these resources. There is a companion website for this book and the above resource sites are linked www.wiley.com.

Many clients travel extensively and eat out frequently. Their dining experiences shape their menu choices when planning functions. They expect the catering executive to keep pace with trends in menu, event planning, and design. These challenges must be met by any catering executive who strives to be successful in either the off-premise or on-premise arena.

Markets and Marketing

Chapter

2

Catering is a consumer-driven market, stimulated by clients who demand exceptional quality and excellent value for a reasonable price. Value is determined by the buyer, not the seller. Buyers' perceptions are sellers' realities. This means that the potential clients' impression of the catering ability of your facility, be it a restaurant, hotel, club, or other facility—whether positive or negative—is what is real for them and will influence their buying decisions. Most of your potential clients will comparison shop when they are considering the location of their events. Your facility must be perceived as the best choice because you are reliable, consistent, and creative and you can execute the best-quality event.

The number and types of potential catering clients are unlimited. New markets are emerging constantly. On-premise caterers service all types of events, from the smallest business meeting to the largest industry convention and exposition.

A hotel often has an advantage over other types of caterers because it can handle several types of events simultaneously and in the same location where most guests are staying. Convention centers also have a wide selection of available space to service very large groups. Restaurants, on the other hand, often have only one banquet room on the premises.

Catering clients are everywhere. Our society has a never ending love affair with parties, meetings, conventions, celebrations, ceremonies, and various other special events.

 # BUSINESS MARKET

The corporate business market represents approximately 75 percent of total catering sales in the United States. It is generally divided into three segments: shallow, midlevel, and deep.

Shallow Market

The shallow segment is characterized by low-budget functions. Groups in this category have limited resources and are very cost conscious. Their events usually involve a short lead time for the caterer. These clients usually shop around for the best price, often requesting the least expensive selection on the menu—the ubiquitous "mystery meat and buttered noodles," or "rubber chicken" entrees. This does not mean that they ignore quality and service; however, they are typically on a limited budget and cannot afford the very best. The shallow market generally includes social, military, education, religious, and fraternal groups; these segments usually have low budgets, as does the government market, which limits per diems.

A large portion of this market is the fraternal group. Fraternal organizations abound. Most areas of the country have Rotary, Kiwanis, Lions, Seroptomist, and similar service organizations. They represent a good source of steady business because of their desire to meet at the same location each month. They do not like to move around. They like their members to know, for example, that their meeting is held on the third Tuesday of the month at a local restaurant. This avoids confusion. It also makes it easier for members to plan their personal calendars—an important point, as some members tend to belong to more than one fraternal organization.

The military segment is also a good source of catering business, particularly in cities that house major military bases. There are many awards functions, Armed Forces Days, and birthday events. For instance, every November 10th, or on the closest weekend, the Marine Corps holds its Marine Birthday Ball. Although it is true that most military bases have club facilities capable of providing catering services, other local catering facilities can expect to attract some of this business by providing a welcome change of pace.

The education segment can also generate a respectable amount of revenue and profit. There are many continuing education seminars, symposiums, graduation parties, and fraternity and sorority events. There are also many high school functions. For instance, proms can represent considerable revenue in April and May. Many of today's youth have considerable amounts of disposable income, but security at events of this type is essential.

Caterers can use shallow market groups to fill in the gaps during slow periods (i.e., the "shoulders") between more lucrative events. And, because many of the attendees are bona fide business and/or community leaders, their exposure to your facility may persuade them to use it for other catered functions instead of a competing facility.

Because this market has less profit potential, new, inexperienced catering salespersons are usually assigned to it. These neophyte salespersons, however, should not be turned loose on any market segment without proper training and guidance from top management. Without the right training, a new salesperson tends to promise products and/or services to clients that are unwarranted by their budgets or that cannot be handled adequately by the facility. A poorly sold event can increase product and payroll costs. As catering salespersons gain experience, they quickly learn what can be sold and how they can maximize revenue and profits. Experience with officials of civic, political, church, school, museum, senior citizen, charity, condo association, and similar groups is invaluable and necessary for the catering professional who intends to advance to the business and/or special events markets.

The shallow segment customer of today can very easily be the corporate meeting planner of tomorrow. As a result, the caterer who does a good job with these groups is apt to win repeat patronage and to gain an inside track on securing potentially more profitable functions in the future.

However, a caterer should not undertake any event that may damage his or her reputation because of a low budget. If you can not present yourself in the best way possible within the budget, do not book the event.

Midlevel Market

The local association market and local businesses that have regularly scheduled training meetings and seminars generally fall within the midlevel category. Events at this level are usually planned well in advance. Although price is important, clients may not quibble over a few dollars; it is imperative that the event be memorable and consistent with the attendees' status in the business community.

A midlevel function can quickly lead to repeat business. For instance, an executive business luncheon can easily become a monthly affair. The caterer who provides excellent value will more than likely become the favored provider for such clients. Business people are trained to shop around for the best value; however, when it comes to their personal pleasures, they are no different from the rest of us in that they will not switch loyalties on the spur of the moment. Furthermore, these small functions can lead to bigger and better things in the future.

Deep Market

The deep segment involves especially fancy, upscale business meal functions. These are expensive events where cost takes a back seat. The incentive travel market fits this category. Functions of this type often represent repeat business. Although most large conventions and similar events tend to move around the country, many are likely to patronize the same locations or geographical areas on a regular schedule.

Even though many large business events are booked years in advance, the caterer who specializes in the deep segment must be prepared to service a client at a moment's notice. A loyal client expects this consideration and is willing to pay for it. Caterers in casino hotels are often asked to produce a "high roller party" with only an hour's notice.

BUSINESS MARKET EVENTS

Companies and corporations may have a variety of catering needs. Business functions range from small meetings to lavish conventions. Typical business events are described in the following paragraphs.

Meetings and conventions.   These events represent the bulk of the business market. Some, such as sales meetings, can be rather routine affairs that are easily serviced. Others, however, such as an annual stockholders meeting, can severely test the catering executive's skill and ingenuity.

The largest market segment is national and international associations, followed by major corporations. Probably the greatest advantage of working with the corporate meetings segment is that clients of this type can usually give you more accurate predictions. They can ordinarily quote a precise number of attendees. For instance, if a company plans a meeting for 100 persons, it will usually have 100 attendees. If a person cancels, he or she will normally be replaced at the function by the company. Corporations do not have to market and sell registrations as associations do. A corporate group also tends to allocate more money per attendee than other types of clients. As a general rule, corporate events are usually attended by businesspeople accustomed to judging overall value without concentrating solely on price.

The corporate meeting segment is also considered to be a more stable market group than others. There are many events that must be held periodically.

Business-related associations generate a tremendous amount of meetings and conventions business. Caterers encounter two major types of business-related associations: the trade association and the professional association.

A trade association represents persons employed in a particular trade. Membership is usually sponsored and paid for by the member's employer. For instance, the American Culinary Federation (ACF) is a trade association, for which membership dues are generally paid by the chefs' employers.

A professional association represents persons who practice a particular professional activity. Membership is usually paid for by the individual member. For instance, the American Medical Association (AMA) is a professional association in which each doctor pays his or her own membership dues.

The association market is the largest segment of the meetings and conventions trade. Association members participate in local chapter meetings, educational events, charitable works, and regional, national, and international conventions. Most have conventions and/or meetings at least once each year.

There is an association for almost every vocation or avocation in existence. According to the American Society of Association Executives (ASAE), about 70 percent of Americans belong to one association, about 50 percent belong to two, and about 25 percent belong to four or more. There are more than 20,000 national associations based in the United States. In addition to their membership rosters, they employ approximately 500,000 people to manage their affairs.

Incentive events. The purpose of incentive events is to encourage company employees to meet or exceed sales and/or production goals. When goals are met, a celebration is planned to honor those who contributed to their successful achievement.

A company's marketing department usually plans such events, which are typically used to motivate salespersons. In addition to a special celebration, high achievers can also be rewarded with a free trip (incentive travel) or some other prize.

Incentive events are very profitable business for catering. Companies usually reward their star performers with lavish functions. Economy is not in their vocabulary, but they do not waste their money. Maximum reward leads to maximum effort and results.

New product introductions. Events held to introduce new products range from film premieres to new software releases. These are usually very elaborate, expensive events. First-class food, beverage, entertainment, and decorations are standard fare—all designed to attract maximum media coverage.

Many companies periodically hold news conferences. These also represent potential catering business. Reporters are more likely to show up if food and beverages are being served.

Building openings. Most companies celebrate ground breakings, topping-offs, and grand openings with gala parties. Many of these are off-premises functions; however, there are usually many preopening functions that can be held within a facility. For example, a building developer's leasing department may host a party to promote interest among potential tenants.

Recognition events. Recognition events are similar to incentive events, but are generally less elaborate. They typically involve awards dinners and other types of ceremonies intended to recognize several employees at various levels of performance. For instance, many companies and associations hold an annual luncheon to recognize long-term employees and to honor the employee of the year or someone who is retiring.

Some recognition events are actually a form of public relations. A company or association may hold a function that, although it is designed to honor someone, is also used to generate publicity. For example, the National Academy of Motion Picture Arts and Sciences holds Oscar parties and similar events that generate interest among the movie-going public while honoring industry members. There is a major banquet for Academy Award nominees and movie business insiders before the awards ceremony. Other parties are spawned by this event, with movie studios, agents, and other entities producing after-event parties with exclusive guest lists.

Training sessions and seminars. If an educational event is expected to last one day or more, the company usually will want to hold it at a place where food and beverages are readily available. Catered functions in this case can offer pretty basic fare. Most of these events are held by the midlevel market.

Anniversaries. Most companies celebrate decade anniversaries, as well as silver, golden, diamond, centennial, sesquicentennial, bicentennial, and tricentennial anniversaries. Coca-Cola's 100th birthday celebration held in Atlanta was an incredible event. Coca-Cola executives and other guests from around the world were feted at parties over a period of several days. The celebration encompassed events at all the major hotels and culminated in a reception for 16,000 people at the city's convention center.

ICW (in conjunction with). Many smaller events "piggyback" onto larger events. They are ancillary to a main event. Trade show exhibitors often host events during conventions. For example, during the COMDEX computer show in Las Vegas, IBM or Microsoft may throw a party for potential customers or host a dinner for their best clients. This business does not come directly from COMDEX per se, but is generated because of COMDEX. For shows that meet in the same location each year, it is quite easy to go to the convention center and pick up an exhibitor directory that you can use during the year to solicit ICW business for the following show. Now, with the advent of the web, you can also go to the trade show web site and obtain a listing of exhibitors.

This type of business is not booked in advance by a sales department, but is "up for grabs." All participating properties usually try to book this segment, as it is among the highest revenue producers for catering. The smart caterer researches this segment at least one year in advance, often by paying a visit to the current year's meeting location to find those customers, to meet and greet them and establish a relationship. Although each convention has rules as to how their affiliates can book at the hotels, these efforts generally pay off and generate extensive revenues.

Traveling exhibitions. There are many "traveling shows," such as music or entertainment extravaganzas and sports events. Sports teams are a particularly good market segment. Whether major league, college, high school, or intramural, when their participants are on the road they tend to have healthy appetites. Although at times they may be difficult to service because of their scheduling constraints, their catered functions generally involve very specific types and quantities of foods and beverages and relatively simple service procedures.

SPECIAL EVENTS—SOCIAL MARKET

According to Joe Goldblatt of George Washington University, "a special event recognizes a unique moment in time with ceremony and ritual to satisfy specific needs." In his book *Special Events: The Art & Science of Celebration,* he states that all human societies celebrate, privately and publicly, individually and as a group.

To some extent, every catered event may be considered a special event, at least for some clients and their guests. For instance, a convention may book several "refueling" functions, such as breakfasts and luncheons, but may also schedule one special event such as a surprise birthday party for the company president.

Special events differ from daily, ordinary events in at least three ways. A daily event generally occurs spontaneously, whereas a special event is always planned in advance. A daily event does not necessarily arouse expectations, but a special event always does. And although a daily event usually occurs for no particular reason, some type of celebration is the motivating force behind a special event.

Types of Special Events

Many special events are life cycle events. Birthdays, anniversaries, reunions, and the like mark times in our lives. They are usually celebrated with specific ceremonies and rituals. Many are celebrations catered by off-premise social caterers at clients' homes or other locations. Some use restaurants, clubs, and other small to mid-size facilities. And others are larger affairs, which would be of interest to the typical hotel or convention center catering department.

Among the special events that caterers handle are the following:

Weddings. Today's wedding lasts longer and is more expensive than ever before. Many couples are marrying later in life and thus have more time and money to devote to this special day. A recent national survey conducted by *BRIDE's* magazine indicated that approximately $42.4 billion was spent on weddings in the year 2000. The survey also revealed that there are approximately 2.4 million weddings per year in the United States and that the average wedding reception has approximately 186 guests. Facilities that can provide a one-stop service are apt to have a competitive edge among today's active women, who have many demands on their time.

Facilities with unique surroundings, picturesque views, and/or romantic settings are especially preferred by wedding planners. For example, the Del Coronado Hotel in Coronado, California, is located in an absolutely beautiful area—a stone's throw from the ocean. It is such a favorite spot for weddings that it is not unusual for two or three such events to be held each day, one right after the other. Many weddings have specific religious requirements. For instance, the Jewish wedding ceremony requires a *chuppah* (canopy), and the reception requires special service of the *challah* (ceremonial bread) and the breaking of a glass. The caterer will have to be aware of traditions like these to avoid disappointing and/or insulting guests. Ethnic weddings, such as Italian and Greek weddings, are quite often very extravagant affairs.

The wedding is the ultimate theme party, as discussed further in Chapter 3.

Wedding anniversaries.   Wedding anniversaries are often surprise celebrations hosted by adult children to mark milestone years. The silver 25th wedding anniversary is especially popular. The "party planning children" generally need a good deal of advice on putting together their celebrations. The caterer may consider advising them to center a theme on what was going on in the world at the time their parents were married. This is usually a very popular theme, especially with guests who are contemporaries of the anniversary couple. The web and the local library have plenty of information about what was happening during the wedding year, as well as on the specific wedding date. The Catering Research Institute of the National Association of Catering Executives (NACE) provides research services to members on menus and theme ideas (http://www.nace.net).

Reunions.   The reunion market encompasses many areas, including high school, college, family, military units, and former work groups. High school reunions are especially popular these days because of the recent emergence of private reunion planners that specialize in locating alumni and planning memorable events, tasks that a few well-intentioned alumni are usually unable to perform well.

Reunions require a great amount of preplanning. A successful event usually needs a one-year lead time. There are usually a few faithful alumni who shoulder the bulk of the planning burden, or they may engage a professional reunion planner. A caterer, however, is often part of the overall planning process.

Reunion organizers usually benefit from any advice a caterer can offer. Many clients are amateurs and have no experience in planning and organizing events of this type. Consequently, a sales representative must be able to recommend a number of little things that will be a big hit with attendees. For instance, a very popular technique is to put each school reunion attendee's original graduating class yearbook picture on a name badge. Another strategy sure to please the school reunion attendee is to recreate the yearbook by taking each attendee's picture at the reunion and including it in the revised yearbook along with the graduates' activities since graduation.

Bar and bat mitzvahs.   A bar mitzvah is the traditional Jewish ceremony celebrated on a Jewish boy's 13th birthday. It marks the coming of age in the Jewish faith. During the ceremony the young man publicly recites benedictions from the Torah, the Jewish Scripture, and accepts personal responsibility for observing the commandments set down in the Torah. A bat mitzvah, for young Jewish girls, is similar to a bar mitzvah.

The celebrations of these events are traditionally very serious and glamorous, similar in scale to large wedding receptions. Important elements include the blessing of the bread and wine and the lighting of candles. Menus and food preparation and service may adhere to the kosher dietary restrictions or may be of kosher style.

Bar and bat mitzvahs are discussed in more detail in Chapter 3.

Baptisms and confirmations.   A baptism is the Christian rite that results in the acceptance of the baptized person into the faith. A celebration, following the rite performed in a church, is most often held at the parents' home; larger functions may have to be held at a hotel or similar location.

A confirmation is the Christian rite confirming a child's infant baptism into the faith. The ceremony allows the young person to confirm that he or she knows right from wrong and that Christ is the chosen savior. Receptions are usually very popular, with the confirmed receiving gifts and a considerable amount of attention.

Graduations and proms.   Graduations and proms can be a very attractive market segment these days, especially because many older persons are graduating from college. They have fulfilled lifelong dreams and usually are eager to celebrate. Proms, which are high school affairs, are not usually high on the priority list of caterers. Underage adolescents, coupled with tight budgets, do not normally result in profitable, successful affairs. However, many companies are specializing in marketing "prom packages" or "post-prom party packages."

Birthdays.   Large, expensive birthday celebrations tend to be surprise parties. The caterer must be involved in a considerable amount of preplanning and subterfuge. An emerging trend is the "turning 40, 50, or 60" party, along with special themes and menus, as baby boomers in our society are aging.

Gourmet clubs.   Groups such as the Chaine des Rotisseurs and the American Institute of Wine & Food (AIWF) host extremely upscale, high-priced meals. When evaluating a caterer, the members give priority to those establishments that are fellow members and that hold menu design and execution in high esteem. Consequently, the facility seeking this type of business must see to it that the chef, director of catering, and/or food and beverage director hold active memberships in such organizations.

Customer appreciation parties.   Another type of unique, corporate special events are customer appreciation parties, which are quite common in some industries. They are occasionally based on a theme of some kind. For instance, a company may throw a "Thanksgiving Day" party for current clients as a way of showing its appreciation for their patronage. Customer-appreciation parties can also be used by a company to solicit future business. For example, an equipment manufacturer may host a party that also includes a brief display of its collection of equipment prototypes. This presentation can encourage its current and potential customers to preorder the merchandise. It is also a good bet that these customers will provide profitable referral business for the client and for the caterer.

Fund-raising events.   Fund-raisers and other types of good cause, charity events continue to be popular. The facility is often a partner in these events, in that it contributes all or part of the products and/or services needed. These events create a "showcase opportunity" for the caterer. Some of these functions are multifaceted events. For instance, a fund-raiser may include a reception, dinner, silent auction, or dance.

Fund-raisers can be very profitable over the long run. You may not earn a fair profit on each one, but if you develop a reputation for considering the many disparate interests involved with a particular charity and organizing them into a successful affair, eventually you should generate profitable repeat and referral catering business.

Mega-events.   A mega-event involves several simultaneous events coordinated by the caterer. For instance, for Super Bowl 2000, the caterer at the Georgia Dome handled the NFL Corporate Hospitality Village (16 corporate parties ranging in size from 50 to 1,500 guests), the NFL Tailgate Party (approximately 10,000 guests), concession stands in the NFL Experience, and approximately 80,000 spectators in the stadium, including 6,000 guests in 210 hospitality suites. A mega-event can also be a multicity event. For example, in early 2000, the Mercedes Benz company repeated the same party in 12 cities over a 14-day period, with each party having the same menu.

Other events.   Holiday, costume, farewell, and similar parties represent potential catering business. Sometimes they are held in conjunction with another event. For instance, a corporate awards banquet can double as a farewell party for recent retirees.

CLIENT DECISION MAKERS

Who makes the purchase decision? This is one of the first things to find out when soliciting catering business. In some instances this person may be the company secretary. In other cases the chief executive officer (CEO) may be the decision maker.

Usually, the type of function dictates who will make the purchase decision. A secretary may plan the office Christmas party, whereas the CEO may plan the annual board of directors meeting.

Some companies employ a meeting planner. Meeting planners, depending on the size of the company and the amount of meeting/training/convention activity, may or may not have other job responsibilities. The meeting planner who concentrates exclusively on this activity is easier to work with, as the planner with other company responsibilities often has less time to concentrate on meetings.

Some very large companies employ a corporate meeting planner to plan and organize functions for all company-owned satellite locations. The corporate meeting planner is normally based at the corporate headquarters; for instance, Coca-Cola's corporate meeting planner is based in Atlanta. However, even though the planner resides in Atlanta, this person has responsibility for planning and organizing events for all regional Coca-Cola bottlers.

Many associations have professional meeting planners on staff, but some are too small to afford this type of support. Consequently, they tend to hire independent or contract meeting planners to help them. Such an association may use an independent contractor to handle all of its events, including its meetings and conventions needs. There are also multimanagement contract companies that manage several associations.

Association meeting planners on the national level are concentrated in a few cities. They move their meetings around the country, but are usually based at the association's national headquarters. Most national associations are based in Washington, D.C., because lobbying is often one of their main activities. New York, Chicago, Atlanta, and San Francisco also have high concentrations of associations' headquarters staffs.

The ASAE, an association for association executives, publishes a membership directory (*http://www.asaenet.org*). Gayle Research publishes an annual *Encyclopedia of Associations*, which can usually be found in the reference section of the local public library. Another online source for association information is at *http://www.association-central.com*.

The regional, state, and local chapters of national associations also have catering needs. Regional and state chapters usually have one or two functions per year. The meeting planner at the national level often helps the regional and state chapters plan and organize their events.

Local chapters typically have monthly meetings at which association business is discussed. These functions usually include a meal or a reception, as well as a guest speaker. For instance, NACE has 47 chapters that plan and organize these types of monthly events (*http://www.nace.net*).

Local chapter meeting planners are usually volunteers. Caterers experience a great deal of variety with local chapters; some volunteers are well versed in planning and organizing events, whereas many are willing to work but require considerable care and attention.

Travel agencies are planning more catered events today. Some travel houses have evolved into full-fledged meeting planning companies. They actively seek to attract corporate meeting planner clients, especially the large corporate clients.

Some corporations and associations believe that it is good business practice to use travel agents to plan meetings because, theoretically, it is much more efficient to deal with one person for travel, catering, and sleeping room needs. Unfortunately, some travel agents do not understand the catering part of the overall meeting. They usually do not comprehend the subtle differences between planning a banquet and planning a tour. For instance, the typical travel agent may be unaware of the difference between meal couponing and meal guarantees and might therefore, be placed in an embarrassing position.

With the meal couponing procedure, when a travel agent books a meal function, he or she presells event tickets to the guests and reimburses the caterer for each ticket redeemed. If some guests do not use their tickets, the travel agent keeps the "breakage,"—the money paid by guests to the travel agent but not given to the caterer.

With meal guarantees, however, there is no breakage. The caterer must be paid according to the number of guests the agent guaranteed. The travel agent must pay, regardless of the number of guests who attend the catered function. This is troublesome for the travel agent accustomed to earning considerable breakage income. It is even more disturbing to the travel agent who books a great deal of breakfast business, as there can be a very large "no-show" factor for this meal.

Another difference with travel agents is their concept of professional compensation for their services. They have a commission orientation, whereas meeting planners do not. For instance, a travel agent usually receives as much as a 10 percent commission for sleeping room business booked for a hotel. If a travel agent books a meal function or two, he or she may expect a commission for each function.

The client decision maker in the social and special events markets is not always easy to identify. For instance, just because a bridal coordinator may be the first person to make contact with the caterer, it does not necessarily follow that he or she is empowered to make decisions. The caterer must make sure to avoid wasting valuable time with the wrong person by qualifying each caller.

Some special events market segments employ event managers and/or event coordinators. For instance, sports leagues usually have hospitality and special events coordinators—some are employed full time at league headquarters, with other local independent coordinators hired to handle temporary assignments on location.

Sports leagues represent profitable catering opportunities. For example, the hospitality coordinator for the U.S. Open Championship arranges about 100 parties during each tournament; the director of special events for major league baseball plans several banquets throughout the year, some for as many as 3,500 persons. The Super Bowl generates a legion of parties in the host city.

Years ago, most persons in the food and beverage industry paid less attention to marketing than they do today. Many who entered the business then concentrated almost exclusively on production management and customer service. The industry has entered the mature stage of the product life cycle. Potential catering clients have a myriad of choices today, and some of them think that one caterer is as good as another. The successful caterer must develop a competitive edge in order to dispel this image and stand out in a crowded field.

Many clients do not simply purchase a meal, they buy an experience. They buy fantasy. They buy fun, service, ambience, entertainment, and memories. Buying food and beverages is only a component of the fun and fantasy. Much of what a caterer sells is intangible. The client cannot touch or feel an event beforehand. The caterer is selling something that has yet to be produced and delivered; it cannot be resold, restocked, or returned. Clients purchase what they think will happen. It is a gamble for them. They are understandably nervous and need to be reassured that they have made the correct decision. The caterer must create a sense of trust with his or her clients.

Caterers who consistently achieve their revenue and profit goals are those who understand these unique characteristics and develop marketing procedures to exploit them. In today's business environment a strong price/value relationship must prevail in order to attract a profitable share of the market. A facility's services must be equal to or better than its competition's. The sales staff must be completely familiar with the services offered, their costs and benefits, and their impact on the facility's overall performance.

Catering functions, when properly priced, are usually quite profitable. The type and quality of cuisine offered, ability to accommodate large groups, entertainment attractions, and variety of services offered are the major factors a client considers when selecting a caterer. The successful catering department will ensure that these aspects are clearly defined and articulated to potential clients.

THE MARKETING PLAN

Michael Roman, president of CaterSource, Inc., notes that the successful caterer develops a well-defined marketing plan and follows it closely. He maintains that the marketing plan must include three major aspects: (1) getting the job, (2) performing well, and (3) following up.

Getting the Job

Before a facility can solicit catering business, it must first define clearly the market(s) it wants to service. Many facilities mix and match several markets. This affords the opportunity to maximize revenue and profit. However, specialization can lead to increased efficiency as well as a unique reputation and image in the marketplace.

The desired market(s) should be examined closely to determine the extent of its catering needs. For example, if a facility wishes to cater to the business market, it should examine closely and quantify the supply (i.e., other competing caterers) and the demand (i.e., potential business clients) to see whether it is economically feasible to concentrate on that segment.

After determining the desired market(s), the next step is to set financial goals. There should be revenue and profit goals. There also should be attention paid to other income that can be generated indirectly from catering; for instance, a wedding party can generate sleeping room business for a hotel, as well as bar, gift shop and parking revenue. Additional income may also be generated by up$elling, thank-you gift baskets for parents, and the like.

Revenue and profit goals must be reasonable. "Booking pace" is the term used to describe the amount of business a catering sales manager is expected to sell within a prescribed time frame. It is useless to set unrealistically high goals, because the certain failure to attain them can deplete employee morale and badly skew business projections. By the same token, the catering executive must be willing to take some risks when setting these goals. If or she is unduly conservative, the facility's overall performance will suffer in the long run.

Getting the job—booking business—also includes creating a particular image. If, for example, a caterer wants to specialize in the weddings business, it should develop logos, menus, decorations, room layouts and designs, employee uniforms, and so forth, to complement and enhance this image. This clientele segment will identify with these details.

The catering department must set standard procedures, which sales representatives should use to solicit business. These procedures must be consistent with the desired image. For example, a caterer seeking clients in the deep end of the business market must tailor its sales solicitation efforts accordingly, which may even include its representative's image, attire, and vehicle used, as well as collateral material presented.

It is important to develop standardized procedures to (1) canvass for new clients, (2) qualify leads, (3) make sales calls, (4) advise clients, (5) develop contracts, and (6) provide required products and services. A complete description of all catering policies and procedures must be prepared and distributed to the catering staff and all other relevant operating departments.

Performing Well

Once bookings are obtained, the emphasis shifts from sales to execution and service. Clients and their guests want to be treated with care. They want their needs to be handled in a professional manner. Above all, function hosts want the caterer to make them look good. Michael Roman says a catering client's greatest fear is the fear of being embarrassed by the caterer with poor food quality, inadequate amounts, poor service, and/or poor presentation.

Performing well involves standardized procedures designed to ensure that (1) service is punctual, (2) foods, beverages, presentations, sanitation, cleanliness, and ambience meet established quality standards, (3) professional attention will be paid to all details, (4) the function host will be made to feel like a guest at his or her event, and (5) all last-minute requests and/or crises will be handled calmly, professionally, and to everyone's satisfaction.

A caterer's performing well is the bottom line for clients. They have entrusted their events to outsiders. They have relinquished control. Consequently, they will be understandably nervous and anxious. The caterer who can satisfy clients and make them look good will enjoy several benefits. Referral business is an obvious benefit, as is repeat patronage. It cannot be over emphasized that it is much harder and much more expensive to get new customers than to keep old ones. Referral and repeat business lead to a profitable catering operation; they are critical to the life of any catering business.

Following Up

Following up is another very important part of the marketing plan. Standardized procedures must be developed to ensure that (1) thank-you calls are made, (2) individual, personalized follow-up letters are written and sent, (3) event assessments are performed, one with the client and one with the catering staff, wherein all aspects of the function are fairly evaluated and critiqued (See the Appendix for a Post Event Critique example.), (4) referral business is solicited, (5) appropriate souvenir gifts are presented to clients, and (6) accounts are settled.

Many industry experts believe that the follow-up stage is the most critical part of the marketing plan. The caterer and the client have been working together for some time. It is inappropriate simply to give the client an invoice at the end of the event and say, "See you around." The relationship should not be ended abruptly; it must be continued. The few moments spent with clients during the follow-up stage will pay huge dividends.

This is the time when the caterer can learn something from or about the client that can be used to improve future events. It is also the time when long-term relationships are cemented. The seeds of referral and repeat business are planted and cultivated during the follow-up period.

THE MARKETING BUDGET

Marketing expenses usually represent a significant percentage of expected sales revenue. For instance, the average U.S. foodservice operation spends about 2 to 5 percent of sales revenue for direct marketing expenses such as advertising, promotion, public relations, franchising fees, royalties, and other fees and commissions.

Some hospitality operations allocate a set percentage of expected annual sales revenue for marketing at the beginning of the year. The caterer is then expected to use these funds to accomplish the stated objectives. Sometimes there is some flexibility with these funds, whereby monies can be shifted from one marketing expense to another. Other properties, however, assign a "line item" budget—that is, the department head has no flexibility; for example, the catering manager cannot spend less money for brochures and shift the savings to radio advertising.

Some catering departments are allocated a specific dollar amount for marketing expenses, rather than a set percentage of expected sales revenue. Prior to the beginning of a fiscal year, the director of catering, in conjunction with top management, prepares an annual budget for the catering department. This budget includes all anticipated departmental incomes and expenses.

As a general rule, the sales forecast is based on tangible factors, such as business already booked, and expenses, such as food, beverage, and payroll costs, that are expected to be a certain percentage of these projected sales. If estimated sales increase or decrease, most expenses (except those that are completely fixed) must follow the curve and stay within their allocated percentage. If there are any variances, you usually do not change the budget. You document them, pay the extra costs (if necessary), and learn from them so that the next budget does not suffer the same fate.

Some facilities may revise the annual budget periodically. For instance, after three or four months the director of catering and top management may agree to shift funds from one expense category to another if business warrants. Or these executives may decide in midstream to allocate additional funds, say, to advertising, in order to combat a new competitor who plans to open soon.

When allocating the marketing budget, management generally considers historical trends as well as new business opportunities. As a general rule, past performance is the key variable influencing the budget. An analysis of previous revenues and expenses can reveal expected future trends. The marketing budget's accuracy depends primarily on effective sales analyses. A thorough sales analysis includes the following:

○ *Total revenue.*   Monthly revenue totals should be evaluated with an eye toward determining trends. This helps to ensure that marketing dollars are directed to the seasons with the most sales potential, based on market conditions and any changes or trends noted.

○ *Average revenue per function.*   This statistic will reveal average productivity per function. If there is a consistent shortfall between the actual average revenue and the potential average revenue, marketing dollars can be devoted to reconciling this inequity.

○ *Average revenue per type of function.*   This figure will indicate which functions carry the greatest sales potential; marketing funds can therefore be allocated appropriately.

○ *Average guest count per function.*   Some functions have few guests. Unless they are paying a large amount per guest, it may be more profitable to ignore them and concentrate on larger groups. More guests mean more exposure.

○ *Average check.*   The per-person price for different types of functions is a good measure of labor productivity. It also can reveal opportunities where marketing dollars can be spent in an effort to increase the average revenue per guest.

○ *Average contribution margin.*   This is similar to the average check. The difference is that it is the amount of money available from the average check after you pay the cost of food and beverage used to serve a guest. Most foodservice experts agree that the average contribution margin per guest is more important than the average check because it represents the amount of money left to cover all other expenses and a fair profit.

○ *Number of functions.* A monthly analysis can indicate how well the facility manages and sells its available space. Trends will reveal where marketing dollars should be deployed; for instance, if February is a slow month, perhaps a slight change in the marketing plan can significantly improve sales and profits during this time period.

○ *Space utilization percentages.* This analysis can indicate periods of time when certain function space is underutilized. For example, if a particular meeting room is vacant almost every Wednesday and Thursday, a change in the marketing plan should be considered to increase business on those days.

○ *Popularity of different types of functions.* These statistics can indicate the catering department's strengths and weaknesses. If, for instance, weddings are the most popular function, it is obvious that clients view your facility as a good place to hold these events. This can be a mixed blessing. On the one hand, it can give you a competitive edge for this type of business. But on the other hand, it may eliminate you from consideration by other types of potential clients.

○ *Percentage of repeat business.* It takes more time, money, and effort to acquire a new customer than it does to retain an old one. Turning a customer into a repeat patron is a major challenge. However, the rewards are substantial.

○ *Percentage of referral business.* You know a product is good when you can recommend it to your friends. The caterer who receives a considerable percentage of referral business is obviously doing something right.

The primary purpose of performing this type of sales analysis is to determine the success rate of the current marketing plan. If the results of the analysis suggest that changes should be made, then future marketing efforts will have to be altered to reflect a new direction.

If the marketing plan requires significant alteration, the director of catering should ensure that a thorough market and competition analysis is performed before taking any steps to change it. The analysis can reveal potential opportunities and suggest profitable changes that should be considered. A market and competition analysis involves a thorough evaluation of (1) the facility's capabilities, (2) the types of markets available, (3) potential sales trends in these markets, (4) number and types of competitors, (5) the facility's strengths and weaknesses, as compared with its competitors, and (6) trends in sales solicitation efforts.

Alterations to a marketing plan should never be made hastily. Once a plan has been established, it should be given a fair chance to work. You should not make a habit of second-guessing your marketing efforts. Changes in the marketing plan should be considered only after evaluating past trends and future opportunities. They should be made only if there is a reasonable expectation of increasing sales revenue and profits.

MARKETING RESEARCH

Marketing research should be an ongoing activity. It involves a continuing analysis of the potential clients and competitors that reside within the facility's market area. A catering department's trading area, however, is not easy to define. Theoretically, it could be the world; realistically, it is a lot closer to home.

Foodservice operations sometimes separate their trading areas into primary trading areas and secondary trading areas. The primary area generates at least 50 percent of the foodservice's business, with the rest coming from the secondary area.

Restaurants also tend to segregate their trading areas into meal segments, such as lunch market areas and dinner market areas. Those who analyze potential restaurant locations usually note that lunch customers will not travel more than 10 minutes to a preferred restaurant, whereas dinner guests generally will travel up to 30 minutes.

Caterers do not have such neat rules of thumb to guide their marketing research efforts. However, they usually maintain adequate records that can help them determine as accurately as possible the sales revenues and profits they can expect to earn in the future. The major records needed are (1) group history files, (2) lost business files, (3) tracer files, and (4) market and competition surveys.

Group History Files

A group history file should be created whenever initial contact is made with a prospective client. Eventually, this file will include all facets of the business relationship with the client. The file involves a synopsis of all relevant aspects of the catered event, from initial inquiry to final disposition.

A catering department usually uses a standardized format to record client information. For instance, when a potential client calls the caterer for price quotations and space availability, the important details are recorded. A sales representative follows up on the inquiry after studying these details. If the initial inquiry results in a booked event, the appropriate entries are made in the function book and in the group history file. Much of this detail is kept on a computer.

A group history file is also created when a sales representative solicits catering business from a prospective client. In some instances, there may be tentative group history files created for potential clients; for instance, sales representatives may develop open files of potential clients whose names and group affiliations are obtained from mailing lists, directories, and/or referrals.

The group history file should contain all relevant information, such as correspondence, client decision maker, attendance figures, contracts, potential for future business, credit history, business referrals, testimonial letters, and other similar data. Group history files help the marketing effort because they reveal consumer desires, trends, and price sensitivity. They usually contain information that, when analyzed carefully, can indicate future business opportunities. The information noted in such files can lead directly to additional catering business.

Group history files represent the caterer's major source of repeat patronage. The wise director of catering will ensure that the client decision makers noted in these files are not forgotten. He or she will personally maintain some sort of communication link with them or assign this responsibility to another member of the catering staff. For instance, birthday cards, direct mail flyers, and/or holiday greeting cards should be sent to these individuals. Thanksgiving cards should be considered in lieu of, or in addition to, Christmas cards. Thanksgiving cards stand out, instead of being lost in the jumble. Because clients are from a variety of faiths, always opt for "Season's Greetings" instead of "Merry Christmas."

This is called "relationship marketing"; in other words, you develop professional friendships and positive rapport with your clients. Clients should feel that they have a "friend in the catering business," because then they will tell others about you.

Lost Business File

If client inquiries or sales solicitations do not lead to booked business, the group history file should be transformed into a lost business file. These files must be evaluated periodically to determine why potential business did not materialize. If certain patterns—such as space unavailability, high prices, or inadequate menu offerings—are discovered, perhaps the facility can do something to improve the underlying problems. For instance, if there is a consistent problem with space availability, the facility can use this information to support a proposal to construct additional function rooms, erect a permanent tent, or create a poolside or roof patio area for outdoor events. Future marketing plans, highlighting the additional space, may thereby lead to a significant increase in business.

Some lost business files will be created after the catering event is booked. For instance, an event is scheduled, but the client cancels at the last minute. The director of catering will want to know why the client had a change of heart. It is inappropriate merely to retain the client's deposit—some further contact with the client must be made to determine why the cancellation occurred.

Tracer Files

Tracer files (sometimes referred to as tickler files) are similar to a manager's personal list of "things to do today." For instance, if a current client books catering business on a fairly regular basis, the manager's tracer file will include this information. These files are typically kept on a computer, using one of the excellent software packages available. (See our companion web site.) The file will also note when the client should be contacted, how he or she should be approached, any special considerations that must be offered, and so forth. A tracer file should be established for tentative bookings so that space is not held more than, say, two weeks without a deposit or definite option. Similarly, a tracer file can be developed that will trace the number of bookings per market segment.

A market segment that provides 5 percent or more of total catering business should be monitored closely for trends and other indicators of future business. Furthermore, if the facility has, say, 18 separate market segments, it should consider developing a specific marketing plan for each one.

Lost business files should be part of the facility's tracer filing system. Lost business should be coded according to the reason that it was lost. The individual lost business events should be "tickled," that is, they should be put on a calendar so that a catering sales representative will be prompted to go back to the file the same time next year and attempt to solicit the client's future business.

Catering sales representatives usually update the tracer files daily, adding information to them as it is obtained. They will also use a system whereby the group history files will be traced and reviewed a few days before client decision makers are contacted.

Some catering departments use a secretary to monitor the tracer filing system. He or she is then responsible for planning part of the catering sales representatives' workdays.

Market and Competition Surveys

Market and competition surveys consist of detailed descriptions of potential clients and current and potential competitors.

Sales representatives are expected to canvass for new clients; that is, they are responsible for "sourcing" new clients by studying consumer trends, client desires, and similar data. The best way to obtain these data is to conduct a market and competition survey. A market survey can be a simple questionnaire sent to potential clients, asking them about their catering needs and the amount of money they would be willing to pay for these services. More elaborate, professionally conducted surveys are very costly, but they do reveal considerably more information. A local college with a hospitality program can often provide assistance at a nominal cost. Frequently, a marketing class will do this as a class project. Contact faculty members to see whether they can help or can direct you to other resources. Often, graduate students are looking for funded projects.

Food and beverage trade associations, such as the National Restaurant Association (NRA), conduct market surveys that may be useful to the director of catering.

A competition survey should be an ongoing effort. Catering executives must know as much as they can about the competition. The caterer's marketing plan cannot be completed without some knowledge of competing products and services.

A competition survey should include the following information for each competitor, whether hotel, club, or other type of venue:

1 Competitor name and address
2 Amount and type of function space available
3 Guest capacity
4 Major markets serviced
5 Franchise or chain affiliation, if any
6 Number of catering employees (service level)

 7 Average checks, or other similar data
 8 Main products and services offered (menus, package plans, etc.)
 9 Daily analysis of any reader boards in the facility's lobby or foyer
10 Style of decor (rustic, elegant, trendy, traditional, etc.)

When gathering data on competitors, you must not violate federal, state, or local antitrust laws. You cannot get together with a competitor and discuss your pricing strategies. Nor can you agree to charge the same prices that a competitor charges.

The competition survey will reveal any unmet market niches. For instance, if a director of catering learns that no one seems to be specializing in the civic events market segment, or the after-theater dinner crowd, he or she may decide to explore the possibility of targeting this pool of potential business.

The competition survey also lets the catering executive know what he or she is up against. It is important to differentiate yourself from your competitors. *Differentiation* is being the best, in comparison with your competition, on the criteria valued by your customers. It is like "branding." Today's consumer looks to brands, such as Coca-Cola, Black Angus Beef, and Provimi Veal. They trust these products when making purchasing decisions. Consumers are loyal to brands that stand for something, such as quality and reliability. In today's competitive hospitality business, it is necessary to carve out a unique reputation, image, and/or specialty. However, any attempt to do so should be initiated only after analyzing the competitive environment.

THE FOUR P'S OF MARKETING

An effective marketing plan includes a description of a facility's (1) *Place*, (2) *Products* and services offered, (3) *Prices* charged, and (4) *Promotion* policies and procedures. The director of catering, either alone or in conjunction with other management personnel, must develop and implement these four P's of marketing.

Place

Place refers to the facility's location, amount of function space available, and the type of environment and ambiance provided. Clients are very much interested in a property's space availability, particularly the number of persons that can be accommodated, as well as the speed with which they can be served. They also are interested in other space issues. For instance, meeting planners may want to know how long it takes for 1,000 conventioneers to ride the elevators from a hotel lobby to the 14th floor during normal meal hours, or whether a restaurant has adequate parking or offers valet parking services.

A property's environment and ambiance include its sanitation, cleanliness, decor, view, and other related factors. Many facilities must consider the implications of the appearance, level of crime, safety, and/or prestige of their neighborhoods. The director of catering cannot do anything about the facility's location, but he or she can ensure that the controllable variables meet established quality-control standards.

Products and Services

The facility's *products and services* are probably the most flexible parts of its marketing plan. A large facility usually enjoys the ability to provide an unlimited number of menu items, meal service styles, and other ancillary services. The property that offers clients a one-stop shopping opportunity usually has a significant competitive edge in the marketplace.

Price

Price is perhaps one of the most important and troublesome parts of a marketing plan. It is of major concern to clients. It can also present several problems for caterers, particularly because it is risky to quote prices too far in advance.

How does your facility establish prices for your catering brochure? Every business must grapple with the question, "How much do I charge?" Pricing is not an easy task; there are many variables in the decision-making process. There is also a delicate balance between client demand and price level. Prices can be calculated by any of the following methods, then reviewed for competitive factors, reasonableness, potential acceptance, and profitability.

What things should you consider when determining prices? Any method should account for inflation, menu printing costs, waste, and changing markets. The mechanics of menu pricing usually begin with determining the cost of the product (food) and the cost of labor to prepare and serve the meal.

Profit requirements should be factored into the price and treated as a cost, just like any other cost of doing business. Pricing is a function of both marketing and cost accounting.

Some restaurant operators like to estimate their total annual expenses (except food costs), add in a fair annual profit, and divide this amount by the estimated number of customers expected during the year. This figure is the average amount of contribution margin (CM) needed from each customer. A menu price for any particular item, then, is the food cost for one serving plus the average CM.

For example, assume the director of catering needs to earn an annual profit of $250,000, the forecasted annual expenses (except food costs) are $1,500,000, and 125,000 guests are expected during the year. In this case, the total amount of CM needed is $1,750,000 ($250,000 + $1,500,000) and the average CM is $14.00 ($1,750,000/125,000). A menu item with a food cost of $4.50 would be priced at $18.50 ($4.50 + $14.00) plus applicable consumption taxes, gratuities, and/or service charges.

When using this type of pricing procedure, the menu planner assumes that all costs of doing business, except food costs, are fixed. Realistically, food is not the only variable cost incurred by the typical foodservice operation; for instance, labor cost is at least a semivariable cost. However, the conservative menu planner realizes that semivariable costs are more fixed than variable. To open the doors of a facility, a certain critical mass of labor, utilities, and so forth, must be made available, and this critical mass can be quite expensive.

A catering sales representative may use this type of pricing procedure when computing competitive price quotations and preparing proposals. Alternatively, he or she could use a variation of this method. For instance, a total CM can be calculated that does not include food costs or labor costs. The average CM can then be added to the estimate of payroll and food costs needed for the catered function.

For instance, assume a client wants to book a party for 100 persons and that the catering sales representative knows from experience that the average CM per person must be $5.00. Initially, then, we know that the function must earn a total CM of $500 (100 × $5.00). Next, we determine that we will need about 6 servers and food production workers, which are priced out at, say, $460. If the menu desired is precosted at $6.00 per serving, the total food cost is $600 (100 × $6.00). The price quotation will be $15.60 per person (($500 + $460 + $600)/100) plus applicable consumption taxes, gratuities, and/or service charges.

Another way to price a meal function is to charge one price for the meal, one for labor, one for room rental, one for equipment rental, and so forth. This type of pricing is more common with off-premise caterers than with on-premise facilities. As a general rule, on-premise facilities do not use this pricing strategy primarily because it is too cumbersome. The typical on-premise client does not want to be burdened with an itemized list of charges, even though it tends to be less expensive to negotiate for each charge separately. The client prefers a price-per-person bottom line. It is more convenient, and it makes it easier for him or her to compare price quotations from several caterers. Off-premise caterers, who must rent tables, chairs, china, flatware, and so forth, are more likely to quote charges separately.

Pricing objectives can be classified as follows:

○ Financial, such as covering all costs and earning a targeted profit
○ Volume driven, such as maintaining a high level of activity in order to sustain maximum profits
○ Competitive factors, i.e., retaining a customer base and increasing market share
○ Client's relative perception of value, i.e., ensuring that clients are offered the appropriate price/quality/service combination

All of these variables must be weighed carefully in establishing prices. It is important not to lean too heavily on just one variable. Any method should account for inflation, menu printing costs, waste, and changing markets. The mechanics of menu pricing begin with determining the cost of the product (food), including the seasonality of ingredients, and the amount of labor cost, influenced by the complexity of the preparation of the dish.

Clients generally want good-quality products at the lowest possible price. A person who would not think of haggling over price at a restaurant will nickel and dime you over a catering menu. Prices established by management must strike a fine balance between the client's need for value and the facility's need for maximum return on investment.

Sometimes prices are influenced by your competition. In this case, pricing usually begins with reviewing competitor prices. Competitors can be defined as those caterers who offer similar products, services, and atmosphere to a client in the same market area. You must first identify your competitors, study their menus, and know their selling prices.

Before quoting a tentative price to a potential client, you may want to revise it in light of any recent competitive pressures. For instance, if your direct competitors are selling the same product for one dollar less than your price estimate, you may need to meet this competitive price or, alternatively, convince the client that you provide additional value to justify the extra dollar.

Experience shows that competition may be the most important element in the pricing formula. Often, it is the major influence on the final price quoted.

One way to address competitors' prices is to use your price quotation as your competitive bid, subject to negotiation. For instance, you may give potential clients several price/quality options and let them mix and match according to their needs.

Another way to beat the competition is to differentiate your facility from similar establishments, be they local hotels, restaurants with banquet facilities, or freestanding off-premise event venues. One way to differentiate is to offer flexible pricing or higher value.

Sometimes prices are a function of management intuition. The following are examples of intuitive pricing procedures:

○ *Reasonable Price Method.*   Setting a price to represent a value to the client. Asking, "If I were a customer, what would I be willing to pay for this meal?" This method does not consider profit requirements, food cost, or labor cost.

○ *Highest Price Method.*   Setting the highest price you think the customer will pay. This method does not consider profit requirements, food cost, or labor cost. It relies on the principles of supply and demand (or whatever the market will bear).

○ *Loss Leader Price Method.*   Marking the price of an item or items unusually low with the rationale that clients will be attracted by the low price and will subsequently purchase other items at regular or inflated prices. This method does not consider profit requirements, food cost, or labor cost.

○ *Trial and Error.*   Taking a wild guess, and if that price does not work, trying another price. This method does not consider profit requirements and can affect the client's perception of the operation.

○ *Management's Guidance/Policies.*   Conforming to the constraints of higher-ups. This approach does not consider profit requirements.

Many caterers use a food cost method to price menus. However, food cost should not be the only consideration. Production cost and the amount of variety offered are also important. For instance, lengthy preparation time caused by difficult menu items or large varieties will increase your labor cost.

A typical food cost method involves the use of a food cost formula. However, this method does not consider the cost of labor or other expenses. It considers only the cost of the products.

To determine the selling price of each menu item, the following formula is used:

Plate cost ÷ % food cost = selling price

For instance, if a menu item costs $1.25 and you desire a 32 percent food cost, the menu price will be $3.91 *($1.25 ÷ 32% = $3.91 selling price)*.

Unfortunately, this is not the most effective method of pricing, as shown in the following example:

Menu Item	Food Cost	Menu Price	Food Cost % Margin	Contribution
Chicken	$1.50	$4.50	33%	$3.00
Steak	$3.00	$7.00	43%	$4.00

Even though the food cost and the food cost percentage on the steak is higher, the dollar amount of the contribution margin is much higher.

Another formula that is sometimes used is adding a *flat percentage* to the cost of food, beverages, and services. But this may not be an effective pricing method, because, like most formulas, it does not always consider the cost of labor and other expenses. Still another formula that can be used is the *prime cost method*. This method takes into account the combined cost of the product (food) and the cost of labor to come up with a "prime cost" equal to approximately 55 to 60 percent of the menu price. This formula forces you to account for labor; you cannot ignore it or separate it from the final price.

There are many other things to consider in establishing or recommending menu pricing:

○ What is your net income objective?
○ Should you set prices to generate additional business (quantity)?

○ Do you try to price so updates do not have to be done very often?

○ Is the chef determining all pricing?

○ When revising, should you take your last price and add a certain percentage more? All menu items should be evaluated and reviewed on a regular basis and prices changed as necessary.

○ What does your competition charge for similar products and services? The pricing of your menu is where competitive shopping comes heavily into play. If your prices are too high, then you are forcing your clients to the competition. Always keep in mind what your competitors are doing.

○ Whom are you trying to target with your catering brochure? What are their preferences regarding selections, and what level of affordability are they prepared to accept?

○ What will be your menu mix (high volume, high profit versus low volume, low-profit)? Your brochure should target all economic levels.

○ What items take more/less preparation, therefore affecting labor cost?

○ Have you developed a brochure in which you start building a basic menu and accompaniments and which lends itself to enhancements and up$elling opportunities?

○ Are you looking at the total income from all arrangements and services, or from only the sale of the food itself? Price is not the only gauge utilized by your clients. Value pricing, that is, value as related to quality and service, is very important to your clients. All of these items should be taken into consideration in pricing your menu. Value pricing is a direct response to increased competition at all levels. Value is defined as the perception that quality and service equal or are on a par with price. Does your pricing strategy include built-in provisions for complementary "upgrades" (added value to the client at no cost to the facility)? In New Orleans, the term *lagniappe,* which means "a little bit extra" is commonly used. Always try to add a lagniappe to your pricing. The unexpected, pleasant surprise can produce client satisfaction and goodwill, resulting in repeat business. You might include a glass of wine, increase portion sizes, provide a complimentary centerpiece, or upgrade the breads, for example.

○ Do you use market price for items with fluctuating costs, such as fresh swordfish?

Experience shows that taking all of the following features into consideration will assist you in creating a brochure/menu that is not only cost-effective, but something you and your staff can take pride in:

○ *Mark-up Factor:* The amount that food costs must be increased to cover direct food expense, other allowable costs, and contributions toward the facility's total profit needs.
○ *Profit Centers:*
  ○ Food
  ○ Beverage
  ○ Extra services
  ○ Facilities (if room rental charges are applied)
    It is important to determine whether you want to charge one price for all or to use itemized prices.
○ *Breakeven Analysis:* The point at which revenues match costs. Includes fixed and variable costs.
  ○ Fixed costs—costs that stay the same, regardless of business fluctuations, such as mortgage payments, interest, employees' salaries, etc.
  ○ Variable costs—costs that change, depending on business fluctuation, such as costs for casual labor, food, etc.
  ○ The breakeven point = Fixed costs ÷ (fixed costs ÷ total sales).
○ *Desired Contribution Margin*
○ *Elasticity of Demand:* If a reduced selling price leads to the sale of enough additional items to increase the product's total revenue, the price usually should be lowered. However, if a higher price results in decreased revenues because fewer items are sold at the higher price, then it is not effective.
○ *Marginal Revenue:* Managers are often tempted to reduce prices in the hope that more clients will book their events and the result will be increased gross sales. Marginal revenue is the difference between the gross sales at the old price and the gross sales at the new or "special" price.
○ *Cost Margin Analysis:* Each menu item is examined based on three factors:
  ○ Popularity
  ○ Food cost percentage
  ○ Weighted contribution margin or total contribution to profit

The following information is needed from the facility's sales history and accounting records:

○ Number sold of each menu item
○ Food cost of each item
○ Selling price of each item

Each menu item is compared with other available items. Menu items that sell above the average number of items sold are classified as popular. If the average number of each entrée sold was 400 in a month, the entrées that sold in excess of 400 would be considered popular, whereas those selling at less than 400 would be considered not as popular.

Then each menu item's potential food cost is calculated. Items with potential food costs below the average potential food cost are considered low-cost menu items, and those with costs above the average are considered high-cost menu items. Alternatively, the potential food cost percentages can be compared.

The purpose of this analysis is to evaluate the need for menu changes. For instance, unpopular items may be repriced or dropped from the menu.

Many variable costs in our industry fluctuate widely. This is especially true of food costs, which tend to undergo seasonal price changes and are subject to the vagaries of weather. Some facilities have long-term relationships or contracts with a few of their suppliers, so a certain amount of long-term predictability can be achieved. However, many suppliers are just as unwilling as catering directors to offer long-term price guarantees.

A catering department has several costs that must be covered. In addition to food and beverage costs, it will incur costs for payroll, payroll benefits, direct operating supplies, music licensing and entertainment, advertising and promotion, utilities, administrative and general, repairs and maintenance, rents, property taxes, property insurance, interest, depreciation, other taxes, and miscellaneous deductions.

Appropriate prices must be charged in order to cover the fixed and variable costs, and to leave a fair profit for the business. The director of catering must also ensure that prices are competitive. It is a delicate balancing act.

Often the total price quoted for a catered event is the sum of several prices for individual client needs. For instance, a conference center's total price may include charges for food and beverages, room rentals, deposits, security, setups, audiovisual (AV) equipment, lighting, entertainment, and printing. With so many aspects to consider, there is ample room for negotiations between clients and the caterer.

Computing the total price can be somewhat complicated. The catering executive must have a good understanding of costs in order to compute competitive and profitable prices. For instance, when computing food menu prices, the catering manager must work closely with the chef to (1) precost the menu, (2) factor in other variable costs (often called the "Q factor" in restaurants), such as payroll, payroll benefits, and direct operating supplies, and (3) factor in an allowance for fixed costs (i.e., overhead) and profit.

Menu precosting involves costing out each food item recipe in order to compute the food cost per serving. This cost is multiplied by the number of servings needed. The amount of other variable costs needed to service the particular type and size of event must be added, as well as the additional charge needed to cover overhead and profit. If applicable, charges for room rental, security, setups, and so forth must be included. The total price can then be divided by the number of attendees to obtain a per-person price quotation, or the manager can quote the total price for the event for a fixed number of guests.

Computing prices can also be very challenging if you are calculating them for customized menus. Some caterers use a component pricing procedure, illustrated in the chart on page 61, to guide their pricing decisions.

Once a total food cost is calculated, the caterer typically multiplies it by a factor of 4.5 to 5 to determine the total price for the event. This ensures that the food cost percentage will be approximately 20 to 22.5 percent. The resulting total price in this example is a bit higher than the total for comparable foods and beverages listed on a standardized catering menu; however, it is necessary to compensate the property for the extra work needed to create and serve a unique menu.

If applicable, the director of catering must also determine room rental rates and other similar charges. The basic pricing format is the same as that used for setting menu prices. The total price is a compilation of variable costs, fixed costs, and profit. For instance, when setting room rental rates, one would consider the variable costs—such as utilities, setup, cleaning, and security—and the fixed costs—such as insurance, depreciation, and taxes. A profit margin would then be added.

Usually, the fixed-cost portion of any price is calculated only once in a while. For instance, the director of catering will generally have a good idea of the amount of fixed charges he or she will incur whenever a particular banquet room must be opened, set up, readied for service, torn down, and cleaned. These costs are usually determined by upper management. When calculating a price quotation for a meal

CUSTOM MENU/ITEM COST SHEET

Event Name: _____ Event Date: _____ Sales Rep _____

Function Type: ____ Breakfast ____ Lunch ____ Dinner ____ Plated ____ Buffet ____ Reception ____ #PP

Appetizers/Soups	POR SIZE	COST		POR SIZE	COST
_____	_____	____	Rolls and Butter	_____	____
_____	_____	____	or		
_____	_____	____	Sliced Breads and Butter	_____	____
_____	_____	____	Beverage		
Salad			_____	_____	____
_____	_____	____	Dessert		
_____	_____	____	_____	_____	____
_____	_____	____	_____	_____	____
_____	_____	____	_____	_____	____
Entrée/Sauces			_____	_____	____
_____	_____	____	Miscellaneous		
_____	_____	____	_____	_____	____
_____	_____	____	_____	_____	____
_____	_____	____	_____	_____	____
_____	_____	____	_____	_____	____
Vegetable/Starch			Total Food Cost	_____	
_____	_____	____			
_____	_____	____	Retail Cost	_____	
_____	_____	____			
_____	_____	____	Cost %	_____	

Comments

_____
_____
_____

_____ _____
Approved Executive Chef   Director of Sales or Operations Director

61

function, the catering sales representative divides these fixed charges by the number of guests to get a per-person overhead charge. To this charge he or she adds the variable costs needed per person to determine a tentative price quotation.

The same pricing strategy can also be used in determining menu prices for a standardized menu. You can compute the variable costs for one serving and add to it the standard set charge to cover overhead and profit. For example, some menu items' prices are set to reflect a 25 to 30 percent food cost. The remaining 70 to 75 percent (i.e., the contribution margin) is usually sufficient to cover all other costs and leave a fair profit for the facility.

Some caterers prefer a *level pricing* technique. This method allows for comparison shopping at your facility. For example, the following chart gives clients many price quality options within prescribed limits.

	Popular	Up-scale	Value Based
Chicken	Picatta	Oscar	Dijon
	$24.00*	$32.00*	$22.00*
Staff	B-team	A-team	C-team
	$500.00	$700.00	$400.00
Linen	Color choice	Overlays	White only
	$250.00	$400.00	$125.00
Chairs	Stacking	Ballroom	Padded
	$850.00	$1,400.00	$600.00
Floral	Roses	Orchids	Carnations
	$400.00	$600.00	$300.00
Music	Duo	Trio	Solo
	$550.00	$750.00	$375.00

*per person.

The *range pricing* method is recommended when a client gives you a count with a wide range of expected guests. For instance, the following chart gives clients an idea of how fluctuating guest counts can affect the total bill.

Prime Rib Dinner	Number of Guests	Price per Guest
	235 or less	$29.75
	236 to 265	$27.45
	266 and up	$24.25

Using a traditional restaurant pricing method, you might quote a per-person price on a banquet whether 200 or 300 guests are expected. This method works well with the higher count, but not as well if the count drops, because fixed costs are divided by a smaller number of guests. So if a price of $24.25 per person was quoted, based on 200 to 300 guests, and the final count is 208 guests, your revenue would be $5,044.00 (208 × $24.25).

Using range pricing, your revenue would be $6,188.00 (208 × $29.75), permitting you to pick up an additional $1,144.00 that you normally would not have received. This additional revenue is necessary because your overhead expenses do not vary much; they would be about the same even if you served 200 to 250 guests.

Many events are booked years in advance at convention centers and hotels, and it is not feasible to quote catering prices more than three months in advance. In this case, the agreement (contract) can be written to state, "If this meal were purchased today, the price would be $25.00. At the time of your meeting, the price may be higher or lower, depending on the fluctuation of the consumer price index (CPI), with a maximum cap of $30.00." The CPI is then noted, and if it is 3 percent higher at the time of the event, the price of the meal is increased by 3 percent. If the CPI is 2 percent lower, the price is decreased by 2 percent. This puts an independent variable in charge of the final price, which is fair to both parties.

There are times when the catering department prices its goods and services to break even or to incur a loss. For instance, catered events for charities may be provided free of charge, or they may be priced to cover only the prime cost (i.e., food, beverage, and payroll expenses). This loss-leader pricing strategy is a typical procedure used whenever customers are solicited for other types of profitable business or for the public relations value.

Deposits, guarantees, cancellation fees, gratuities, tips, and refund policies must also be detailed by the director of catering and reviewed by senior management. These rates are usually influenced by the season, opportunity costs associated with last-minute cancellations, employee union contract provisions, and the facility's credit policies.

The profit margins for catered events are generally greater than those in the typical restaurant operation. However, the catering department has many more slow days—even days when there is no business—with which to contend. As a result, even though the director of catering may sympathize with clients' budgetary constraints, the fact remains that there is only so much he or she can do to accommodate them. The key to success, for all pricing methods, is to give your clients as many pricing options as possible at your property and to do what the competition is not doing.

Some larger facilities use computerized yield management procedures to calculate suggested prices for meal functions, beverage functions, function room rentals, and so forth. A computerized system essentially systematizes the intuitive process an experienced catering executive would use to calculate prices by hand. Although the catering manager could personally take into account several cost and market demand factors when preparing a competitive price quotation, he or she could accomplish the same feat electronically by feeding these data into a computerized yield management system and letting the system perform the necessary data analysis.

Computerized yield management incorporates artificial intelligence, and the formulas used to analyze the data and compute suggested prices are based on the procedures experienced managers use in doing the work by hand. The computer speeds up the decision-making process. Yield management, whether computerized or performed by hand, seeks to maximize total profits by manipulating suggested prices based on perceived demand for the goods and/or services. It is a demand-oriented process, in that the price charged should be higher if the demand is high, and lower if demand is low. The foodservice manager who discounts prices during the early evening hours in order to spur demand during this normally slow period is practicing yield management. The director of catering also applies yield management principles when he or she reduces prices during the slow seasons or discounts the function room rental rates in order to book profitable food and beverage business.

Computerizing the process ensures that all relevant data are considered and that the best decisions are made. The person booking this type of business can input the client's requests, and within a few moments the computer will determine an appropriate price quotation.

Computerized yield management is not a new concept. It has been used extensively over the years in the airline and rental car industries. Several large hotels, especially chain properties, use it to calculate sleeping room prices. Several yield management software packages have been developed that specifically address the needs of hotel catering departments. These systems can electronically manipulate prices for new bookings according to variations and fluctuations in demand patterns by different markets. The end result is maximum revenue and profit as well as more predictable, consistent business.

A smaller facility, however, will have to justify the expense of computerization. Unfortunately, with this program, the learning process requires a substantial amount of time. And, like many computer applications, it is not very friendly to users. The computerized yield management systems that handle group history files, tracer files, competitor profiles, recipe costing, and related functions also require a considerable amount of start-up data as well as continual data revision. To maintain current recipe costs, you have to load all recipe formulas, inventory data, and current purchase prices into the system. As purchase prices change, you must update them. Once updated, all recipes will be recosted by the computer, thereby ensuring that you always have the most current food and beverage costs. Yet if you fail to maintain the data files, your conclusions will be based on inaccurate information.

Promotion

Promotion includes the cost of developing and maintaining a web site; advertising in newspapers, magazines, telephone directories, and trade media; outdoor billboards and other signage; radio and television advertising; fees paid to advertising and promotion agencies; entertaining business clients (such as hosting a customer appreciation party for meeting planners); memberships in professional associations and civic and other business groups; and promotional materials, such as sales brochures, menus, photographs, videotapes, direct mail pieces, and written solicitations for catering business. If the facility is a franchisee or part of a chain or referral group, the franchising and/or referral fees and royalty payments that must be paid to the parent company are part of promotion expenses.

Public relations and publicity constitute another type of promotional effort. The costs of preparing press releases to be sent to food editors; writing books, columns, and articles about the catering industry; and hosting charity and media events are considered part of promotion expenses.

Salespersons' salaries and commissions are also included in the promotion budget. In some cases, a catering salesperson earns no salary, or a minimum salary; commissions make up the bulk of his or her paycheck. With this income arrangement, the facility usually expects the salesperson to concentrate solely on selling directly to one or more market segments.

Salespersons may also be paid commissions for developing leads. They may be hired to generate interest among potential corporate clients. Once a lead is established, it is turned over to a catering manager, who would handle proposals, planning, contracts, and so forth.

Possibly the most effective and efficient type of promotional plan a catering department can use includes (1) effective brochures, (2) well-designed, imaginative menus, (3) an effective, up-to-date web site, (4) creative proposals, (5) videotapes and photos, (6) word-of-mouth advertising, and (7) soliciting future business at current events.

These types of promotion are not given in order of importance here. For instance, you cannot say that a brochure is always more important than word-of-mouth advertising. It would be if you were using a mass-mailing campaign, but it would be much less effective than word-of-mouth advertising if you wanted to solicit specific local civic events.

Sales Brochures.   Sales brochures generally include a considerable amount of information that potential clients can evaluate when they are in the market for catering services. A brochure should include the facility's logo, slogan, catering policies, available rooms, suggested menus, prices, credit information, and service procedures.

Because a brochure may be the potential client's first contact with the catering department, it must be professionally prepared. It is an invitation to potential clients that can create a lasting impression. It should be complete and attractive, especially if the caterer is soliciting the deep segment of the business market. If a brochure is mailed, it absolutely must be sent to a specific person, not to "Manager." A great brochure is not an expense, it is an investment that pays!

Your brochure is your best marketing tool, your opportunity to show what your facility can offer. It includes your menu, which is your single most important piece of advertising. If your menu is not merchandising your catering offerings, you are doing your facility an injustice. A high-quality brochure entices the client and generates sales.

A brochure often creates the first impression of a facility and its services. In many cases, catering brochures are reviewed by potential clients in their homes or offices without the assistance of a catering sales manager to guide their choices. Often, by the time the catering manager meets with the client, initial choices have already been made.

The brochure is an integral part of any successful marketing strategy and must convey a stimulating message that will be understood by the market you are addressing. The copy should be both tasty and tasteful—the words should convey mouth-watering images—delivered hot and fresh. It is important to create and maintain an image in the client's mind. Descriptions of menu items should generate both interest and sales. The copy must talk to the consumer in his or her own words. Avoid clichés, such as "the best-kept secret," "chef's special," or "as you like it." Clients must be able to understand the names of food items, or a descriptor should be included, such as:

Kartoffel Kloesse
(Savory Potato Croquettes)

Brochures and menus include the following design elements:

- Cover
- Design format
- Layout
- Typeface/font
- Paper stock
- Colors
- Illustrations/graphics
- Copy

A brochure should be printed on a good-quality, durable paper stock. Few things bring a better return on investment than a high-quality brochure printed on high-quality paper. The heavier the paper, the better impression you will make. There is a fine line here, however. Although you want your brochures to be elegant, they should not convey the idea that your service is too expensive or that you are spending too much money on fancy brochures. On professionally printed materials, about 40 percent of the cost is for the paper. The two basic choices are cartridge paper, which has a matte finish, and coated paper, which has a shiny finish. Coated paper looks really nice, but when folded it tends to crack. Parchment has a lush texture.

Be sure you see the color print on the actual paper you will be using, as colored ink looks different on different types of paper. If you provide a sample of the color you want, a printer will be better able to best decide which ink to use to match the color. Color adds variety and interest. However, production costs escalate as you add colors, so it is usually preferable to stick with two colors, one paper color and one ink color. Dark ink on white or light-colored paper usually provides the best contrast and is easiest to read.

The colors themselves are important. Choose classic colors. For the cover of a brochure, deep royal purples, rich dusky blues, dark greens, and chocolate to mahogany browns are elegant, conveying reliability and a sense of permanence. Insipid colors, such as lime green or hot pink, create a faddish look. A rich cream paper stock for menu pages has a more cultured appearance than a stark white finish. Pantone has an excellent web site on color: *http://www.pantone.com/ allaboutcolor.*

Desktop publishing is great, if there is someone in-house who can do it attractively. This technique allows the flexibility of changing brochures and menus often. There are hundreds of typefaces (fonts) available. Choose an appropriate, easily readable style and font size. It is best to stay with the same font family, using the following variations:

plain lowercase

PLAIN CAPITALS

bold lowercase

BOLD CAPITALS

italic lowercase

ITALIC CAPITALS

bold italic lowercase

BOLD ITALIC CAPITALS

An attractive font is New Times Roman, which is the standard font on Windows-based PCs and is part of the Times family of fonts. There are also extended families, such as Goudy, Century, Swiss, Gill and Garmond. The nice thing about extended families is that they work well together when printing name plates, headers, bodies, and captions.

Brochures must be easy to read. The smallest type size used should be 12 point. Avoid the Courier font, which looks typewritten and not as professional. *Script type can be difficult to read.* ALL CAPITALS CAN BE DIFFICULT TO READ AS WELL.

Be sure the print "jumps off of the page." There should be a contrast between the paper and the print. Red print on a dark pink background would be impossible for a color-blind client to read.

Leave adequate spacing between items. Menus that are difficult to read may be discarded quickly. Many backgrounds do not fax well, so test a fax copy to see what it looks like and be sure that it is legible. Red and yellow print generally do not fax well.

Pages and brochures should incorporate graphics and/or color photographs. Photographs can help stretch the imagination. Clients should be able to picture themselves in the setting. Photographs of activities are more effective than photographs of just the facilities. If you plan to include food in the photographs, use close-up photos of finished products, not just the ingredients. Avoid the overdone, common scenes, such as the smiling chef standing next to the buffet table. Strive for a fresh approach. Bad photographs are worse than no photographs.

The best-quality photo is four color. When you are looking at a four-color photo, you are actually seeing a lot of colored dots. If you look through a magnifying glass, you will see the groups of dots—thicker where the colors are darker. The color separation during the printing determines the quality of the photograph. Be sure the food represented in the photographs looks like the food people actually receive.

The brochure should not appear crowded or cluttered. It is best to have at least 50 percent of the page blank, including wide margins and space between menu items. Be sure to include the name of your facility, address (and map), phone number, e-mail address, web site address, and any other pertinent information in a prominent position.

Be concise in your verbiage, but make your points. Be consistent in your style of writing. Mixing casual phrases with dignified statements can confuse the client.

Tell the client the benefits of holding his or her events in your facility. Give the client the information that will sell the services you can provide. You must maintain credibility. Mention any awards or favorable reviews received. Include testimonials. Tell the client the background of your chef and any other relevant information.

It is important to paint word pictures in your brochures, such as the following:

The Georgia World Congress Center and Georgia Dome offer unlimited possibilities in creative use of space and unforgettable special events. The combination of unique environments and extraordinary catering capabilities provide you with opportunities to let your imagination soar. So, whether an event takes place on the floor of the Dome, in the GWCC ballroom, or in Centennial Olympic Park, whether it's for 50 people or 50,000, we can provide the service to make a memorable experience.

The cover can be designed as a folder, and the letter of agreement, correspondence, flyers, and so on, can be placed in the pockets. The two-panel 9″ × 12″ cover is a popular size, in which standard 8½″ × 11″ stationery will easily be accommodated. This size will also fit into a standard business-size mailing envelope. Before having odd-size brochures printed, check with the post office to see what the mailing cost will be. Sometimes a fraction of an inch can greatly increase postage costs.

Standardized banquet menus are usually included in sales brochures. If so, they should be well written and attractively presented. The smart catering executive will resist the temptation to create a laundry list of menu items; he or she will include one or more examples of menu formats that clients can select for their functions.

Menus should also include mention of the facility's ability and willingness to create a personalized custom menu. The successful, competitive caterer is generally one who can accommodate specific client needs.

A facility's restaurant menus can also be used as an effective marketing tool. For instance, a creative menu from a hotel's gourmet room or from a restaurant's dining room can impress meeting planners who are visiting the facility on a fact-finding mission. Restaurant menus can also carry discreet notations that advertise catering services.

The menu portion of the brochure is vitally important. Nutritional claims must be verifiable. Be sure there are explanations for any items with which the client may not be familiar, such as ingredients or preparation method.

The menu, as well as the entire brochure, is a promise of excellence. Your menus should be user friendly. This means avoiding a separate page with prices on it. Although it may be less expensive to simply reprint a single price sheet when prices change, it is inconvenient and annoying for the client to have to look back and forth. These are called "bingo" menus because meals are identified as B-1, L-1, D-1, and so on. The client usually ends up writing the prices on the menu him- or herself, or the price sheet may become separated from the rest of the menu. Suggest complementary wines by listing them after each entrée item. Include several price ranges. Identify wines by sweetness or dryness, in addition to color or variety.

What you can offer on your menu depends on the resources you have available, such as the following:

Facility Layout/Design and Equipment.   Do you have the proper equipment, in good working order, to produce the type and quality of menu items desired?

Available Labor.   What is the skill level of your kitchen staff? Do you have enough labor to produce the volume required?

Ingredients.   Are the items on your printed menus always available? If you include seasonal ingredients, you will pay a premium for them during off-seasons.

Menus should be centered symmetrically for aesthetic appeal. Symmetry is pleasing to the eye, and this arrangement leaves blank spacing, which is easier on the eye than a page filled with print.

Menus should be written in the following order:

Menu Order for American Service

Appetizer
Soup
Salad
Main Course
Starchy Vegetable
Vegetable   Vegetable
Bread
Dessert
Beverages

Example

Shrimp Cocktail
Chicken Consommé
Caesar Salad
Roast Prime Rib of Beef
Baked Potato with Sour Cream
Steamed Broccoli   Honey-Glazed Carrots
Hot French Bread with Garlic Butter
Strawberry Shortcake
Coffee, Assorted Teas

Menu Order for French Menus

Appetizer
Soup
Intermezzo
Main Course
Starchy Vegetable
Vegetable   Vegetable
Salad
Bread
Dessert
Beverages

Example

Shrimp Cocktail
Chicken Consommé
Champagne Sorbet
Roast Prime Rib of Beef
Baked Potato with Sour Cream
Steamed Broccoli   Honey Glazed Carrots
Caesar Salad
Hot French Bread with Garlic Butter
Strawberry Shortcake
Coffee, Assorted Teas

Course headings should be in a larger and/or bolder type than the rest of the menu. Course headings serve to divide the menu into particular areas, such as appetizer, salad, main course, and dessert. The names of menu items should stand out. Descriptive wording identifying the menu ingredients, method of preparation, or other applicable information should follow. Do not overestimate the extent of your customers' knowledge; explain items they may not understand, such as Beef Wellington or Veal Oscar.

Restaurant customers typically select menu items more or less on impulse. Catering clients usually give much more thought and deliberation to their selections, and there is often more than one person involved in the decisions.

- Do not use the word "starch" with a client or on menus (starch is for shirts).
- Do not use "w/" for "with" or "&" for "and"; in general, avoid abbreviations.
- Never give a client a duplicated copy of a menu on computer paper.
- Do not use documents with typographical errors, misspellings, or grammatical errors.
- Be consistent with capitalization.
- Do not list prices from least to most expensive. This will encourage your clients to shop for price instead of for specific menu items.
- Use appropriate descriptors for menu items. Be specific. The second example that follows is much better than the first.

Assorted Cheeses

An Array of Creamy Brie, Tangy Muenster, and Sharp Cheddar Cheeses

Descriptive wording evokes an image—for example, *crisp, hot, flaky.* Be careful about using words that may worry weight-conscious people, such as *rich, heavy* and *thick.*

Tender Chateaubriand with a velvety rich gravy

Melt-in-Your-Mouth Maple-Cured Smoked Ham

Use only words that actually describe an item. What is a "surprise omelet"? What is a "delicate sauce"?

Printed menus include your normal offerings and are usually incorporated into your brochure. Most menus show prices for complete meals. However, à la carte menus price each food individually. The client may choose from a variety of options for appetizers, soups, salads, main courses, vegetables, desserts, and so forth. This is most common when clients are ordering a buffet meal instead of a sit-down function.

Custom-printed menus are developed especially for particular clients for particular events. The customized menu is designed primarily for those clients who want something different. Clients often prefer to incorporate their own personal preferences into the menu. For instance, a client may want to assemble a unique set of menu items and print a souvenir or commemorative menu. This is typical with awards dinners, anniversaries, and weddings. Customizing a menu also allows the caterer to work within a client's specific budgetary constraints.

A client may want to develop a special printed menu to include a certain logo, advertising, and or/style. For instance, a computer convention may want menus printed in the shape of a personal computer. If you are asked to develop a customized menu, you should have menu items printed symmetrically in the center of the page, not on one side or the other like a laundry list. It is important to create an attractive visual presentation.

Convention clients who book several meals may want to communicate the menus to attendees ahead of time. A professional association's convention may last several days. The convention program can list each day's menus so that attendees will know in advance what to expect. Attendees with special dietary needs then have enough time to order a special meal or make alternate plans.

Every page with a price on it should also be dated. Clients often have old menus in their files. When you talk to a client, be sure he or she has a menu with current prices.

Direct Mail Campaign.   Many facilities use direct mail efforts to solicit catering business. Specific names, titles, and addresses can be obtained from several database sources to construct mailing lists of potential catering clients.

Mailing lists are the key to an effective direct mail campaign. Facility executives are often active in many local associations and fraternal organizations; their membership rolls can be excellent, fruitful mailing lists. You can obtain mailing lists from trade shows; for instance, a bridal show would be a good source for wedding business.

Lists also are available from the local chamber of commerce, economic development authorities, and local charitable groups and foundations. Local department stores also have mailing lists; for example, some of them have bridal registries that they may be willing to share.

Access to member mailing lists are often a member benefit of association involvement.

Mailing lists also can be obtained from companies that specialize in developing them. For instance, American Business Lists, Inc., a division of American Business Information, Inc., prepares and sells business mailing lists and mailing labels encompassing just about any type of group, industry, or profession a catering executive may wish to solicit.

Direct mail is an effective marketing tool. It can be personalized, a specific audience can be targeted, and the results of a direct mail campaign are readily measurable. However, it is an expensive marketing tactic; the cost of the brochure, other inserts (such as a cover letter, response card, and/or promotional flyer), envelope, postage, labor, and other ancillary expenses can be quite high.

Web Site.   An effective, up-to-date web site is invaluable. A web site is a living brochure, which should contain photos, menus, contact information, and descriptive information. Too many web sites are merely bulletin boards on the information highway. If your site does not provide your customers with the information they are looking for, it is useless. If the content is not kept fresh and up-to-date, it reflects poorly on your operation. Web sites are easy to create and maintain as long as you keep the format simple. Stay away from expensive frames, java, and the bells and whistles that the professional web masters promote. Search engine "robots" do not "crawl" sites with frames, which will keep your site off many search sites. Many computers cannot access all of the deluxe capabilities without downloading a program, and the novelty soon wears off. And with the move to web appliances and hand-held access, text-based web sites will become simpler by necessity. Provide an e-mail address, and answer messages in a timely manner.

Be sure that the web site diagrams of your function space show columns, doors, electrical outlets, and any other obstructions or features. Include parking information and directions from the airport.

When planning a web site, consider the following: Do you want to build it yourself or to hire someone to do it for you? If you do not have the interest or skill, the better choice is to hire someone. However, most colleges and many private concerns offer classes that can teach you the basics, using a page maker. There is no need to learn *html.* One of the authors of this book created the web site for the entire Hotel College of the University of Nevada, Las Vegas, using Netscape (*http://www.unlv.edu/Colleges/Hotel*).

If you are part of a much larger entity, see if upper management will give you permission to create a separate web site just for the catering department. When you create your own web site, you have more control and can keep information timely and relevant to avoid displaying a static site. Your site can be linked to the main site for the facility. It is important to register your own domain name; thus your web address should read: *http://www.myfacility.com*, rather than *http://www. internetprovide.com/myfacility*. If you use the latter, it appears that your facility is not willing to pay $35 a year to register its own domain. You can go to *http://rs.internic.net* to register your name. If your facility name is no longer available, try a variation, such as *http://www. mynamemycity.com*. You can also choose a *.com* or a *.net* extention.

You can then select an Internet provider. This is where your site will reside. Depending on the size of your site, it should cost $25 to $50 per month. To choose a provider, ask for references from satisfied clients.

Your web site should be consistent with other marketing efforts as to colors, logos, fonts, and so forth. Provide content that is useful, informative, and entertaining. Include interior and exterior photos, photos/descriptions of plate presentations and theme parties, your menu, and contact information.

Target your market. Remember market segmentation. You can create additional pages for different markets and use them as "back doors" to your site. Each individual page on your site can be submitted to the search engines. You can create a separate page for weddings, one for meeting business, and so on, and link them all through your main page.

Avoid garish colors and backgrounds that clash with or make reading the text difficult. Do not use backgrounds with the *.bmp* extention, as they take an inordinate amount of time to load and people have no patience for slow-loading sites. Look at other sites to see what you like and don't like. Just go to any search engine and type in "catering," and you will get thousands of sites to view. Type in "catering" and the name of your city, and you will be able to do a competitor analysis online. Many sites include their prices, but we do not recommend this practice.

Do not participate in banner ads; they cheapen a site. Do not submit your site to the search engines until it is finished. A half-ready site creates a negative image. You can submit it free by going to *http://www.addme.com.*

There is a tutorial for making web sites on Netscape at *http://www.unlv.edu/Tourism/facweb.html.*

Proposals.   A proposal is an "offer" to provide specified goods and services, explaining the terms, the costs, and the ability to satisfy clients' needs. The proposal is an attempt, in writing, to persuade a potential client to give you its business—it is a written sales presentation. A proposal is the first serious written understanding of a client's desires. If the client accepts the offer and signs an agreement, the proposal ceases to be a proposal and becomes a contract for specified services.

What is a "winning" proposal? One that will beat your competition and ultimately award you the contract for the event. It typically includes one or more options that the client can consider. For instance, if a qualified client is in the market for a company holiday party, the caterer may prepare one or more competitive bids for his or her perusal. If the client selects one of the options, he or she signs a confirmation notice, usually included in the proposal, and returns the agreement to the caterer.

In general, a proposal is prepared only when there is serious client interest. Normally, a sales representative does not prepare and send one to a client until both parties have met once or twice to explore possibilities.

Because the proposal is the first major step toward a signed catering agreement (contract), it must include all relevant information. Nothing should be left to chance or assumption. And, of course, there should be no verbal side agreements; if a certain element is worth negotiating, it is worth writing down. This will prevent misunderstandings, which can result in unhappy clients and cloud the facility's reputation.

If proposals are part of the sales solicitation efforts, they should include sales brochures, menus, and photos. A videotape or audiotape may also be included, which can feature sales presentations, previous and/or suggested plate presentations, function room setups, and so forth.

Generally, however, a proposal is a direct response to an inquiry by a serious shopper. Beware of potential clients who are merely "trolling" for new ideas to relay to the cheapest caterer. Sales brochures and similar materials are normally sent to persons who represent potential business but have not actively sought to use your facility for their catered events.

Shelley Pedersen, owner of Beyond Cuisine in Atlanta, recommends sending proposals in mailing tubes, tossing in a few hard candies. She also hand delivers proposals in gift bags related to the theme she is proposing. In the bag, she also places tissue paper and a few cookies or brownies.

Videotapes and Photos.   Videotapes and photos are excellent promotional materials that should be part of all sales representatives' sales kits. Although they may be expensive to produce, they are exceptionally useful marketing tools. They can also be used in direct mail campaigns. Today's digital cameras make photos easy and inexpensive.

Videotaping is very popular. Many catering clients are willing to spend a considerable amount of money to tape their functions, especially for weddings, bridal showers, and similar events. The caterer should consider taping some of these functions and using them to impress potential clients. For instance, if a videotaping company is hired to tape a wedding, the catering executive may make some arrangement with the bride and groom and the videographer to prepare a short version of the final tape for the facility's marketing purposes.

The facility should also consider developing a video sales presentation. For example, a video walk-through of the facility can be a very persuasive part of the marketing plan. Successful videos are usually no more than three minutes in length, as most people today have short attention spans. If a videotape is too expensive, a short slide or photo presentation with an accompanying audiotape may be an acceptable compromise. Alternatively, a short full-motion video presentation can be included on your web site.

Glossy color photos are another very effective marketing tool. The photos should include some food items, especially the facility's specialty products. They should also highlight the property's function space and other amenities.

Wherever possible, people should be included in these photos because, psychologically, clients will identify more closely with them. Photos that do not include people are said to be "cold," whereas those with people are seen as "warm." Presumably, the warmer the photo, the more positive its effect will be on the intended audience.

The director of catering should see to it that a binder is maintained for sales use that includes photos of suggested plate presentations, lavish parties that were previously served, and similar pictorial materials. The binder should also include testimonial letters. A copy of this binder should always be on display in the catering sales department's waiting room or conference room.

Word-of-Mouth Advertising.   Word-of-mouth is by far the most effective form of advertising. Many foodservice operations, especially table service restaurants, rely exclusively on this type of exposure. Word-of-mouth advertising is the prelude to referral business. Most catering clients put great stock in current and previous customers' recommendations. This is especially true if the client knows the customer and trusts his or her opinion. No other marketing effort will carry as much weight as the opinions and recommendations of a trusted colleague or friend.

Soliciting Future Business at Current Events.   All of us at one time or another have attended catered functions at which the caterer, disc jockey, florist, and other outside contractors have discreetly placed brochures, business cards, and so forth around the room, hoping that today's impressed guests will become tomorrow's profitable clients. This is an effective strategy, but it must be handled tastefully. The sales materials should not detract from the event. The current client and his or her guests cannot be ignored. And discussions, negotiations, and other similar activities with potential clients should not be carried on at this time. If a potential client is interested, try to set an appointment as soon as possible before the memories of the current event begin to fade.

 SALES PROCEDURES

One of the nice things about the restaurant business is that once a guest enters the establishment, he or she most likely will buy something. Other retailers would love to be in this enviable position. Unfortunately, many of them, especially department stores, must put up with a great number of casual shoppers who are just browsing and are not interested in buying anything.

Many potential catering clients are also casual shoppers. This is understandable; you cannot assume that a person is apt to purchase a catered event just because he or she walks in the door seeking information. Unlike the restaurant patron who is willing to risk a bit of money to try out a new foodservice operation, the potential catering client cannot afford to do this. A potential client feels obligated to do a bit of research, because there is no second chance to hold the event again next week if something goes wrong. So, before the final agreement is signed, he or she must be "sold."

Client Inquiry

Potential clients often call or stop by, seeking information about the catering department's products and services. Such clients can be categorized as off-the-street business, and the rest are usually referral business.

The director of catering should develop a standard procedure for catering staff members to follow when handling these inquiries. This procedure should be based on the assumption that a booked event will be the obvious result.

Sometimes potential clients inquire about dates, meals, and other services the facility is unable to accommodate. The word "no" is probably the hardest one to utter when dealing with potential clients. You do not want to lose any type of business. The skillful catering executive should be able to negotiate with the potential client to the satisfaction of all parties.

There are five ways a potential client can contact a caterer: (1) letter, (2) phone, (3) fax, (4) e-mail, and (5) in person.

If a potential client inquires with a letter or fax, the caterer should always respond with a phone call. If other caterers have also been contacted by this client, you will want to get back as soon as possible in order to avoid being upstaged by a competitor. A phone call follow-up is also necessary because additional information will most likely be needed in order to prepare a proper proposal. For instance, the client's objective, budgetary constraints, dietary restrictions, and so forth must be considered before advancing to the proposal stage.

A phone call follow-up also allows the catering executive an opportunity to invite the potential client to visit the facility. You should make every effort to get the potential client to make a site visit. Your selling task may be much easier if you have potential clients on-site where you can control the presentation and eliminate interruptions. While there, they can be treated to lunch, given a tour of the facility, and allowed to visit with other catering staff members. If you visit potential clients in their homes or places of business, you do not enjoy this "home court advantage."

If a potential client inquires by phone, ideally the receptionist will answer before the third ring. The voice should be pleasant, modulated, and unhurried. "Good morning/afternoon, this is Mary Smith in the

Catering Department. How may I help you?" When you are away from the office, make a call and see how many times the phone rings before it is answered. What does the person answering say? What is the tone of voice? Are you put on hold? For how long? Ask a question. Does the person know the answer? If not, does he or she find out for you? Whoever answers the phone must be able to answer basic questions. At the very least, the receptionist must be able to route the call to the right person as quickly as possible. There should always be someone in the office who can handle such calls adequately. A knowledgeable person should always be present. Too often the lowest paid, least knowledgeable persons answer the phone. They may be unable to answer questions because they have not been trained to do so. Many times the caller is not even asked to leave a message or number when the person he or she is trying to reach is unavailable. Consequently, a considerable amount of business is lost.

For times when no one from the catering department is available, develop a form for the receptionist or hostess to fill out during a phone conversation to obtain initial information, such as date, type of function, number of guests, and so forth. This can then be given to the sales manager, who can check on availability prior to returning the call. However, the director of catering should ensure that a manager is assigned to each shift who is able to process these inquiries properly.

Voice mail is both a blessing and a curse. You must learn how to use it effectively to avoid playing phone tag. For incoming voice mail: (1) Change your message when you are out of town so clients will know why you are not returning their calls, (2) in your message, leave a time when they can reach you, and (3) provide alternate means by which they can contact you if necessary, such as your e-mail address or your secretary's phone number.

When you are leaving a voice mail message, (1) tell the client the purpose of your call; if that person needs to find information for you, it will save an extra call, (2) let the client know when he or she can reach you, when you will be available to take the call, and (3) leave your phone number; even if a person has it, he or she may have to hunt for it.

The fax machine has become a necessary business tool. You can respond immediately without interrupting the client or wasting long distance time chatting. Faxes should not be scribbled notes; they should be typed as professionally as anything else you send via regular mail. Faxes speed up your possible response time to clients, but they heighten their expectations of speed. A caterer may not be at his or her creative best when a client is impatiently waiting for a fax.

When an inquiry is by e-mail, respond by e-mail. The client who uses e-mail generally loves technology. The advantages of e-mail are that (1) you can print off and have hard copy of all information exchanged, (2) you can provide an immediate reply, (3) you can forward messages to others, (4) you can archive information in folders, (5) it is less expensive than long distance phone calls, (6) you don't have to worry about time zones, and (7) you can retrieve messages at your convenience without interruptions.

If a potential client inquires in person, it is imperative that someone sees this person as soon as possible. The inquirer should be made to feel comfortable. He or she should be offered coffee, soda, or other refreshment. An accurate estimate of waiting time should be indicated. The receptionist or hostess should be instructed to use a form to take some preliminary information from the inquirer, such as name, company, type of function, date needed, and number of guests. This activity gets the client involved—a positive step toward consummating a sale.

To be able to sell effectively, you must present a well-organized catering office. Sales staff must be trained and goals must be set. You never get a second chance to make a first impression. The appearance of your office is a reflection of your personality and job performance. A messy, cluttered office does not instill confidence in prospective clients. A client's initial impression of the office affects his or her perceptions of how well the facility will handle an event.

It is essential to maintain a good filing system. You can not keep everything on a computer. Filing cabinets should be arranged in such a way that needed information is at your fingertips. Information should be current and comprehensive.

Your office should serve as a marketing tool. The pictures on the walls should be of events you have produced, to show unique or interesting room setups. The top of a credenza should have a sample place setting; empty bottles of quality champagnes and wines that you offer make a nice display and assist you in up$elling the event.

An office projects an image. It should be tastefully furnished and decorated. An office that is too elegant or too plain may not be suitable in your environment. Offer the client a comfortable chair with a convenient place to take notes. If you have a waiting area, a testimonial book (binder with photos, suggested menus, catering policies, testimonial letters, and so forth), along with linen samples, china, stemware, and the like, should be strategically placed on the coffee table for the potential client to peruse while waiting. Testimonial books should contain not only positive letters from satisfied clients, but photos taken at events. Photo binders should be displayed in a creative, elegant, or eclectic manner, depending on the image of the facility. The binder should always be in good condition and free of dust and fingerprints.

It is important to project a competent and professional image to your client. Colors play an important role. Hot colors, such as reds and oranges, stimulate, whereas cool blues and greens tend to be calming. Choose classic shades, not current fads that will quickly date your decor.

Whenever possible, it is preferable to meet prospective clients by appointment. This allows the catering staff time to prepare and to give their full attention to the client. It also provides adequate time to discuss arrangements and answer questions. Be ready to meet with the client when he or she arrives. Be familiar with the client's file. Avoid interruptions. Have coffee and tea available.

Make sure to have all necessary information at hand so that you do not have to hunt for it while the client is waiting:

o Color charts for linens, both in-house and rentals.
o Types and quantities of various china patterns and colors available.
o Rental brochures for props, dance floors, platforms, risers, etc. Salespersons should know costs and sources of all rental equipment.
o Referral lists of recommended suppliers, such as florists, photographers, etc.
o Information on audiovisual equipment and services.
o Precise floor plans, along with sample configurations.

All materials mailed from the office must be on good-quality paper in pristine condition. The appearance of a letter reflects the professionalism of the writer. This means that misspelled words, incorrect punctuation, typeovers, or visible corrections are not acceptable.

When using spell check on the computer, always proofread, as spell check does not differentiate between words like *their* and *there* or *here* and *hear*. Spell check does not note mistakes in tenses or plural words.

The punctuation mark that follows the salutation is a colon, not a comma (Dear Major Smith:). However, a comma follows the closing (Cordially,).

A letter should never start with *I* or *We*. Psychologically, it is preferable to draw the client into the letter before presenting yourself.

Thank you for the opportunity to create the enclosed proposal . . . ,
not: *I am pleased to have the opportunity to submit . . .*
Your wedding will be in good hands with . . . , not: We look forward
to your wedding reception . . .

Everything mailed from your office should be checked for accuracy. Be sure that brochures, menus, and other items are not outdated.

Client Solicitation

Some caterers are in the position of not having to solicit business. They do not use outside sales representatives. They currently have all the incoming calls they can handle. In fact, they usually have to turn away potential business. They are basically order takers.

Most catering executives, however, cannot wait for business to walk in off the street. Nor, for that matter, should the facility that has all the business it can handle rest on its laurels. It should always plan ahead and have a system ready to use for those times when its business cycle is expected to bottom out. Furthermore, the type of current incoming business may not be the best business for maximizing profits.

There will always be a certain amount of off-the-street, referral, and repeat business. However, in order to maximize the catering department's profit potential, client solicitation is usually needed. It is especially necessary if you want to book business during the shoulder (i.e., slow) periods.

Many facilities assign sales quotas to their sales representatives that cannot be satisfied with walk-in business. Generally speaking, there should always be a certain amount of solicited business because this ensures that you continue to get the business you want, not just the groups that walk in the door.

Client solicitation takes many forms. Sales representatives canvass for new business with telephone solicitation, direct mail, cold calling, and sales blitz techniques.

A national sales survey discovered that 80 percent of all new sales are made after the fifth call on the same prospect. Yet 48 percent of all salespersons make one call and cross the prospect off their lists. Thirty-five percent quit after the second call. Only 10 percent keep calling. Result: On average, 10 percent of salespersons make 80 percent of new sales. Persistence and patience pay off!

Direct mailing with telephone follow-ups, sales blitzes (whereby the catering staff works the phones once or twice a year in marathon solicitation efforts), and cold calling (whereby a sales representative personally calls or visits potential clients unannounced) are the most common forms of client solicitation efforts.

A direct mailing involves sending out a stock information kit (such as a sales brochure with menus, prices, photos, and so forth) to potential clients whose names were gleaned from a mailing list. The most effective type of mailing is the personalized one. A sales representative should not send out an information kit until he or she finds out something about the potential client so that the mailing can be personalized. This tends to generate more positive responses. It also enhances the caterer's image and reputation, which is certain to pay huge dividends in the future.

The direct mail piece should have some unique physical characteristics to distinguish it from those sent by competing facilities. Printed material can be inserted in an attractive, uniquely colored folder that will stand out in a potential client's files.

Some direct mailing efforts are aimed at previous clients who have not visited the facility lately. For instance, a tracer file can be kept that shows customers who have not held an event at your facility for more than a year. An information kit, with telephone follow-up, can be sent as a courtesy so that these old friends do not forget that the facility remains ready to satisfy their needs.

Some repeat customers should receive an occasional telephone solicitation. For instance, if the facility is in the process of booking next year's Christmas party business, it can call former customers to let them know that space is filling up fast and that the catering staff looks forward to booking space for them and servicing their events.

Sales blitzes and cold calls can yield considerable catering business if they are handled correctly. The most important aspect of these sales techniques is to use a process whereby you can quickly identify potential business. You do not want to waste anyone's time, but to be successful, you need to ask the right questions. For instance, you need to know: (1) Who is the decision maker? (2) How often are events planned? (3) Is your type of facility ever booked? (4) What is the size, type, and budget of the typical event? (5) How are events planned? (6) How far in advance does the potential client start planning an event? This information will help streamline selling efforts and make them more productive.

Canvassing will result in a certain percentage of prospects. Off-the-street and referral business will also generate a list of prospects. To streamline the list, the sales representative may ask potential clients to complete a credit application and ask their permission to run a credit check with a credit reporting service, such as Credit Bureau/Equifax, Dun & Bradstreet, TransUnion, and/or TRW. A call to these organizations can reveal a potential client's creditworthiness as well as other useful information. There are standard credit applications used to uncover important credit data, such as the credit applicant's bank branch and the name of a financial official who can provide a credit reference.

Credit verification is an important part of the selling effort. As soon as possible, you should ask the potential client for permission to verify credit. If he or she refuses to grant permission, you must be certain the potential client understands that the facility will expect payment in advance for any catering services booked. In some cases, if permission is denied, you may want to end discussions with these potential clients and remove them from your list of prospects.

The sales representative can also cull prospects from the list by checking references. For example, if a potential client's name was drawn from the membership list of a local civic association, someone in the association probably knows something about this group, as well as who in the group should be contacted for a reference.

Once the prospect is qualified, the sales representative should set an appointment to meet with him or her. Ideally, the appointment is at the facility so that the client can tour the function rooms, visit a restaurant, and personally witness the facility's capabilities to handle the proposed event.

After the initial appointment, the sales representative may have enough information to prepare a formal proposal. If necessary, there may be one or more additional meetings before a competitive bid can be submitted to the potential client.

When submitting proposals, it is important to recognize that the presentation is in itself a major part of a caterer's promotional efforts. The "packaging" is critical. According to Michael Roman, of Cater-Source, Inc., the catering executive should:

1 Use an overnight service to deliver the proposal, even if the client is in the same city.

2 Avoid folding the proposal document.

3 Offer a home telephone number or cell phone number so that the potential client can get in touch, if necessary.

4 Show a copyright statement on the proposal document.

5 Use stamps in lieu of a postage metering machine.

6 Send a hand-written thank-you note before the potential client receives the proposal.

7 Send photos or videotapes showing events similar to the one desired by the potential client.

8 Consider hand-delivering the proposal instead of sending it in the mail or faxing it.

9 Create a sense of urgency by indicating the proposal's expiration date.

Once the proposal is presented, the usual next step is to commence negotiations. If all goes well, a formal agreement that is mutually acceptable to all parties will be signed.

Client Contact

Serious contact with potential clients usually begins with a general discussion of the event. Specific details are then discussed, such as prices, times, room availability, and other customer requirements. Eventually, there will be a meeting of the minds and a signed contract or letter of agreement will be prepared. (*Agreement* is a more palatable word than *contract* to many catering clients.)

For this process to become reality, sales representatives must be knowledgeable. They must be able to answer clients' questions. They cannot afford to lose face. A stumbling, bumbling answer leaves a terrible impression.

Sales representatives must be thoroughly familiar with food and beverage production and service. They must also know and understand the facility's limitations, especially those restricting the types of functions that can be hosted properly.

Sales representatives must also be enthusiastic and likable. They must be polite and friendly. And they should exude the proper amount of sophistication consistent with the facility's competitive position.

Sales representatives should sell benefits to the client. They should not wait for the client to ask about them. Rather, they must take the initiative and see to it that clients know that, for example, whether parking is free or whether there are special prices available for some functions, or that the facility has a unique view that will dazzle their guests.

Clients want to know that they are being treated correctly and professionally. They want to trust someone to do a good job and make them look good in the eyes of their guests. They expect to pay a reasonable price for a catered event, but they must be satisfied with the results. Consequently, an effective sales representative will make sure that he or she knows exactly what the client wants.

A checklist of things to ask the client is an essential part of the sales representative's sales kit. The list should contain the obvious questions, such as the number of guests, the event's starting and ending times, and the required room setup. It should also include questions about more particular items, such as dietary and religious restrictions, entertainment needs, and the number and type of outside contractors that will be used. Ask why the client is holding the event; what is it the client hopes to accomplish? Is he or she seeking to raise money? Wishing to provide a networking opportunity? Does the client have a web site you can check out for more information on his or her organization?

A sales representative must find out as much as possible about the potential client before advancing to the negotiating and proposal stages. This information will indicate the potential for up$elling, how many other competing caterers the client is considering, and any unusual service needs that must be met.

Meeting with Prospective Clients

In meeting with prospective clients, be friendly. Smile, be enthusiastic and outgoing. People want to do business and work with those who seem to enjoy what they do for a living. Address clients by name. This shows your personal interest in them. Be helpful. Go out of your way to offer service, and tell clients about products and services. Be flexible. Do it the client's way. Put the client first. Be patient. Maintain good posture, make direct eye contact, open doors for others, say *please, thank you,* and *you're welcome.* Never argue. Speak clearly, use appropriate language, and avoid bad habits.

Determine the client's needs and objectives before you begin promoting your food, beverages, and services. It is important to know what the client is trying to achieve with the function. The client wants to be assured that the event will be well done. Clients' concerns may include the following:

○ Does the catering manager understand my needs?
○ Does he or she show a willingness to ease my concerns?
○ Will the food be good?
○ Will the servers be courteous and attentive?
○ How much is this going to cost?
○ Are there any hidden costs?
○ What happens if something needs to be changed?
○ Will this person be there during my event?

Face-to-face contact is the most effective method of selling. It is more personal, and communication is visual as well as verbal. Body language can communicate a person's mood or interest. Rapport is developed through in-person contact.

When calling or visiting a potential client without an appointment (cold calling):

○ Introduce yourself.
○ Inform the potential client immediately of the purpose of your call or visit.
○ Explain the variety of special events you can cater (i.e., picnics, themed events, etc.).
○ Listen carefully to what the person says.
○ Keep your presentation brief and to the point unless the prospective client asks for additional information.
○ Thank the person for his or her time.
○ Leave (or offer to send) brochures and menus.

When meeting with prospective clients, try to obtain the following information:

○ What type of functions they plan
○ Minimum/maximum number of guests at each
○ Date(s)
○ Time(s)
○ Where they have held previous events

Although the purposes of cold calls are primarily to inform and to gather information, appointments are made to sell. When scheduling appointments, it is preferable to meet at your facility. Extend a warm welcome. Phrase your initial questions to obtain a clear understanding of what the client is seeking. A sales presentation is not complete without a tour of the facility. Describe the full scope of the facility's catering products and services. Provide the client with a copy of your catering brochure. You can also introduce the client to the chef, the banquet manager, and perhaps the food and beverage director.

Potential clients who have made an appointment with you already have an interest in your facility/product/service. It is up to you to provide the information and reassurance that will nudge the prospective client from undecided to committed.

Begin the menu suggestions and selection process. In addition to the regular catering menus, extend the opportunity to the client to custom design his or her menu. Designing a special menu for clients makes them feel special and pampered. You can also take advantage of seasonal foods that may be at their peak of freshness and at their lowest price.

Always accept (or offer) a beverage during a meeting. It buys you time with the client. Courtesy requires that you (or the client) be allowed to finish a drink that is provided.

Be sure the rooms you are going to show the prospective client are in good order, clean, and with the lights on. The client needs to envision how the room will look during his or her event. Stacked furniture or dirty rugs will not convey a positive image.

Shop the competition. How can you compete effectively if you do not know your competition?

- What menu items do they offer?
- What are their specialties?
- What are their prices?
- What types of services are available?
- How do they respond to inquiries?
- What policies do they have that make you more (or less) competitive?
- How do their facilities compare to yours?
- How do their brochures and other materials compare to yours?

If you are serving the same menu items as your competitor, yours should look better, taste better, and be served better. Add unique touches to your menu. Try to place yourself in the position of the client. Does the competition's presentation paint a better picture than yours? What are the differences that you need to address in your own presentation?

Clients expect quality, value, and attention. Knowing your facility's strengths and your competitor's weaknesses will give you an advantage. Distinguish your catering operation by offering more and better service and personalized assistance.

Avoid "bad mouthing" your competition. This is unprofessional and will be perceived negatively by the prospective client. It may also leave you open to charges of slander. Instead, emphasize your positive benefits in areas in which the competition cannot compete.

Do not overlook important details that can help you close more sales. Listen more and talk less. If you listen to people, they will tell you what to sell. Say, "I would like to hear what your ideas and needs are before I propose any ideas." Then be inventive!

There are many points at which communication can break down. There are certain "filters," that influence and cloud a person's perception of a communication. Filters may affect communication:

- When you are very busy
- If you are preoccupied with personal or business matters
- When you are not feeling well
- When you are biased or hold preconceived notions
- When you are in an emotional state
- When you do not understand or comprehend the information
- When environmental factors, such as noise, temperature, etc., intrude
- When your level of sensitivity is less than it should be

Watch for body language that indicates that the potential client is not listening. Be aware of positive and negative signals. When you meet someone, the first few seconds are critical in projecting a positive first impression. Body language communicates attitude much more powerfully than the sound of the voice or the words that are used.

You must project confidence. Direct eye contact communicates confidence. Leaning forward slightly communicates that you are listening intently. A friendly smile can make you seem attractive and open. Nodding when a client is expressing his or her needs conveys understanding.

Complaints are opportunities. The client is saying, "Will you help me?" Every successfully resolved complaint increases customer satisfaction. Never allow the client to make you upset. Listen to the complaint and make sure you understand what the client wants. Accept responsibility, even if you are not at fault, and take immediate action. Always thank the client for bringing the matter to your attention.

Selling

Service can be defined as "the manner in which the client is treated." Good service is often felt, rather than seen. Making the sale is the ultimate goal, and serving the customer is the means to achieving that goal. Service is something you do that results in a sale or a rebooking.

Selling is both an art and a skill. Not everyone excels at selling; however, with practice, you can develop a sales presentation to accomplish the task successfully. The average catering manager spends approximately 60 percent of his or her time selling, and 40 percent servicing catered events.

Focusing on Benefits

It is important to focus on benefits rather than features. Features are information about your facility, menu, and service. Benefits explain why the features are important to the client. Never sell what your catering is—sell what your catering does. When you are focused on features, you would say things like:

"We have a great chef and a great service team."

"We have a great view."

But when you focus on benefits, you would instead say:

"Our chef will prepare a wonderful meal that will please your guests, and our staff will make them feel like VIPs."

"The view of the mountains and the water will be the perfect romantic backdrop for your wedding reception. Just think about your wedding photos in this setting."

Remember, clients purchase a happy bride, not a wedding.

You must know everything about your facility, including:

○ Room sizes and capacities
○ A variety of setup alternatives
○ Ingredients, preparation method, and price of every menu item
○ Electrical capacity, number, and location of outlets

- Audiovisual availability and capability
- Floor load capacity
- Sizes of doors
- Skill level of the kitchen staff
- Skill level of the servers
- Availability of equipment, etc.
- How long it takes to turn a room (for example, from a classroom set to a banquet set); many caterers do not know what their facility can do during a crunch, and so often do not leave enough time between events.

The sales manager should, without hesitation, be able to say, "Mrs. Nelson, this room will seat 160 banquet style and accommodate 200 at a reception." Should the desired booking date be unavailable, you may be able to offer the prospective client a discount, a complimentary food item, or another incentive if the client is willing to hold the event on another date.

Closing the Sale

For many, closing the sale is the most difficult part of sales. You must ask for the business and get the commitment. After all details have been noted, and all questions answered to the satisfaction of the client, the last steps before presenting the agreement for signature include the following:

- Verbally recapping the specifics of the function and what has been agreed upon. At this point, review the arrangements and the sequence of the events that will occur during the function. To avoid possible misunderstandings, make sure that the agreement contains all arrangements and the sequencing and timing of events.
- Confirming the items you will check on and agreeing as to when you will get back to the client.
- Recapping the information the client will provide to you.
- Asking for the client's business.
- Getting a commitment.

Overcoming Objections

Objections are based on fear of nondelivery. If you do not overcome clients' objections, you will not get their business! *Ask* clients whether they have any concerns or objections. The following are the concerns that cause client hesitation most frequently:

○ Availability of dates
○ Adequacy of space
○ Price
○ Menu suggestions
○ Whether the event will be done correctly.

Techniques for Overcoming Client Objections.   First, listen for the objection. It may not be immediately obvious. Ask questions and address the objection. Change the objection to client acceptance by using the following techniques:

○ Review features and benefits with the client.
○ Review how you plan to meet the client's needs.
○ Guarantee satisfaction.
○ Build trust.
○ Refer to testimonials.
○ Refer to visual presentations.
○ Supply a referral list for client use.
○ Close the sale by asking direct questions.

Solutions to Objections.   If the objection is based on price:

1   Determine the client's budget; if it is reasonable, build a menu that fits the budget.
2   Be specific. Ask what it is that the client thinks is too expensive.
3   Ask how the client would propose to lower the cost.
4   Offer suggestions—read the client's reactions.
5   Explain and show value for items under consideration.

If the objection is based on space:

1   Offer an alternate date when more space is available.
2   Suggest a different type of service (for example, a station buffet with cocktail tables vs. a sit-down meal).
3   Change the time of the event so that another room may be used.
4   Adjust the layout.
5   Look for alternative locations, such as poolside or in a tent.
6   Look for an innovative solution.

If the objection is based on the menu:

1   Ask whether the client has any suggestions. Does the client have favorites or items preferred to yours? Can he or she supply you with pictures or recipes?

2   Discuss and resolve any dietary concerns.

3   Know your competition's product, presentation, and pricing. If possible, meet or beat its offerings. If not, offer value alternatives.

4   Involve the chef if customized menus are under consideration.

Examples of Closing Statements.   It is important to restate an objection and counter it with positive action.

> "Mrs. Hamilton, I understand your concern about backup space for the ceremony. If we can make arrangements for a tent and include the string ensemble as well, will you commit to having Kimberly's ceremony and reception here at our club?"

> "Mr. Tuttle, if we can get white chair covers and pink satin bows for the ceremony, and make it within your budget, may I consider your date with us firm?"

> "Miss Reed, I understand your concern about having hot food served to 150 guests within 20 minutes. I will guarantee it can be done, and you are welcome to call or visit other satisfied customers. If I give you a 100 percent guarantee that all 150 guests will be served hot food in 20 minutes, will you confirm your event here at our club?"

Close the sale by asking, "Now that we agree on the menu, the timing, the room arrangements, and the entertainment, are you ready to sign the agreement?" Provide provisional choices:

> "If I provide x, y, and z, will this satisfy your (budget, taste, concern, etc.)?"

> "If we change the Balsamic vinaigrette to a raspberry vinaigrette, will the salad be to your liking?"

If client answers yes—close.

You are ready to close the sale when:

○   Client needs and wants are met.

○   Menu and beverage arrangements are satisfactory.

○   The price is right.

○ The atmosphere and decor are acceptable.
○ The date, time, and agenda are confirmed.
○ Trust and confidence have been established.
○ Value and anticipated satisfaction are perceived.

IDENTIFYING YOUR MARKETS AND HOW TO REACH THEM

You must know the weaknesses of your competition (prices, furnishings, skills of the banquet staff, etc.). You must also be aware of the strengths of your own catering operation.

Products and Services

What products and services should your catering department offer? A critical first step is to review previous bookings to identify the menus, services, and types of functions that were most frequently booked. These historical data serve as the primary basis for determining product and service selection.

Which products and services does your facility do best in terms of quality, cost, and presentation? Remember that it is better to offer a limited number of items that are done well, than to offer many items without the ability to guarantee that the facility will provide quality preparation, presentation, and service.

A major consideration in determining the menu items to be offered depends on the skill level in the kitchen as well as the available equipment. What items can the kitchen staff prepare well, and what are the equipment limitations? Many restaurants do not stray from their regular menus. Banquets are restricted to what the kitchen already produces and what they do best. Other facilities have separate catering menus and/or are willing to create custom menus for their clients.

MARKETING TOOLS

As you know, a satisfied guest is the best advertisement for your catering operation, but you cannot rely only upon word of mouth to increase your catering business. You should also develop publicity and advertising materials to generate additional awareness and sales.

Direct Mail: This may consist of a specially prepared flyer or a minibrochure, describing the availability and advantages of using the facility for catered events.

Local Newspapers: A well-written text, accompanied by an eye-catching illustration or photograph is an excellent reminder about your facility's catering program. Send press releases to various media regularly, featuring menus, creative themes, and even a popular recipe. If you or your chef have some writing skills, offer to provide a weekly or monthly food column to the editor. Advertising of this nature has the potential to be seen and read by a large audience. Whenever you pay for an advertisement, the copy and illustrations should be professionally prepared if you do not have desktop publishing capabilities on your computer. Be sure the copy is eye-catching and appropriate for your target audience. When considering the cost, remember that your ad is competing for attention with other professionally prepared ads.

Posters and Flyers: Professionally designed posters and flyers placed at entrances of high-traffic areas such as at the elevator or in the lobby will heighten awareness of your catering operation. For example, you may say something like this:

> *Let us cater your special event. For your next function or party, leave the planning and preparation to us. Whether it is a function for 10 or 300, we can make it a memorable occasion. For more information, contact our catering manager, (name), at (phone number).*

Telephone Recording: If your facility uses an answering machine or voice mail for after-hour messages, a brief, friendly invitation can be extended to callers, suggesting they consider holding their next special event in your facility.

> *We invite you to host your special event at (name). We will make your event a memorable occasion. For information about our catering program, please call (name) at (phone number).*

Inserts: For catering operations in clubs, attractive inserts can be prepared for enclosure with monthly statements, dues notices, or when sending out your calendar of activities.

In-House Opportunities: Sunday brunches, live entertainment, or catering services can be promoted with table tents and high-quality flyers.

Presentations: The catering manager should contact local and national groups to inform them about your catering services, facilities, and special amenities. Remind them that your clients and their guests have fun, social interaction, and cohesiveness at catered functions. Presentations should be accompanied with handouts, catering brochures, and photos or videos that convey the facility's success stories and show people having fun.

Video Presentations: A continuous video presentation in high-traffic areas, depicting successful events, banquets, decorations, and special theme parties, offers an excellent merchandising opportunity. It can increase awareness of catering for a wide variety of events. When used in the catering office, a video presentation can be a visually persuasive sales tool with prospective clients.

Employees: Employee recommendations can result in additional bookings. Make sure your employees know about your catering program and offer them an incentive (e.g., a $50 award) if an event is held because of their recommendation.

Word of Mouth: This is a powerful and effective means of generating additional business. A successful event will often result in repeat business and positive recommendations to others by the sponsor and his or her guests. However, if the word of mouth is negative, it can work against your catering program. A less than successful function may produce negative comments and a loss of future business. After-event follow-up is critical.

CLIENT RELATIONS

The catering manager should develop relationships within the community and become a central part of the social and professional fabric of the group of people with whom he or she does business. Positive community relations pay off. A potential sale often begins with a casual inquiry.

There are many alternatives among which clients may choose for their events. Most of your clients will comparison shop. They want assurance that your catering team has the professional skills to make their events enjoyable, memorable, and hassle-free.

As soon as a client's event is completed, you should be trying to book the next function with that client. Providing customer service is an art. Providing customer service profitably is a science. We cannot talk about marketing without discussing service. The best marketing plans in the world will fall short if high-quality service is not part of the equation. High-quality service is your invisible asset. Good service adds value to the purchase and brings the customer back.

A marketing definition of customer service is "Giving your clients what they want, when they want it, where they want it, at a price they are willing to pay." The purpose of customer service is:

○ Customer satisfaction (how we did)
○ Customer retention (striving to secure repeat business)
○ New customer development (word of mouth and firsthand observance of the facility's performance)

Quality service is not tangible and cannot be stored. Our "product" is the service we offer our guests. Service is effort expended to provide a memorable experience for our guests. Every effort should be made to meet and exceed the client's needs and expectations.

Poor service just happens; good service is an ongoing effort. Training service personnel is a continuing process. The more you expect from your staff, the greater the requirement to provide ongoing training, feedback, and two-way communication. It is your staff that determines whether you retain your clients for future events.

RELATIONSHIP MARKETING

Retain records of comments concerning clients' events, as well as any personal information, in the clients' files. Always refer to these files prior to contacting clients. Clients appreciate being asked how their golf game is going, or how their daughter is doing in college. This is called "relationship marketing."

Establishing a personal link with a client is important for repeat business. You should strive to establish rapport with your clients and potential clients, as well as their spouses. Find a common interest to discuss. Establish a "professional" friendship.

Networking

Networking is an attempt to tap into a large group of like-minded folks. It is part of the selling process. It is relationship building. It offers an opportunity to establish rapport, find a common interest, and generate a business friendship with potential clients as well as other catering professionals.

In catering sales, you will be attending many lunches, dinners, and receptions. These are all opportunities for relationship marketing. You must be sure you know the rules of etiquette. Letitia Baldrige's *Guide to Executive Manners* is an excellent resource. A business reception may look like a party, sound like a party, feel like a party, and taste like a party, but it is *not* a party. It is a social business environment. It is a vehicle to relax attendees so they can meet in a casual manner, instead of across a desk in an office. Remember your good or bad manners are always with you. Do not overdrink, station yourself at the food, or otherwise make a spectacle of yourself. People have long memories. You need to make people feel at ease. People gravitate to other people who make them feel comfortable. No one wants to feel ill at ease. Know when to say *please*. Know how to say *I'm sorry*. Know how to say *thank you*. Know how to give and receive a compliment.

Audiotape Proposals

Most people have tape decks in their cars. With the average commute time of 35 to 60 minutes each way, a person would have ample opportunity to listen to your audiotaped proposal during that time. You can describe the event in detail, without interruption. But always include a written proposal and a brochure along with the tape. Identify what you want to talk about and script an outline with key points to describe the highlights of different aspects of your catering program. Up$ell the features you wish to promote, such as flowers, decorations, and so on. You might develop one tape for weddings and others for various theme party options. The tapes should not exceed 20 minutes in length. Practice voice modulation so that you will speak expresively.

TELEPHONE MARKETING

Telephone marketing can be an excellent source of new business. First, you need a plan that includes whom you wish to target, what information you want to convey, and the results you expect to achieve. You have only a brief opportunity to state the reason for your call, describe the catering services you offer, and create enough interest to gain a positive response from the potential client. To improve opportunities for successful selling, prepare a script containing the key points you wish to convey. Rehearse what you plan to say until it sounds natural and not as though you were reading from a script. Be clear, concise and gracious. Use the following guidelines:

- Prepare a list of items you wish to discuss or points you want to make.
- Be as specific as possible.
- Complete each point before moving on to the next subject.
- Be sure to take notes and date them.
- Follow up immediately.
- Every telephone call should be logged for future reference.

A sample script might consist of the following:

"Good Morning, Mrs. Benson. This is Carl Whitman from the catering department of the Bountiful Hotel. I noticed the announcement of your daughter's wedding in the newspaper, and I would like to extend our best wishes to the family. We are proud of our catering department and would like to offer our catering services for the reception. As you may know, we specialize in wedding receptions and we are very competitive. Our mission is to make every reception a memorable one. I'd like to extend an invitation for you to visit our catering office so that we can show you the many attractive services we offer. It would be our pleasure to cater your daughter's reception."

This type of telephone marketing can be applied to almost any situation, person, or group. For example, suppose the call is to a person whose name just appeared in the newspaper. The following approach may be appropriate:

"Good afternoon, Mr. Duffy. Congratulations on your promotion to Vice-President. This is Mary Forese, from the catering department of the Bella Napoli Restaurant. I'd like to offer our catering services for your promotion party if you haven't made other arrangements already. I would like to extend a personal invitation for you to visit our facility so that we may show you our full range of party services."

The ideal outcome of this type of inquiry would be a tentative reservation or a firm appointment to discuss the special event further. Your minimum goal should be to obtain the prospective client's approval to send him or her a copy of the catering brochure. Always follow up if a potential client needs to talk to a spouse or with the family prior to making any decisions.

 ## VALUE

Recall that value is a function of price/quality/service. There has been a gradual shift from guests focusing strictly on price to looking more at quality service. This involves the enhancement of quality and service so that they will be perceived as a greater component of overall value. It is less expensive to improve service and/or amenities than it is to discount prices. Sell service first. Assure the potential client that you will provide dependable, knowledgeable, experienced personnel to ensure that his or her event will be successful.

When your price is too high, customers will tell you—and not buy. When your price is too low, customers buy—and never tell you they would have paid more.

The perception of value is greater when you offer something extra, as opposed to merely discounting prices. If a client asks for a reduced price, offer complimentary centerpieces, decor, microphones, or the like, instead. Value-added menus can reflect environmentally sound practices, such as serving free-range chicken and/or organic vegetables, not using disposables, using napkins made from recycled paper, donating excess food to a shelter, and so on.

 # Up$ELLING

A crucial skill is the ability to "up$ell." Up$elling is painting a mental picture of enhancements to convince the client that by spending a little more money on extra service or elaborate presentations, increased guest satisfaction will result. Up$elling is suggestive selling to upgrade the menu, arrangements, decorations, or other items, by recommending specific "extras" or enhancements. It may involve changing the entrée from chicken to prime rib, adding a fancy specialty dessert, or serving a better-quality wine. Up$elling also includes adding extra courses, such as an intermezzo, cheese cart, cordial service, hot hors d' oeuvres, petits fours, ice carvings, or flavored coffees. Up$elling pertains to anything associated with the event; it may include extra staffing, a separate service station, specialty linen, or serving equipment such as a champagne fountain. Instead of asking, "Do you want to serve wine?" ask the client, "What type of wine will you be serving?" or "Do your prefer a red or a white wine?"

Up$elling increases the per-person selling price. There are several methods that can be used to achieve this goal. Although each is effective individually, combining methods can help you retain more revenue for your bottom line and deliver a more complete service to your client and his or her group. Effective methods include the following:

Upgrading individual items. Clients' budgets are often focused more toward the chicken price range than the beef range. Some clients want to feel more involved in their menu planning than simply ordering the standard menu from the brochure. To facilitate upgrading, it is important to have the appropriate sales tools. Each manager should have lists of prices and be prepared to upgrade appetizers, suggest showy dessert presentations, add specialty salads, such as Caesar salad prepared tableside, relish trays, and the like.

Upgrading entrée items. Have choices available, including a variety of fresh seafood and fish items, Cornish game hens, quail (now widely available in ready to heat and serve packaging), and a number of chicken and turkey preparations using different stuffings, sauces, or accompaniments. Top-end up$elling would include veal, prime rib, beef filet, pork loin, Peking duck, or venison (For example, add two jumbo butterfly shrimp to a filet mignon.) After a lull in popularity, beef has had a resurgence.

Upgrading refreshment breaks.   Offer special beverages, such as lattes, cappuccinos, flavored coffees, juices, or imported bottled waters. Suggest food items to go with the beverages in a per-person price. For instance, $10 per-person coffee/refreshment breaks can contribute more to your end of month statement than an upgraded appetizer. Themed refreshment breaks are discussed in Chapter 3.

Upgrading ambiance.   Special china, glassware, linen, and props are potential reusable money-makers. These items should be of special interest because they can greatly increase menu price without any additional food cost. The cost of a special item can usually be recovered after its first use, and the following rentals can be considered pure profit.

Custom proposals.   All catering operations have standard menus. Flatter your client with the attention and creativity of custom proposals. Always seek to custom design at least one or two items on the menu. It removes the pressure of dealing with printed lists and pre-suggested prices. Within the first few conversations, ask the client for his or her budget. This question will save you time and effort and allow you to imaginatively exceed your client's expectations.

Early involvement.   Offer to assist the client in making arrangements for flowers, audiovisual equipment, photographers, and so forth, and create a budget including these items with a minimum markup of at least 10 percent for the facility. You are providing a service—one-stop shopping and added convenience for the client. Always let the client know that there will be a markup on these services.

Pre-packaged theme parties.   A package eliminates the client's need to handle details like props, entertainment, and menus. Many of your clients may be unaware that you offer such complete services and will be impressed and more confident with your range of services, as well as your ideas and proposals. Theme parties are discussed in Chapter 3.

SPACE UTILIZATION

Is it possible to use your available space better? Many facilities use their available space only 20 to 30 percent of the time, owing mainly to lack of business. A number of factors may contribute to this situation, including the following:

- No incentive for the catering manager to seek additional business
- Seasonal business fluctuations
- Limited market
- Lack of staff/skilled serving staff
- Waiting for business to come into the facility rather than seeking it out
- Limited operating hours for food operations
- Lack of flexibility in turning rooms over into new setups

Banquet space has potential for being occupied at least 3 times a day, or 21 times a week, per room. You can also break this out by meal period, such as dinner. If you had 150 dinners a year in a particular room, your occupancy percentage for that room for the dinner meal period would be 41 percent.

You can calculate space utilization by the number of covers (place settings) served divided by the number of available seats. However, remember that banquet setups vary from function to function. Dance floors take up room, for instance.

Empty banquet space does not produce revenue. The space is there to be sold. You cannot wait for someone to walk in and book a party. Walk-in business may not produce the most revenue. Business that comes to you may be a luncheon for 25 guests, whereas you may be able to find a luncheon for 100 guests. Or you might seek out and book a wedding instead of a coffee reception. Therefore, to increase utilization, it is important to market outside the facility and be a salesperson, not an order taker.

You have to keep up with what is happening in the economy to know which industries have money to spend on catered functions. For example, the munitions industry was "flying high" until the cold war ended. Industries that today are considered on the upswing, with money to spend, include the following:

- *Infrastructure.* Most bridges, tunnels, and roadways were built in the late 1800s and early 1900s, and many are now more than a century old and crumbling. This infrastructure will have to be replaced, creating business for engineers, construction companies, materials companies, and heavy equipment manufacturers and sales forces.

○ *Technology.*   This area is advancing so rapidly that it is difficult to keep up with all of the new high-tech companies that are sprouting up and thriving.

○ *Energy.*   The world will continue its dependence on all types of energy for the foreseeable future.

○ *Health care (including pharmaceuticals).*   As the baby boomers age and the population continues to live longer, medical care needs will increase.

○ *Environment.*   The earth must be saved from centuries of neglect and ruin. Companies that recycle and otherwise work to protect the environment (cleaning up oil spills, for example) will be needed in the twenty-first century.

Most of your potential clients will comparison shop when they are considering the location of an event. You must be perceived as the best alternative—because you can create the best-quality event.

What You Need to Know About Your Clients

○ Where have they gone in the past?
○ What features can your facility offer to create value for the client?
○ How do they measure success?

Explain everything:

○ Operating procedures
○ Type of services provided
○ Menu design
○ Room setup
○ Key points in the agreement
○ Deposits and payments
○ Special arrangements
○ Rental items
○ Choices of rental items offered

Establishing trust is critical. Remember, a client purchases what he or she thinks will happen. So, clients must trust that you will provide what you say you will provide. The party does not exist at the time of purchase.

To earn additional income consider these options:

- Selling more beverages
- Charging room rental
- Bringing services in-house
- Raising prices
- Adding off-premise catering

What are the strong selling points of your facility?

- Location?
- View?
- Decor?
- Pricing?
- Excellent food?
- Great service?

 ## FUNCTION BOOK

The function book (diary), i.e., the main list of bookings, is critical for the smooth running of a facility's operations. There are basic books of various sizes and complexity to suit the need of every type of operation. The traditional function book is gradually being phased out in favor of a computerized version that is available on many software programs. See Chapter 10 for information on computerized office.

Regardless of whether your function book is high tech or low tech, the basic principles apply:

- Only one person should be allowed to make entries and changes.
- Tentative bookings should be in pencil, or so indicated on the computer.
- The book (or computer version) must be readily accessible so that available dates and space can be determined.
- A phone should be installed in close proximity to the book (computer).

When a potential client inquires, the first order of business is to see what space is available on the date and time requested.

Prospective entries are inquiries. Tentative entries actually hold space for a certain period of time and indicate that a proposal and/or contract has been sent. Confirmed entries are made when the signed contract is returned and/or the deposit arrives. All entries should be initialed or otherwise coded. In actual books, tentative bookings are usually in pencil and confirmed bookings are in ink. In computer software, generally the letters *T* and *C* are used, or color coding is employed.

Theme Parties, Weddings, Outdoor Parties, and Other Special Events

Chapter 3

Catered events—from banquets to receptions—need excitement and drama in addition to delicious food. For this reason, themed events are very popular. A theme party transports the attendee to another dimension, another place and time, away from the mundane and ordinary world. Themed events create a magical space of fantasy and fun. Caterers have an opportunity to show their creativity and expertise by developing one-of-a-kind events for their clients.

Before developing a proposal or planning a function, it is necessary to know the reason for the event and who will be attending the party. The demographics of the group (age, income, ethnicity, etc.) will influence the selection of appropriate elements.

Every function or party should be treated as a special event. According to Joe Goldblatt at George Washington University, author of several books on special events, "A special event recognizes a unique moment in time with ceremony and ritual to satisfy specific needs." A caterer may create 200 parties a year, but this is probably not the case for the client. It may just be another party for the caterer, but for the client, it is truly a special occasion. The bride wants a perfect wedding to remember; the association meeting planner wants a spectacular closing event to the convention to wow the attendees; the corporation wants to impress clients and potential clients.

 THEME PARTIES

The majority of attendees may not be able to tell you what they had to eat the day before. What they do remember, sometimes for years to come, are creative themes, unique presentations, and outstanding entertainment. Themed events create memories.

Theme parties are events that tie in:

○ Creativity
○ Food
○ Beverage
○ Entertainment
○ Decor
○ Activities

Event elements include:

○ Fun
○ Flavor
○ Excitement
○ Action
○ Color
○ Sound
○ Entertainment
○ Showmanship
○ Surprise

A caterer should strive to involve all five senses: sight, sound, taste, touch, and smell.

Whenever possible, create something out of the ordinary for each such event. You can use a visual object, something as simple as the mashed potato "duck" that was served to us on a plate at the Contemporary Hotel at Disney World. The key is to *involve* and *excite*.

A themed event also provides an opportunity to up$ell by adding additional components to the presentation. Guests like interactive events. John Steinmetz, a caterer from southern California, once produced a party using bubble wrap as an overlay on a tablecloth, then topped the table with Lucite cut to fit the entire tabletop. The centerpiece was an assortment of soap bubbles, Silly String, water pistols, and other fun toys. As the evening progressed, one could hear the bubble wrap being popped all around, making the room sound like a giant popcorn popper. Guests soon got into the mood, blowing bubbles, shooting Silly String, laughing, and having a great time.

Lights are Magic

Whether they are tiny Italian Tivoli lights, pin spots, strobes, black lights, beacons, rope lights, fiber optics, neon, laser lights, or other types, lights attract and dazzle the eye. Lights are truly "eye candy." Gobo lights are portable spotlights that can create colors or focus pattern projections on a ceiling, wall, or floor, depending on the metal templates affixed to the lens. The images can be trees, cityscapes, or any object relating to the theme of the event. They are also available in versions that rotate slowly, back and forth, 180 degrees, creating changing patterns that pulsate in tempo with the music.

A portable "light tree" contains a base with two pipes forming a T. Lights hang off the crossbar. A par light is used for short distances (throws) and creates a wide beam of light. A leko light is used for a longer throw and creates a narrow beam of light. Gels are heat-resistant colored cellophane sheets placed in front of a lens to bathe an area in a particular color.

Chapter 8 includes information on electrical requirements for lighting. The Star Light and Magic web site provides many photos and valuable information on a variety of lighting options (*http://www.starmgc.com/*).

You can also use a *soundscape*—that is, decorate with sound. Sound can envelop a space and create a mood. Commercially prepared tapes are available with the sounds of foghorns, rainstorms, ocean waves, sea gulls, tropical birds, clopping horses, the clickety-clack of a train on the tracks, and a variety of other background elements. Music playing in a room as guests enter reinforces the theme, such as Dixieland jazz for a New Orleans theme, Arivaderci Roma for an Italian motif, or the "Tara" score for a *Gone with the Wind* theme.

A *moving decor* can be created by people in costumes. These can simply be the servers and bartenders in costume and/or actors hired to roam around and entertain. They are part of the décor and add life to the theme.

Entrance

The entrance to an event sets the mood. If the client's budget allows, a few props relating to the theme may be placed in proximity to the doors. Entering a room through a prop of a plane fuselage set the tone for an *Indiana Jones and the Lost Temple of Doom* event that was held at the Sheraton in Boston.

Budget Considerations

In the 1980s and 1990s, the mood was "eat, drink, and be merry." As we move into the new century, however, budgets are tighter; the average catering budget per person has dropped by about 25 percent, while costs have escalated by about 25 percent. However, expectations are as high as they were in the latter part of the previous century. Clients want freshness, quality, service, and creativity.

Theming allows creativity to make up the difference. "Where we used to use 12/16 jumbo shrimp, we now offer 26/30 'blackened shrimp' for New Orleans night—or 'coconut breaded shrimp' for Tropical Nights," stated Ricky Eisen in an *Events Solutions* article (*http://www.event-solutions.com/*).

Themes with Low Food Cost

○ Old Mexico. Taco bars, chili bar with toppings, interactive fajita bar, chips and guacamole, etc. Think of how many shrimp a guest could eat in the time it would take to construct and eat a taco.

○ Fifties, Sixties, State Fair, Carnival, Circus, Super Bowl, Fourth of July Variations on the usual menu: hot dogs, hamburgers (grilled to order), pizza, floats, etc.

○ Pioneer Party. "Chuck wagon"—serve beef stew, sourdough bread, apple brown Betty; use tin plates and cups.

○ M*A*S*H. "Chow line" food: chicken à la king, creamed chipped beef on toast; serve on tin plates.

○ Patriotic Themes. All-American foods: fried chicken, barbecue, apple pie, etc.

- Oktoberfest. German beer, bratwurst, Weiner schnitzel, apple streusel, etc.
- Halloween. Hot dogs, hot cider with cinnamon, hot cocoa, caramel apples, pumpkin bread, etc.
- Ethnic Themes. All ethnic cuisines have a low end and a high end. When you are trying to save money, go for the low end. Forget sweet-and-sour shrimp; serve lo mein and stir fry. Serve spaghetti instead of veal scallopini.
- Cajun Theme. Go for the low end here as well. Instead of blackened red fish, shrimp, pecan pie, etc., serve seafood gumbo, red beans and rice, fried catfish with hush puppies, po'boys, muffalettas, sweet potato pie, banana pudding, etc.

Other Theme Party Ideas

- Gay Nineties—The Victorian Era.
- TV Classics—Any television show can be a theme: *The Untouchables, I Love Lucy* (Cuban music and servers in red wigs and poodle skirts), *Saturday Night Live, Gunsmoke, Bonanza, Miami Vice, Streets of San Francisco, Ozzie and Harriett, Father Knows Best, The Wonder Years, The X Files, Funniest Home Videos, Little House on the Prairie,* etc.
- Game Shows: *Jeopardy, Wheel of Fortune, Beat the Clock, the Gong Show, The Price Is Right, Hollywood Squares.*
- Movie Classics—Any movie can be a theme: *The Wizard of Oz, Shootout at the O.K. Corral, Alice in Wonderland, Rambo, Indiana Jones and the Lost Temple of Doom, Titanic, Shogun, Fargo.*

Be careful about possible copyright infringement if trademarked images are used. Disney has aggressively protected Disney images and characters. When in doubt, contact the marketing department of the studio that produced the show. This type of information is available at the Internet Movie Database, which is also a great place to look for ideas: (*http://www.imdb.com*).

- Music Themes—Elvis Tribute, Beatles Forever, Fly Me to the Moon (1960s, with Sinatra).
- Western Theme (great for a barbecue)—Rodeo, Hoe Down, Frontier Days, On the Trail.
- Roaring Twenties—Flapper, Betty Boop, *Great Gatsby.*
- Las Vegas Night—Casino, *Viva Las Vegas, Honeymoon in Vegas, Ocean's Eleven, Vegas Vacation.*

○   Great Romances—Antony and Cleopatra, Elizabeth Taylor and Richard Burton, Romeo and Juliet.

○   Science Fiction—Beam Me Up, Scotty (*Star Trek*), *Star Wars*, Flash Gordon.

○   Famous Fads—Hula hoops, pet rocks.

○   Highway 101—Highway 101 runs down the California coast. You can have food and beverage stations representing stops along the way. At the Napa Valley station, you might serve wine, cheeses, and breads. At the San Francisco stop, serve Chinese food to eat right out of a takeout container, and Italian food or cracked Dungeness crab cocktails. At the Santa Barbara station, you might serve fajitas and tacos. End up in Hollywood with a salad bar and yogurt.

Variations: Use your imagination. A theme can be based on any highway or coastline. Route 66, the legendary old highway immortalized in song, wended its way from Chicago to Los Angeles. The Chicago station can serve Chicago deep-dish pizza, ribs, or other appropriate items. The Oklahoma City station can serve carved steamship round, and Albuquerque can present Mexican food. California pizza can be at the last stop in Los Angeles.

Caterers on the East Coast might do an I-95 theme. Starting in Boston with seafood, one stop can be Baltimore for crab cakes, and you can end up in Miami with Joe's Stone Crabs.

Another variation can include the Orient Express—an elegant train ride with food stations based on the stops along the route, perhaps including a "murder mystery" interactive entertainment and decor.

This theme can also work internationally—perhaps Marco Polo's trade route, circling the Mediterranean, all of the islands in the Caribbean. The possibilities are limited only by the imagination and the budget.

○   Putting on the Ritz—Big Band, Art Deco, mirror balls, tap dancing, trains, tuxedos, top hats, nightclubs, long slinky dresses (à la Erté, an Art Deco artist famous for painting tall ladies in slinky long dresses), nightclubs, champagne, veal Oscar, prime rib, Cherries Jubilee, Caesar salad, shrimp cocktail, lobster.

○   *Wizard of Oz*—Attendees enter the room on a "yellow brick road" made from a roll of yellow vinyl. They are greeted by the Scarecrow, the Tin Man, and the Cowardly Lion handing out lollipops. Music from the movie is playing in the background: "Somewhere

Over the Rainbow," "Follow the Yellow Brick Road," "Ding, Dong, the Witch Is Dead." Props around the room simulate scenes from the movie: for Kansas, bales of hay, pitchforks, an old wagon wheel; a wicked witch hanging from the ceiling on a broom, and so forth. On the buffet table, food can be elevated using yellow bricks. Centerpieces can be ruby slippers (shoes painted red and decorated with red glitter and a red bow).

○ Theming with Color—Coordinate linens, candles, menus, flowers, lights, and so on. Rhapsody in Blue, In the Pink, Black and White Ball, Silver Threads Among the Gold, Paint the Town Red, How Green was My Valley, Green Berets, Red Herring, Blue Velvet, Red Hot Mama, Deep Blue Sea, Blue Danube, Yellow Rose of Texas.

○ Location Themes—Paris, Rome, London, Hong Kong, Singapore, New York/New York, New Orleans, Midnight in Moscow, MacArthur Park, Panama Canal.

○ Themes-Within-Location Themes—At a recent convention for the National Association of Catering Executives, held in Seattle, several Seattle themes were presented, including a Purple Haze Lunch (Jimi Hendrix was from Seattle), a "Rain" breakfast, satirizing the famous Seattle climate using upside down umbrellas as centerpieces with water and rubber duckies inside. New Orleans caterers are well versed in the Mardi Gras theme, as Atlanta caterers are with the Gone with the Wind theme. In Dallas, a popular theme is Denim and Diamonds, with attendees asked to wear items of clothing such as tuxedo jackets with jeans, denim shirts with rhinestone necklaces, and velvet skirts, or sequin dresses, with boots.

○ Time Themes—1890s, 1920s, 1950s, 1400s.

○ Time and Location—San Francisco in the 1960s, New York in the 1930s, Hollywood in the 1940s, Paris in the 1700s, New Orleans in the 1920s, Berlin in the 1930s.

○ Historical Themes—Stanley and Livingston , Ghengis Khan, Attila the Hun, The Renaissance, Marco Polo, the Pirates of the Caribbean.

○ Cultural Themes—The Bolshoi Ballet, The Opera, French Impressionist Painters, Picasso, Salvador Dali, Swan Lake.

○ Sports Themes—Monday Night Football, Superbowl, the Americas Cup, Wimbledon, the Masters Golf Tournament, Soccer Madness.

With these theme ideas as a starting point, think about what you could use to create a decor and ambiance. Let your imagination run wild. The more creative the better.

Props

Facilities with sufficient storage space can develop a prop collection for signature themed events. Most major cities also have one or more prop houses that maintain warehouses full of every imaginable type of prop, from rickshaws to Grecian columns or trellises. For a Western theme, corral fencing may be used to separate the reception area from the seating area. It is important to place props correctly and to highlight them with Gobo lights, rather than just sticking them up against a wall.

Take a tour of a prop house to get an idea of what is available. The use of props is an excellent vehicle for up$elling. Remember, the client pays for the the props, or you build them into the cost of the event.

If you want to keep your own props in-house for often used themes, and you have sufficient storage space, there are a number of places you can look for bargains. Remember, whatever clients do not have to spend from their budget with a prop house, can be spent with the caterer. You can find props at party centers, ethnic food stores, arts and crafts shops, sports clubs, junk shops, antique shops, Goodwill stores, military surplus stores, auto supply stores, import shops, toy stores, garden centers, garage sales, travel agencies (destination posters), flea markets, and pawn shops.

You can pick up discontinued fabric remnants for about $1.00 per yard to decorate buffet or refreshment break tables and add a special touch to the visual display. Fabric is available in an amazingly wide variety of prints that fit various themes. Always be sure that the fabric meets the fire code. Ample fabric creates the look you are after; skimpy attempts with fabrics will harm the overall effect. Typically, a 6-foot buffet table will need 10 yards of fabric to achieve the right look.

Dècor

In developing a decor, stay within the planned budget. It is very easy to add "just one more thing" and overspend the budget. The most common error in costing events of this type is to underestimate the labor involved.

With any decor, be mindful of safety issues. Do not create a hazard whereby guests may trip on cords or otherwise injure themselves.

Guests eat more food in brightly lit, colorfully decorated surroundings. Vibrant colors (red, hot pink, bright yellow) stimulate the appetite. Dark tones (deep green, dark blue, brown, gray, black) dull the appetite.

Fun Food

Guests like to be surprised. Fun food makes your guests say, "Wow!" There are many things you can do to add visual interest to the shape of certain foods for plate presentations: noodle cages for deep-fried shrimp, julienne of carrots in scallion-tied crepe pouches, chocolate pianos (available ready-made from specialty food suppliers) filled with fruit and chocolate sauce. Fun food often requires guest participation—sloppy ribs, ice cream cones, taco bars—all change the context of social eating. This usually works best when guests will be in casual dress.

Signature Items

Providing something people cannot get elsewhere can give your facility a reputation for unique presentations. This is an example of "niche" marketing. There is a dairy in Atlanta that makes signature ice cream for clubs and restaurants in the area, including muscadine ice cream exclusively for Callaway Gardens. Lawry's Seasoned Salt started out as a specialty blend of spices at its Los Angeles restaurant; the item became so popular that the company produced it for the mass market. Every chef should be encouraged to develop two or three items he or she is particularly proud of, and they should be featured on the menu. Such an item may be hot, fresh signature breads, a pâté, a special house salad dressing, or a specialty dessert, such as the bourbon bread pudding at Atlanta's Omni Hotel.

Themed Refreshment Breaks

Coffee breaks can add significantly to total revenue, and should therefore be considered an integral part of food income. Turning them into unique refreshment breaks can be a strong selling point in obtaining and improving business. The traditional coffee break, including Danish or doughnuts, is often expected or required. However, the same items presented over and over again can become boring. The purpose of the break is to provide refreshment between periods of work so as to improve concentration. Offer the client a selection of refreshing ideas for breaks to add variety to the standard fare; it can enhance the client's impression of you as a professional. Here are some ideas:

○ Beignets (doughnuts from New Orleans), malasadas (Portugese doughnuts popular in Hawaii) or crepes with unusual fillings

- Hot muffins—blueberry, date nut, bran, gingerbread, pumpkin, banana
- Hot pretzels directly from a conveyer belt
- Special breads—scones, English muffins, brioches
- Flavored cream cheese, whipped butter
- Fruit in tart shells
- Sticky cinnamon buns
- Ice cream bars

In addition to special food items, the decorative setting should be a selling point. Unique break settings should include flowers, linen, unusual food containers, and anything else that surprises guests and enhances the presentation.

Innovative Themed Refreshment Breaks

- *Greek*—Grape juice, feta cheese, spanakopita, baklava, mounds of grapes, melons, blue and white checked linen, Greek coffee, *Zorba the Greek* music, Grecian columns
- *Southwestern United States*—Tacos, cactus, pottery, Indian baskets
- *German*—Apple juice, beer steins, strusel, ceramic pictures, cheese, polka music, cold cuts, white linen
- *New York Deli*—V8 Juice, hanging sausages, bagels and lox, hanging cheese balls, pound cake, checked linen
- *French*—Fresh-squeezed juices, crepes, fresh flowers, croissants, white porcelain china, French bread, wicker baskets, melted Brie cheese, accordion music, café au lait
- *Mexican*—Papaya juice, churros, exotic fruits, sopapilla (fried dough), sombreros, serapes, piñatas
- *English*—Fruitcake, tea, plum pudding, fruit compote, crumpets, scones, spicy iced tea, tin boxes, teapots
- *Circus*—Caramel apples, popcorn, peanut butter cookies, fruit punch, balloons, clowns
- *Flower Drum Song*—Chinese fortune and almond cookies, Chinese green tea, Chinese calligraphy, lacquer umbrellas
- *101 Dalmations*—Nuts and candy served in dog food bowls; cut churros and cinnamon bow ties, simulating dog chews
- *Biker Break*—Biker food, such as donuts, beef jerky, Twinkies, coffee from a thermos; props: a motorcycle; music: Steppenwolf's "Born to be Wild" and Bruce Springsteen's "Born in the USA"
- *Other Creative Food Ideas*—Miniature waffles, Scotch eggs, chocolate cigarettes, strawberries dipped in chocolate, trail mix, marshmal-

low roast, root beer floats, banana splits, lemonade and ginger snaps, sundae bar, cheese ball, flavored coffees, espresso, cappuccino, Irish coffee, nuts in the shell with nutcrackers, ice cream cones, peanut butter and jelly finger sandwiches, hot cider, hot chocolate with marshmallows, caramel apples, Cracker Jack, peanut brittle, popcorn, pomegranate juice.

WEDDINGS

The wedding is the ultimate theme party. Wedding receptions are excellent revenue generators. The average spent on wedding receptions in the United States in 1990 was approximately $15,000 and in 1999 approximately $19,000. It is interesting to note that at any given time period, the price of an average car often equals the price of a typical wedding.

Because the occasion is so special to the bride and groom, their families, and their friends, the quality of the event often takes precedence over the cost of the reception. *Memorable weddings don't "just happen"! They are "created" as the result of careful attention to detail.*

Use the following guidelines for your initial meeting with a prospective client:

- Develop ideas for presentation at the first meeting or visit.
- Build trust and confidence in your initial conversations.
- Listen and take lots of notes.
- Touch the clients' lives—get excited and share their enthusiasm for the wedding.
- Involve the clients' senses—use visual proposals (*photos, table settings, cake decorating*).
- Describe the advantages of using your facility versus the competition's.

A wedding is one of the most important events in a person's life. Choosing a caterer and location for the wedding reception is a major decision. A wedding reception requires the utmost skill, attention to detail, and careful coordination with the bride and groom and their respective families. Some couples prefer an informal, relaxed reception, whereas others will request a more dignified affair. Each couple's tastes will be different. Many couples pay for their own wedding expenses today, and grooms are becoming more involved in wedding planning.

With the costs of renting a church escalating, many couples are opting to hold the ceremony, as well as the reception, at a hotel, club, or other facility. Do you have an area that is particularly well suited for a ceremony? Perhaps a gazebo or an area with a spectacular view? Gazebos can be rented from prop houses, professional floral houses, and decorators. Outdoor receptions can be beautiful, especially in the spring or fall. There are advantages to holding the ceremony at the same place as the reception:

○   Provides one-stop shopping.
○   Everything is under one roof.
○   Guests do not have to travel from the ceremony at church or temple to the location.
     No limousine costs
     Saves time and travel arrangements
○   You can charge a setup fee and/or a coordinator fee.
○   You can be inventive and imaginative with tents, canopies, fabric-lined ceilings, rented foliage, bridal runner, etc.

Saturdays and Sundays are the most popular days for weddings. Afternoon weddings are often sold at a lower price.

According to Shelley Pedersen, CPCE, owner of Beyond Cuisine in Atlanta, the five basic elements of all wedding receptions are as follows:

1   Menu
○   Start with your menu. Be accommodating by offering custom menus.
○   Listen to the client—what should the menu accomplish for the client?
○   What does the client want his or her guests to say about the event?
○   Involve the senses: sight, sound, taste, touch, smell.
○   Be aware of trends in the marketplace and the popularity of certain foods, as well as innovative preparation methods.
○   Keep traditional menu approaches in mind, as some clients will prefer an "old-fashioned wedding."
○   Up$ell.

2   Beverages
○   Be aware of beverage trends in your marketplace.
○   Describe the special features you offer.

    o   Learn your client's preferences.

    o   Discuss wedding traditions with your client, such as toasts.

    o   Up$ell.

3 Disposables

    o   Describe options (personalized matches, napkins, etc.).

    o   Present samples to your client.

    o   Be familiar with "trendy" items in the marketplace.

    o   Draw upon favorite, traditional wedding items (e.g. Jordan almond favors).

    o   Up$ell.

4 Equipment

    o   Make the most of your facility's equipment strengths (e.g., silver service, outdoor grill, etc.).

    o   Be aware of trends in the wedding market (Champagne fountains, etc.).

    o   Up$ell.

5 Service

    o   Know how the service you propose and the menu will work together.

    o   Be knowledgeable about different styles of service and offer choices (up$ell).

    o   Train your staff in different service styles.

    o   Suggest new trends in styles of service (e.g. action stations, etc.).

    o   Offer traditional styles of service (e.g. French, Russian, etc.).

    o   Up$ell.

In addition, consider the following items:

o   Enhancements for each element—Up$ell.

o   Trends and traditions (especially for ethnic weddings).

o   Processions, recessions, blessings, candle lighting, communion, gift tables, toasting table, guest book table.

o   What will make a reception perfect in the eyes of your client, and what can you do to make it happen?

o   A representative from the catering office or management should be present from the moment the first guest arrives until the bouquet has been thrown. The single most important role of the catering staff should be the sincere assurance that the wedding reception is in the capable hands of an experienced staff and that it will be done right.

○   The finale: To ensure a lasting impression of the event, make it a "wow" by creating a memorable finale (e.g., a live butterfly release, indoor fireworks, or other spectacular feature).

Decorations, table settings, room layout, and flow are often major concerns of the bride and family. Discuss each topic in detail with the parties concerned, and once agreement has been reached, the parties should initial the diagram or the agreement specifying how these arrangements will be carried out.

Develop a checklist that covers virtually every facet of planning and execution of the wedding reception. This helps to avoid last-minute problems and reduces the chances of major omissions in the planning and arrangements. Is there to be a head table? What service style is preferred? When is the limo arriving? Is there scripting for the "first dance"? When will the champagne toast be made? Will there be a groom's cake? A sample wedding checklist is shown on pages 133–138. This checklist should be used by catering staff to record all appropriate information that will eventually become part of the wedding. It is a good idea to have this handy whenever you discuss any element of the event. In fact, it may be fun to get the client involved in completing the necessary entries; interactivity always seems to enhance a client's comfort level.

Developing A Wedding Brochure

It is wise to develop a separate wedding brochure. By doing this, your facility conveys the importance it places on wedding receptions. The needs and desires of this client segment differ greatly from those of a corporate client, and your wedding brochure should reflect the fact that you, the catering professional, recognize and acknowledge these critical differences and stand ready to address them.

In your wedding brochure, use descriptive language that evokes warm emotions and visual images, such as the following:

○   Reminiscent of a Victorian Garden
○   Crackling fire in our fireplace
○   Soft sunlight
○   Sparkling moonlight
○   Panoramic view

- Grand staircase
- Attentive staff
- Knowledgeable, experienced service
- Let us custom tailor a wedding as individual as you are!
- Offers intimacy and charm
- We are at your service
- Let us take care of all your needs
- We cater to your needs at an affordable price
- A wedding of style and grace
- A romantic setting
- The wedding your love deserves
- Weddings of sophisticated simplicity
- An event of perfection
- Complimentary champagne toast
- Book early and get the date and location of your choice for the wedding of your dreams
- Romantic weddings
- Something old, something new
- The room is aglow in a festive fashion
- Be the center of attraction surrounded by friends and family
- Our elegant ballroom provides the perfect ambiance
- Fairy-tale wedding
- Cathedral ceilings
- Crystal chandeliers
- White-gloved waiters
- Award-winning chef
- A dream come true
- One-on-one attention
- A custom-made package just for you
- We will make it perfect for you
- Weddings are our business
- Save your $$$ for your honeymoon
- More than 25 years' wedding experience
- We'll do it your way
- Professional sound system
- Personalized planning
- Free wedding planning
- Affordable elegance
- Custom-tailored menus for your special day
- Memories destined to last a lifetime!

Wedding Package Plans

A facility should offer a minimum of three complete plans for each of the following wedding functions:

o   Hors d' Oeuvres Reception: "tray-passed only" or a combination of tray-passed and buffet
o   Stand-Up Reception
o   Seated Buffet
o   Seated Luncheon or Brunch (possible buffet or combination)
o   Seated Dinner

Complete plans should include everything: food, beverages, live entertainment, champagne toast, wedding guest book, color-coordinated linen, matchbooks, embossed napkins, wedding cake, groom's cake, floral arrangements, photography, and any other items required.

Promote your "personalized wedding planning services" and discuss all of the "little extras" (up$elling) that you can provide.

One-Stop Shopping

Position yourself as a wedding consultant who will handle all of the wedding details and take the care and worry away from the bride. Develop a list of vendors who will grant the facility discounts for providing services, including:

o   Entertainment
o   Wedding and formal attire
o   Videography and photography
o   Limo and innovative transportation
o   Baker for wedding cake, groom's cake, petits fours, guest favors
o   Decorations
o   Floral designer
o   Wedding and social stationery
o   Invitations
o   Calligraphy (invitations, menu cards, and place cards)
o   Embossed napkins, match books
o   Candy favors, keepsakes, mini-bubble bottles for guests to blow bubbles
o   Upgraded china, flatware, glasses
o   Rented linens—double cloths, overlays, runners, swagging

- Red carpet in entryway
- Upgraded chairs—slipcovers
- Candelabra—silver, brass, gold
- Horse and carriage ride from church
- Fireworks display
- Skywriting message
- Hot air balloon sendoff
- Luminarias to line the footpath (after dark)

Independent wedding consultants typically charge 15 to 20 percent of gross wedding costs. If you provide this service and earn the discounts from vendors, both you and the client benefit.

Entertainment

Music sets the mood. When suggesting entertainment, do not think merely of the reception. A harpist or a chamber orchestra is ideal when the wedding ceremony is being held at the facility. A band can play at the reception, but calming, soothing tones are best for the ceremony. Most churches have organists, but organs are not portable. The ceremony music is important because it creates the mood for the wedding. Music should start about half an hour prior to the ceremony and continue while guests are arriving. The music can be religious, contemporary romantic, or classical. Discuss the selections to be played with the bride.

Soft background music is appropriate for the receiving line and during the meal when people are trying to talk.

Types of music available for ceremonies and receptions include the following:

Classical ensembles	Chamber music
Harpists	Strolling strings
Herald trumpets	Jazz combos
Vocalists	Ethnic bands
Big bands	Dance orchestras
Top 40 bands	Country and Western music
Disc jockeys	Pianist
Classic rock bands	Bluegrass music
Guitarists	Dixieland bands
Mariachi bands	Bagpipers

Other Opportunities and Ideas

Do not forget that there are usually a variety of other functions surrounding a wedding, such as an engagement party, showers, bachelor and bachelorette parties and a rehearsal dinner.

Disposable cameras for use at weddings can be purchased in quantity for a reasonable price. Do not stop with the floral needs for the reception; flowers will also be needed for the church, the bridal party, and the bridal bouquet, as well as for the reception.

The Language of Flowers:

Unity	Red and white roses, double daisies
Gaiety	Yellow lilies
Expectation	Purple anemone
Hope	Bachelor's button
Consistency	Bluebell
Riches	Buttercup
Gratitude	Camellia
Pure, deep love	Carnation
Sharing feelings	Daisy
Fidelity	Ivy
Grace, elegance	Jasmine
Affection	Jonquil
Purity	Lily

How to Manage a Successful Catering Business by Manfred Ketterer (New York: VNR, 1991) contains an excellent chapter on weddings with specific instructions and diagrams of how to set up for a Christian wedding and a Jewish wedding. It also includes detailed instructions on how to cut the wedding cake, throw the bridal bouquet, and throw the garter.

When champagne is served only for a toast, it is preferable to save the toast until the cutting of the wedding cake. It will reduce the probability of the guests going to the bar for unavailable refills. The champagne toast can also begin a seated meal, as guests will probably not get up for refills.

A sample wedding package plan is shown on pages 127–132.

PLANNING YOUR WEDDING

You are about to begin planning one of the most important days in your life—your wedding! We at the _____(name of your facility)_____ want to assure you that our attention to detail will make your wedding reception one of the most cherished memories of your life.

We offer several complete, all-inclusive plans in several price ranges. You may also custom design your arrangements or use your ideas in combination with one of our plans. We offer seated dinners, seated buffet dinners, and stand-up receptions. In each category, there are various menus and options that enable you to tailor your reception as you like. Trust us to make your arrangements and planning smooth, stylish, and worry-free.

Room Selection: Room capacities vary according to the table, bar, and entertainment requirements. For your planning purposes, room capacities are listed here

Room	Seated Dinner	Seated Buffet	Stand-Up
Azalea	350	320	500
Dahlia	75	65	110
Rose	110	80	150

Wedding receptions are normally booked for 4 hours for seated functions, and 2½ hours for stand-up receptions.

Reservations/Deposits: Wedding reservations and arrangements are provided on a first-come, first-served basis. Reservations for a particular room are determined by the number of guests, the arrangements, and the services to be provided. A tentative reservation may be made by phone, fax, e-mail, or in person. The reservation for a particular room or date is tentative and may be offered to another party until a deposit of _____($ or %)_____ is made and the sponsor signs a catering agreement. The agreement should be signed at least _____(number)_____ days prior to the wedding date.

Menus and Pricing: Pricing for the all-inclusive plans is based on the menu and type of reception selected. The menus available for seated dinners, seated buffets, and stand-up receptions follow this section.

Beverage/Bar Service: An open bar is included in the package price. The bars are open for the entire 2½-hour period for stand-up receptions. For seated dinners and seated buffets, the bars are open for 3 hours; during the meal period, carafes of wine are provided for each table of 10 guests. A champagne toast is also included with these plans.

Live Entertainment: All plans include live entertainment. When there is a final count (guarantee) of 100 or more guests, a trio is provided; if your plan is for fewer than 100 guests, a pianist is included.

Flowers: For seated dinners and seated buffet dinners, floral decorations are provided for the bridal and cake tables. For stand-up receptions, a buffet centerpiece is provided in place of the bridal table centerpiece. The remaining guest tables are furnished with candles.

Linen: Napkins are available in a variety of colors for seated functions. Tablecloths are normally white, and tables that require skirting (cake, gift, book, etc.) are skirted in white. Additional decorations are available, if desired, for a nominal charge.

Your wedding reception will be supervised by a trained, professional catering sales representative. Each plan includes the wedding guest book and all service charges and setup fees (except those related to package plan modifications).

Rice: Rice or birdseed may be thrown. A cleanup fee of $____(amount)____ will be added to the invoice. Because of the slip/fall danger for guests when rice or birdseed is used, insurance is required for their use. Recommended alternatives are confetti, flower petals, or soap bubbles.

Additional Touches: The following optional items are available upon request for a nominal charge:

○   Additional appetizers
○   Hot hors d' oeuvres
○   Ice sculptures
○   Silver candelabra
○   Champagne fountain
○   Lace overlays for the cake table
○   Take-home deli tray for the family
○   Premium champagne (Moet et Chandon or Mumm's)
○   Additional or specialty desserts

STAND-UP BUFFETS

Regency Buffet
Cubes of Sharp Cheddar, Rounds of Creamy Brie, and Blocks of Swiss Cheese
Stone-Ground Wheat Thins and Water Biscuits
Spicy Deviled Eggs
Carrots Julienne, Celery Strips, Cauliflower and Broccoli Florets, and Cucumber Rounds
Creamy Ranch and Dill Dips
Hot Chili con Queso with Taco Chips
Choice of Two Hot Hors d' Oeuvres:

Crab Puffs	Sweet-and-Sour Meatballs
Shrimp Egg Rolls	Breaded Mussels
Italian Meatballs	Mini-Quiche Lorraine

Coffee and Tea
Wedding Mints
$ _____ per Person

Deluxe Buffet
Fresh Fruit Tree with Melon, Strawberries, and Pineapple Chunks
International Cheese Station
with Stilton, Muenster, and Roquefort
Assorted Canapés with Sliced Smoked Salmon on Rye Bread
with Horseradish Butter and a Dill Garnish

| Cauliflower Florets | Crab-Stuffed Mushrooms |
| Deviled Eggs | Chicken Fingers |

Carrots Julienne, Celery Strips, Cauliflower
and Broccoli Florets
Assorted Finger Sandwiches,
including Chicken Salad, Ham Salad, and Chopped Olives
Hot Chili con Queso with Chips
Carved Tenderloin of Beef with Tea Rolls
Choice of Two Hot Hors d' Oeuvres:
Pizza Puffs   Sweet-and-Sour Meatballs
Shrimp Egg Rolls   Breaded Mussels
Italian Meatballs   Mini-Quiche Lorraine
Petits Fours
Wedding Cake
Coffee and Tea
Wedding Mints
$ _____ per Person

International Buffet
Pineapple Tree with Melon and Strawberries
Vegetable Bleu Cheese Dip, Cubed Sharp and Cheddar Cheese,
Rounds of Creamy Brie, and Blocks of Swiss Cheese
Pâté de Maison
with Party Rye and Pumpernickel Breads
Assorted Canapés Consisting of:
Smoked Oysters and Clams, Chicken, Ham,
and Shrimp Mousse in Pastry Puffs
Smoked Salmon, Red and Black Caviar
Crab Aspic, Cornets of Salami
Corned Beef and Cream Cheese Roulettes
California Walnut Pâté
Assorted Tea Sandwiches
including Chicken Salad and Ham Salad
Hand-Carved Steamship Round of Beef
Fried Maryland Crab Puffs
Bacon-Wrapped Chicken Livers
Clams Casino   Chicken Nut Puffs
Bourbon Franks   Barbecued Riblets
Sweet-and-Sour Meatballs
Tempura Fried Vegetables
Mushroom Caps Singapore
Sourdough Rolls, Mini Wheat and Pumpernickel Breads and Condiments
Apple and Almond Fritters
Coffee and Tea
Wedding Mints and Almonds, Cashews and Peanuts
$ _____ per Person

SEATED BUFFETS

Brunch Buffet
Fresh Fruit including Cantaloupe, Honeydew, Watermelon,
Pineapple, Grapes, and Apples
Fresh-Squeezed Orange, Grape, and Apple Juices
Ham, Bacon, and Sausages
Scrambled Eggs
Hashed Browned Potatoes
Creamed Beef
Hot Biscuits with Honey Butter
Belgian Waffle and Omelet Station
Coffee and Tea
$ _____ per Person

Dinner Buffet
Assorted Iced Relishes
(Olives, Sweet Gherkins, Kosher Dill Pickles)
Peach Aspic with Walnut Dressing
Fruited Gelatin Molds with Cottage Cheese
Green Beans with Vinaigrette Salad
Tossed Garden Salad
Choice of Dressing:
(Ranch, Thousand Island, Italian, Bleu Cheese,
French, and Vinaigrette)
Beef Stroganoff
with Buttered Egg Noodles
Broiled Filet of Sole Amandine
Potatoes au Gratin   French-Cut Green Beans
Glazed Petite Carrots
Sourdough and Pumpernickel Rolls with Whipped Butter
Strawberry or Chocolate Mousse
Coffee and Tea
Wedding Mints
$ _____ per Person

Deluxe Buffet
Assorted Iced Relishes
(Olives, Sweet Gherkins, Kosher Dill Pickles)
Gazpacho Aspic with Sour Cream
Peach Aspic with Walnut Dressing
Fruited Gelatin Mold with Cream Cheese
Fresh Fruit Salad Bowl Consisting of:
Cantaloupe, Honeydew, Watermelon, Oranges,
Pineapple, Grapes, and Apples
Cucumber and Tomato Salad
Roast Top Sirloin of Beef
Breast of Chicken Normandy
Seafood Newburg au Sherry
Rice Pilaf, Potatoes au Gratin, Peas
with Pearl Onions, and Glazed Petite Carrots
Sourdough and Pumpernickel Rolls
Whipped Butter
Parfait
(Your Choice of Cordial Liqueur)
Coffee and Tea
Wedding Mints
$ _____ per Person

SEATED DINNER MENUS

Select one in each category

Appetizers and Soups
Frosted Fresh Fruit Cup Consisting of:
Cantaloupe, Honeydew, Watermelon, Oranges,
Pineapple, Grapes, and Apples
with Cointreau
Fresh Strawberries
French Onion Soup or Seafood Bisque

Main Courses
Breast of Chicken Veronique
with Seedless Grapes
Breast of Chicken Stuffed
with Apple and Almonds
Veal Princess
Sauteéd with Asparagus and Hollandaise Sauce
Veal Cordon Bleu
Stuffed with Swiss Cheese and Ham
Roast Top Sirloin of Beef
with Mushroom Sauce
12 ounce Boneless Prime Rib au Jus
with Creamy Beefeater Sauce
Sourdough and Pumpernickel Dinner Rolls and Butter

Vegetables
Broccoli, Peas, Green Beans, Glazed Petite Carrots

Potato or Rice
Baked, Oven Roasted, Boiled New Potatoes or Rice Pilaf

Desserts
Crème de Menthe Parfait
Chocolate or Strawberry Mousse
Lemon Sherbet or Coconut Ice Cream
Coffee and Tea
Wedding Mints
$ _____ per Person

PAYMENT:

Cash/Check: Payment for the event is due on the day of the function (or) within (number) days following the event.

Charge Card: Visa, MasterCard, American Express, In-House

See the Appendix for a listing of appropriate action station menu items.

WEDDING CHECKLIST

Day and Date of the Wedding:

_____

Bride's Name: _____

Bride's Address: _____

Phone Number (Home): _____ Fax: _____

e-mail _____

Phone Number (Work): _____ Fax: _____

Name of Groom: _____

Future Name of Bride: _____

Contact Address: _____

Phone Number: _____

Location of the Wedding Reception:

_____

Minimum Number of Guests Expected: _____

Location of the Ceremony:

_____

Ceremony Start Time: _____

End Time: _____

Transportation: _____

Type: _____

Company: _____

Driver's Name: _____ Phone Number: _____

Reception Start Time: _____

End Time: _____

133

Location Planning

Receiving Line/Introductions

_____ Time: _____

Gift Table: _____

Guest Book Table: _____

Escort Table: _____

Bridal Table: _____

Equipment Requirements: _____

Tables for Guests:

Seats per table: _____

Number of tables: _____

Size of table:

60-inch round (seats 6 to 10, recommended for 8) _____

72-inch round (seats 8 to 12, recommended for 10) _____

6-foot rectangle (seats 8 with one on each end) _____

Type of Chairs: _____

Chair Covers: _____

Napkins: Color _____ Size _____ Quantity _____

            Color _____ Size _____ Quantity _____

Tablecloths: Color _____ Size _____ Quantity _____

                Color _____ Size _____ Quantity _____

                Color _____ Size _____ Quantity _____

Overlays: Color _____ Size _____ Quantity _____

Skirting: Color _____

Total Footage _____

China Color and Pattern: _____

Glassware Type: _____

Flatware: _____

Ancillary Services

Support Staff:

Number _____ Location _____

Responsibilities: _____

Music:

Name: _____

Phone: _____

Start Time: _____ End Time: _____

Hourly Play Time: _____

Family Tables: _____

Proposed Menu: _____

Hors d'Oeuvres: _____

Type of Bar: _____

Champagne Toast: _____ Time _____

Cake Cutting: _____ Time _____

Meal

Buffet _____   Served _____

Cocktail _____

Proposed Food Items:

Hors d'Oeuvres: _____

Passed: _____

On Tables: _____

Appetizer: _____

Soup: _____

Salad: _____

Intermezzo: _____

Main Course: _____

Dessert: _____

Wines: _____

Floral Requirements

Centerpieces:

Tables: Number _____ Size _____ Type _____

Buffets: Type _____ Quantity _____

            Type _____ Quantity _____

Bridal bouquet: _____

Groom: _____

Bridesmaids: _____

Wedding Party: _____

Best Man: _____

Bouquet: _____

Cake: _____

Other

Photographer: Name _____ Phone _____

                  Time of Attendance _____

Videographer: Name _____ Phone _____

                  Time of Taping _____

Wedding Cake: Bakery _____ Phone _____

                  Type _____

Special Requirements _____

                  Delivery Time: _____

Refrigerate: Yes _____ No _____

                  Number of anticipated servings _____

Groom's Cake: Bakery _____ Phone _____

                  Type _____

Special Requirements _____

                  Delivery Time: _____

Refrigerate: Yes _____ No _____

                  Number of anticipated servings _____

Cake Knife and Server: _____

Bride and Groom Glasses: _____

Cocktail Napkins: Color _____

Quantity _____

          Inscription _____

          Printer _____ Phone _____

          Fax _____ e-mail _____

          Date Promised _____

Matches: Color _____ Quantity _____

          Inscription _____

          Printer _____

          Phone _____ e-mail _____

          Date Promised _____

Floor Plan: _____

Anything Else? _____

OUTDOOR PARTIES

Outdoor parties can be held on a patio, balcony, golf course, beach, by a swimming pool, or at another off-site location.

If the event is held in the evening, outdoor lighting will be necessary. Visit the site at the time of day of the party to determine whether auxiliary lighting is required. You can use strategically placed spotlights, Tiki torches (that are also insect repellent), or strings of tiny Tivoli lights in trees. Outdoor lighting is often controlled by an automatic timer, and you may have to arrange to have lights turned on earlier or left on later.

Most facilities do not have off-premise liquor licenses, and thus their in-house licenses are not valid for events held off property. Be sure to obtain a one-time-only license for any off-premise event at which you will be serving alcoholic beverages, as your municipality may dictate.

Facilities doing a "cater-out" should rent tables and chairs and build the cost into the price, instead of transporting these items from their properties. Transporting involves labor costs and damage and loss costs, and because you will most likely need the equipment simultaneously, additional purchase costs and storage space.

Fiesta-type receptions, which are popular in the Southwest, call for grills and smokers (which generally require a 110 v outlet, gas, Sterno, Bunsen burner, or propane).

Whether you spell it Barbeque, Barbecue, Bar-B-Q, or just BBQ, this is a popular item for outdoor events. Barbecue can be loosely defined as "meat plus fire plus a secret sauce."

The meat can be a variety of cuts and types, including pork ribs, a side of beef, a half chicken, or shrimp kabobs, depending on where you are and what your mood is. The meat should be precooked, either by oven baking or boiling. This will keep the outside from overcharring and becoming crusted while the inside is allowed to tenderize.

There are two basic types of barbecue. One style is to cook the food by direct heat and flame over a grill. The other way is to use indirect heat and smoke, usually inside a cylinder-style smoker.

Barbecue experts abound, each with his or her own closely guarded secret sauce. Many of these recipes have been handed down through generations. Some are vinegar based, and others are tomato based. Vinegar based sauces tend to be absorbed more readily by the meat and act as a tenderizer when marinated. Red meats also marinate well in red wine and olive oil with garlic and other spices. Rosemary goes well with lamb. Poultry and seafood marinate well in white wine, olive oil, and spices.

International versions of barbecue include tandoori cooking from India. Tandoori is food on skewers, marinated overnight, then either baked in a clay oven or grilled. The sauce is yogurt based and includes white vinegar, garlic, onions, ginger, and fresh herbs. Greek barbecue includes shish-ka-bob, which is lamb chunks cooked on skewers.

Always have an alternative or backup location in the event of rain, high winds, or extreme heat. This can be a room in your facility or a tent with transparent vinyl siding that can be raised or lowered as needed. Tents are discussed in Chapter 6.

Do not forget to provide an adequate number of portable lavatories for off-site events. Attendees can get rather uncomfortable without proper facilities. A rule of thumb is to provide one portable lavatory for every 100 attendees. It is important to provide directional signs that make them easy to locate. You can also rent hand-washing sinks with portable water tanks. Be sure these amenities can be removed easily and when placed on the truck, the truck is not heavy enough to damage the ground.

Be careful not to serve a hot, heavy meal on a muggy, humid day. Likewise, on a hot day avoid foods that spoil quickly, such as raw shellfish, mayonnaise-based items, or cream pies and cakes. Humidity also quickly wilts pretzels, potato chips, and cut cheeses. Meat, especially if it is raw, attracts bees, so if you are cooking steaks, keep them covered until they are tossed on the grill.

To be sure food is served fresh and hot at sit-down off-premise events, preplate the appetizer and dessert, but you may wish to serve the other courses with French service. Preplated food that sits in hot carts loses presentation value.

Be sure your clients are aware that they should specify a dress code and let their attendees know what types of shoes to avoid or whether they should bring a light sweater. A woman in high heels can sink right into a grassy area. If it is likely that some women will be in high heels, arrange the area so that part of it covers a solid area, such as a sidewalk or parking lot. An alternative is to lay out a portable dance floor, just to be sure the ladies have something solid to stand on.

Make certain that any automated sprinkling systems are turned off to avoid drenching guests. It is also a good idea to avoid excessive watering for a few days prior to the event so that guests don't sink into squishy ground. Request that the lawn be mowed rather short, so that tables are level, linens hang properly, and mosquitoes do not hide in the grass.

An added benefit with outdoor parties is that the site is the decoration, especially in a garden in full bloom. If you are using cut flowers in very hot weather, avoid very delicate blooms, as well as camellias, gardenias, and similar varieties that do not draw water. You can enhance the site with Italian twinkle lights in the trees, Japanese lanterns, flowers floating in a pool, or maypoles festooned with ribbons. Gelatin molds with hollow centers can be used to create centerpieces on umbrella tables.

If insects may be a problem, have the area sprayed six hours before the event. If this is not feasible, ask the host to advise the guests not to wear perfume, which attracts insects. Perfumes are flower based and attract all kinds of winged insects, including bees and wasps. Bright colors also attract bees. Likewise, although it may be nice to hold the event in the middle of a flower garden, remember that bugs and bees also find flowers attractive.

Plan your party so the guests can see and enjoy the flowers without being close enough to upset stinging creatures. Mosquitos love warm, moist, moving bodies. They also love carbon dioxide (produced by breathing) and favor dark, nonreflective clothing. Guests who are warm, perspiring, and wearing perfume are the best targets.

Use pyrethroid insecticides, which are deadly to mosquitoes. Or you may suggest that clients incorporate sprigs of the citrosa plant into centerpieces and floral arrangements. The citrosa emits an odor of citronella that repels mosquitoes, but because of its odor, it should be used some distance from food. For an environmentally safe pesticide, there is a fogger available that vaporizes, an insecticide called resmethrin, which has a low toxicity, is people-friendly, and has less impact on the environment.

Bees and yellow jackets are attracted to food and will sting the hand that shoos them away. At buffet tables and close to each dining table, place a saucer filled with equal parts of honey and beer. This will draw the bees away from guests' plates; the insects will circle woozily around the saucer and eventually fall in. The saucers must be changed constantly, as a saucer full of dead bees would be an unappetizing site on a buffet.

Mini aluminum tart pans can be fastened to wooden tabletops or railings with thumbtacks or pushpins to create makeshift ashtrays that won't blow away in the wind.

Water attracts children, so if children will be present, stay away from areas such as reflecting pools, swimming pools, and golf course water hazards.

When going off-premise, pre-site work is essential. Plan travel time by driving to the site on a day and time that matches that of the event. Take a sketch pad and/or a camera. Draw the area, including where you plan to place food, bars, and so forth. If the event is a wedding, be sure that neither the bridal couple nor the guests will be squinting into the sun. Plot the traffic flow.

Outside surroundings should also be evaluated for sources of contamination, such as vermin, bird harborage areas, drainage problems, odor problems, debris, refuse, smoke, and dust. Appropriate steps must be taken beforehand to contain and control these potential problems.

The smartest thing is to plan the party partly indoors and partly outdoors, or have a backup area in case of inclement weather. Rain or wind can put a damper on any party.

BAR AND BAT MITZVAHS

A bar mitzvah is a rite of passage whereby a 13-year-old boy of the Jewish faith becomes a man. A bat mitzvah is the corresponding rite for girls. The religious service is often followed by an elaborate event, sometimes rivaling the pomp and ceremony of a wedding.

The bar/bat mitzvah usually commences with either the Friday evening, Saturday morning, or Saturday afternoon service. It can also be held on a Monday morning or Thursday morning—any time the Torah is read. The celebration that follows is often a breakfast, luncheon, or dinner with entertainment on a grand scale.

Many bar/bat mitzvahs serve kosher or kosher-style food, depending on whether the family observes the rules of kashruth, (keeps kosher).

True kosher food must follow stringent rules and pass the approval of a *Mashgiach*, who does not have to be a rabbi but must be recognized in the community as a person authorized to give certification for kashruth. For example, in kosher serivce, meat products must not be served on any plate, with the exception of glass and some china that can undergo a curing period, that has ever had dairy products on it. Pork, shellfish, rabbit, and the hindquarter cuts of beef and lamb are not allowed. Kosher-style food may use traditional Jewish recipes but does not necessarily follow the kosher rules. Kosher food conforms to strict Jewish biblical laws regarding the type of food that may be eaten, as well as the kinds of food that can be combined during a meal. In addition to designating the kinds of animals considered kosher, the laws also state that the animals be fed organically grown food and killed in the most humane manner possible.

A web site with Jewish recipes is *http://www.cyber-kitchen.com/rfcj/.*

Meal Functions | Chapter 4

The ability to provide outstanding food and exceptional service is a major marketing advantage in today's competitive catering environment. All aspects of a catered function are important, yet it is reasonable to assume that the quality of food and guest service makes the deepest and most lasting impression on attendees.

The caterer who strives for a competitive advantage would do well to emphasize consistent-quality food, because this consistency is something some caterers cannot offer. Although it may be easy for most facilities to offer clients similar function space or meeting times, such is not the case with food. Other factors may initially attract clients, but food and service are the key variables influencing return patronage.

143

PURPOSE OF A MEAL FUNCTION

One of the first things to consider when planning a meal function is the client's reason for hosting it. Does the client want a meal function primarily to satisfy hunger? create an image? provide an opportunity for social interaction and networking? showcase a person, product, and/or idea? present awards? honor dignitaries? refresh convention attendees and resharpen their attention? provide a receptive audience for program speakers? keep people interested in other nonfood activities? increase attendance at conventions?

The list of reasons is endless. The catering executive, however, should query the client about his or her particular reason(s) so that the appropriate menu and production and service plans can be created. If the catering executive knows about these considerations and concerns, he or she can tailor the function around them.

MENU PLANNING

The director of catering is often responsible for developing standardized menus (in cooperation with the chef), as well as unique menus customized for particular clients. He or she must also see to it that the standardized menus are revised periodically in order to keep them current with changing consumer trends. Many upscale properties are abandoning printed menus and use only custom proposals for their clients.

It also is a good idea to get input from other department heads, such as the purchasing agent, the food and beverage director, and the facility sales director.

The types of menu items a facility can offer its guests depend on several factors. Before adding a menu item to a standardized menu, or before offering to accommodate a client's particular need, the menu planner must evaluate all relevant considerations that will affect the facility's ability to offer it and the guest's desire to eat that food.

Food Cost

Ideally, the catering department will offer a variety of menu prices to suit its target markets. However, these prices must also be consistent with the target market's needs and desires. Many clients appreciate the opportunity to work with several price options when allocating their meal budgets. These clients tend to shuffle their budgetary dollars back and forth among events; this routine is easier to accomplish if the catering department cooperates by offering several price variations. Food cost margins affect profitability. Caterers should be aware of ways to modify their standard menu, such as including a less expensive entrée, or eliminating a course. Pricing is discussed in detail in Chapter 2.

Guest Background

A menu planner should consider the demographics of the group ordering the meal function. Average age, sex, ethnic background, socioeconomic level, diet restrictions, where the guests come from, employment and fraternal affiliations, and political leanings can indicate the types of menu items that may be most acceptable to the group. Psychographics—guests' life-styles and the way they perceive themselves—are also useful indicators.

Age is often an excellent indicator. For example, senior citizens usually do not want exotic foods or heavy, spicy foods. In this case, you should avoid excessive use of garlic, hot spices, and onions. You would want to avoid other distress-causing foods, such as monosodium glutamate (MSG), cabbage-family vegetables, beans, and other legumes.

Guests sometimes require special diets, which will influence the types of foods served. Some persons cannot tolerate MSG (allergic reactions), onions or garlic (digestive problems), certain spices or peanuts (allergic reactions), sugar (diabetic reactions), salt (high blood pressure, heart problems), fat (weight problems, high cholesterol), and/or milk products (allergic problems, lactose intolerence).

Some guests adhere to special diets for religious or life-style reasons. For example, devout Muslims and Jews do not eat pork or shellfish. Orthodox Jews require kosher-prepared foods. Some persons do not eat red meat, but do eat poultry and seafood. Some vegetarians (referred to as "vegans") do not eat anything from any animal source, including cream, eggs, butter, and honey. Other vegetarians (referred to as "lacto-ovo" vegetarians) do not eat animal flesh, but do eat animal by-products such as eggs and dairy products. Accommodating some ethnic or religious requirements may create added expense because of the need to engage specialized personnel (e.g., a rabbi to supervise kosher preparations) or acquire special food items. (See the Appendix for a sample Special Meal Request Form.)

If a group is coming from a previous function where heavy, filling hors d'oeuvres were served, the meal should be lighter. If guests are coming from a liquor-only reception, then the meal can be heavier. If a group will be going to a business meeting immediately after the meal, you should serve foods that will help keep attendees awake. Protein foods, such as seafood, lean beef, and skinless chicken, will keep the guests alert. Carbohydrates, such as rice, bread, and pasta, tend to relax people and put them to sleep. Fats, such as butter, whipped cream, and heavy salad dressings, also tend to make guests sleepy, sluggish, and inattentive.

Politics can play an important role in menu planning. Some groups will not consume certain types of foods. The catering department and the function planner must see to it that politically correct foods are available. Serving veal to members of animal rights organizations can anger them, because these groups believe that veal is raised and processed under inhumane conditions. Politically active groups may insist that the facility purchase and serve politically correct products. You may be prohibited from purchasing beef raised on recently deforested rain forest land. You may be asked not to purchase tuna from countries that use drift nets that trap and kill dolphins and other sea life indiscriminately. And for your clients with "green" concerns, you may be prohibited from packaging finished food products in disposable containers; you may have to use reusable containers without charging a premium for this service.

Nutrition Concerns

Nutrition is always a consideration for caterers, but especially when they are serving groups that will be at a hotel or conference center for several days during a convention. Because virtually all meals during their stay will be consumed on the premises, special attention must be paid to nutritional requirements when planning menus.

Dietary restrictions abound. Many customers will appreciate it if the facility provides alternatives, including some low-fat, low-calorie, or high-protein meal options as well as a variety of low-carbohydrate foods. Some caterers list information on calories, fat, carbohydrates, and sodium for some menu items.

Whenever possible, serve sauces and dressings on the side so that guests can control their own portion sizes. Use fresh ingredients instead of processed foods that contain preservatives and other additives. Today's consumers want fresh choices. They also are becoming more adept at recognizing pre-prepared, processed foods.

Caterers notice that many guests are reluctant to give up their dessert course. Ironically, when people are "good," they like to reward themselves with a rich dessert. In spite of the fact that people are becoming more health conscious, fancy desserts are expected at a catered meal. The typical guest feels cheated if the meal ends without a dessert or if the dessert offered is viewed as mediocre.

The dessert creates the last impression of the meal and should be spectacular. A small portion of a rich dessert is sufficient if the presentation is artistic. For instance, desserts can be quite impressive if served decoratively on an oversized plate and/or prepared at tableside.

Always consult with the fire marshal when planning to use an open flame. Be sure that the station where flaming is performed is not set up directly under a sprinkler head or smoke detector.

Special service presentations can be very effective. For instance, a baked Alaska parade, for which the lights are dimmed and the servers carry in the flaming dishes, is a dazzling sight.

Dessert action stations (i.e., for performance or exhibition cooking) are certain crowd pleasers, guaranteed to have a favorable impact on guests. Chefs working at these stations can prepare hot crepes with different fruit sauces. Or they can prepare bananas Foster, fruit beignets, and/or cherries jubilee to order.

Dessert buffets are also a nice touch, especially when served with champagne, flavored coffees and teas, liqueurs, and/or brandies. This type of service allows the guests an opportunity to move around, a good idea if you expect the meal function to be more than 1½ to 2 hours.

If you provide a dessert buffet or a dessert action station, you should prepare bite-sized "taster" dessert items. Guests will appreciate this, because many of them will have a hard time choosing. You do not want them to take two or three full desserts, because this will increase waste and food costs.

When stocking a dessert buffet, a good idea is to display full-sized desserts on an upper tier of the table, then on the lower tier place duplicate miniature versions of the showcased items. This type of presentation is especially effective if the taster samples are placed on mirrored platters. Cheesecake, tarts, tortes, cakes, baklava, cannoli, butter cookies, chocolate leaves, and fresh fruit are especially attractive and inviting when presented like this.

Hard-to-Produce Foods

Certain delicate items cannot be produced and served in quantity without sacrificing culinary quality. For example, lobster, soufflés, rare roast beef, medium-rare tuna or salmon steak, and rare duck breast are almost impossible to prepare and serve satisfactorily for more than a handful of guests.

If a client insists on having these types of items, the facility may need to implement a creative, and possibly costly, procedure to accommodate the request. For instance, flaming desserts do not lend themselves easily to quantity production. However, the caterer can install an action station on an elevated platform safely away from tableside, but not near sprinkler heads. Guests can view the flaming displays without worrying about getting burned. And servers can retrieve the completed desserts when the chefs are finished.

Standardized Menu Offerings

If the facility has a restaurant, the catering sales representative should encourage budget-conscious clients to order menu items offered in the restaurant. This will keep food costs under control, inasmuch as banquet leftovers can be utilized elsewhere and you will have extra inventory on hand if needed.

The chef usually prepares enough food to serve more than the guaranteed guest count. This overproduction is necessary to avoid stockouts. Unfortunately, if the menu includes unusual foods that cannot be used in the facility's restaurant outlets, a client will have to pay a higher price to defray the extra food costs. With a standardized menu, clients may not have to worry about paying for overproduction.

Length of Meeting

If guests will be at a hotel for several days eating mostly catered meals, the most important rule is, Do not repeat the same preparation, presentation, or product. You must be careful not to repeat food items from meal to meal or from day to day. For instance, you would not want to serve carrot cake for dessert if you served a carrot and raisin salad and/or glazed carrots last night, serve chicken for dinner if you served it yesterday for lunch, or serve beef two nights in a row. Similarly, you should not use the same ingredients in more than one course unless the meal is specifically designed for such repetition. For instance, a convention group visiting Atlanta may be pleased if more than one course includes Georgia peaches. Likewise, for a group visiting Seattle; the creative director of catering may be able to include Pacific salmon in two or three courses. These instances should be marketed as such, so that attendees understand the reason for the repetition.

The most important consideration is to provide variety and nutrition options. The longer the meeting, the more critical these factors become.

Meeting attendees often do not eat every meal in their hotel. If you are an off-site facility hosting a group for one meal, you should try to find out what attendees are scheduled to eat at other meal locations before they come to your function. This will prevent your using too many of the same ingredients. For example, when Prince Charles once visited the United States, he was taken to several places for meals. Each facility served him a veal dish, which caused the prince to wonder aloud whether veal was the only meat that Americans eat.

Seasonality

A catering sales representative should always try to recommend seasonal foods. The quality of food items is greatly enhanced when they are in season. In-season foods are also less expensive. Lower food costs will increase profitability. Moreover, lower food costs will allow you to pass on some of the savings to the client in the form of lower price quotations, thereby possibly capturing catering clients who would not purchase standard-priced meal functions.

Easy-to-Produce Foods

The director of catering should resist the temptation to emphasize only easy-to-prepare foods. Clients may think that these menus lack creativity and flair and may have doubts about the catering department's capabilities.

Chicken is a very common item served on banquet menus, primarily because it is easy to prepare and can be prepared and served in so many ways.

Beef is another common menu offering for at least three reasons. First, it is usually a safe choice for meeting planners; most people will eat beef at least once in a while. Second, a tremendous variety of cuts are consistently available. And third, it can be prepared and served in many ways.

In general, catering executives tend to favor poultry, beef, and similar items that lend themselves to assembly line production and service. If nothing else, such a menu offers no disastrous surprises and can usually be prepared and served very efficiently.

Some clients will be satisfied with these tried-and-true menu options. For instance, a survey conducted by the Marriott Corporation revealed that association meeting planners prefer familiar products. However, this same survey indicated that corporate meeting planners are more adventurous when they develop menus for meal functions and are more receptive to unique cuisine. It is risky to offer items such as fish or lamb to a large group, as these items are not universally appreciated. If you want to be a bit adventurous, you might try a split entrée, i.e., half portions of 2 entreés. This is sometimes called "dualing menus" or twin entreés. It would provide something "safe" for the meat-and-potatoes diner. An example is surf and turf, perhaps a small filet mignon with three grilled jumbo shrimp. Avoid wacky or unusual entrée duets, such as sea scallops with buffalo medallions or lamb with ahi tuna. Usually, such offerings simply increase the number of requests for an alternate or vegetarian meal, which can throw the kitchen into a tailspin.

Product Shelf Life

Because catered events do not always run on time, it pays to have foods that will hold up well during service. This is also an important consideration whenever a banquet is scheduled for a large group and you anticipate a few minor logistics problems.

Large pieces of food hold heat or cold longer than small pieces. Solid meats hold temperature better than sliced meats. Lettuce wedges stay fresher and colder than tossed salad. Whole fruit and muffins stay fresher longer than sliced fruits or sliced cake. Whole vegetables hold up better than julienne cuts.

Generally speaking, cold foods retain cold temperatures longer than hot foods hold heat. Moreover, cold foods will stay cold longer if they are served on cold plates, and hot foods will stay hot longer if they are served on warm plates.

Sauces tend to extend a hot food product's holding capacity and keep foods from drying out. A sauce can also add color to a finished dish. However, if not planned properly, a sauce can run all over the plate, skin over, and/or pick up flavors and odors from other foods or heating fuels. Topping a main course with a hot sauce just before serving can bring the dish back to life, as well as raise the temperature.

Market Availability

Before committing to a specific menu item, the catering executive must ensure that the food is available. It is especially imperative to check the availability of any ethnic products needed before preparing a proposal for the client.

At times there are seasonal restrictions, product shortages, and/or distribution shortcomings that interfere with acquiring some products. For instance, although vine-ripened tomatoes may be in season, there may be a temporary shortage and local purveyors may be unable to satisfy your needs.

Menu Balance

A menu planner should try to balance flavors, textures, shapes, colors, temperatures, and so forth. Appetites are stimulated by all of the senses. You should not plan meals that tend to overpower any one of them. Color is pleasing to the eye. How appetizing would it be if you prepared a plate of sliced white-meat turkey, mashed potatoes, and cauliflower? Guests would be turned off by the lack of color contrast.

Be cautious of strong flavors that clash. For instance, you would not want to serve broccoli with cabbage, cauliflower, or Brussels sprouts at the same meal. These are all strong-flavored vegetables and in the same vegetable family. You would need more variety and contrast to create a successful menu.

You should strive to have something mild, something sweet, something salty, something bitter, and/or something sour on the menu. Textures also are very important. Ideally, you would have a pleasing combination of crisp, firm, smooth, and soft foods.

Product forms, shapes, and sizes should be mixed and matched. Offer as much variety as possible. For instance, a menu may include a combination of flat, round, long, chopped, shredded, heaped, tubular, and square foods. A temperature contrast will also appeal to most guests. A menu should offer both hot and cold food options.

The type of preparation offers an opportunity to provide several pleasing contrasts. For instance, an appropriate combination of sautéed, broiled, baked, roasted, steamed, sauced, and smoked foods will be more pleasing to customers than foods prepared only one or two ways.

The menu planner also should offer several types and varieties of food courses. A client should be able to select an appropriate combination of appetizer, soup, salad, main course, starch, vegetable, bread, dessert, and beverage from the standardized menu offerings. Ideally, a catering sales representative will be able to offer more than one combination.

Avoid the common mistake of serving two or more starches, (i.e., potatoes, rice, pasta, stuffing, corn, etc.). Remember that the word "starch" should be used only in-house, never in speaking with the client.

Equipment Limitations

Certain foods require special equipment to prepare and/or serve properly. For instance, a standing rib roast dinner for 2,500 people usually requires a battery of cook-and-hold ovens. Buffets cannot be set up properly unless sufficient steam table space and/or chafing dishes are on hand. And a large banquet that requires several hundred deep-fried appetizers cannot be serviced adequately unless you have sufficient deep fryer capacity and/or automated deep fryers.

The size of your food and beverage production and service facilities and their layout and design also affect menu-planning decisions. For instance, although you may have a sufficient number of cook-and-hold ovens, if they are not located correctly, your ability to serve large numbers of guests may be severely limited.

If there is any question about equipment capacity, an equipment specialist can usually provide the correct answer. An equipment manufacturer, dealer, designer, sales representative, or leasing company can usually help you estimate your facility's capacity and recommend minor, inexpensive changes that can increase it significantly. The chef may also be able to offer useful suggestions. If your facility is large enough to have an engineer, he or she may also be helpful.

Labor

Some menu items are very labor-intensive, especially those made from scratch in the facility's kitchens. It is not unusual for payroll costs to be as much as a third or more of a meal function's total price.

Payroll is expensive in the foodservice industry. There are many labor costs that are not readily apparent. To say the least, there is a great deal of pressure in our industry to hold the line on payroll costs. Unfortunately, this puts you in a very awkward position when planning the menu. To control payroll, you may need to purchase more convenience foods, reduce menu options, eliminate menu items that require a great deal of expensive expertise to prepare and serve, or charge the client more. It is not an option to schedule fewer servers or to compromise on other services.

The director of catering must stay within his or her payroll budget, but it is equally important to avoid alienating guests. Instead of cutting labor to the bone and possibly incurring the customer's wrath, it is much better to charge the client a modest labor surcharge so that the meal can be prepared and served professionally. If you believe that a labor surcharge is a client's best option, you should suggest it and plan for it in advance; it should not be a last-minute consideration.

Matching Food and Wine

Generally speaking, delicate, less flavorful foods should be served with white wines. Red meats, pastas with meat and tomato sauce, and other strong-flavored foods should be served with red wines.

Some wine lists are not based on the color of the wine. A list may note wines according to their degree of sweetness, lightness, alcoholic strength, or other relevant factors. In fact, it is a good idea to have many wine options available for a client's selection.

The catering sales representative should be prepared to suggest food and wine combinations to clients. Because many people are unsure of these selections, it is important to help them make the right choices. Some wine companies provide assistance to food-service professionals, sending a company representative to your establishment to help you pair all of your wines and foods. These purveyors will usually pair all wines, not just those you purchased from them.

Some clients have personal preferences that may interfere with selecting appropriate wines for the meal. For instance, a client may want to serve red wine with fish. If so, the catering executive should persuade him or her to have alternative wines available; otherwise, some guests may not embrace this unconventional pairing and think that the caterer is incompetent. Furthermore, some guests cannot tolerate the histamines and tannins in red wine (which can upset some people's stomachs); they will appreciate having a choice.

Entertainment Value

Some menu items lend themselves to entertaining displays in the dining room. For instance, action stations are very popular. Seafood bars and other similar food stations are attractive and tend to generate enthusiasm among guests. And flaming dishes, when prepared safely, are always well received by the dining public.

Any form of entertainment is bound to be expensive. For instance, the aforementioned examples can be very costly. They involve considerable setup and teardown work, labor hours, and labor expertise, all of which can strain a client's budget.

On the other hand, however, special touches may promote attendance. For example, the association meeting planner who wants to attract the maximum number of attendees, and spouse attendees, must be willing to provide an extra incentive. Special foods, prepared and served in an entertaining, exciting way, are sure to enhance attendance. Furthermore, this form of entertainment may be the least expensive way to motivate guests to attend the event.

Menu Trends

It is important to keep up with trends, but it is equally important to be able to differentiate between a trend and a fad (or "craze"). Trends seem to be more permanent. They are like roads, providing direction—a way to go. Fads, on the other hand, are like highway rest stops, which appear and fade away along the route.

The move to a healthier diet is a trend. Significant numbers of people want less fat, salt, and sugar in their diets. Chocolate is a trend. Many persons who eat healthfully all week reward themselves on the weekend with rich, gooey chocolate desserts.

Nouvelle, Cajun, Southwest, and spa cuisines were fads. Although grilled food is a trend that is still with us and thriving, mesquite grilling was a fad. Complicating matters is the possibility that a certain style can be popular in one part of the country and disdained in others. It may take a fad or trend started in California a long time to catch on in the Midwest. Menu planners, trying to lead the pack, often take a chance. For instance, someone had to get on the cutting edge and introduce goat cheese pizza with sun-dried tomatoes. At the other extreme, if you are risk averse, you may be classified as a laggard or someone woefully behind the times. Some chefs, trying to make a name for themselves, come up with outlandish combinations such as lamb chops dipped in Japanese tempura batter and fried, then set afloat on Italian-style tomato sauce with Moroccan spices. This is an example of good ingredients being manipulated to create unnatural combinations. Most facilities take the middle ground by staying close behind the leader.

Style of Service

The style of service clients want often influences the types and varieties of foods the menu planner can offer. For instance, foods that will be passed on trays by servers during an afternoon reception must be easy to handle. They must also be able to hold up well. In this case, sauced items that can drip should not be served, but easy-to-eat finger foods would be appropriate.

The service styles that can be used for a catered meal function are discussed in the follow paragraphs.

Reception.   Light foods are served buffet-style, displayed on a table, or are put on trays in the kitchen and passed by servers. Guests usually stand and serve themselves. They normally do not sit down to eat. These events are sometimes referred to as a "walk and talk." Food is "finger food" and/or "fork food." It is inappropriate to serve food that requires a knife.

Butlered Hors d' Oeuvres.   Food is passed on trays by servers. Guests serve themselves, using cocktail napkins provided by the server. This is a typical style of service used for upscale receptions. This style of service is appropriate only for finger food.

Buffet.   Foods are arranged on tables. Guests usually move along the buffet line and serve themselves. When their plates are filled, the guests take them to a dining table to eat. Servers usually provide beverage service at tableside. A very elegant buffet would have servers carry guests' plates to their tables for them.

Action Station.   Similar to a buffet. Chefs prepare and serve foods at the buffet. Items that lend themselves well to action-station service include wok stations, mashed potato bars, fajitas, pastas, grilled meats, omelets, crepes, sushi, flaming desserts, and spinning salad bowls. These stations are sometimes called "performance stations" or "exhibition cooking."

Cafeteria Service.   Similar to buffet. Guests stand in line, but do not help themselves. They are served by chefs and/or servers and sometimes use trays to carry their food selections to the dining tables.

Plated Buffet.   Selection of preplated foods, such as entrées, sandwich plates, and salad plates, set on a buffet table. They may also be placed on a roll-in (i.e., rolling cart) and then moved into the function room at the designated time. Because the food is presented on individual plates, trays are usually used. This is a particularly good idea for groups who want "working" meals.

Plated (American).   Guests are seated. Foods are preportioned in the kitchen, arranged on plates, and served by servers from the left. Beverages are served from the right. Used dishes and glasses are removed from the right. This is the most functional, common, economical, controllable, and efficient type of service. However, if servings are plated too far in advance, the individual foods can run together, discolor, or otherwise lose culinary quality.

Family-Style (English).   Guests are seated. Large serving platters and bowls are filled with foods in the kitchen and set on the dining tables by servers. Guests help themselves from a lazy Susan or pass the foods to each other. Occasionally, a host carves the meat.

Preset.   Food is already on the dining tables when guests are seated. Because preset foods will be on the tables for a few minutes before they are consumed, you must preset only those that will retain sanitary and culinary quality at room temperatures. Most common are bread and butter, but often the appetizer will be preset as well. For lunches with a limited time frame, salad and dessert will occasionally be preset.

Butlered Table Service.   Foods are presented on trays by servers, with utensils available for seated guests to serve themselves (often confused with Russian service). Sometimes used to describe tray passed hors d'oeuvres at receptions.

Russian (Silver) Service.   Guests are seated. Foods are cooked tableside on a rechaud (portable cooking stove) that is on a gueridon (tableside cart with wheels). Servers put the foods on platters and then pass the platters at tableside. Guests help themselves to the foods and assemble their own plates. Service is from the left (often confused with French cart service).

Banquet French Service.   Guests are seated. Platters of foods are assembled in the kitchen. Servers take platters to the tables. Guests select foods, and the server, using two large silver forks in his or her serving hand (or silver salad tongs if the forks cannot be coordinated with one hand), places the foods on the guests' plates. Each food item is served by the server from platters to individual plates. Guests are served from the left.

French Cart Service.   The type of French service that is used in fine-dining restaurants but not usually in a banquet setting. Guests are seated.

Foods are prepared tableside. Hot foods are cooked on a rechaud that is on a gueridon. Cold foods are assembled on the gueridon. Servers plate the finished foods and serve them to guests. This is the only style of service in which food is served from the right. Some foods, such as desserts, are already prepared. They are displayed on a cart, the cart is rolled to tableside, and guests are served after making their selections.

Hand Service.   Guests are seated. There is one server for every two guests. Servers wear white gloves. Foods are preplated. Each server carries two servings from the kitchen and stands behind the two guests assigned to him or her. At the direction of the captain or maître d' hôtel, all servings are set in front of all guests, or dome covers are removed, at precisely the same time. This procedure is followed for all courses. This is a very elegant style of service that is sometimes used for small gourmet meal functions. It is sometimes called "service in concert."

The Wave.   This is a method of serving whereby all servers start at one end of the function room and work straight across to the other end. Servers are not assigned workstations. In effect, all servers are on one team, and the entire function room is the team's workstation. The wave is typically used in conjunction with plated and preset service styles. Large numbers of guests can be served very quickly.

There is a good deal of confusion between butlered, Russian, banquet French, and French cart service. The authors had difficulty in determining the exactly correct interpretation after talking to many caterers around the country. The key is that you and your client have the same understanding so that there will be no surprises. If clients are not knowledgeable about service styles, the catering sales representative may wish to explain some of them so that they can make informed choices. Of course, you should describe only those service styles your staff is equipped and trained to comfortably execute properly. Moreover, when pointing out service options, you must inform clients of any extra labor charges associated with them.

The service style plays an important role in the success of a catered event. Clients can choose a style that may be less expensive (such as preset) or can splurge with French or Russian service. Furthermore, some service styles (such as action stations) are quite entertaining and can contribute significantly to guest satisfaction.

For variety, you can mix service styles during a single meal function. For instance, you might begin with reception service for appetizers, move into the banquet room where the tables are preset with salads, rolls, and butter, use banquet French service for the soup course, use Russian service for the entrée, and end the meal with a dessert buffet.

Truth-in-Menu Guidelines

A menu planner must ensure that he or she does not inadvertently misrepresent menu items. Printed menus, photos, illustrations, signage, verbal descriptions, and other media presentations must not deceive or mislead clients.

The National Restaurant Association (NRA) recognized the problem of menu misrepresentation in 1923. At that time it issued a report entitled *Standards of Business Practices*. In 1977 it published the *Accuracy in Menus* report, which reaffirmed its position decrying menu misrepresentation.

In some parts of the country, local governments have enacted truth-in-menu legislation. For instance, in Southern California, health district sanitarians are empowered to inspect a restaurant's menu items and determine whether customers are receiving the advertised value.

The NRA has identified 11 potential menu misrepresentations, as discussed in the following paragraphs. The menu planner must see to it that menu offerings adhere to these guidelines. By doing so, ambiguity will be eliminated and guests will not be unpleasantly surprised.

Misrepresentation of Quantity

If portion sizes are listed on the menu, they must also be noted on the standardized recipes. The sizes noted must be as-served sizes. Alternately, a size can be noted with a qualifier, such as "weight before cooking."

Sometimes you may get in trouble if you use terms that are recognized sizes. For instance, you cannot use the term "large egg" if in fact you are serving the medium size. According to federal government guidelines, large eggs must weigh 24 ounces per dozen, and medium eggs must weigh 21 ounces per dozen. Anyone using the description "large egg" must serve a 2-ounce egg.

Some terminology, such as "jumbo tossed salad," can be misleading. There is no established government standard for marketing qualifiers of this type, so you must be careful when using such language.

Some terms have implied meanings. For instance, when a customer notices that you offer a cup of soup and a bowl of soup, he or she has the right to assume that the bowl contains the larger portion. Likewise when you list the terms "small," "medium," and "large" for soft drinks.

Qualifiers, such as "mile-high pie," or "world-famous giant strawberry shortcake," usually do not mislead consumers because they tend to view these terms as a permissible form of trade puffery. However, the menu planner may want to avoid even the appearance of impropriety and not use any term that cannot be supported.

Misrepresentation of Quality

The federal government, through the U.S. Department of Agriculture (USDA) and the Food and Drug Administration (FDA), has established quality-grading procedures for many foods. For instance, meats, poultry, and fresh produce have standardized quality grades that can be noted on the menu only if you purchase products that have received these grade designations from a government inspector. You cannot, for example, note that you serve U.S. Grade AA butter unless you can prove you are purchasing this type of item.

Misrepresentation of Price

You will run into problems if you do not disclose all relevant charges. For instance, if there will be an extra charge for each cook at an action station, for all-white-meat chicken, and so forth, the client must know about it before he or she signs the catering agreement.

Misrepresentation of Brand Name

You cannot advertise that you serve a particular brand if in fact you do not offer it. For instance, you cannot say that you offer Sanka coffee if you serve another brand of decaffeinated coffee.

Sometimes we are guilty of using brand names as generic terms. For example, we tend to use casually the terms "Coke," "Ry-Krisp," "Tabasco Sauce," and "JELL-O," not realizing that they are proprietary brand names. One major foodservice company was sued and eventually had to pay considerable monetary damages because guests were not informed when generic cola was served instead of the Coke product advertised or requested.

Misrepresentation of Product Identification

The standard of identity defines what a food product is. The federal government has established standards of identity for more than 300 foods. For example, maple syrup is not the same as maple-flavored syrup, beef liver differs from calf liver, and half-and-half cannot be served if cream is noted on the menu.

Misrepresentation of Point of Origin

Some menu items traditionally note specific points of origin—areas of the world where the foods were harvested and/or produced. For instance, seafood menu items are often preceded by their point of origin. Idaho potatoes, Florida oranges, Maine lobster, Alaska crab, and Colorado trout are mainstays on many restaurant menus. You cannot make these claims, however, unless you can prove you are purchasing the items from appropriate suppliers.

Sometimes a misunderstanding can arise if you use a geographic term that describes a method of preparation. For instance, Manhattan-style clam chowder indicates that the chowder is tomato-based, not milk-based or cream-based. Yet a naive client may misinterpret this designation; it is up to the menu planner to foresee problems of this type and, if necessary, explain the situation to the client beforehand.

Obviously, French fries do not come from France, Russian dressing does not come from Russia, and Swiss steak does not come from Switzerland. The typical consumer realizes that these terms reflect a method of production and/or service. However, some qualifiers are too close to call and may confuse some guests. For instance, some customers may wonder about the origin of "imported Cheddar cheese" and others will not give it a second thought. The astute menu planner should not flirt with potential problems of this type.

Misrepresentation of Merchandising Terms

Sometimes you can get in trouble if you use too much trade puffery when describing menu items. For instance, saying that you serve "only the best-quality meat" implies that you serve the highest government quality grades. You should avoid using terms such as "fresh daily," "homemade," "center-cut portions," and so forth, unless you can substantiate these claims.

Misrepresentation of Means of Preservation

When you say something is fresh when in reality it is frozen, canned, bottled, or dried, you are misrepresenting the means of preservation. The word "fresh" is probably the most overworked and incorrect term noted on the typical menu. It is easy to fall into the freshness trap. You cannot indicate "fresh" on the menu if the foods you purchase and use to make the menu items are pre-prepared, processed products.

However, phrasing such as "freshly prepared" or "freshly baked" is fine.

Misrepresentation of Means of Preparation

Guests consider several things when selecting items from a menu, and the way a dish is prepared is an important determinant in the selection process. When a guest orders a broiled food, he or she will not be happy with oven-fried, pan-fried, or baked food. Likewise, if the customer orders deep-fried food, then roasted, barbecued, or sautéed food is unacceptable.

Sometimes we encounter difficulty when, for instance, we book a party of 2,000 for broiled steaks. The large volume usually necessitates browning the steaks on a broiler and then finishing them in a convection oven. Some customers will be able to identify the browned, baked steaks and may be unhappy with the result.

Food preparation terms can also be used indiscriminately. For instance, it is tempting to note on the menu the words, "made from scratch." However, the prudent menu planner will avoid this description because it may be impossible to obtain raw food ingredients consistently. If a processed substitute must be used once in a while, some guests may notice it and be disappointed.

Misrepresentation of Verbal and Visual Presentations

A catering sales representative must be careful when describing menu offerings to clients. If there is any doubt, he or she should contact the chef. At no time should you promise something that cannot be delivered.

Photos should be a major part of the caterer's sales effort. But because they always display items at their very best, the difference between a picture and the real thing can sometimes be significant. Even when you try to live up to a pictorial representation, there may be times when it is impossible. For instance, a picture may show seven different vegetables in an oriental dish. But if one of them is temporarily unavailable, a few guests may notice it and cause you an embarrassing moment or two.

Misrepresentation of Dietary or Nutritional Claims

No dietary or nutritional claim can be made unless you can prove that the menu item meets the prescribed standards. In addition to being deceptive, false claims can be dangerous for your guests. For instance, if you note "salt-free" on the menu, persons on a sodium-free diet can be harmed if they consume an item that does not live up to expectations.

MENU PRICING

A menu price must cover the cost of food, payroll, and other variable and fixed costs, plus a fair profit for the caterer. As a general rule, however, the price charged for a particular menu item is based primarily on its food cost.

By and large, if the food cost for a catered event is estimated to be $9.00 per person, the menu price for this function will range between $27.00 per person (i.e., a 33 percent food cost) to $36.00 per person (i.e., a 25 percent food cost), plus applicable consumption taxes, gratuities, and/or service charges.

There are also less common menu-pricing procedures that can be used. Pricing is a marketing function and is more fully discussed in Chapter 2.

TIPS AND GRATUITIES

It is important to note the required amounts of applicable consumption taxes, gratuities, and/or service charges when quoting prices to potential clients.

Consumption taxes usually include local and state sales taxes. Some parts of the country also levy an entertainment tax, cabaret tax, and/or luxury tax on commercial foodservice meals. These taxes are usually equal to a set percentage of a catered function's net price. (The net price does not include consumption taxes or gratuities.)

Although consumption taxes are usually a set percentage of a function's net price, there are some states and local municipalities that require you to charge taxes on the net price plus the gratuity. Generally speaking, if a gratuity is noted separately on the final bill, and if it is dispensed entirely to employees, you will not have to charge consumption taxes on it. But if you note a service charge on the bill, and if you use this money to pay all employees a flat rate of compensation, then chances are you will need to charge consumption taxes on the function's net price plus the service charge.

In most states, if a commercial foodservice operation extracts a service charge from each guest in lieu of a voluntary tip, the restaurant must charge consumption taxes on it. In effect, the service charge becomes part of the net price, whereas a tip or gratuity does not.

To say the least, the variations in taxing procedures between states and local municipalities can cause a great deal of confusion for clients, especially those who book events in several parts of the country.

It is conceivable that a specific meal may involve both flat-rate employees and gratuity-earning employees. For instance, employees on a facility's A-list usually receive gratuities, whereas B-list employees often work for a flat rate. In this situation, the client may be paying a bit more in consumption taxes than he or she might have to pay if the event were booked at another facility in another state or local municipality.

The terms "tips" and "gratuities" are often used interchangeably. However, gratuities are mandatory charges, whereas tips are discretionary. Gratuities are usually equal to a mandatory 15 to 19 percent of the catered function's net price. The gratuity is divided among various facility employees. Internal policies and traditions usually dictate who receives a share, and what the value of the shares will be. In some facilities, catering managers receive a share, whereas in other cases managerial personnel are excluded. Servers, and sometimes setup staff, are typically the primary beneficiaries.

Generally, at government-owned convention centers, tipping is not allowed in any form. In some parts of the United States, state laws govern the distribution of gratuities. For instance, in California, gratuities are "owned" by the service staff. Hotels and restaurants can keep service charges but cannot retain any portion of gratuities. Check with the local state restaurant association to determine the pertinent regulations in effect in your area.

A client may wish to award voluntarily a tip to one or more catering employees because some additional service, or exceptionally good service, was provided. Some clients may also wish to reward noncatering employees because of their help in making the function an especially memorable one.

Professional meeting planners recommend that convention clients also consider tipping the "unseen" employees who do not participate in the gratuity pool, yet whose services can sometimes make or break a function.

Caterers should have clear policies regarding the method used to split gratuities, service charges, and tips. Usually the gratuities/service charges are distributed among the servers, banquet crew, bartenders, and sometimes the catering managers. Tips are usually pooled and distributed among the servers only. However, some facilities include management in the pool. In fact, a recent decision by the Nevada Supreme Court upheld the Reno Hilton's policy of including all staff and managers in the tip pool.

Generally speaking, convention clients are advised to budget 1 to 3 percent of their master bill (i.e., total bill) for voluntary tips. For example, if a convention costs $100,000, the client should expect to award at least $1,000 to other employees, especially the "heart-of-the-house" employees (such as technicians, PBX operators, and so forth) if their services were particularly timely and beneficial.

Given that the total tip is to be 1 to 3 percent of the total master bill, a suggested distribution is as follows (each area will vary, depending on the size of the meeting and complexity of responsibilities):

20 to 25 percent of the tip: convention coordinator

20 to 25 percent of the tip: sales or catering manager (if active during the meeting)

10 to 15 percent of the tip: house setup crew

5 to 10 percent of the tip: audiovisual (AV) technician

5 to 10 percent of the tip: housekeeping (for VIP suites, staff rooms, and public areas)

3 to 5 percent of the tip: receiving department

2 to 5 percent of the tip: for movement of convention materials, deliveries, etc.

20 percent of the tip: miscellaneous

Convention clients are also encouraged to distribute these tips after the function ends, not before. This is the traditional procedure. Once the tips are given, there may be less incentive for employees to provide above average service.

A client can give money, gifts, or both. For example, he or she can see to it that when the tip money is distributed, employees also receive small mementos.

In addition to giving tips, the client should write a letter to the general manager, praising the employees' special efforts. In most cases, letters of this type can be the most valuable "tips" employees receive.

Some facilities require tips to be pooled and then distributed to members of the pool, whereas others allow the individual recipient to keep his or her entire amount. All tips received must be declared by staff members so that management can withhold the appropriate amount of income and Social Security taxes from the tip earners' paychecks.

If the caterer is a government facility, such as a state-operated convention center, employees are not allowed to accept cash tips. However, it is sometimes acceptable for clients to send key employees thank-you gifts, such as T-shirts or pens, that are of low to moderate value. Some government facilities may have an employee fund set up to allow contributions by clients who insist on distributing cash tips. A fund of this kind is typically used to pay for a holiday party for the staff.

Service charges are not gratuities, nor are they tips. In restaurants they are added to the customer's guest check in lieu of tips. In catering, however, service charges represent a separate charge for labor and are typically part of an itemized price quotation. For instance, a service charge for extra servers may be added to a client's bill if he or she requested special service, or additional service, for some VIP guests. And, as noted earlier, the appropriate consumption taxes must be charged on these amounts.

Usually when a catering sales representative quotes a price, he or she will note a "price, plus, plus." The price is the price per person, and the plus, plus represents the taxes and gratuity. For instance, a price quotation of "$20.00 + +" in Las Vegas tells the client that the total price per person will be $24.85 ($20.00 menu price, plus 7.25 percent sales tax ($1.45), plus 17 percent gratuity ($3.40).

TYPES OF MEAL FUNCTIONS

Each type of meal presents a unique set of challenges and opportunities. When planning a meal, the catering sales representative must know and understand the meal planner's objectives so that the appropriate menu, room setup, service, and timing can be provided.

Breakfast

Speed and efficiency are extremely important to breakfast-meal planners. This is especially true if the attendees are conventioneers who will be going to a business meeting, seminar, or other event immediately after the meal. The last thing a client wants is to start the day's activities late and throw off the whole day's schedule. Everything must be ready at the appointed time in order to avoid this problem.

Many attendees skip the breakfast meal. Some of them regularly do not eat breakfast. A few may be in the habit of engaging in early-morning exercise workouts and cannot make the scheduled breakfast time. And others may have been out late the night before and would rather sleep than eat.

Breakfast is a functional meal. Guests need to energize the brain cells. If they skip breakfast, chances are that their attention spans will decrease and they will become irritable by ten o'clock.

The menu should contain energizer foods, such as fresh fruits, whole-grain cereals, whole-grain breads, and yogurt. As a general rule, a person should try to start the day with these types of foods because, in addition to providing a bit of energy, they are much easier to digest than fatty foods. A breakfast like this will keep attendees awake and ready to tackle the morning's business.

There is a trend away from sweet rolls toward whole-grain, blueberry, and oat bran muffins and fruit breads, such as banana or date bread. Sugary and fatty sweets, such as Danish, doughnuts, and pecan rolls, give only a temporary lift.

Yet there must be some variety at breakfast. Although many persons will not eat sugary, fatty foods, they may want to have at least a little taste of one. As much as possible, the menu should accommodate all guest preferences. For instance, you can offer bite-sized portions of several types of foods on a breakfast buffet table.

A buffet is the best type of service for breakfast functions because it can accommodate very easily the early riser and the latecomer. In some cases a buffet may cost less than sit-down service. And it can be just the thing for guests who are in a hurry because, if there are enough food and beverage stations, a breakfast buffet can be over in less than an hour.

The traditional breakfast buffet includes two or three types of breakfast meats, three to six varieties of pastries, two styles of eggs, one potato dish, and several selections of cereals, fresh fruits, cold beverages, hot beverages, and condiments.

An English-style breakfast buffet usually includes the traditional offerings along with one or more action stations. For instance, an action station where chefs are preparing omelets, Belgian waffles, or crepes is very popular with guests. This type of service, however, can increase significantly the food and labor costs, so it can be offered only if clients are willing to pay an extra charge.

For the cost-conscious client, the more economical continental breakfast buffet is appropriate. The traditional continental breakfast includes coffee, tea, fruit juice, and some type of bread. A deluxe version offers more varieties of juices, breads, and pastries, as well as fresh fruits, yogurt, and cereals.

If a breakfast buffet is planned, you should separate the food and beverage stations so that persons who want their coffee quickly, or do not want a full meal, will not have to stand in line behind those who are deciding which omelet to order. You should also separate condiments, such as cream, sugar, and lemons, and flatware from the coffee urn areas. Because it usually takes a guest about twice as long to add cream and sugar as it does to draw a cup of coffee, this type of layout will prevent traffic congestion. If separate beverage stations are not feasible, you should have food servers serve beverages to guests at the dining tables.

Conventional sit-down breakfast service usually includes a combination of preset and plated service. This is an appropriate procedure if the guests have more time and want to savor the meal a little longer. Served breakfasts, though, make greater demands on the catering and kitchen staffs. More servers are needed, and more food handlers are required to dish up the food in the kitchen. However, unlike buffet service, sit-down service allows greater control of food costs because you, not the guest, control portion sizes.

Many clients, especially corporate clients, want some added luxury touches at breakfast. For instance, they often appreciate things such as mimosa cocktails, virgin Marys, exotic flavored coffees, puff pastries, and fresh fruit in season.

Many people are not very sociable at breakfast. Moreover, if guests trickle in a few at a time, they may spread out in the banquet room so that they can be alone with their thoughts or with some last-minute work. The catering department may want to make newspapers available, such as *The Wall Street Journal* and/or *USA Today*, for those who do not wish to fraternize so early in the day.

Refreshment Break

A refreshment break is an energy break, intended to refresh and resharpen attention. It also helps to alleviate the boredom that tends to develop when guests are engaged in tedious business activities during the day.

Refreshment breaks are typically scheduled at midmorning and midafternoon and usually located near the meeting and conference rooms. They generally offer various types of "mood" foods—foods that increase guests' enthusiasm to tackle the rest of the day's work schedule.

Ideally, a refreshment break station includes hot and cold beverages, whole fruits, raw vegetables with dip, yogurt, muffins, and other types of breads and pastries that will hold up well and will not dry out. Chewy foods, such as peanuts, dried fruits, and sunflower seeds, should also be available because these types of products are thought to relieve boredom.

The caterer should strongly suggest to the client that water, soft drinks, and other cold beverages be available for each refreshment break, no matter what time of day the break is scheduled. Many guests prefer cold beverages throughout the day. Bottled water has become a very important amenity. Most of those who drink soda prefer diet beverages. In fact, the soft drink industry notes that typically 50 to 75 percent of guests selecting cold beverages choose a sugarless drink, such as diet soda, bottled water, or club soda.

Some refreshment breaks include only beverages. This is especially true with the midmorning coffee break. A beverage-only break does not distract convention attendees as much as one at which several foods are available. Guests who get a beverage only are apt to return to business quickly, whereas foods take longer to select and consume, thereby slowing service and possibly throwing off the rest of the day's schedule.

Speed is a major consideration for some refreshment breaks. If so, the menu should not offer any foods that will slow service and cause attendees to arrive late at their next business activity. For instance, when you have a short break, you would not want to offer sliced fruit on a tray. Instead, you should offer fruit kabobs or whole fruits, which can be picked up quickly and easily as "walk-away" snacks.

Another major consideration is to locate the refreshment break station so that it serves the client's needs. Ideally, it should be placed in a separate room or in the prefunction space. It should not be located at the back of a meeting room. The reason is that if attendees are lingering too long around the food and beverage stations, a speaker will have a hard time getting started. The speaker may also find it difficult to compete easily with the food and beverage stations; guests are liable to sneak a quick trip to the back of the room and disrupt the proceedings. Furthermore, there may be a lot of noise when tables are replenished.

Be sure to provide trash receptacles for waste and trays for used tableware. A server should check the refreshment setup periodically and replenish foods and beverages as needed. He or she should remove trash and soiled tableware and not let them stack up. Someone also must be responsible for tidying the break area regularly. Few things are as unattractive as finding, for example, a half-eaten pastry on a tray next to whole, untouched pastries.

Many clients, especially corporate meeting planners, want refreshment breaks available all day so that they can break at will instead of at a predetermined time. In effect, they want permanent refreshment centers. Meeting planners who are accustomed to conference centers expect permanent refreshment centers. If other facilities want to compete favorably with conference centers, they must offer similar amenities. Of course, the client must be willing to pay the added cost.

Clients reap many advantages with permanent refreshment centers. For one thing, clients think this will keep attendees around all day. If attendees go off to a restaurant outlet for a beverage, they may never return for the business activities. A permanent refreshment center usually stocks coffee, tea, and cold soft drinks all day, with foods being offered only at certain times, say at 10:00 A.M. and 3:00 P.M. All-day nonalcoholic beverage service provides an attractive, comfortable social atmosphere for attendees to congregate and discuss the day's activities.

Some clients want the traditional refreshment breaks, but they also want them to be preceded by exercise periods. For instance, just before the midmorning refreshment break, a corporate client may schedule an exercise leader to come in and lead attendees in a few stretching exercises.

Themed refreshment breaks are popular and provide an opportunity to up$ell. Themed breaks are discussed in Chapter 3.

Luncheon

Luncheons are often quite similar to breakfasts in that they are intended to provide a convenience to convention attendees and to ensure that they will not roam away and neglect the afternoon's business activities.

If a luncheon is intended solely to provide a refueling stop for attendees, the menu should not include an overabundance of "sink-to-the-bottom" foods. If attendees eat too much heavy food, they will most likely become drowsy and inattentive later in the day.

Sink-to-the-bottom foods are greasy, fatty foods, such as cheese omelets, and complex carbohydrate foods, such as rice and pasta dishes. These products take a long time to digest; for instance, fats can sit in the stomach for 12 hours or more. Conversely, fruits and vegetables are digested more quickly. Complex carbohydrates are somewhere in between, in that they digest more rapidly than fats, but not as quickly as fruit and vegetables.

"Working" luncheons usually rely quite a bit on white meats and salad greens. Breads, pastas, heavy sauces, and so forth, are usually deemphasized. If served, they are usually served on the side so that guests can take a small taste. Serving these products on the side tends to discourage guests from consuming too much.

Yet you should have some fatty foods on the menu. Some guests will be disappointed if, for example, they cannot have a few French fries or butter pats. The wise director of catering will see to it that alternatives are available to satisfy everyone. A crowd pleaser is the deli buffet. It serves the dieter, the hearty eater, and everyone else in between.

Whatever strategy is followed by the working luncheon meal planner, it is important to remember that attendees may be eating several luncheons during their stay at the facility. In this situation, variety is mandatory.

Most guests are satisfied with the few traditional breakfast selections, but they normally seek greater variety when selecting luncheon menu items. If they do not get it from you, they will go to a restaurant or bar for lunch and be late getting back to the afternoon's business sessions. (This also throws off the meal guarantees.) In some cases, they may get sidetracked and not come back at all.

Many luncheons are not working luncheons, for which refueling and keeping attendees on the property are the major objectives. The "nonworking" type of luncheon usually involves some sort of ceremony. For instance, many luncheons include speakers, audiovisual (AV) displays, fashion shows, awards, announcements, and so forth, that may overshadow other objectives.

When a ceremonial type of luncheon is booked in your facility, the logistics are more complicated. For instance, you must ensure that head tables and reserved tables are noted correctly, name badges prepared, AV equipment installed and ready to go, all lighting synchronized properly, and printed materials, if any, set at each guest's place. You also have to ensure that sufficient labor is scheduled to handle the food and nonfood service demands adequately.

Buffet, preset, and plated services are the typical service styles used for luncheon meals. In most cases, luncheon service is similar to breakfast service. Speed is usually a major concern. Consequently, menus and service styles are usually selected with quickness and efficiency in mind.

Reception

Receptions are often predinner functions designed primarily to encourage people to get to know one another. For instance, most conventions schedule an opening reception—an ice-breaker party, to allow attendees to make new friends and renew old acquaintances. If an opening reception is not scheduled, an attendee will usually meet only the handful of people sitting at his or her dining table.

Some receptions are not predinner functions. For instance, many conventions have hospitality suites that are open late in the evening. Hospitality suites are similar to receptions in that they encourage participants to mingle. They can also be hosted by sponsors to introduce new products and/or build goodwill. For example, a book publisher at a book sellers convention may sponsor a hospitality suite to introduce new authors or to allow guests to meet established authors. This is a type of business that restaurants can seek out if they are conveniently located in relation to the hotel. In Las Vegas, many independent restaurants with banquet facilities are located right inside the hotels.

One of the strongest complaints heard at a convention's opening reception is that the music is too loud. Many attendees have not seen each other for a year and want to talk, and there are generally a lot of introductions being made. The reception is typically a networking event, but attendees end up having to shout over the music to be heard. If loud music is desired, save it until later in the evening or for the final-night banquet.

Some receptions, referred to as "walk and talks," are held during standard dinner hours and are intended to precede or take the place of dinner. A reception allows guests to have a drink, eat a little, and get to know one another.

One thing most receptions have in common is that they usually include alcoholic beverage service in addition to food. Another common feature is that rarely are they scheduled during business hours; most receptions do not begin before 5:00 P.M.

When planning a reception, it is best to locate several buffet stations around the room, each with a different type of food. This encourages guests to move around and socialize. If possible, include one or two action stations. There should be a server at each station to replenish foods, bus soiled tableware, remove trash, and be a psychological deterrent to curb guests' tendencies to heap their plates and/or return several times.

If beverages are served, the bars and nonalcoholic beverage stations should also be spaced around the room. Place them a sufficient distance from the food stations so that people have to change locations in order to get a drink. This further increases guest participation and mingling.

If the reception is intended to take the place of dinner, offer a complete balance of food types, colors, temperatures, preparation methods, and so forth, to suit every taste. And, because this type of reception normally extends for a longer period of time than a predinner reception, and people will in effect be consuming the equivalent of dinner, sufficient backup food and beverage supplies must be available to prevent stockouts.

The selection of foods offered should have broad appeal. Be careful when serving exotic foods that some guests may not recognize. For instance, if you are serving unusual fish items on a buffet table, you may want to identify them with name cards in a font large enough to read in subdued "party lighting." Similarly, if unusual foods are passed by servers, the servers should be able to answer any questions posed by guests.

Menu items should be bite-sized. This allows guests to sample a wide variety of foods without wasting much of it. It also ensures that the foods will be easy to consume. Ease of consumption is very important, as most guests must balance plates, glassware, handbags, and business cards while moving around.

Menu items must be easy for guests to hold and to eat. For instance, although kabobs are popular items served at receptions, if they are not prepared and assembled properly, guests will have a frustrating experience trying to eat them. If you serve kabobs, put the food ingredients on only half of the skewer. Otherwise, guests will be unable to get all the food off the skewer without making a mess. Never hand pass kabobs, baby lamb chops, rumaki with toothpicks, or similar items. Once the food is eaten, the guest is left holding a skewer, greasy rib bone, or annoying toothpick, which must now be disposed of. These discards can create slip-and-fall problems, generate litter, and can later be found tucked down into potted plants, in seat cushions, or in other unsuitable locations.

Foods should also not be messy or greasy. Nor should they leave stains on clothes or teeth. For instance, you should be careful not to oversauce foods, such as barbecued chicken wings, that may drip when guests are eating them. Instead, offer boneless chicken "fingers" that are lightly coated or served with a stiff sauce on the side.

Oversized plates can add up to a third to your food cost. Be certain not to use dinner-sized plates for receptions without the client's knowledge. Larger plates encourage overeating and excessive waste, because a guest may fill a plate, eat some of the food, set the plate down somewhere, forget it, and then go back for another plate of food. Guests with plates full of food tend to sit down to eat and do not mingle and network very much, if at all. Using plates, you can serve "fork food"—food for which you need a fork to eat. Caterer Gayle Skelton states, "A caterer's dilemma is not what quantity people eat, it's how much they put on their plate!"

Rarely would you serve food at a reception that requires a knife, as guests are generally eating while standing up, and often balancing a drink while trying to exchange business cards.

Seating should be minimized at receptions. You do not want to encourage guests to sit and eat; remember, you want to promote mingling and networking. Seating should be provided for 25 to 30 percent of the guest count. Cabaret-style seating (i.e., cocktail tables), or park benches, both of which provide little or no table space, can be suitable.

To encourage mingling and to control food costs, suggest having servers pass foods in addition to, or instead of, placing food buffet stations throughout the room. Guests tend to eat less if the foods are passed. Generally speaking, if the foods are displayed on a buffet table where guests can help themselves, they will eat twice as much as they would if all foods were passed butler-style by servers.

Ordinarily, you would not have all foods passed, although passing foods makes it easier to retain control of food quantities. By alternating quantities of expensive items with low-priced items, you avoid the food excesses that buffets require. Generally, at least one or two food stations and/or action stations can enhance the appearance of the function room. To save the client money, expensive items should be passed, and inexpensive food (such as cheese cubes, vegetable trays, and dry snacks) should be available on tables. A client without budgetary concerns would probably prefer his or her guests have access to a mountain of shrimp on ice and a sliced tenderloin action station.

If you offer butlered foods, place only one type of food on a tray; otherwise, guests will take too long to make their selections. If they cannot decide easily what to select from a tray with a number of foods, they may take one of each. This will slow service because the servers will not be able to work the room quickly and efficiently. It might also encourage overconsumption and food waste. Butlered food should always be "finger food"—food that can be consumed without eating utensils. The server should always carry a small stack of cocktail napkins.

With butlered service, the client's labor charge will be a bit higher. However, this should be offset with a lower food cost. As noted earlier, guests will consume less if foods are passed. Passing foods also allows you to control the pace of service. For instance, you can stagger service by sending out servers with trays every 15 minutes instead of sending out all the food at one time. Furthermore, the catering sales representative should remind clients that passed foods lend an air of elegance to the reception that many guests will appreciate. Be sure servers are assigned areas of the room to cover, or one side of the room may get all of the food.

Receptions can be tailored to any budget. Unlike other meal functions, they give clients flexibility. There are many opportunities to be extravagant or frugal. For example, clients can control the time allocated for the reception; they can offer a seafood bar with a few shrimp and a lot of inexpensive mussels arranged on crushed ice, or they can start with expensive hors d'oeuvres and back them up with cheese and dry snacks. The breakfast, luncheon, and dinner planner generally does not enjoy such a wide array of options.

Generally speaking, if you are charging clients according to the amount of foods consumed, you would opt for buffet tables, dinner-sized plates, and self-service. At the other extreme, passed foods are appropriate if the client is paying a per-person charge for unlimited consumption. Because most clients prefer paying a per-person charge for foods, your service strategies will tend toward passed foods. However, you and your clients can usually find several mutually agreeable positions between these two extremes to satisfy everyone's quality and cost requirements.

Dinner

Dinner is the most typical catered meal. Although it has many similarities to breakfast and luncheon, a dinner is usually a longer, more elaborate affair.

A client will be more adventurous when booking a dinner function than when arranging a breakfast or luncheon, because he or she usually has more money and time to work with. For example, Russian and French service styles are more likely to be requested for a dinner than for other meals. Even the buffet, preset, and preplated service styles are enhanced. Furthermore, entertainment and dancing are more common at dinner.

Many dinners are part of a theme, ceremony, or other type of major production where foodservice is only one part of the event. Rarely are dinners scheduled merely for refueling purposes.

Dinner guests are not usually on a tight time schedule. They normally do not have to be at a business meeting or any other sort of activity later in the evening. As a result, some tend to wander in late, and others tend to linger well after the function ends. Catering staff must be aware of these tendencies and plan accordingly.

The catering sales representative should be prepared to work closely with the client in developing a dinner event. Many clients do not have sufficient background or expertise to plan a major function. Nor do they have the creative talents necessary to plan an unforgettable experience. For instance, most conventions reserve one night for an awards banquet. Clients and catering executives must find ways to take the boredom out of awards presentations without sacrificing the recognition that winners deserve.

An awards banquet is often part of a grand banquet given on the convention's last night. Unfortunately, this approach has several drawbacks. For one thing, attendees have just survived an intense few days of meetings and other business activities and are ready to party. Most of them have probably been to one or more receptions earlier in the day and have consumed a few alcoholic beverages. And if wine is served with the meal, the group may become boisterous.

The catering sales representative should suggest ways to avoid these problems. For example, there is a trend in the industry to present awards early in the convention, perhaps on the first day. This ensures rapt attention from attendees. It also allows the recipients to bask in the limelight throughout the rest of the convention.

Awards can also be given at a breakfast or a luncheon. Guests are a bit more alert during these times. Furthermore, they then can have the last night free to have fun and unwind. If there are several awards to be given, another tactic is to spread the presentations throughout the convention. You might begin with the minor awards and save the most important, prestigious one for the last night.

If a client insists on the traditional final-night awards banquet, suggest that the presentations be staggered between courses instead of scheduling them for the end of the meal. As mentioned earlier, dinner meals tend to run overtime; thus, if all awards are presented at the end, chances are that the program will have to begin before or during dessert. Some guests may not be paying attention, and, embarrassingly, conversation may continue throughout the program.

The catering sales representative also must be aware of the protocols, seating arrangements, and other considerations associated with various ceremonies so that the client can be advised correctly. The catering sales representative should also be prepared to suggest themes that can be used by clients to increase interest in their dinner functions.

Theme parties will promote dinner attendance. For instance, some convention attendees may be motivated to register because one or two theme parties are being offered. Furthermore, convention attendees' spouses are also more eager to go to a convention if this type of entertainment is offered.

Theme parties are in vogue. They add interest and provide a good deal of fun for the guests. Although some themes are elaborate and pricey, you do not need to spend a great deal of money to throw a theme party. Some clients want to design themes that will enhance the image of the group booking the dinner. For example, a dairy convention may want to hold an "ice cream social" theme party to introduce new frozen dairy products. The catering sales representative will need to work closely with the client to ensure that this party runs smoothly. Chapter 3 focuses on themed events.

A dinner is usually much more than a meal. Food and beverages constitute only one part of it. The catering executive must be able to juggle many attractions when helping clients to plan these major events.

OFF-PREMISE CATERING

Some facilities go beyond the traditional on-premise meal functions and offer off-premise options. However, very few facilities offer this service. The typical restaurant, club, conference center, or hotel is generally unable to perform this service adequately.

Off-premise catering is a very involved business that is much different from on-premise catering. It requires quite a different form of management. To do it correctly, you must have a considerable amount of special equipment that the typical restaurant or hotel does not have. For example, the off-premise caterer needs on-site preparation and service equipment and transport equipment. The full-service off-premise caterer also needs power generators, fresh-water and brown-water (non-potable) wagons, portable furniture, and tents.

Some hotels will not solicit off-premise catering business because they do not want to be put into the unpleasant position of being unable to get maximum use from expensive fixed assets. To perform adequately, you must invest a great deal of money in transport equipment, especially trucks and vans. Portable hot-holding and cold-holding equipment that can be transported off-site is also very expensive. Unless these assets can be rented for a reasonable price, it could be economically disastrous to own them if they are going to be used infrequently.

In addition to investment considerations, the off-premise caterer encounters many problems foreign to the typical restaurant or hotel caterer. For instance, the off-premise caterer must visit the site in advance to check the layout and design, see what utilities are available, determine what, if any, type of cooking can be performed on-site, have a backup plan in the event of inclement weather, hire qualified drivers, secure communications equipment (such as cellular phones), obtain the appropriate insurance rider, obtain a temporary liquor license, obtain union permission to use on-site employees off-site, and cover a host of additional related details.

The off-premise caterer also encounters many sanitation and safety problems that do not afflict an on-premise catering department. For example, an off-premise caterer cannot reuse any leftovers (except sealed condiments), whereas an on-premise facility may be able to salvage some. Only foods that transport well can be used. The off-premise caterer does not have complete control over the function site, so his or her product liability insurance will be very expensive. The typical on-premise caterer is not set up to remove finished foods safely from the kitchen, to the back door, and onto a waiting vehicle. It may be difficult to secure a potable water source. Garbage and trash removal is more difficult to handle at off-site venues. In addition, equipment used to transport finished foods usually cannot be used as serving containers on a buffet line; the foods must be removed from the transport containers and put into serving bowls, trays, and/or pans designed for service.

Other operational problems unique to the off-premise caterer include tying up the property's loading dock and receiving area when stocking the catering vehicle(s); pre-preparing products in-house, transporting them, and handling final preparation and service on location; making sure all employees get to the right place at the right time; transporting, setting up, and tearing down all furniture and equipment; controlling shoplifting; setting up and tearing down tents; installing and removing portable heating or cooling equipment; installing and operating electric power generators; packing foods very carefully to eliminate breakage; and qualifying for the relevant business licenses, liquor licenses, and health permits.

Usually, the greatest barrier facing the on-premise caterer who wants to get involved with off-premise catering is the lack of adequate vehicles. One way for hotels or convention centers to get around this stumbling block is to borrow another department's truck or van. Another method is to rent old UPS vans, milk trucks, or laundry trucks; they work well because they back up readily to loading docks and equipment can be rolled in very easily. The only problem with these strategies, however, is that unless the vehicles meet local health district codes, you cannot use them to transport foods.

If a regular client requests off-premise catering, it is not smart to refuse the request. If you, as an on-premise caterer, cannot handle the request, you should refer the client to a reputable off-premise caterer whose standards and reputation parallel yours. It is a mistake to refer the client to an unknown off-premise caterer who does not share your standards.

Even though off-premise projects may be minimally profitable for some properties, a few may be willing to get involved with them in order to satisfy good clients. These facilities may decide to maintain vending machines, prepare box lunches, cater an off-site picnic, stock the sleeping rooms' in-room bar cabinets, and so forth, rather than divert this business to competitors.

One form of off-premise catering provided by many on-premise caterers is the preparation of box-lunches. For instance, a group may request individual box lunches for a day when they will be taking a bus tour. Alternately, a catering and/or kitchen employee may pack a few foods and beverages, ride with the group, and set up a small picnic-style buffet at a rest stop location.

Another type of off-premise catering provided by many on-premise caterers involves a food or beverage function held outside the banquet areas, but within the facility's property. For instance, a client may be able to book a poolside party, garden wedding, or picnic barbecue.

Most on-premise caterers are usually able to handle an outdoor function so long as it is on the property. For instance, if there are many requests for picnic barbecues, the hotel may build a permanent outdoor grill and shelter, complete with hot and cold running water, refrigeration, and storage space.

Another form of off-premise catering that may be thrust upon the director of catering is the type that starts out being an on-premise function and eventually ends up being a combined on-premise and off-premise event. For instance, a major banquet may suddenly require more floor space than a hotel has available. To accommodate it, a tent and other related equipment can be rented. Tents are aesthetically pleasing and come in all shapes and sizes. They can be used solely to shelter the foods, or they can house the entire party. Some can be heated, air-conditioned, and floored with wood or Astroturf. They also can be used indoors to enhance the decor.

Sooner or later, most on-premise caterers get involved with some type of off-premise catering function. As the costs of business increase every year, so too does the need to seek out other forms of business. At the very least, you must be prepared to handle the occasional request or else risk losing current and future business.

According to off-premise caterer Shelley Pedersen, owner of Beyond Cuisine in Atlanta,

---

The most daunting element of off-premise catering for on-premise caterers is their inexperience in full event operations, both front of the house and back of the house. They are uncomfortable with the many checklists required so nothing is overlooked, not packed or loaded, or simply forgotten. The lack of venue/weather/ conditional control they enjoy on property sometimes unnerves them, and they find it difficult to tackle the operational logistics needed, because other departments in a facility take care and plan for the very details that make off-premise events so challenging, exciting and rewarding.

Beverage Functions | *Chapter* 5

Beverage functions today almost always include food. It is very unusual for a beverage function to offer only alcoholic and nonalcoholic drinks. At the very least, clients want to include a few hors d' oeuvres or dry snacks.

In view of increasing host and host-facility liability, the wise catering executive will not book events that offer only alcoholic beverages. For instance, all-evening drinking parties, such as fraternity bashes and bachelor parties, are inappropriate and ripe for liability lawsuits.

PURPOSE OF THE BEVERAGE FUNCTION

The purpose of a beverage function will give the catering sales representative an insight into the client's wishes. This information is invaluable when working with a client to create an exciting, memorable event.

There are many reasons that clients schedule beverage functions. However, unlike meal functions, beverage functions tend to have at least one common purpose: These events usually serve as a way for guests to socialize and practice networking.

A beverage function is not a refueling stop. It is not scheduled primarily to give guests an opportunity to recharge their batteries. After all, no one needs to consume alcoholic beverages to survive.

Rather, beverage functions offer guests a chance to visit with others in a relaxed, leisurely setting. New acquaintances are made and old ones rekindled. Job openings are circulated. Hot tips are exchanged. And the seeds of many successful business deals are planted.

Another aspect that most beverage functions share is the time of day they are offered. They are usually scheduled after 5:00 P.M. Every once in a while you will be asked to offer poured-wine service, and/or specialty drinks such as mimosas or Bloody Marys, at a brunch or luncheon meal function. However, it is less common today for a client to request liquor service before the end of the normal business day.

Still another commonality among beverage functions is that many of them are scheduled before a meal. Premeal cocktail functions, such as receptions, allow strangers an opportunity to get acquainted. For instance, if a guest is invited to a meal function where he or she knows very few of the other guests, it is much easier to meet them while strolling through a reception area than by sitting at one dining table for the whole evening.

Some receptions are intended to take the place of a meal. For instance, a cocktail reception scheduled from 5:00 P.M. to 8:00 P.M. usually must offer a reasonable variety of foods so that guests can select enough of them to satisfy the appetite and create a meal. Even if these guests expect to go out to dinner later, it is usual for the host to see to it that sufficient foods are offered to suit those guests who will not make alternate dining plans.

A host may schedule a short reception in order to provide some sort of transition period from a long workday to an enjoyable meal function. For instance, as the wise convention planner realizes, some attendees who were working very hard during the day may not stick around for a dinner function scheduled to begin at 8:30 P.M.

Even though there are several aspects common to most beverage functions, the catering sales representative must still query clients regarding their perceived primary objectives for scheduling them. By knowing as much as possible about clients' needs, desires, and objectives, the catering executive can suggest the types of functions that will satisfy them adequately.

MENU PLANNING

It is relatively easy to develop a drink menu. Generally speaking, if a client wants a particular type of drink, you can provide it. If you do not have the necessary ingredients in stock, you can usually get them before the date booked for the function. And if you have sufficient production and service equipment to handle a standard drink menu, you essentially have enough equipment to prepare and serve just about any type of drink clients and guests may request.

Note the current trends in regard to alcoholic beverages:

○ Declining hard liquor sales
○ Flat wine sales
○ Increase in light beer, imports, and microbrews
○ Increase in specialty drinks
○ Quality vs. quantity (i.e., selection of finer vintages)
○ More neutral beverages (nonalcoholic)

Spirits (another term for "hard liquor"). This category includes distilled beverages, such as bourbon, scotch, gin, vodka, brandy, rum, and a variety of blends.

The most popular spirit among females is vodka, and the most popular for males is Scotch, followed by vodka.

Spirits can be taken straight, on the rocks, or as highballs or cocktails, mixed with a variety of ingredients.

Spirits consumption trends suggest that overall consumption will average three drinks per person during a normal reception period. Assuming that 50 percent of the people will order spirits, you should stock the following quantities for every 100 guests:

Number of Bottles	Type	Number of Bottles	Type
1	Blend	2	Scotch
1	Gin	1	Rum
1	Canadian	2	Bourbon
3	Vodka	1	Brandy/Cognac

Take demographics and the group's history into account as well. Remember that these figures are averages and will not apply to every group. Whenever possible, try to obtain the history of the group for a more accurate estimate. A group composed mainly of women will tend to drink more wine than spirits.

There are also geographic differences in spirits consumption. Following is a list of local markets, showing the number of drinks consumed on average per person at a black-tie gala with a reception and dinner.

○ Las Vegas 5.5
○ Chicago 5.0
○ Washington, D.C. 4.5
○ Orlando 3.5
○ San Diego 3.0
○ Honolulu 3.0
○ San Francisco 2.5

Wine consumption trends show that overall consumption averages three glasses per person during a normal reception period. Assuming that 50 percent of the people will order wine, you should order thirty 750 ml bottles for every 100 guests. Wine consumption trends also suggest that 30 to 40 percent of people consuming wine will drink red wine.

Beer is classified as domestic or imported. Domestic beers include Budweiser, Coors, and Michelob. Do not forget to add light beers, such as Bud Light, Miller Lite, or Coors Light. Imported beers include Heineken, Molson, and Corona.

There are also specialty beers from microbreweries that you may be asked to order. These products are usually available only in the regions in which they are brewed. Catering managers should know what is available in their areas.

Beer is no longer considered "low-class," and an increasing number of women are drinking this beverage. The varieties and subtleties of beer can be as complex as those of wine. Beer can be pale and sparkly or dark and coppery.

Kegs of beer are appropriate for an outdoor barbecue or picnic, or where a low price is a key factor.

Neutral beverages are nonalcoholic beverages. This category includes effervescent or still mineral waters; citrus-flavored, carbonated, sugar-free beverages; herbal and decaffeinated teas; nonalcoholic wines and beers; juices; and sodas.

Most clients are satisfied with the standard drink menu. This menu usually includes a red wine and white wine, a domestic light beer and a domestic regular beer, a few soft drink brands, drink mixers, and at least one brand each of Scotch, gin, vodka, bourbon, rum, tequila, and Canadian whiskey.

A more elaborate drink menu usually includes the standard offerings plus one brand each of blended whisky, rye, brandy, champagne, and imported beer. On-premise caterers may also offer some specialty drinks, such as piña coladas, margaritas, frozen daiquiris, and grasshoppers. Specialty drinks can be a challenge at an off-premise event without the proper equipment.

The top-of-the-line drink menu offers a wide selection of liquor brands, both imported and domestic. A guest at a function with the most extensive drink menu, who wants a gin and tonic, for instance, does not have to settle for the one brand offered on the standard drink menu (i.e., the caterer's "well" brand). Chances are he or she can choose from among two or three brands of gin. In other words, guests are offered the choice of pricing levels in "well," "call," and "premium" brands.

Some clients may want to specify each brand of liquor and non-alcoholic beverage offered during a beverage function. However, when shopping for beverage service, most clients do not want to select all brands. Some of them will choose only those few that absolutely must be offered in order to satisfy specific guests. Clients will often want to specify the exact varieties and brand names of wines served at catered meal functions, but not those liquors served during the premeal receptions.

Instead of specifying each brand name of beverage that must be served at a catered event, most clients would rather concentrate on the price per drink, price per bottle, labor charges, specific needs (such as a particular style of cocktail service), and/or the price charged for each hour the bar is open. This does not mean, however, that you should ignore the subject of well liquor versus call or premium liquor. You will need to broach this subject with potential clients. One way to do this is to develop a drink menu that notes all brand names and the prices charged per container. For instance, you may note that a well brand costs $40.00 per liter, plus, plus, and that a call brand costs $55.00 per liter, plus, plus. If a client desires, he or she can then mix and match well brands and call brands and create a unique drink menu.

Occasionally you will encounter clients, or guests, who have personal drink recipes they want your bartenders to prepare. For example, a guest may prefer a unique type of martini made in a special way.

Menu Pricing

Beverage functions can be priced several ways. The catering sales representative can usually offer a few alternatives to clients. However, before discussing pricing procedures with clients, it is important to determine whether the beverage function will be offered as a (1) cash bar, (2) open (or hosted) bar, (3) combination of cash bar and open bar, or (4) limited-consumption bar.

A *cash bar* is sometimes referred to as a no-host bar. To obtain drinks at a cash bar, guests pay for them personally. Alternatively, guests may purchase drink tickets from a separate cashier and give them to the bartenders in exchange for drinks. At a small beverage function, the bartenders may take cash and prepare and serve drinks, thereby eliminating the cashier position.

An *open bar* is sometimes referred to as a host bar. Guests do not pay for their drinks. The client (i.e., host) or a sponsor pays for them. Guests usually can drink as much as they want and what they want during the beverage function without having to pay.

A *combination bar* includes elements of the cash bar and the open bar. The typical combination bar arrangement involves the host paying for each guest's first two drinks, and the guests then paying for any subsequent drinks. For instance, the host may purchase the first two drink tickets and issue them to each guest. After that, guests are on their own. If they want more drinks, they will need to purchase their own drink tickets.

The combination bar is the logical solution for the client who does not want to provide only a limited number of types and brands of liquor at an open bar, yet cannot afford to allow guests unlimited choices and consumption. The combination bar is also a good way to limit liability for the client and the facility by not providing unlimited consumption.

A *limited consumption bar* is priced by the drink. The host establishes a dollar amount that he or she is prepared to spend. When the cash register reaches that amount, the bar is closed. The host may decide to reopen the bar as a cash bar. This is feasible only on a per-drink basis when a cash register is used.

Beverage Charges

The way in which liquor charges are set varies somewhat from food menu-pricing procedures. Generally speaking, with food, the menu price offered to potential clients includes all relevant charges for food, labor, and direct and indirect operating expenses. With beverages, however, potential clients usually choose how they want to pay these relevant charges. They can pay one price for everything, or they can opt for an itemized list of charges and pay for each one separately.

Most establishments pour between ⅞ to 1¼ ounces per drink of hard liquor. Hard liquor generally comes in liters (33.8 ounces). It is recommended that absent a computer bar system, usually found only at permanent bars, portion control measuring pourers, such as a Posi-Pour, be used. This type of bottle measuring system ensures that bartenders do not "free pour" and decrease the number of drinks per bottle. Some bartenders favor the measuring jigger, which is preferable to free pouring, but bartenders usually overpour (keep pouring a little bit) while simultaneously emptying the contents of the jigger into the glass.

Charge per Drink.   The typical pricing procedure used for cash bars is to charge per drink. Normally, the price charged per drink is high enough to cover all other relevant expenses. A per-drink charge is either tallied and a single check presented to the function host, or guests pay individually by the drink. In either case, prices are negotiated in advance.

Individual drink prices usually are set to yield a standard beverage cost percentage set by the facility. For instance, mixed-drink prices are typically based on a beverage cost percentage ranging from approximately 12 to 18 percent; wines and beers are usually priced to yield a beverage cost percentage of approximately 25 percent. The menu prices will be lower only if a client pays separately for other relevant charges.

The client can sometimes negotiate away some of these extra charges if a certain level of sales is attained, unless he or she requests something special not normally provided by the facility. Some facilities will waive bartender charges if the beverage sales reach a predetermined dollar amount. A meeting planner may attempt to have the facility waive corkage fees.

The price-per-drink method can also be used for open bars. Bartenders can keep track of all drinks prepared and served by ringing up each one on a precheck machine. At the end of the beverage function, a total count is computed and extended by multiplying the number of drinks consumed by the agreed-upon price per drink. Consumption taxes and gratuities are added, and the final accounting is presented to the client for payment.

Some clients may want the facility to charge a relatively low price per drink at cash bars in order to minimize the financial impact on guests. The caterer can accommodate these requests by charging clients separately for the bartenders, cocktail servers, cashiers, security personnel, and/or room rental. Alternatively, he or she can suggest that the client directly subsidize the drink prices by, for example, paying the facility $2.00 for each drink served.

When charging per drink, the caterer may offer a sliding scale of prices, depending on the size of the beverage function. For instance, you might charge $5.50 per drink for the first 500 drinks, and then $5.00 per drink for those served thereafter. An example of a "by-the-drink" menu follows:

Cordials, Cognacs, International Coffees, Polynesian Drinks $5.50

Premium Brand $4.50

Call Brand $4.00

Well Brand $3.50

Wine by the Glass, Beer, Imported or Domestic $3.50

Perrier, Juices, Soft Drinks $2.50

Charge per Bottle.   The most common pricing procedure used for open bars is to charge per bottle. The charge-per-bottle pricing method is also typically used when poured-wine service is offered during a luncheon or dinner meal function.

A physical inventory of all liquor is made at the beginning and end of the beverage function in order to determine liquor usage. Many facilities charge the client for each opened bottle even though all the liquor is not used. In a hotel, the remaining liquor can be sent to the host's suite or to a hospitality suite. Alternately, if a client has booked several catering events during a convention, the leftover opened liquor can be used at the next function. It is not a good idea to let clients take home the opened bottles; this is illegal in most areas. Even if the facility has an off-sale liquor license, open containers are usually not allowed in automobiles.

If the client pays for each bottle, instead of per drink, he or she may save a bit of money in the long run. For instance, if a liter of gin yields approx. twenty-seven, 1¼-ounce drinks at a price of $5.00 each, the expected revenue is approx. $135.00 per liter, plus, plus. Generally, however, a facility does not charge this amount if the client purchases the gin on a per-bottle basis. Usually, the per-bottle charge in this situation will be a little less. However, it cannot be significantly lower unless the client is willing to pay separately for other relevant charges.

Charge per Person.   The charge-per-person pricing option is usually available to clients who want to offer open bars to their guests. Since the open bar reduces the facility's control over liquor consumption, the price per person is typically set fairly high to ensure profitability.

The amount charged per guest may include a charge for food and beverages. The client's final billing is usually based on the type and amount of foods and liquors desired and the amount of time the bar must remain open. For instance, if a client wants unlimited amounts of shrimp, expensive canapes, and quite a few premium brands, and/or wants the bar to remain open longer than normal, the catering executive will charge much more per person than if the client settles for standard offerings.

Charge per Hour.   The charge-per-hour method is similar to the charge-per-person pricing procedure. The major difference is that this pricing method usually includes a sliding scale of charges. For instance, for 150 guests, a client may have to pay $2,500 for the first hour of standard bar service and $2,000 for the second hour. Because most guest consumption usually takes place in the first hour, the caterer can offer a lower price for the second hour and still earn a fair profit.

When using this pricing procedure, the catering executive must consider the number of guests expected. For instance, you might charge $2,500 for the first hour if there are 150 guests or fewer. If you do not consider the number of guests, you have no control over the number of people who can show up at the event. You must have a guaranteed maximum number of guests expected before quoting a specific charge per hour.

To some extent, then, the charge-per-hour pricing strategy must be combined with the charge-per-person pricing strategy. For instance, you might charge $25.00 per person for the first hour, $20.00 per person for the second hour, and so forth. This combination strategy will usually satisfy those clients who prefer a fixed charge per hour. It also ensures that the caterer will retain control over sales, expenses, and profits.

Flat-Rate Charge.   Using a flat-rate charge is similar to the price-per-guest pricing procedure. With this pricing method, however, the client pays one bottom-line charge for the beverage function.

A flat-rate charge is usually based on the assumption that guests will consume an average of two drinks apiece during the first hour and one drink apiece per hour thereafter. The charge usually varies according to the number of guests expected and the amount of call and premium brands requested by the client.

Some clients prefer the flat-rate charge to other pricing methods because it is the easiest way to purchase a beverage function. No matter how many drinks guests consume, clients know in advance what the price will be. They do not have to worry about exceeding their budgets. Moreover, there is no need for them to wait for an inventory of empty liquor containers or an audit of the number of drinks prepared and served. There are no unwelcome surprises.

Labor Charges

Sometimes labor charges are waived by a caterer. For instance, a very large party that generates considerable food, beverage, and, in the case of a hotel, sleeping room revenues, may be provided with complimentary bartenders and cocktail servers.

Labor charges may also be waived if the beverage function generates a specified amount of business. For instance, the caterer may charge the client for three bartenders to staff a cash bar, but note in the catering contract that half of the charge will be rebated if 300 drinks are consumed, and all of the charge will be rebated if 500 drinks are consumed.

One bar/bartender per every 85 to 100 guests is standard. If all guests are arriving at once, or the host does not want the guests standing in long lines, you can provide one bar/bartender for every 50 or 75 guests. Unless this is a very lucrative event, you would pass these labor charges to the client.

Charge for Bartenders. Generally, clients must hire a minimum number of bartenders for a minimum number of hours. For example, a hotel may have a policy that all beverage functions must have at least one bartender working a four-hour shift.

The labor charge for bartenders is typically based on a sliding scale. For instance, if two bartenders are scheduled, the client may have to pay $125.00 for the first hour, $75.00 for the second hour, and $50.00 for every hour thereafter.

Charge for Bar Backs. Generally speaking, there is no separate charge for bar backs. Their cost is normally included in the charge assessed for bartenders. For instance, if two bartenders are purchased by a client, their cost will normally include the cost of one bar back needed to assist them in replenishing ice, stock, glasses, and so forth.

Charge for Cocktail Servers.   Cocktail servers can cost almost as much as bartenders. For instance, if a client wants a few cocktail servers to pass trays of filled wineglasses, this little touch of luxury will add significantly to the final bill.

Some clients view cocktail servers as an unnecessary cost. If a beverage function has two or three portable bars set up throughout the room, it may be more convenient to let guests give their orders directly to bartenders instead of to cocktail servers. In fact, the additional layer of service imposed by cocktail servers can slow service as well as increase a client's costs.

One way to use servers to an advantage is to have them circulate with trays of poured wine or champagne. This will keep wine drinkers from clogging bar traffic, slowing down the mixed drink service.

Charge for Cashiers.   Some facilities do not allow clients to schedule cash bars unless they agree to employ at least one cashier. They do not let bartenders handle cash, inasmuch as the extra work of making change will slow down beverage production and service significantly. Bartenders handling cash also creates additional security problems. Separate cashiers are an excellent form of financial checks and balances and must be used if tight cost control is desired. Furthermore, money is dirty and can create a sanitation problem with bartenders handling money and beverages simultaneously.

Clients may be able to have cash bars without cashiers, however, if state and local liquor codes allow them to purchase the drink tickets in advance and resell them to their guests. If you allow clients to purchase drink tickets for resale to guests, you should exert some control over the resale prices. If local laws allow, a client may decide to add a profit markup to the prices you charge, thereby leaving the impression with guests that the facility's prices are too high, when in reality the client is creating the excessive prices. You should ensure that resale prices are not exorbitant or, if they are, make certain the client informs his or her guests that the facility is not responsible for them. If the client is repricing to earn money for charity or other fundraising activities, make sure the guests realize this. If a client decides to use a repricing strategy, he or she may need a temporary business license.

Charge for Security. It is unusual for a catered function to have extra security assigned to it. However, if a large beverage function has a cash-bar arrangement, and/or there are minors expected at the event, a client may be more comfortable if the facility provides an extra margin of safety. Because in this situation the facility may be at risk, a client may expect the catering department to absorb the added security costs. However, inasmuch as the typical facility employs a standard in-house licensed security service to patrol the entire property, the client will usually have to pay for anything beyond this.

Some clients may be more than willing to pay a few extra dollars to hire additional security so that they have one less thing to worry about. The catering sales representative should broach this subject with clients, as some of them may be unaware that they can employ additional plainclothes and/or uniformed security and thereby gain additional peace of mind.

Charge for Corkage. Some clients may want to bring in their own liquor and have it served at their beverage functions. Some think they will save money by avoiding the higher prices charged by the facility. In other cases, however, clients are not concerned about cost, but are motivated strictly by the desire to serve something special that only they are able to obtain.

Some facilities have policies prohibiting guests from bringing in and serving their own food and beverage products. And some state and local government agencies, especially health districts, may prohibit this type of thing. If there are no restrictions and the facility is willing to allow clients to use their own liquor, there is usually a corkage fee.

The corkage fee charged is typically based on the facility's estimated cost of labor needed to handle the products. For instance, you may need labor to receive a special delivery, store it, possibly refrigerate it, and deliver it to the portable bar. You may also need labor to set up a clean drink area, keep it clean, maintain clean glassware and sufficient ice, and so forth. The more expense involved, the higher the corkage fee must be. As a general rule of thumb, if your corkage fee is equal to the retail value of the product, less your cost to purchase the same product wholesale, the dollar amount should be enough to compensate you for your trouble.

Part of the corkage fee may represent a type of "luxury" or "privilege" tax levied on clients. For instance, you may want to charge something for the "privilege" of bringing personal liquor into your licensed establishment to compensate for the profit you would have made selling your own items.

Clients who want to bring in and serve their own liquor most often do so when serving wines. For instance, it is not unusual for a convention to have a few corporate sponsors, one of which may be a winery. Naturally, the winery will want its own wines served at one of the catered events. And to keep the peace and accommodate a good client, the facility usually makes arrangements to honor this request.

A corkage fee is generally quoted on a per-bottle basis. For instance, you might charge $10.00 for each outside wine bottle brought in by the client and served by your staff.

A corkage fee may also be extracted from clients in the form of "drink setup" charges. For example, if a client brings in a very special, very old brandy that is unavailable locally, you may agree to handle it only if you can charge $2.00 per setup every time you use the liquor to make a finished drink.

Package Plans.   Most hotels offer a package plan. See the sample of a package plan shown below.

▪AZALEA HOTEL COCKTAIL RECEPTION PACKAGE PLAN▪

The Azalea Hotel Cocktail Hour is a package designed to ease your budgeting plans for groups of 50 or more attendees. You will be provided a full-service cocktail reception with portable bars, experienced bartenders, and full set-ups.

Choose the package you prefer, and we will charge per person, based on guaranteed attendance or actual attendance, whichever is higher.

The Azalea complete bar set-up includes call or premium brand liquors, California wines, domestic beers, bottled water, and soft drinks. Bar service includes vermouth, mixers, juices, and garnishes.

Per person charges:

Number of Hours	One	Two	Three
Premium Brands	$15	$18	$20
Call Brands	$12	$15	$17

Prices are subject to a 17 to 19 percent gratuity/service charge and 8 percent sales tax. There is a bartender charge of $75 for the first hour, $50 the second hour, and $25 for each additional hour, which includes the cost of the bar back.

What Is the Best Option?

Each catering executive will have to determine the best method of pricing for every particular event. As an example, consider the following:

○ If a caterer charges $80.00 for a bottle of bourbon that yields approx. twenty-seven 1¼-ounce drinks, each drink costs the client about $2.96.

○ If guests are expected to drink 2 drinks per hour, for a one-hour reception for 1,000 people, the client purchasing by the bottle would pay approx. $6,000.

○ If the client purchases by the drink, at $4.00 per drink, he or she would pay $8,000.

○ But if the bourbon is purchased at $10.00 per person (no food), the total billing would be $10,000.

The caterer in this example makes more money selling per person.

TYPES OF BEVERAGE FUNCTIONS

Like the various meal functions, each type of beverage function presents unique challenges. In some cases, the number of challenges increases considerably if the beverage function must be arranged around a meal function. For instance, not only must a predinner cocktail reception go off without a hitch, it must also set the stage for the dinner that follows. Any guest dissatisfaction erupting during the reception may carry over to the banquet service and cause additional unhappiness.

Cocktail Reception

The cocktail reception is one of the most common types of beverage functions. Cocktail receptions held during the workweek are usually scheduled during the early evening hours, just after the end of the normal business day. On weekends there is more flexibility, but as a general rule, cocktail receptions are usually scheduled after 5:00 P.M.

Cocktail receptions often precede a dinner event. They are usually scheduled for only about 45 minutes to an hour. And in almost all instances, at least a few foods are served along with the beverages.

Hospitality Suites

Hospitality suite functions are usually set up in a client's hotel suite that can accommodate the reception's production and service equipment, supplies, employees, and guests.

In some cases, a hospitality suite is located in a public area, such as a small meeting room converted for this purpose, or in a restaurant banquet room. Using these locations may be less expensive for the client than reserving a hotel suite. In addition, they may be more convenient for guests to locate. Other benefits include room for a band or disc jockey, room for a dance floor, and room for a buffet.

If a hospitality suite is located in a hotel suite, the hotel's room service department usually handles the event. Private hospitality suites are not ordinarily serviced by the banquet staff. Generally speaking, catering is involved only when selling the event and/or when the hospitality suite is located in a public area.

The hotel suite on a sleeping room floor is generally set up like a home living room, with sofas, chairs, and coffee tables, which may become impediments to the flow of the event when overcrowded. However, these suites usually have great ambiance, are comfortable, and often provide a great view.

Some hotels and restaurants have designated employees in the catering department whose primary function is to market hospitality suites to major conventions. In a hotel, the food and beverage service may be handled by the room service department, but the selling, planning, and coordinating activities in these hotels are usually the responsibility of the catering department.

Hospitality suites are an inextricable part of convention business. Conventions have exhibitors, sponsors, and/or attendees who want to hold "open houses." These affairs are primarily social events, but they also present opportunities for guests to network and discuss business.

Hospitality suites are normally open only in the evening, after the regular convention business day is over. Attendees who wish to expand their social horizons like to make the rounds of these hospitality suites in order to meet friends, acquaintances, and business associates, and to cast their networking web as widely as possible.

Some hospitality suites are ongoing affairs. For instance, a convention sponsor may have an open house virtually around the clock. During the evening, the open house serves alcoholic beverages, but during the rest of the day it resembles a refreshment break, with a continental breakfast in the morning and soft drinks and snacks in the afternoon. In this case, the sponsor is competing for attendees with other refreshment breaks and other attractions located in the convention area.

Some hospitality suites have a full bar, others offer beer and wine only. Some offer a wide range of food, others provide only dry snacks.

If convention attendees have an open evening, you can promote more food. If they are coming directly from a dinner, you can suggest desserts, flavored coffees, and cappuccino.

Many hospitality suites are not connected to meetings. A tourist destination city may wish to host a hospitality event for local travel agents to promote travel to its location. A corporation may wish to hold an event as a "thank you" to its best clients.

A sensitive issue that tends to arise with hotel hospitality suites is that of the convention attendee who wants to offer surreptitiously his or her own "underground" hospitality suite. It is not uncommon for attendees to go out to the local supermarket or liquor store and purchase a few wines, beers, spirits, paper and plastic supplies, and dry snacks. Not only does the hotel lose this revenue, the underground hospitality suite puts a big dent in the hotel's complimentary ice stock. Furthermore, these clients and guests can create extra noise, a nuisance to other hotel guests, and increase the hotel's liability exposure.

Poured-Wine Service

A poured wine beverage service is part of a meal function. Many dinner events include one or two wines. In some instances, the wines are opened and preset on the dining tables. Guests may serve themselves, or the food servers may be responsible for serving the wine.

At more elaborate meals, cocktail servers, supervised by a sommelier, may be in charge of wine service. This is especially likely if guests are offered a choice of wines. It is also more common when a rare and/or expensive wine is served with each course.

According to a *Meetings and Conventions* survey of meeting planners, the most popular white wine, by far, is Chardonnay. The most popular red wine is Cabernet Sauvignon, followed by Merlot.

Caterers usually uncork all of the wine that is ordered for an event. Some cost-conscious clients will ask you to uncork wines as needed so that unopened bottles can be returned to stock at no charge.

It is important to be familiar with your wine list (see Figure 5.1). You should be prepared to recommend wines that will complement your client's menu choices. You should match the body of the wine with

Foods	Compatible Wines
Asparagus with hollandaise	Pouilly-Fuissé, Pouilly-Fumé, blush wines
Capon	Montrachet, white Burgundy
Cheeses:	
Blue, Gorgonzola	Claret, Burgundy, Port, Brandy, Chianti, Champagne
Brick	Rosé, white wines, Cream Sherry
Brie	Dry port, Cognac, Calvados, Burgundy, Champagne, Riesling
Camembert	All ports, red wine, pink Champagne, Champagne, Cognac, Riesling
Cheddar	Ports, Sherry, Madeira, Claret, Burgundy, Italian reds, St.-Émilion
Colby	Ports, Sherry, Madeira, Claret, Burgundy
Cream	Sparkling wines, Rosé, sweet wines
Edam	Tokay, Cold Duck, Claret, Muscatel
Gouda	Tokay, Cold Duck, Rosé
Gruyère	Sancerre, Beaujolais
Liederkranz	Dry red wines
Limburger	Dry red wines
Monterey Jack	Rosé, white wines, Cream Sherry
Muenster	Rosé, white wines, Cream Sherry
Neufchatel	Sparking wines, Rosé, white wines
Port du Salut	Light, dry, fruity wines
Provolone	Dry red wines, dry white wines
Roquefort	Châteauneuf-du-Pape
Stilton	Fruit wines, Port, Burgundy, Cognac, Sherry
Swiss	Sauternes, Brut Champagne, dry or sweet white wines, Sparkling Burgundy
Chicken, veal	Dry white Bordeaux, very light red Bordeaux, dry whites
Clear soups, consommés	Dry or medium sherries
Cold meats	Dry Alsatian whites
Coq au vin	Volnay, red Graves, light reds
Fish with white sauces	Dry Alsatian whites
Heavy pâté	Red Bordeaux
Lamb, beef, roast chicken	Light dry reds
Leg of lamb	Heavy reds, Cabernet Savignon
Light pâté	Soave, Alsatian, light reds
Lobster	Meursault, Muscadet, dry whites
Nuts	Ports, light red Bordeaux
Oysters	Chablis, dry Riesling, Pouilly-Fuissé
Roast pork	Valpolicella, Beaujolais
Roast veal	Red or white Beaujolais
Salmon	Dry whites
Shrimp	White Burgundies, Muscadet
Steak, beef	Chianti, Bordeaux, Burgundy, Pinot Noir, Merlot
Turbot, trout, bass, sole	White Burgundies, dry whites
Turkey	Light, dry reds or whites, blush wines
Veal scallopini	Beaujolais, fruity reds
Vegetable soups	Soave, dry whites

FIGURE 5.1. Example food and wine pairings.

the body of the dish. The body and acidity of wine are as important as its flavors in matching it with food. A high-acid wine, such as Chianti, would be best suited to a high-acid food, such as tomato sauce.

White wines and blush wines are served chilled and are best served with light dishes and delicately flavored foods. Red wines are served at room (cellar) temperature and are best served with medium to hearty foods.

Varietal wines are named for the grape varieties that are used in making them. U.S. regulations require that at least 75 percent of the grape variety must be used in making a wine so designated. Examples of white varietal wines are Chardonnay and Reisling. Red varietal wines include Pinot Noir, Merlot, and Cabernet Sauvignon. Blush wines include White Zinfandel and Rosé.

Offer wines with good value for the client. Many caterers are eschewing the traditional high markup and charging the wholesale price plus $10.00. Offer wines of several price/quality levels. Include simple taste descriptors on your wine list.

Blush wines, such as Rosé, popular for decades, were in decline until the introduction of White Zinfandel, a pinkish sweet wine. White Zinfandel is currently one of the most popular wines at receptions.

Generally, a drier wine is preferred with a meal. There is also increasing demand for wine coolers at receptions.

A problem with serving well-known wines is that consumers know how much they pay at their local liquor stores and do not understand the overhead and handling costs that a caterer must add, which, of course, makes them more expensive. One way around this difficulty is to stock a label that is sold wholesale only to food services—for example, Whispering Peak's domestic wines.

According to *Food Arts*, wine generally should not exceed 20 percent of the total food and beverage billing for a typical catered affair. Many caterers use a standard formula for a seated affair—about half a bottle per person. They add 10 percent to cover emergencies, then divide the number of bottles into the total wine budget to determine the appropriate price range.

The nature of the event should also be considered, including the average age of the guests (younger groups tend to drink more wine and beer, older crowds more hard liquor), their occupations, nationalities, and so forth. Also consider the location (at an outdoor party more white wine will probably be used as a thirst quencher) and the season (red wine is consumed more in winter).

Occasionally, you can offer a good client a special deal on wine if your facility has broken cases in its inventory.

Pay attention to your glassware. Glass size affects consumption. Larger glasses tend to promote more consumption. Use the correct glass for the type of wine.

According to Korbel Champagne Cellars, when serving champagne, the best method of chilling is with ice. To achieve the greatest benefit from ice, fill an ice bucket or tub with equal parts of cold water and ice. Adding cold water allows a more rapid dissipation of heat from the wine or champagne. Serving temperature can usually be achieved in 20 to 30 minutes, depending on the number of bottles, size of the icing bin, and amount of ice and water.

Chill only what you will need. A rise and fall in temperature can lower the quality of the wine. Champagne bottles should not be left in the water indefinitely, or the water will soak off the glue on the label.

When chilling large quantities of champagne for an outdoor party, you can use the cardboard case in which the product was shipped. Simply remove the champagne and cardboard dividers, line the box with two plastic trash bags, and place the wine back in the box with water and ice. Never allow champagne to get warm before chilling with ice. The sudden change in temperature may cause the champagne bottle to fracture, with explosive results.

The champagne cork is treated with a lubricant to allow easy extraction. Warm conditions, such as direct sunlight on a bottle neck, will cause the lubricant to soften to a degree that will permit the cork to fly out of the bottle when the bale or wire hood is removed. This is a dangerous condition that can cause injury, so it is important to keep champagne buckets, tubs, and cases shaded while the bottles are chilling. Drape the bottles with linen cloths to reduce the exposure of the bottle necks to warmth and sunlight. An opposite effect is produced when bottles fall over in the iced water and become extremely cold. Now the cork lubricant hardens, making it very difficult to pull the cork. Never remove the wire hood prior to uncorking the bottle. You can pull away the lead foil in advance, but always leave the wire in place, as it is holding the cork down.

As part of pre-event planning, you can taste various wines with your client. Tasting wine along with menu choices can demonstrate how wine enhances the meal. If this is not feasible, at least include suggested wine pairings on your menu.

Special Events

Alcoholic beverages, especially wines, are often the stalwarts of special functions. For instance, many fund-raising events are centered around wine and cheese tastings, meet-the-winemaker dinners, and introductions of new wineries and new wine products.

Unique alcoholic beverage presentations are also used by convention clients to generate excitement and enthusiasm at one of their catered events. For example, you may encounter a client who wants to book a dinner at which Beaujolais Nouveau, the first of the season, is served. Or some clients may request special setups, such as martini bars, vodka imbedded in ice carvings, Bloody Mary breakfasts, or champagne parties.

LIQUOR LAWS

Of all the products and services sold by caterers, none are subject to more governmental control and regulation than liquor sales and service. Every facility must adhere to the liquor laws enacted by the federal, state, and local governments. Although there is some similarity in liquor laws throughout the nation, each state, and particularly each local municipality, usually has its own liquor codes. Catering salespersons must know these regulations.

Illegal Liquor Sales

No matter where a facility is located in the United States, there are at least four types of illegal liquor sales that it must avoid.

Sales to Minors. In most parts of the United States, it is illegal to sell alcoholic beverages to anyone under 21 years of age. There are a few exceptions to this rule, however. For instance, in some states, it is legal to serve a minor if his or her parents are present, or if his or her majority-age spouse is present.

The law generally allows you to refuse liquor service to anyone you suspect is underage. This is true even if someone shows you what appears to be a true and correct identification card that indicates legal drinking age.

Most parts of the country also prohibit minors from being inside a tavern or liquor store. The catering staff must ensure that minors are not allowed near the portable bar areas.

Admittedly, it is very difficult to police guests' movements during a catered function. Although public bars are ever vigilant, there is a tendency to relax normal crowd control procedures when serving a private party, especially if there is the feeling that clients will be upset if you adhere strictly to the letter of the law. However, the catering executive must not surrender to a temptation to relax standards. If you are caught serving minors, you can rest assured that the "private party" defense will receive a cold reception from the legal authorities. Furthermore, the client will probably be the first to complain that you failed to exercise reasonable care. The caterer/facility is increasingly vulnerable to risk and litigation.

Sales to Intoxicated Persons. It is illegal to serve alcohol to a person who is legally intoxicated. In fact, the law generally stipulates that you cannot serve alcohol to anyone who *appears* to be intoxicated.

In most states, a person is legally intoxicated if his or her blood alcohol concentration (BAC) is one-tenth of 1 percent, or a BAC of .10. In some parts of the country a person is legally intoxicated if his or her BAC is .08.

It is impossible for you to assess accurately each guest's BAC. For instance, after consuming one drink, a young person may appear intoxicated, whereas an older guest who has considerable drinking experience may be legally intoxicated yet show no outward signs.

The average person's liver needs about one hour to eliminate the alcohol in one drink. If he or she has more than one drink per hour, the BAC will increase quickly. For instance, if a person weighing 125 pounds consumes three average drinks (i.e., a drink that contains approximately one-half ounce of alcohol) in one hour, his or her BAC can be .10 or more. Unless this person reduces his or her liquor consumption significantly, or refrains from drinking during the rest of the catered function, the liver will not have enough time to reduce the BAC to a legal level before the function ends.

Caterers use many strategies to prevent overconsumption. For instance, instead of dictating the number of drinks a guest can consume, you might offer "minidrinks", low-alcohol frozen drinks, and/or use low-alcohol liquors in all prepared drinks.

There is a budding trend in the beverage industry toward offering smaller drinks at lower prices. For instance, if you normally charge $4.75 for a highball with 1¼ ounces of liquor and 6 ounces of mixer, you might offer one with ¾ ounces of liquor and 5 ounces of mixer and charge only $3.75. In the long run, guests will probably spend just as much money. If you alter the consumption pattern, however, the guest is more likely to remain sober.

Another trend is for bars to offer frozen concoctions that have only a hint of alcoholic beverage. When a drink is frozen, the guest is less able to determine the amount of alcohol present. Furthermore, many guests seem to love drinks of this type. Unfortunately, they may be much harder to prepare and serve, so you may have to charge more to cover the additional expense. They also take longer to drink, as the typical guest cannot take too much cold too fast. Consequently, because you serve fewer frozen drinks, you will have to charge more for each one in order to compensate for this revenue shortfall.

Some states and local municipalities allow the sale of low-alcohol products. For instance, instead of using an 86-proof bourbon, you might be able to purchase a 56-proof product in your area. Even though this product has less alcohol, its use is a better choice than merely adding more mixer to an 86-proof product. Excess mixer tends to give a finished drink a "washed out" character. The low-alcohol alternative, however, tends to retain the characteristic flavor of the original beverage even though it contains less alcohol.

If there is any doubt about a person's BAC, you must "cut off" that person. When this is necessary, try to use peer pressure to your advantage. Attempt to check with the host of the function before taking action with an intoxicated guest. Ask another guest, or the client, to help you handle the situation. Be courteous to the guest and minimize the confrontation. State that you cannot serve any more alcohol, but you can offer food or nonalcoholic beverage alternatives. Or you can see to it that the guest gets a safe ride home. Retain a professional demeanor and do not prolong contact with the guest any more than is necessary.

Your company should have a policy on handling intoxicated guests. Some facilities participate in a designated driver program, whereby at least one guest in a party consumes no alcohol so that he or she will be able to drive everyone home safely. You can offer free, fancy nonalcoholic drinks that make it attractive and fun to be a designated driver.

Unfortunately, this concept can sometimes backfire. For instance, if you cut off a guest who is part of a designated driver group, he or she may become quite agitated. The guest may assume that the designated driver program allows him or her to get completely sloshed. The fact that it is illegal to serve visibly intoxicated persons is at odds with the customer who has arranged ahead of time for a safe ride.

You may encounter a similar problem with conventioneers who do not plan to leave the hotel after the catered function. Instead, they plan to go directly to their rooms and straight to bed after a long night of partying. They believe that they should receive special consideration because they will not be driving that evening.

Our liquor laws are sometimes contradictory, as are some of the solutions we have developed over the years to combat drunk driving. But that does not alter the fact that you cannot serve liquor to an intoxicated guest, even if that person is chained to a table and cannot drive. To do so puts your liquor license, not to mention your career, in jeopardy.

Hours of Operation.   Most local municipalities restrict the hours during which liquor can be served in a commercial beverage establishment. For instance, many areas have "blue laws" and you may be unable to accommodate a client's request for a champagne brunch because no liquor can be served before noon on Sunday. Or a late evening event may have to stop liquor service at 2:00 A.M. Some areas prohibit liquor sales while the polls are open on election day.

You will have to check the local codes to determine whether these restrictions apply to private parties. If they do, you must ensure that catering sales representatives do not book beverage functions during the prohibited hours.

Liquor License.   To serve liquor, you must hold the appropriate liquor license. For instance, a full tavern license, or hard liquor license, is usually needed to serve spirits, wines, and beers for consumption on-premises. The typical hotel or club usually holds this type of liquor license.

If the facility holds only a soft liquor license (a wine and beer license), it cannot serve distilled spirits. To say the least, this puts a crimp in your ability to sell full-service catering functions. It is possible, however, that under these conditions clients may be able to bring in their own spirits, in which case you can earn your revenue by charging corkage fees or drink setup fees.

In some parts of the country a hotel or conference center may be unable to serve liquor unless it holds a private club license. In this case, you cannot serve anyone who is not a member or a member's guest. Usually, however, you are able to grant memberships to any qualified clients and their guests. But because this adds to your administrative burden, you may need to charge a bit more for catered beverage events.

You may be in an area where a facility cannot purchase its own liquor. In this case, you usually must have a private club license, or similar license, in order to prepare and serve liquor brought in by the client. For instance, in some parts of the country, the client must buy liquor at a state-operated liquor store, bring it to the facility, and give it to the bartender. The client then pays a drink setup charge for each drink prepared and served. At the end of the function, the client carries home any unopened leftover product.

It is important to note that a liquor license attaches to a specific location. An on-premise facility cannot produce an off-premise event in a park across town and assume that its existing liquor license covers it—it does not. You may need to obtain a temporary license for each event of this type.

Facilities with on-sale licenses (i.e., alcohol must be consumed on the premises) cannot sell liquor to be taken off-premise and consumed. Some hotels have both an on- and off-sale license, which is very expensive. You will usually see a bottle shop in the lobby at these establishments. Liquor stores have off-sales licenses, which means alcohol must be consumed off the premises.

Potential Liquor Code Violations

A catering executive must ensure that all local liquor laws are obeyed when booking and serving group functions. Although the prohibited sales noted earlier are common throughout the United States, each local municipality usually has one or two unique regulations that place additional controls on the local liquor licensees. Those that usually affect caterers are discussed in the following paragraphs.

Food Served with Beverage.   In some parts of the country, the local Alcohol Beverage Commission (ABC) may prohibit beverage functions that do not offer foods. In these areas, a person applying for a liquor license to sell and serve alcoholic beverages for on-premise consumption must show that he or she intends to serve foods as well.

Alcohol should never be consumed on an empty stomach. Without food to slow the rate at which alcohol is absorbed into the bloodstream, guests run the risk of becoming intoxicated very quickly. If such guests leave the function and drive away in their cars, unfortunate, preventable traffic accidents may occur. By requiring you to serve foods at all beverage functions, the local government authorities are giving society one more weapon to fight these tragic situations.

Bring Your Own Bottle.   Before allowing clients to bring in their own liquor, you should check with the local ABC to see whether the liquor code permits this. In some parts of the United States, you are not allowed to use liquor purchased from a retail liquor store in a bar operation that serves liquor by the drink for on-premise consumption. In this case, you must purchase all liquor from licensed liquor wholesale distributors or, in control states, from the authorized state liquor agency.

Free Liquor.   You may be prohibited from giving away any liquor during a catered function. Similarly, you may be prohibited from offering sliding-scale pricing; you must sell the beverages at a fair market price. For instance, you may be unable to offer the first 250 drinks for $5.00 apiece and anything over that amount for $4.00 apiece.

Free liquor or reduced-price liquor tends to encourage overconsumption. By outlawing pricing practices of this type, the local ABC keeps a tight rein on the sale and purchase of alcoholic beverages.

Self Service.   To further control overconsumption of alcohol, some local municipalities may prohibit guests from preparing their own drinks at group functions. If this restriction exists in your area, it usually does not infringe upon the hospitality suite host's ability to allow guests to mix their own beverages.

Alcoholic Content of Liquor Used.   There may be a regulation prohibiting the purchase and use of closed containers of liquors that have exceptionally high alcoholic contents. For instance, some parts of the country prohibit the use of any distilled spirit that exceeds 100 proof.

Some clients may be unaware of this type of restriction, so it is up to you to inform them. This is especially important for conventions that attract attendees from all over the country. You should let these clients know that some drinks, such as a traditional Zombie, cannot be prepared and served.

Similarly, if an out-of-town client wants to bring in his or her personal liquor—assuming the liquor code and your facility policy permits this—you must ensure that anything brought in does not violate alcoholic-content restrictions.

Amount of Alcohol per Drink.   Some local municipalities may restrict the amount of alcohol you can put in each drink. For instance, doubles, boilermakers, and pitchers of beer may be outlawed because they can cause overconsumption of alcohol. Likewise for drinks that contain more than one type of liquor. For instance, you may not be allowed to prepare and serve drinks such as traditional mudslides, Long Island teas, and scorpions because they contain multiple liquors.

The major problem with a multiple-liquor drink is that one of them can have the same clinical effect on a person's central nervous system as three or four average drinks. Recall that the average person's liver can eliminate alcohol from the body only at the rate of about one average drink per hour. Also recall that the average drink contains about ½ ounce of alcohol. A typical highball contains about ½ ounce of alcohol, but a traditional mudslide contains approximately 1½ ounces of alcohol. If a guest consumes two mudslides in one hour, his or her BAC may exceed .10.

Leftover Liquor. The local ABC may prohibit letting clients or guests take home any leftover liquor. In this case, if a client books a beverage function and agrees to pay for each bottle served as well as each bottle opened, you must let him or her know up front that no leftovers can leave the facility.

If you face this situation, you can charge clients the standard price for each full container consumed and a prorated amount for each partial container used. This will probably satisfy all clients except those who order something special that cannot be reused at one of the facility's other bars or other events.

Alcohol Awareness Training

Some local municipalities require anyone who sells, serves, distributes, or gives away alcoholic beverages to take an approved server-awareness training course before he or she is allowed to work in a licensed alcoholic beverage establishment. These courses are similar in concept to the sanitation courses that some local health districts require all food handlers to take before they can work in a public food-service establishment.

The typical server-awareness training involves instruction in the following areas:

○ Dealing with minors
○ The telltale signs of intoxication
○ Dealing with intoxicated guests
○ Clinical effects of alcohol on the human body
○ Local liquor codes

Server-awareness training courses offered throughout the United States vary from about 4 hours of instruction to 20 hours. They usually follow the format initially established by the TAM (Techniques of Alcohol Management) course, the Serving Alcohol with Care course developed by the American Hotel & Motel Association (AH & MA), or the Bar Code program developed by the National Restaurant Association Educational Foundation.

Before hiring a permanent beverage-staff member, or putting anyone on the A-list or B-list, the catering executive must ensure that the job candidates have the appropriate training. Trainees usually receive a pocket card after taking the course, which they can show to potential employers to prove that they have been certified.

Third-Party Liability

If you serve an intoxicated guest or a minor, and he or she goes out and hurts an innocent third party, the facility, server, and host may be liable for damages to the injured person.

Some states have passed dramshop laws that specify exactly your liability in these instances. Under dramshop legislation, if it is proved that you served a minor or legally intoxicated person who causes damage to a third party, you will usually be held at least partially responsible. For example, if a minor you served gets into a traffic accident and injures someone, the injured party can sue the driver, the server, the facility, and even the host. Chances are that the minor does not have the same financial resources as the facility. Consequently, the facility stands to lose a great deal because it often has the "deep pockets" that a judge or jury can tap for huge financial awards.

In a dramshop state, the facility usually cannot defend itself if it is proved that its employees served a minor or a legally intoxicated guest. You cannot, for example, tell the judge that the minor presented what looked like a legitimate ID card. Nor can you plead, "Your Honor, the person appeared to be 30 years old." Such defenses are usually not permitted where absolute liability has been legislated. As a result, if you serve a minor or legally intoxicated person who causes damage to an innocent third party, you can count on being held responsible.

It is important for clients to realize that some states have passed social-host laws. Social-host laws hold function hosts liable for private functions hosted in their homes or at other locations. For instance, if a minor served at a private party held at a facility inflicts damage on an innocent third party, the function host and the facility may share responsibility for the injury.

Most states do not have dramshop or social-host laws. However, the facility, server, and client may still be held liable under common law. Under common law, an injured third party can sue you for damages. However, it is up to him or her to prove that you were negligent in serving the person who caused the injury. For instance, if you can prove that a minor whom you served proved his or her age by showing what appeared to be a legitimate ID, chances are you will be absolved from liability, especially if you can also show that the minor appeared to be older than 21.

Unlike dramshop or social-host laws, common law mandates that the burden of proof shifts to the plaintiff. He or she must prove that you were negligent and did not exercise reasonable care. As long as you followed generally accepted beverage-service principles and practices, you can usually mount an adequate defense. In a liquor liability situation, it is most likely that everyone involved in the incident from the lowest to the highest echelon, will be sued, with all parties hiring and paying lawyers to determine who is ultimately culpable.

In addition to the facility and the person causing the accident, hosts and servers can also be named parties to a lawsuit under common law. Hosts with deep pockets can rest assured that, one way or another, they will be defendants.

It is imperative that clients realize the types of risks they incur when booking beverage functions. In some cases they may have to be reminded of this if they expect you to cater a wild affair, such as a stag party. Entertainment options may be restricted if alcohol is served; for example, in Las Vegas, there is a regulation against have a female dancer emerge from a cake at a function if alcohol is served. A few minutes spent discussing liability and the legal issues faced by our industry should dispel these requests quickly.

Function Room Selection and Setup

The catering sales representative must select an appropriate function room to hold an event. Along with the client, he or she must consider several things when making this selection. The major factors influencing the selection process are a function room's appearance, location, utilities, and amount of floor space.

APPEARANCE

A function room's appearance is high on most clients' priority lists. In fact, a potential client is often attracted to a facility primarily because of the ambience provided.

For instance, a function room in Caesars Palace in Las Vegas overlooks the Las Vegas Strip. At night the view is phenomenal. Of course, many clients want to book this room regardless of any other advantages or disadvantages it offers.

Room dimensions; ceiling height; number of columns, exits, and entrances; the proximity, number, and quality of rest room facilities; the colors and types of floor and wall coverings; sound insulation; and lighting are also important, especially in those facilities whose function rooms do not enjoy breathtaking views.

The overall appearance of the room is critical. Consider the room in regard to the following factors:

○ Lighting
○ Sound
○ Colors
○ Walls
○ Temperature
○ Smell
○ Visibility
○ Layout

Many clients are turned off by a function room that is long and narrow, imparting the "bowling alley" effect. This room shape precludes the mingling, participation, and networking of guests. It also harms service, because many guests will tend to gravitate toward one end of the room; for instance, the bar at one end may be very busy whereas others are serving only a few guests. It is also difficult to place a platform speaker in a long, rectangular room; in such a room it is preferable for the speaker to be midway on the long wall as opposed to being located at either end of the room. The use of audiovisual equipment is also limited in a long, narrow room.

The typical ceiling height in hotel and convention center function rooms is approximately 11 feet. In many local municipalities the building code may require a higher ceiling. For instance, some building codes stipulate 14-foot ceilings in public areas such as restaurants, theaters, and shops.

Columns are usually a negative in a function room. A few are acceptable, but too many will detract from the catered event unless the caterer can suggest a room setup that will minimize their negative effects. For instance, buffet tables can be arranged between decorated columns, which may enhance the room's appearance. Or buffets can be wrapped around columns with the use of hollowed-out circular tables.

Most function rooms have a sufficient number of entrances and exits because of local fire code requirements. Some clients who have scheduled speakers and audiovisual presentations will want to know how easy or difficult it will be to transport their equipment in and out of the function room. Some rooms have outside entrances and loading docks.

Consider the location in the facility in relationship to the rest of the meeting rooms, phones, rest rooms, and so forth.

A lectern or head table should not be located next to an entrance, because the movement of those coming and going will disrupt the speaker. If a video or power point presentation is planned, try to have the room set up so the doors are off to the side. With this arrangement, a latecomer does not have to walk in front of the projector and interrupt the presentation.

The colors and types of floor and wall coverings are the first things a client sees when viewing a function room. In addition to meeting building code requirements, floors and walls should be free of stains and in good repair. They also should be in good taste and decorated with style.

Guests tend to eat and drink more in brightly lit, colorfully decorated surroundings. Vibrant colors, such as brilliant red, hot pink, and bright yellow stimulate the appetite. Dark tones dull the appetite. Colors that cool the appetite are dark green, navy blue, gray, and black. In regard to the colors used in a function room, some caterers consider how the client is paying for the reception. If the client is paying per person, it would benefit the facility to have the guests eat and drink less; hence, locating them in a darker room would be a wise choice. However, clients who are paying on a consumption basis would benefit the facility's sales in a brighter room.

Table placement at a reception also affects food consumption. An hors d'oeuvre table placed against a wall provides only 180-degree access to the food. A rectangular table in the center of the room provides two open sides and 360-degree access to the food, thus ensuring greater food consumption. A round table in the center of the room gives an appearance of a lavish presentation, but because there is no way for a line to form to circle the table, guests have to work their way in and out at various points for each item they wish to eat, which decreases food consumption.

Unsophisticated clients may not consider the sound and lighting capabilities when selecting a function room. However, if there are any inadequacies, they will be noticed during the event and cause dissatisfaction among the guests. For instance, if platform speakers are scheduled during the meal function, the room used cannot have any dead space, that is, an area(s) in the room where sound is absent or unintelligible.

If the function room directly abuts the kitchen, hallways, or service corridors, steps should be taken to prevent unwanted back-of-the-house noises from filtering into the function room. Employees moving about in these behind-the-scenes areas may occasionally cause distractions. For instance, some guests may be unable to hear a platform speaker if employees are overheard shouting, laughing, or talking. Employees should be trained to tread lightly in these areas in order to minimize noise pollution.

Similar action will also be needed if you have to minimize the amount of ambient light (to prevent light from seeping into a darkened room from around doors, draped windows, or production and service areas).

LOCATION

If the function room is a great distance from the kitchen, the menu planner may be limited to only those foods that hold up well.

The banquet staff also will need to use hot and cold transport equipment in order to preserve the foods' culinary quality en route. Without this equipment, food costs may increase, because finished food items are more vulnerable to quality deterioration when they must be preplated in advance and transported long distances. The extra effort can also increase labor costs.

UTILITIES

Meeting and convention clients are often concerned about the function room's utility capabilities. These clients book functions that tend to tax a room's utilities. The catering sales representative usually has schematic drawings of the room that illustrate the capacities and locations of the utilities. These drawings should be included in any mailed sales solicitation and on the facility's web site.

The catering sales representative must be conversant with each function room's utilities. Clients will be concerned with the following:

1 Types of electricity available in-house.
2 Types of electricity that can be brought in.

3   Maximum wattage available.
4   Maximum lighting available.
5   Number of separate lighting controls. For example, if a client will be using rear-screen projection, you will need to darken the area behind the screen while leaving the rest of the room light.
6   Heating, ventilation, and air-conditioning (HVAC) capacity.
7   Closed-circuit TV, radio, and VCR system.
8   Closed-circuit audiovisual (AV) system.
9   Paging system.
10 Number, types, and locations of:
   ○   Electrical outlets
   ○   Electrical floor, wall, and ceiling strips
   ○   Phone jacks
   ○   Dimmer switches
   ○   Vents and ducts
   ○   Built-in speakers
   ○   Doors (Do they open in or out? Are they single or double doors?)
11 If the function will be held in an exhibit hall, the client will also be concerned with the number, types, and locations of:
   ○   Gas hookups
   ○   Exhaust fans
   ○   Drains
   ○   Water connections
12 Data ports for computers, Internet service providers, and other cutting-edge technology.

SPACE REQUIREMENTS

The amount of floor space available is perhaps the function room's most critical feature. The caterer must assume responsibility for determining the amount of square footage needed. He or she cannot expect the client to make this calculation.

   Several factors influence the amount of space needed, the most critical of which are discussed in the following paragraphs:

Number of Guests

The local fire code will dictate the maximum number of people who can legally occupy a function room. This maximum usually is an excellent guide in planning a stand-up function, such as a cocktail reception. It can also be a good guide in planning theater or auditorium setups. However, some events, such as those that require a banquet or classroom setup, will accommodate fewer persons.

Generally speaking, for most meal and beverage functions, you will be unable to accommodate the maximum number of persons allowed by the local fire code. The room setups required for events of this type will usually reduce significantly the number of guests that can be handled efficiently and comfortably.

Type of Dining Table Used

You will have to allocate about 10 square feet per guest if seating is at rectangular banquet tables. If round tables are used, you will need about 12½ square feet per guest. These estimates will suffice if you are using standard chairs whose seats measure 20 by 20 inches. You should adjust your estimates if you use smaller chairs (seats measuring 18 by 18 inches) or larger armchairs (which usually have a minimum width of 24 inches). Round tables are easiest for the staff to service, and they maximize interaction between guests. Chair backs should be placed 2 to 3 feet apart.

Aisle Space

Aisles are needed for server access and customer maneuverability. Aisles between tables and around food and beverage stations should be at least 48 inches wide.

When planning aisle space, remember to leave enough entry and exit room for guests. Plan to allocate sufficient cross-aisle space—aisles used for guests to gather and funnel in and out of the function areas. A cross-aisle should be approximately 6 feet wide.

Cross-aisle space is used in setting up large functions. For instance, for a function requiring 100 tables, you cannot set a square layout of 10 tables by 10 tables without allowing additional space for guests to maneuver comfortably to the middle tables from the outside perimeter. As a general rule of thumb, if you need 100 tables, you should set up four blocks of 25 tables. Within the 25-table block, 48-inch aisle space is sufficient. However, there should be a 6-foot-wide cross-aisle surrounding each block of 25 tables. Tables should also be at least 48 inches from the wall.

Before making any final decisions regarding aisle space, you must check the local fire code for specific requirements. Many facilities utilize graphic layout software to design a room setup.

Dance Floor Space

If the function includes dancing, you need about 3 square feet of dance floor per guest. If you use lay-out squares, most of these types of portable dance floors come in 3-by-3 foot (i.e., 9 square feet) sections; plan on using one section for every three guests. A 24-by-24 foot dance floor covers approximately 600 square feet of floor space.

For very large functions, a second dance floor is very convenient. Guests at the back of the room will not have to negotiate the long trail leading to the front, where the single dance floor is normally located. On the other hand, this arrangement does divide the group into two subgroups. Two dance floors placed as diamonds with the points abutting keeps separate dance floors connected. Be sure the dance floor is safety-coated with an abrasive to improve traction. Be sure that sections are flush against each other and there are no cracks in which a woman's high heel could get caught. All sides must be completed with trim pieces that slant and will not cause a guest to trip.

Band Stand

For a bandstand, estimate about 10 square feet per band member. Drum sets usually require about 20 square feet. Large pianos, synthesizers, runways, and so forth, need additional space. Disc jockeys may require considerably more space to hold their equipment and music collection. Check the entertainment contract, as it may set forth the floor-space specifications.

Bandstands and similar attractions are sometimes elevated on risers. Stage risers come in many shapes and sizes. Their purpose is to elevate platform speakers, entertainers, or audiovisual (AV) equipment so that a large audience can see what is taking place at one end of the function room.

Most risers are 4 by 4 feet, or 4 by 8 feet. They are folding risers that can be adjusted to several heights. Risers should be set up with steps with attached handrails and light strips. A lawsuit can occur if a guest falls from an improperly set stage.

Other Entertainment

You may need to allocate additional floor space for strolling musicians or similar entertainment. Once again, check the entertainers' contracts for exact space requirements.

Head Table(s)

Head tables usually need about 25 to 100 percent more floor space than regular dining tables. Furthermore, if the tables will be placed on risers, you must increase your space estimate accordingly to accommodate the platform area, steps, and the need to spread the table-and-guest weight properly over the stage. For instance, if you use typical platform sections measuring 4 by 4 feet and 4 by 8 feet, you would need to connect a 4 by 4 and a 4 by 8 to have enough space to accommodate a dining table measuring 3 by 8 feet. In other words, you will need about 48 square feet of platform space to accommodate approximately 24 square feet of dining table space. The 48 square feet will accommodate four guests seated at 24-inch intervals. The 12 square feet per person is usually the minimum amount needed for head table guests.

A raised head table for 12 people, plus a lectern, should be a minimum of 26 feet long. The rule of thumb is 2 feet per person, plus 2½ feet for the podium. For more comfortable seating, allow 2½ to 3 feet per person.

If you have head tables reserved for speakers, dignitaries, and other VIPs who will be addressing the guests after the meal, you may be asked to set up extra dining tables on the floor for these guests, near the head tables, so they can enjoy their meal without feeling as though they are on display. Some guests do not want to sit at an elevated table and eat. If there is enough space in the function room, they can have their meal at regular dining tables and then move up to the head tables just before the program begins.

Setting up extra dining tables allows you to maximize the number of VIPs who can be accommodated at the head tables. For instance, if you have 10 VIPs and 10 spouses, you can set up 20 place settings (i.e., covers) at regular dining tables. And, if the client agrees, instead of setting up a head table for 20, you can set one for only the 10 VIPs. The spouses can remain at the dining tables after the meal.

Bank Maze

A bank maze consists of posts (stanchions) and ropes set up to control guest traffic. You may want to use bank mazes to control traffic around cashier and ticket taker stations. If they are necessary, you will need to allocate more floor space to accommodate them.

Reception Needs

If the function room is used to house a reception and a meal, you will need enough space to handle both phases of the catered event. In most cases, you will be unable to reset the reception area to accommodate meal guests. There is usually insufficient time to do this. Furthermore, the action involved is aesthetically unattractive.

To accommodate a reception adequately, you will need about 6 to 10 square feet of floor space per guest. With 6 square feet, guests will feel a bit hemmed in; they will also have a little less ease in getting to the food and beverage stations. Consequently, they may eat and drink less. If a cost-conscious client is paying on a per-person basis, whereby guests can eat and drink as much as they want for one price, you might consider allocating only about 6 square feet per person to keep the price low and your food and beverage costs under control.

Seven and a-half square feet per person is considered to be a "comfortably crowded" arrangement. It is thought to be the ideal amount of floor space per guest for receptions and similar functions.

Ten square feet provides more than ample space for guests to easily mingle and visit the food and beverage stations. It is an appropriate amount of floor space for a luxury-type reception. It is also an appropriate setup if the client is paying according to the amount of food and beverage consumed. You want guests to have enough room to eat and drink as much as they want so that your revenues are maximized.

Buffet Table

All food stations need enough floor space for the tables and aisles. For instance, an 8-foot-long rectangular banquet table needs about 24 square feet for the table and about 60 square feet for aisle space (if the table is against the wall); about 100 square feet for aisle space is needed if the table is accessible from all sides.

When determining the number of buffet tables needed, as well as the number of buffet lines required, you have to consider:

○ Number of guests expected
○ Length of dining time
○ Amount of service equipment required
○ Type of service equipment required
○ Type of menu
○ Style of service

○ Amount of decor desired on the buffet line
○ Amount of total floor space available in the function room

In general, you must allocate approximately 2 running feet of buffet table for each food container needed. For instance, if you have to display three hot offerings, three cold offerings, and a condiment basket, you should set up a buffet table about 14 to 16 feet long. If you use two standard 8-foot rectangular banquet tables, you will need about 48 square feet of floor space for the buffet table and approximately 150 square feet of standard 3-foot aisle space surrounding the buffet table. The total allocation for this setup, then, is about 200 square feet.

Beverage Station

For self-service nonalcoholic beverage stations, the setups are similar to buffet table setups. For instance, a hot beverage station will need about as much space as a buffet table laden with foods. Bars, however, will require more floor space because you need room to store backup stock, ice, and coolers to hold beer and some wines. You must also allocate enough working space for bartenders and, if applicable, cocktail servers. Generally speaking, the smallest portable bar you can use measures approximately 6 by 7 feet, or about 42 square feet. However, when you take into account the aisle and other space needed, you will have to allocate at least 150 square feet for the typical portable banquet bar setup.

If you are setting up portable bars for a large function, you may be able to reduce your space estimates if you can arrange to locate them in pairs. For instance, you may be able to locate two or four portable bars back-to-back in the middle of the function room so that the bars can share a common area where glassware, ice, wines, beer, and so forth, are stored. This will eliminate duplicate storage areas and free up extra floor space.

Side Stands, Tray Jacks, and Bus Carts

Three square feet will be required for each side stand, tray jack, or bus cart.

Action Station

Allocate a bit more floor space for an action station than for a buffet, so guests can gather and view the chef's performance. Your floor space estimate must also be increased if the action station is elevated on a riser.

Staging Area

You may need to set up a temporary serving line in the function room. A band or disc jockey may need a place to store shipping containers. A client may need space to store convention materials, party favors, and similar items. You may need to allocate floor space to temporarily store lighting and sound equipment. Or you may need to set up a temporary service corridor on one end of the function room to store hot carts, cold carts, and gueridons. If you anticipate any of these needs, you will need to allocate sufficient space to accommodate them.

If you allocate floor space for a staging area, you should block it off with pipe and draping so that it does not interfere with the appearance and ambience of the catered event.

Cashier

Some functions, particularly beverage functions, may require floor space for one or more cashiers. For instance, a catered event may include a cash bar. If so, the facility may require the client to use cashiers to sell drink tickets.

In general, you should allocate at least 25 to 30 square feet for one cashier station. If a security guard will be stationed at the cashier area, you will need additional floor space to accommodate this person.

Display Area

Sometimes clients need space to set up their own cashier stations, registration/information tables, kiosks, booths, or similar structures. For instance, a client may need a cashier station in order to sell meal tickets to guests who have not prepaid, but who decided at the last minute to attend the event.

Selling individual event tickets is typical with convention clients. Most conventions give a book of event tickets (one ticket for each meal function) to each attendee who registers and pays in advance for the total convention. A few attendees, however, may decide to bring a spouse to a meal or register to attend the convention after the preregistration deadline passes. Or some may not want to attend every event; instead, they may show up only for one or two preferred events and pay for only these functions.

If guests need to use tickets to enter a function room, you will have to provide sufficient space for someone to collect the tickets. A ticket taker usually has a spot reserved just inside or outside the front door. This space is sometimes the same space used to locate the client's registration/information station. Guests, therefore, can check in and pay at one station. This is more convenient for guests. It also allows you to economize on your floor space requirements.

If you set up an area to handle all of the client's cashiering and check-in procedures, you must ensure that there is sufficient floor space to accommodate one or more cashiers, desks, tables, chairs, backdrops, service corridors, telephones, waste receptacles, lock boxes (to hold the used tickets and/or receipts to prevent reuse), and so forth. Some clients may have lists of their display needs along with exact dimensions. If not, question them carefully about these requirements so that you do not have to rearrange the function room layouts at the last minute.

Landing Space

A landing space is an area where guests can discard empty plates and glasses, soiled napery, and waste. It can be a tray on a folding tray jack stand located next to a bar or against a wall. Allow 4 square feet for each landing space area. Widely scattered cocktail or tuxedo tables can also accommodate this need. You can reduce the amount of landing space necessary if attendants remove the discards quickly and often during the event.

Landing space should also be allocated on the buffet tables between and in front of food containers. Guests will need some place to set their drinks while putting food on their plates. They will also need room on the table to set their plates temporarily while deciding what foods to take.

Meeting Activity During the Meal

A client may want to have a business meeting and the meal or reception in the same function room. For instance, an association chapter may want the function room divided into two sections: one section housing the reception, and the other housing an auditorium-style setup to accommodate the group's program.

The meeting activity can easily be accommodated if the function room is large enough to be divided appropriately. It cannot be accommodated as readily, however, if the meeting and the meal or reception must share the same space.

One way to handle events where space must be shared is to use a conference-room, U-shaped, or hollow square setup. For instance, with a U-shaped setup, guests can conduct their meeting, and when it is time to eat, roll-ins can be placed in the hollow section of the setup and foods arranged to allow self-service.

A conference-room setup usually requires no more space than the typical meal function; however, a U-shaped or hollow-square setup may need two to three times as much floor space. The U-shaped setup is the least efficient use of floor space. It requires about 42 square feet per person.

To calculate the proper meeting space for an auditorium-set general session, multiply the expected number of attendees by 12 square feet per person. For example, you will need 2,400 square feet for 200 attendees ($200 \times 12 = 2,400$). For a classroom-style setup, plan for 19 square feet per person.

Style of Service

The style of service is important, especially if you are planning to use French or Russian service, as these service styles require up to twice as much floor space than others. Some buffets, especially those where beautiful displays and several tables are used, may also need extra space. For instance, instead of using a typical buffet floor space estimate, you may want to increase it by 50 to 100 percent if the function is very elaborate and you want to provide a luxurious amount of space for all guests.

Audience Separation

If it is necessary to divide or separate the audience, you may need considerably more floor space. For instance, in locations that still allow smoking in public facilities, if you set up smoking and nonsmoking sections, you should set one or two extra tables in each section unless you know exactly how many smokers and nonsmokers to expect. In the worst-case scenario, you will have several half-used tables in each section.

Handicapped Seating

If you expect to have a physically disabled guest, you will need to allocate additional floor space. For instance, a wheelchair-bound guest will need a bit more space at the dining table, as well as a wider aisle in which to navigate.

Props, Decor, and Plants

Some events use large props. In Atlanta, a prop representing Tara (the mansion) is often used for *Gone with the Wind* parties; in San Antonio a prop simulating the Alamo is often used. Even small props scattered around the room take up space that must be considered.

PLANNING THE FUNCTION ROOM SETUP

Function room setups must be established well in advance. Table locations, exhibits, displays, food and beverage station locations, table sizes, head table, seating mix (i.e., number of rounds of 8 (seating for approximately 8 people at a round table), rounds of 10, and so forth), table spacing, table settings, and preferred decor are usually planned by the catering sales representative and the client. With the availability of graphic software, you are likely to encounter clients who bring in their own designs showing how the room should be set up. However, many clients still do not want to be bothered with these details; they are much more interested in the menu, price, and decor.

Using facility floor plans and other schematic drawings that show square footage, dimensions, doors, and other factors that may be important to the client, several visual plans can be developed with the use of a basic template and graph paper. The Room Size Calculator web site will calculate the amount of space you will need: (http://www.mmaweb.com/meetings/Workshop/roomcalc.html).

If your facility can afford it, purchase computer software that will correlate the room's dimensions, location, doorways, service corridors, columns, protrusions, dead space, permanent service installations (such as a permanent bandstand, bar, and/or dance floor), and other limitations, with the client's desires and draw out several suggested layouts for consideration (see Figure 6.1.).

For instance, the typical software program will draw a layout using industry standards as defaults (which can be changed) for such things as distances between rows of chairs or tables, aisle space needed, and the optimal angles that should be set to accommodate video presentations. Most software packages will also automatically generate standard seating styles. If you are unhappy with a computer-generated layout, you can usually alter the data and ask the computer to draw another layout.

Before developing the final function room setup plan, it is important to estimate the amount of time needed to accomplish the

TODAY'S 'ELECTRONIC' MEETING

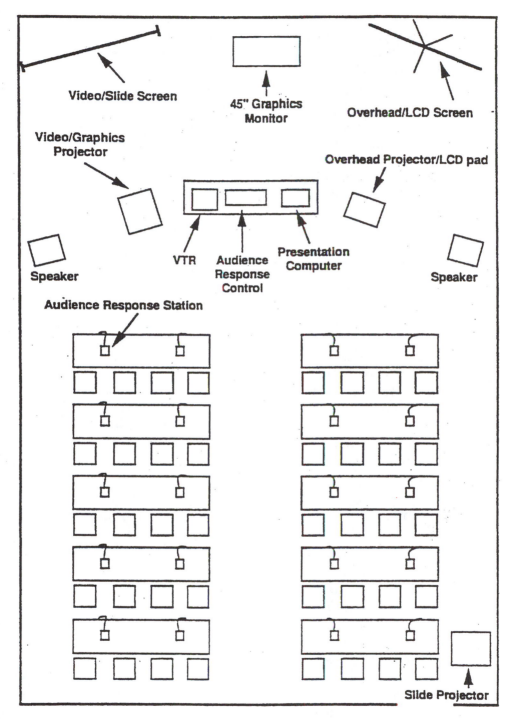

client's layout and design objectives. In scheduling a function room setup, a number of critical factors must be considered, as discussed in the following paragraphs.

1 *Function room status.* Function rooms used as temporary storage or those being repaired or remodeled cannot be used. If a function room has an existing setup, additional time must be scheduled so that it can be torn down. Furthermore, it is important to know how the room will be used after the catered event ends. Similar functions should be scheduled in the same room.

Breaking down one reception setup only to reset it in another function room is a waste of time, money, and effort. When schedules permit and group sizes are similar, a basic setup can be used several times.

2 *Timing of events.* If the function room will be empty several days before the catered event, its setup can be scheduled during slack periods. In this case you have more flexibility. Moreover, you can usually maximize labor productivity.

On the other hand, if there is a meeting scheduled in a function room that ends at 5:00 P.M., and you need to turn over the room for a 7:00 P.M. reception, time is your enemy. This type of scheduling demand can increase your payroll costs unless you plan very carefully.

Before breaking down a room, check to see what the next event in that room will require. You may be able to leave the setup in place, or at least leave the required chairs, tables, and so forth, in the room.

3 *Setup difficulty.* The amount of time needed to perform the final setup depends primarily on the type of setup required. For instance, a theater set requires less time than a schoolroom set, and a reception can be set up faster than a sit-down dinner.

4 *Function room layout and design.* The catering manager or banquet manager is usually responsible for preparing the final function room layout and design for all catered events. In some cases, exact locations of food stations, bars, seating, decor, and other requirements must be communicated to the banquet setup crew well in advance of the function's dates. Standardized and frequently used set-ups, however, do not require complete instructions to be given. Nor do they usually require a significant amount of advance notice. For instance, it is not necessary to draw a diagram of each standard schoolroom set unless there is something unusual or distinctive about the setup.

Record special room setups and decorations by taking digital or instant (Polaroid-type) photos before the room is broken down. Keeping these photos in a file provides a reference and you will not have to rely on memory to recreate a theme or special setup.

5 *Decor.* A theme party or similar function requires additional time to set up properly. Props, plants, flowers, lighting, and so forth, must be delivered and located. The amount and type of decorations, where in the facility they are stored, or whether they must be delivered and set up by outside contractors, will determine when the function room can be set up and how much of the room can be set up at one time. Larger props should be set up first, furniture and equipment next, and smaller props then set up around the furniture and equipment.

6 *Premovement.* Larger functions require additional planning primarily because it takes more time to transport furniture and equipment. Premovement is necessary so that final room setups can proceed quickly. For instance, if a function requires 1,000 chairs, banquet setup personnel, when they have some extra time available, should move the chairs as close to the function room as possible and store them temporarily. The final room setup can be handled quickly and efficiently if a good deal of furniture and equipment are preset this way.

Moving large quantities of furniture and equipment early allows time to handle any unforeseen delays that may occur. Forklift problems, employee sick calls, and equipment mishaps or miscounts can derail a final setup schedule. Time is precious in setting up a function room for a large event. Presetting furniture and equipment will increase productivity, eliminate the need to rush at the last minute, and decrease chances of an accident occurring when moving items.

7 *Teardown.* When a function ends, banquet setup personnel must dismantle the furniture and equipment and return it to storage. Efficient scheduling can reduce labor requirements and increase productivity. For instance, if the next setup in the function room requires chairs, the required number should be left in the room.

The cycle of delivering, setting up, and tearing down furniture and equipment is similar to a chess game, with all pieces subject to constant movement.

8 *Lighting and audiovisual (AV) equipment.* Meetings and meal functions sometimes require extensive lighting and/or AV services. Function room setups that include these services usually require an additional setup time, usually referred to as a "rehearsal set." Although complete furniture and equipment setup is not necessary for a rehearsal set, it can be needed if a band or a keynote speaker wants to test the sound system with all furniture and equipment in place. Re-

hearsal sets significantly increase the time and effort needed to set up a function room properly.

Communication is critical in facilitating a rehearsal set. When will it take place, and how long will it last? Will other setup work continue during the rehearsal set, or must it be postponed until after the rehearsal ends? Unplanned rehearsals can seriously interrupt the overall setup schedule. Productivity is compromised if the setup crew must work in the dark or while a band is checking sound levels.

¶ *Outside service contractors.* If a client is using outside service contractors, banquet setup must ensure that these contractors' work dovetails nicely with the facility's standard operating procedures. For instance, if an outside service contractor is hired to handle all lighting installations and teardowns, banquet setup must coordinate closely with the crew to maximize productivity and eliminate unnecessary downtimes.

Dining Room Layout

When you walk into the setup banquet room, everything should appear symmetrical. Round tables should be evenly spaced so that the eye can view attractive, neat rows. All of the table legs should face the same direction. And the points of square tablecloths should form V-shapes over the table legs. When the banquet room is completely set, the client should be able to look down a row of tables and see a consistent line of V-shapes surrounding each table leg.

The tables used should be the standard ones that measure 30 inches from the floor. The typical dimensions of tables used in catering are as follows:

○ 60-inch round—typically called a round of 8, or an 8-top. It is usually used to seat 6 to 10 guests.
○ 72-inch round—typically called a round of 10, or a 10-top. It is usually used to seat 8 to 12 guests.
○ 66-inch round—a compromise table size, it is designed to take the place of the 60-inch and the 72-inch rounds. It can seat 8 to 10 guests. If a facility uses this kind of table, it may be able to minimize the number of different types of tables it carries in stock.
○ Banquet 6—a rectangular table, measuring 30 inches wide by 6 feet long.
○ Banquet 8—similar to the banquet 6. It measures 30 inches wide by 8 feet long.

Some clients may specifically ask for rectangular dining tables because they want picnic-style seating. Generally, however, rounds are the most popular style of dining tables, except where U-shaped, hollow square, or conference room setups are required. For instance, a small luncheon with a guest speaker can be more readily accommodated with the U-shaped arrangement. The platform, podium, and supporting props can be set up at the top of the U before the meal is served. The speaker can begin right after dessert. Guests will not have to change seat locations, but can remain in their present seats.

○ Schoolroom or classroom table—similar to the banquet 6 and banquet 8. It can be 18 or 24 inches wide and 6 to 8 feet long. Tables of this type are used for business meetings at which classroom presentations are made. Seating is usually on one side only. Such tables can also be used as one half of a buffet table.

○ Serpentine table—a crescent-shaped table. The typical size used is one fourth of a hollowed-out round table. You also can purchase a table that is one fifth of a hollowed-out round table.

Serpentines are used with banquet 6s and/or banquet 8s to make an oval-shaped buffet line. They can also be used to make a snake-shaped buffet line. Four of them can be assembled to create a hollowed-out circle, whereby foods can be displayed on the tables and some sort of attraction (such as a floor-mounted fountain) can be displayed in the hollowed-out center.

○ Half-moon table—a half-round table. This kind of table is typically used to add another dimension to a buffet line. It can also be used by itself to hold, for example, a few dry snacks at a beverage function.

○ Quarter-moon table—a quarter-round table, generally used as part of a buffet line.

○ Cocktail table—a small, round table. Usually available in 18-inch, 24-inch, 30-inch, and 36-inch diameters. You can use 30-inch heights (for sit-down service), shorter tables (for displays), or Tuxedo (bar height; for stand-up service).

○ Oval table—a table of varying proportions, used primarily as a dining table. The typical oval table used for catering measures 54 by 78 inches. It can be used to increase room capacity; for instance, you can fit ten ovals in place of eight rounds. An oval table also allows a more elegant seating arrangement, in that a "host" can sit at its head.

Oval tables, however, do present some drawbacks. For instance, their shape makes it more difficult for servers to work around them efficiently. Guests seated on the narrow ends may feel crowded. And if a few foods are preset in the middle of the table, some guests may be unable to reach them easily.

When taking banquet tables from storage, never roll more than two at a time. When opening and setting them up, be sure that the legs are locked properly. This will prevent accidents that can occur if the tables are not set up and adequately secured. If locking bolts are exposed incorrectly, guests may scratch their legs.

You must also ensure that the table legs lock properly when tearing down the tables and putting them away. And if the tables are stored on a dolly, they must be secured correctly to prevent accidents and damage.

The seats of the chairs used should measure 17 inches from the floor. The most common seat cushion dimension is 20 by 20 inches. The typical banquet stacking chair meets these specifications. Folding chairs usually do not; they are usually lower (15 inches high) and less comfortable. Folding chairs should be used only for outdoor events or for emergency backup.

The placement of chairs and tables in a room can significantly affect the outcome of a function. Unsuitable arrangement or cramped seating can spoil an event. Consider the objective of the function. Is there to be a speaker? Is interaction desired, or are the attendees just expected to listen? Will everyone be able to see the speaker? Will everyone be able to see the audiovisual presentation?

Are the chairs sturdy and in good condition? Are they safe?

Are they clean?

Ultimately, the seating arrangement used will depend on the purpose of the catered event. For instance, awards banquets, celebrations, theme parties, and so forth, will influence the dining room layout as well as the type of tableware, props, napery, floral arrangements, centerpieces, and other decor used.

The purpose of the function will also indicate whether a head table is appropriate. With a head table, it is important to specify whether it is to be on a riser because the platform, just like a dining table, must be set up and dressed appropriately. The appropriate platform height must also be determined.

Before the banquet setup crew is finished, it must be certain that all ancillary tables, chairs, and equipment are set up, such as lecterns, AV equipment, cashier stations, registration/information tables, kiosks, booths, and display attractions.

The room setup is not complete until all outside service contractors, such as decorators and florists, finish their work. You will have to coordinate schedules with these service contractors to ensure that the dining room is ready for service at the scheduled time.

Bar Layout

Bar setups are easier to plan than food events. Unlike food, alcoholic beverage service tends to be quite standardized. Moreover, you do not normally set up portable bars with the wide array of equipment needed to prepare and serve a complete line of specialty drinks. Simple mixed drinks, wines, and beers are more commonly served; unique specialty drinks are not usually offered.

Bar setups are also easier to plan, especially if the facility has permanent, self-contained banquet-bar installations in some function rooms or banquet areas. These bars need only a bartender or two and some inventory, and they are ready to go.

Ideal locations vary, depending on the size of the room, the location of the doors, and the placement of the food and the dance floors. Avoid grouping bars too closely to prevent crowd buildup. In a large room, first open the bars farther from the entrance to encourage guests to move into the room.

Even in function rooms that use portable bars, a facility often has designated specific locations for them that are always used. These locations provide the appropriate utilities, space, and accessibility. When planning beverage service, therefore, the catering sales representative and client need only to work around this preallocated space. In effect, you are working with semipermanent bars that tend to be almost as convenient as permanent bars.

A bar does not pose the same quality-control problems as does food. The product is very standardized. It is a manufactured item, with standardized packaging, quality, and servable yields. And, except for mixers, beer, and some wines, the inventory has a virtually unlimited shelf life.

If portable bars are used, and if you need to allocate space for them, the planning is a bit more challenging. You will have to ensure that they are set up to do the following:

○ *Serve all function needs.* For instance, if there is a reception with dinner following, the bars may have to accommodate both events. This implies that there must be enough room to allow guests to approach the bars during the reception, as well as sufficient service bar area to accommodate cocktail servers who may need to handle poured-wine service.

○ *Provide sufficient working space.*   Normally, you will need at least one bartender and one bar back per bar. If you are catering an upscale function and are using a sommelier, you should allocate some working space so that he or she can handle the wine service correctly. Depending on the type of function, you may also need cocktail servers.

○ *Provide sufficient storage space.*   A busy bar will need a back bar area in which to store additional in-process inventory. Portable refrigerators, portable ice carts, glassware, and paper supplies should be available so that service does not lag.

○ *Enhance cost-control procedures.*   There must be enough working space to eliminate bottlenecks, which can lead to overpouring and spillage. For cash bars, if there are no cashiers scheduled, the facility may bring in cash registers for the bartenders to use to ring up sales and hold cash receipts. If drink tickets are sold by a separate cashier, the bar will need a lockbox to store used drink tickets. Furthermore, sufficient standardized portion-control measuring devices, such as Posi-Pour color-coded bottle pour spouts, and standardized glassware, should be used.

○ *Prevent access to minors.*   A permanent or semipermanent bar installation is usually positioned to avoid this problem. Portable bars, however, may not be so closely watched. Local liquor codes usually demand that you provide some type of separation from the dining area to prevent underage drinking.

○ *Allow adequate space for other items.*   Required cocktail tables and chairs, landing space, cashier(s), and ticket taker(s) will need an appropriate amount of space.

○ *Accommodate special customer requests.*   For example, a client may want you to provide a separate draft beer station, wine tasting station, and spirits and mixed drinks station. In this case, you will need to plan your setup very carefully in order to prevent overcrowding.

○ *Allow for a proper accounting of all drinks served.*   If the bar service is set up to charge the client for each drink consumed by his or her guests, you will have to allocate space for precheck cash register machines to record the number of drinks served.

○ *Enhance security.*   Liquor "shortages" are common in our industry; tight security can minimize this problem. It is best to transport all liquor stock in a portable locked cage. Leave the cage near the portable bar so that if the area must be left unattended, the liquor stock can be secured. You can also have the portable bar and locked cage set up well before the catered event is scheduled to begin; when the bartenders and bar backs come on duty, they can then unload the liquor cage and set up the bar.

Coffee Stations and Refreshment Breaks

Coffee may be the simplest and most profitable service you provide. There are more compulsive coffee drinkers in the United States than there are compulsive liquor drinkers, and they need coffee throughout the day. Coffee drinkers are generally impatient and want their coffee right away, especially in the morning. The setup must be easy to understand. You must make access easy by providing a generous amount of floor space. Traffic must flow smoothly with no backtracking.

Attendees can draw 5 gallons of coffee from a single urn in 15 minutes. You can anticipate twenty 6-ounce cups of coffee per gallon.

It takes twice as long to add cream and sugar as it does to pour coffee, so cream and sugar should never be placed directly in front of a coffee urn. If these items are placed away from the urn, the line will move much faster.

If you are providing food as well as drinks, the food should also be placed away from the coffee urn or on a separate table.

From left to right, items should be placed in this order to facilitate traffic flow:

- Cups
- Regular coffee
- Decaffeinated coffee
- Hot water for tea
- Teabags, sugar, sweetener, cream, lemon slices
- Spoons
- Food

Buffet Layout

Buffets allow guests to choose their favorite menu items. Guests also have some personal control over the portion sizes. However, it is imperative to offer foods that hold up well.

Buffets are generally more efficient than table service procedures, assuming that there are enough buffet lines to accommodate the guests quickly and effectively. One of the disadvantages of a buffet, however, is the possibility that some guests will be finished eating while others are still waiting in line.

Some clients are under the impression that buffets are less expensive to implement than table service styles. However, buffets can be quite expensive unless you use acceptable techniques designed to reduce their costs. Although labor costs may be a bit lower, there is no portion control and you must provide surplus food to ensure an ample supply of each item.

Lower-cost food items, such as salads and breads, should be placed first on the table so that the guests' plates will be full by the time they reach the main course. You can also cut down on consumption by using a 9-inch plate instead of a 10-inch one.

Another cost-saving technique is to put small portion sizes on buffets. For instance, instead of serving whole chicken breasts, or even half breasts, cut them into three or four pieces each. Guests who want to eat another meat on the buffet, but also want to sample the chicken, will not have to take a large piece of chicken, taste part of it, and throw the rest away.

Another cost-control procedure is to have a chef personally supervise the buffet tables. Psychologically, people are less likely to load their plates if they are being watched.

Similarly, the chef may serve the meat course while supervising the rest of the line. For very cost-conscious groups, each guest can be issued an entrée ticket that must be exchanged, for instance, for a serving of roast beef. This eliminates second helpings of the most expensive item.

Regardless of a client's budget, buffets can offer many advantages to both the client and the facility. Buffets provide an acceptable level of customer service. They allow guests to control what and how much they eat. Chefs can use their creative talents to decorate the foods and buffet tables. When laying out the buffet stations, try not to put salads, entrées, and desserts on the same table, because this arrangement will slow service as the guests try to take everything at once. Most guests cannot carry two plates, but this does not stop them from trying. The inevitable result: spillage and other food-wasting accidents.

Avoid setting up buffet tables near doors or other entryways where they can cause traffic jams. If the buffet line will be longer than 16 feet, the space allowed should be two tables wide, that is, about 4 to 6 feet wide. A long, narrow line is unattractive. A wider line allows you to spread out the foods, create a more aesthetically pleasing depth perception, and enhance the setup with decorations and food displays.

If you must use a long, narrow line, use a combination of straight and curved tables to eliminate the "skinny" look.

It is usually more challenging to set up an hors d'oeuvres buffet because, unlike a meal buffet, it offers no natural starting point for guests. Some caterers like to set up V-shaped islands (actually inverted Vs) on the buffet table, perhaps turning two chafing dishes to create an inverted V, with plates, sauces, forks, and so forth for each island. In this way, you can set up multiple points of access at a long buffet table. Guests can move in and out quickly. Such efficiency, though, may strain your food cost budget inasmuch as guests are able to consume more food over the duration of the event.

If the buffet line will include an action station, you will need to allocate enough space to accommodate the in-process inventory of food, preparation and service equipment, the chef, and the guests who will want to congregate and watch the chef create the finished items.

If the action station will be put toward the center of the function room instead of against a wall, you will need more floor space. An action station "in the round" is usually set up with several inside tables and outside tables to allow the chef maximum maneuverability and exposure, and the guests accessibility.

The number of action stations needed depends on the amount of time required to prepare and serve the foods and the estimated number of customers who will want them in lieu of the other foods displayed on the buffet. At the very least, you should expect that half the guests will want something from an action station.

Some buffets incorporate a bit of cafeteria service. If so, there must be enough room allocated so that food servers and chefs can maneuver adequately.

If floor space is at a premium, use double-sided buffet tables. They can save as much as 20 percent of available floor space. They also tend to reduce leftovers because when service slows near the end of the meal, you can close one side of the line and consolidate all foods on the open side.

Whenever possible, beverages, such as wine, hot coffee and tea, and soft drinks, should be served at the table. This provides a bit of personalized table service that guests appreciate. It also makes the overall service much quicker and more efficient. Guests typically take a long time at beverage stations, and bottlenecks are inevitable. If beverages are not to be served, place them on a separate table.

If possible, use small containers of food on the buffet line. Try to use containers that hold no more than 25 to 30 servings. They will be more attractive than large, elaborately garnished containers. Keep in mind that only the first few guests through the line will see the beautifully garnished large presentations before they are disturbed. Small containers will need frequent replacement. Guests will usually take smaller portions from smaller containers, and larger servings from larger containers. The result: You save more on food cost than you spend for any extra labor. Furthermore, smaller containers usually mean fresher, more attractive presentations.

Most meal buffets are usually set up with one line for every 100 guests. (One line is one side of a buffet table; if you are using two sides, that is considered two lines). The maximum number you can serve efficiently with one line is 120 guests. The break point, therefore, is 120 guests. Generally speaking, you should have one line for every 100 guests, and two lines if the number of guests ranges from 120 to 200.

You are courting customer dissatisfaction if you cannot maintain these standardized ratios. This is especially true for luncheon meal functions, because guests usually arrive all at once. In this case, speed is critical.

If you set one buffet line for every 50 guests, you can accommodate the entire group in about 15 minutes. The first guest will take about 5 minutes to go through the line. After that, there will be about 4 guests passing through the line every minute. For some luncheons, it may be a good idea to set one line for every 50 guests.

If hors d'oeuvres are served buffet-style during a beverage function, we recommend setting up one table for every 50 guests. Larger tables, even though fewer are set up, tend to interfere with bar traffic.

If you set one buffet table for every 50 guests, however, you may need more labor to replenish food supplies. You will have more product distribution problems unless you set up enough service corridors to handle replenishment. And you may have more leftovers with several small buffet tables unless you consolidate some tables toward the end of the event.

For breakfast functions, you may be able to get by with one buffet line for more than 100 guests. Unlike luncheon guests, breakfast guests tend to arrive a few at a time. For instance, at conventions attendees tend to drift in throughout the meal. Even though the typical breakfast buffet has a guest rush during the last 15 minutes of the meal period, usually enough guests will have already been served to prevent any service glitches.

Dinner buffets tend to be more elaborate. There are many decorations and more lavish food displays. If you set up this type of buffet, guests will usually take more time to serve themselves. They will want to savor the visual effects and not rush through. Generally speaking, for every hour it takes to serve a luncheon buffet, it will require about 1½ hours to serve a dinner buffet.

It is important to decorate and embellish the tables and their surroundings. Guests will be able to see and appreciate the decor as they move along the table. Add decorative pieces with height that can be seen over the heads of the people in line from across the room. You can create visual interest on buffet tables by placing items at different heights. Fill in blank areas with crunched napkins, ferns and fronds, piled fruit, and similar items. Large displays often tie into the theme of an event.

Buffets should be creative in shape. Use serpentine or round tables to curve the line.

Display tables often need to be skirted. Skirting is draped along the side of a table. It is connected on the table's edges and allowed to fall to just above the floor.

Skirting is usually attached with T-pins or Velcro. Plastic clips with Velcro on one side make installation and removal easy. They come in two sizes, standard and angled. Standard is made to fit a ¾-inch-thick tabletop, and angled is used for ½-inch-thick tabletops.

Some skirting has plastic clips already attached that clip onto the table. Some skirting has Velcro bands intended to hook onto Velcro-strip tapes or the aforementioned clips, which are attached to the table. To avoid sagging, clips are attached at intervals of 2 feet or less.

Although the plastic clips with Velcro are faster and more convenient to use, the T-pin gives a much smoother and more elegant look. A plastic clip does not reflect quality.

Table skirting is usually 29 inches in length to accommodate the standard 30-inch table height. Stage skirting is used to dress risers and is available in lengths ranging from 6 to 36 inches. Longer skirting is available, but if the standard lengths do not meet your needs, you may want to use pipe and draping to dress anything of greater height.

For some skirting, you will need to use a skirting liner. For instance, if you plan to use an elegant lace skirting, you will have to line it so that the uncovered areas do not show through.

Usually, all buffet tables, display tables, and platforms are skirted. Some dining tables may also be skirted. For instance, a head table is usually skirted on three sides. The skirting provides a vanity shield as well as an attractive presentation.

When calculating the amount of skirting needed, you must be very careful to compute the correct total. If, for example, you need enough skirting to cover a banquet-8 table, you will need about 22 running feet (i.e., two 8-foot sides and two approximately 3-foot sides, which equals about 22 running feet).

Try underlighting buffet tables. When using light-colored table skirting, either linen or polyester, place two 60-watt bulbs or two 4-foot fluorescent lights under each table. This arrangement does not work with dark-colored skirting, as the bulbs show through like lighted tennis balls instead of being diffused into a glowing light.

Tablescapes: The Tabletops

The top of a table is "the stage." Once guests are seated, they will spend the rest of the meal function looking at the table. The table presentation sets expectations for the meal and should reflect the theme. The colors of the napery should not clash with the carpet or wall treatments.

Garlands, flowers, or ribbons can be trailed between each place setting. Interesting centerpieces can be made from baskets of bread or fruit, or plates of petits fours. Centerpieces can be highlighted with pin spots (small spotlights) from the ceiling.

Each place setting is referred to as a "cover." The cover should never be empty, or what is called a "naked cover." A show plate, folded napkin, menu, or preset first course should be placed between the flatware.

Planners usually consider color more than the napkin fold. However, the napkin fold and placement of the napkin on the table can add interest. The napkin can be placed in the center of the cover, to the right of the forks. If local health regulations allow, they can be fan folded and placed in stemmed glassware. An interesting twist is to have each napkin a different color, or with a different fold. The layout must be symmetrical and pleasing to the eye.

The type of fold is determined by the formality of the event and the location of the napkin on the table. A flat fold is preferable if a standing menu or a name card is used. Flat folds are usually a better choice for outdoor events, which can be windy.

A nice touch is to have the servers unfold the napkins for the guests and lay them across their laps. If a group is having several banquets, use a different fold for each meal.

All dining tables and buffet tables must be dressed and outfitted appropriately. The type of meal function, menu, and style of service will influence the quality and type of table decor used.

The table setting is the focus of a function room's decor. It is the one thing that guests see throughout the meal. Because it influences the mood in which the patron judges what he or she eats and drinks, you should spend as much time in designing the right look as in developing the most appropriate menu.

Tables should be padded so that table noises are minimized. The typical dining table and buffet table often have pad underliners placed beneath the tablecloths. This pad can be permanent; for instance, you can buy a roll of padding, cut pieces to fit each table, and staple them to the tabletops. Or the pad can be temporary and placed on the table prior to adding the tablecloth. You can also purchase tables that are prepadded. Generally, however, these tables are much more expensive than unpadded ones.

All tables require napery. Buffet tables and display tables need tablecloths, and dining tables will need tablecloths and napkins. You will also need napery for beverage stations. For instance, alcoholic and nonalcoholic beverage stations will need tablecloths. And although both types of stations need coasters and napkins, normally you will use disposable paper coasters or cocktail napkins instead of permanent, reusable napery.

Napery adds warmth and color. In the public's eye, cleanliness is its most important attribute. Crisp, clean, stain-free napery helps create a favorable impression.

Although many refer to napery as linen, only the fabric linen, which is made from flax, is actually linen. Most napery used is made of cotton or polyester.

White is the most common color of napery used. Light colors are used when white does not provide the background desired. Darker colors can be used when a stark contrast is desired or for all-day functions (such as permanent refreshment centers) where the napery, which will become soiled during the day, cannot be changed easily. And darker colors (usually green or tan) are used for schoolroom tables so that convention attendees can take notes without battling the glare given off by white napery.

Sometimes you may want to use two or more colors to dress a table. For instance, a mauve overlay (i.e., contrasting cloth laid on top of the base cloth) may be appropriate for a buffet table; a white tablecloth with a gold overlay may be just right for a table used to display door prizes; and black tablecloths with bright-color napkins (such as fuchsia, gold, or white) provide a contrasting visual effect.

Special napery can be rented in a variety of materials and patterns. A beautiful floral tablecloth with a centerpiece made of the same flowers shown in the tablecloth can make a stunning appearance. Metallic cloths, netting, linen, laces, and plaids can be used to set the mood of a catered event. White lace overlays are appropriate for a wedding.

Many hotels and other facilities own their napery and launder it in house. The alternative most often used by restaurants, convention centers, and clubs, is to engage an outside laundry and linen supply firm that will deliver clean napery items and pick up soiled articles.

When ordering napery or requisitioning it from a "linen" room, you will have to specify the exact measurements needed. For example, if you use round tables, the size of the tablecloth for most functions should be approximately 18 inches wider than the table diameter so that about 9 inches of cloth will drape over the sides. If the tabletop diameter is 60 inches, you should use a cloth 78 inches square. A 72-inch-diameter table should be fitted with a 90-inch round cloth. If you use rectangular dining tables, the tablecloth should also drape about 9 inches over the table's sides.

Because the standard table measures 30 inches from the floor, and the standard chair seat measures 17 inches from the floor, a tablecloth with a 9-inch hem will not touch the chair seats. If this tablecloth is fitted correctly on the dining table, it will not interfere with the guests' comfort. At most, hems should just barely touch the front edges of the chair seats.

For some formal dinners, if floor length tablecloths are desired, allow 29 inches on each side. Thus, for a 72-inch round table, you would order a 130-inch round tablecloth. When using floor-length tablecloths, be sure that the setup crew does not push the chairs in so far that the cloth is not hanging straight down to the floor. (See the Appendix for a Linen and Table Compatibility Chart.)

When placing tablecloths on the tables, keep the hemmed sides down and the creases up. If the tablecloths were pressed incorrectly—whereby the creases and hemmed sides are in the same direction—keep the hemmed sides down even though the creases may not be attractive. In this case, you must select the lesser of two evils. If this is not acceptable, a server would need to iron the cloths in-place.

The napkins used must be laundered and handled correctly so that they have enough strength to hold whatever fold you want to use. For instance, you can use the more common napkin folds, such as the pyramid, goblet fan, or Lady Windermere's fan, or you can use something more adventurous and unusual, such as the rosebud, bishop's miter, or candle folds. There are a variety of web sites with napkin folding instructions linked to this book's companion web site.

For more exotic folds, such as those used to decorate serving trays and buffet containers, you can use a thin-gauge aluminum foil insert to give added strength to the napery. For example, you may want to have two gooseneck-shaped napkins adorning each side of a canape tray. The foil will provide enough tension to make these folds and ensure that they will hold up throughout the function.

If you are using a casual buffet-style service, you may opt to provide the napkins at the beginning or end of the buffet line. For speed and efficiency at casual events, you might roll the flatware inside the napkins.

Napery can also be used to add a touch of class, by having servers use it to cover dirty dishes standing on a tray jack stand in the room, or using tablecloths to drape the tray jack before setting the tray on top.

Dining tables will also need plates, cups, saucers, flatware, water glasses, wine goblets, roll baskets, condiment containers, wine coolers, carafes, show plates, and other appropriate items that must be preset on the dining tables in a symmetrical pattern. As with napkins, however, if you are using a buffet-style service, you can let guests help themselves to some tableware on the buffet line.

There are many other types of tableware needed that usually are not preset on the dining tables. You may need teapots, pitchers, mugs, serving platters, serving bowls, ramekins, and/or specialty utensils.

When selecting tableware, most facilities prefer vitrified china or a similar type of product. China retains heat and cold longer than other materials. China is also impervious to salt, alkali, and acid, all of which attack and corrode metal. It can be produced with dish-washer-safe, lead-free glazes, and with ovenproof, freezerproof bodies. In addition, china resists scratches from knives and other utensils much better than other materials.

Glassware includes stemware, tumblers, goblets, parfaits, decanters, pony glasses, snifters, pilsners, bottles, ashtrays, punch bowls, and cake plates. Foodservice facilities usually purchase glassware that has been produced with a heat-treated, rapid-cooled process that ensures durability and long-term attractiveness.

Glassware is one of the most useful decorating tools. It helps set a mood and carry out a theme. Furthermore, caterers can use specialty glassware as a signature; for instance, the Ritz Carlton is renowned for its cobalt-blue water goblets.

The standard cover includes a plate set in the center with flatware placed on either side. Forks are placed to the left of the cover, knifes and spoons to the right. Some dessert flatware may be placed above the center plate.

Flatware is placed in the order in which it will be used by the guest, from the outside in. The soup spoon is on the outside and far right, as soup is usually an early course. The knife is closest to the center plate, with the blade edge facing the rim of the plate. The smaller salad fork is set to the left of the dinner fork to the left of the plate.

Dessert pieces set above the plate have the bowl of the spoon facing the guest's left, and the tines of the fork facing the guest's right.

The exact place setting depends primarily on the menu and style of service selected by the client. Many catering executives have sample covers set out on credenzas in their offices that can be viewed by clients wishing to see what they are getting. Clients can also redesign the sample place settings to develop something unique.

Coffee cups should not be preset at a formal dinner. They should be placed on the table after dinner when coffee service begins.

Once the desired place setting has been developed, the pertinent information is included in the banquet event order (BEO). Working with these specifications, the room captain usually sets a "Captain's Table"—a sample cover—as a guide for the servers to follow when setting the dining tables.

If you own unique decorative items or serving containers, you must be careful to use only those intended to hold foods. For instance, an imported serving bowl may contain lead in its glaze. Care must be taken to ensure that such containers are used only to hold and/or display nonfood items.

Some dining tables may need place cards and/or personalized menu cards. If you are setting a head table, you must see to it that the head table guests are seated correctly. For the head table at a formal event, the first guest of honor should be seated on the host's or hostess's right, and the second guest of honor seated on the left. If a third guest of honor is present, he or she should be seated to the right of the first guest of honor. If there are other dignitaries, they should be positioned on the left and right according to rank or prominence.

For the head table at a wedding, the bride and groom are seated at the center, with the bride sitting to the groom's left. To the bride's left will be the best man, followed by a bridesmaid, groomsman, bridesmaid, groomsman, and so forth. On the groom's right will be the maid of honor, followed by a groomsman, bridesmaid, groomsman, bridesmaid, and so forth. There should be enough room allocated at the head table to accommodate the entire formal wedding party, but if this is impossible, seat the most important members at the head table, with the others seated at the dining tables closest to the head table.

A table setting is not complete without some sort of additional decoration. Most catered events, especially dinners, have centerpieces on the dining tables. They also have similar attractions on the buffet tables.

Centerpieces should be aesthetically appealing and appropriate for the type of function booked. Floral arrangements of cut flowers, potted plants, or foliage, combined with candles, lights, and/or ice carvings, are excellent centerpieces appropriate for any type of food or beverage function. A bountiful basket of various types of bread also makes an attractive and inviting centerpiece.

Floral arrangements are a manifestation of beauty, adding a dimension to an event that cannot be attained by any other medium. The basics of any arrangement are style, shape, size, color, texture, scent and location. The purpose of any arrangement is to fill the eye with beauty.

Consider how the flowers will look on the day you will be using them. If you want flowers in full bloom, purchase them a few days early to allow them to open fully. If you are going to use roses on the same day as purchased, order "funeral roses," which are at their peak of bloom. Store flowers between 38° and 45° F.

Keep in mind that strongly scented flowers can interfere with the palate, that is, the taste of the food.

Centerpieces on dining tables should have eye appeal, but should never be at eye level. Centerpieces should not interfere with guests' normal sight lines. They should be placed under or over these sight lines. You do not want a guest to feel uncomfortable peering under, over, or around a centerpiece, trying to see the person on the other side. Guests should not have to have a conversation with a disembodied voice. For height, use an epergne, a container with a slender center portion that does not obstruct the view across the table. A centerpiece should not overpower a table.

Unique centerpieces can be conversation starters at events. Indoor pyrotechnics can be placed within centerpieces and all activated simultaneously with a remote control. Crystal ball ice domes can be created with a variety of theme-based items frozen inside, including silk flowers, statues, and even lit candles. Examples can be seen at Ice Magic (*http://www.icemagicinc.com/*) or Ice Occasions (*http://www.iciclesinc.com/*).

A mirror is often used as a base for a centerpiece. It can reflect flickering candles placed around the centerpiece. Mirrors should be clean so that the light does not show fingerprints or dust.

Before setting the tables, the banquet manager must specify the exact setup needed for regular dining tables, head tables, beverage stations, and buffet tables. It is a good idea to diagram in advance the required setup so that the setup crew does not have to scurry around at the last minute for directions. If special centerpieces must be placed on the head table, the setup crew must know about this before it goes to work.

Frequently, a few guests will be having off-menu special meals. These guests should be told to inform their server when they sit down that they are having a special meal. The captain informs the servers ahead of time about these special requests, so there is usually no need to mark their place settings.

The banquet setup crew will also need to know whether there will be a smoking section, if laws still allow. If the client requests one, the crew will need to set out ashtrays on the tables in the smoking section and "Thank You for Not Smoking" signs on those tables in the no-smoking section. (If you do not put these signs out, guests may think you merely forgot to put out ashtrays; they may just go ahead and light up without thinking.)

Dining room layout, bar layout, buffet layout, required table settings, and other pertinent information will be listed on the banquet event order (BEO). Some BEOs also include a room diagram. Although the typical BEO details very specifically the dining room, bar, and buffet layouts, it does not always include an exact description of the required table settings. For instance, if the client wants menus, brochures, and handouts placed at each cover, this information must be noted on the BEO. Every detail, no matter how small, is important to the client. You cannot afford to let any get lost in the shuffle.

Wall and Ceiling Treatments

Many events require wall and/or ceiling treatments. Walls can be draped, floor to ceiling. Ceilings can be given a "tent look" or simply hung with swags or baffles that are transformed by lighting.

Make sure to investigate the fire regulations and insurance considerations for draping fabric. Never hang anything off a fire sprinkler. Tables and chairs should not be in the room until the ceiling treatment is finished. In some cases, when feasible, chandeliers are removed to accommodate production lighting.

Employee Uniforms

A good deal of a catered function's visual impact can be attributed to the type and style of employee uniforms and costumes used. The typical client does not think about this unless he or she requests a specific theme, in which case special uniforms and costumes will be needed to carry out the theme.

Many facilities use a standard server uniform for breakfast and luncheon meal functions, with a slightly different, more formal server uniform for evening affairs. Bartenders, cocktail servers, bar backs, and bus persons also wear standard outfits. These standard uniforms are designed to suit most food and beverage functions adequately.

If the client is a little more adventurous and has a bit more money to spend, the catering sales representative may wish to broach the subject of alternative employee attire if he or she thinks it would add significantly to the function's success. For instance, you can suggest renting special garments specifically for the meal function. This little extra touch can be just the thing to make a good event a great event. Service personnel in costumes are referred to as "moving decor."

Cleaning and Maintaining the Function Room

Dirty windows, walls, or floors can reduce a function room's quality level and cause guest dissatisfaction. Guests notice burned-out light bulbs in chandeliers.

Function rooms must be vacuumed before each function setup (when the room is empty), and given one final sweep or vacuum just before the catered event is scheduled to begin. Postfunction cleaning is equally vital. Trash and leftover materials must be discarded promptly.

Some rooms have a door leading onto a loading dock through which dirt can be tracked into the function area. Trucks, forklifts, and carts that enter the function room will hasten carpet deterioration and generate a considerable amount of work debris.

Covering the floor near the loading entrance with old carpets and plastic sheeting can be an effective way to catch dirt. Precleaning ramps and loading docks can also reduce the amount of dirt tracked into the room.

Rest room, trash can, and public ashtray cleanliness requires constant care during peak periods and must be scheduled to ensure an attractive atmosphere.

All torn wallpaper or carpeting and broken equipment must be replaced or repaired quickly so that the function rooms remain presentable and safe. Quick room turnarounds and constant movement of heavy furniture and equipment will cause damage to doors, floors, ceilings, and walls. These details must be monitored consistently.

Frequent inspection and repair can reduce wear and tear on the facilities as well as create a favorable guest environment conducive to memorable, exciting catered events.

Communication with Function Room Staff

Facilities with several function rooms in various locations require coordination and control of banquet staff. It is difficult to monitor employees who are constantly on the move. Managers must select an appropriate method to supervise and communicate quickly with all employees.

A basic, low-cost method of control is the callback method, whereby an employee must telephone a supervisor when his or her assigned task is completed. The supervisor will know how much time it normally takes to complete the task and can therefore anticipate a pattern of calls from his or her employees. As calls come in, new tasks are assigned on a priority basis. Furthermore, if a last-minute request is received, the supervisor will be able to assign it to the first employee who calls in.

A medium-cost method of control is the beeper method. With this option, beepers are assigned to all setup employees, or the employees are divided into groups with each group leader holding a beeper. This method allows the supervisor to assign a wide variety of tasks to each employee because the supervisor can quickly call all employees when emergencies arise.

Another advantage of using beepers is the ability to assign one to the client. Instead of trying to track down a client to verify a setup or time, information can be checked quickly.

The major disadvantage of using beepers is the time it takes employees to respond when called. When an employee receives a call, he or she must cease working and locate a phone. This stop-and-go action can be time-consuming and frustrating, especially if it is continual. Phone availability is also a consideration; if the only available phone is in a back office, additional time will be lost and labor productivity will plummet.

A more expensive method of communication control is the walkie-talkie method. Walkie-talkies eliminate the need for a person to stop what he or she is doing and locate a phone. Although some systems can cost thousands of dollars to install, the time and efficiency gained can be well worth the expense.

Lead employees and supervisors can be assigned walkie-talkies and, thereby, become instantly accessible. Last-minute changes can be communicated immediately. Clients are quite impressed when their requirements change and employees respond to them instantly.

With walkie-talkies, supervisors can also monitor the conversation between employees and keep up-to-date on the movement of furniture, equipment, and labor. For instance, if a request is broadcast to one employee to locate some equipment, another employee monitoring the broadcast can break in with some pertinent information.

As with beepers, a walkie-talkie can also be issued to a client. Unlike beepers, however, the walkie-talkie ensures instant verification of all details.

In lieu of walkie-talkies, some large facilities may rely on cell phones for communication. However, they must be aware of potential "dead" areas in the building where the phones do not work.

Equipment Inventory

The catering area uses a considerable amount of specialized furniture and equipment to set up a function room and serve a catered event. The department should ensure that complete, up-to-date lists of these items are kept by banquet setup and related departments so that the catering staff knows what is available and what will have to be obtained from a rental company. These inventory lists, which are often kept in a computer software program, should note all chairs, tables, easels, tripods, stanchions, dance floors, AV equipment, gueridons, rechauds, china, glass, flatware, linen, skirting, serving utensils, side stands, trays, bus carts, hot carts, cold carts, permanent centerpieces and other decor, portable bars, and other furniture items kept in-house.

Equipment lists should be updated monthly. A complete physical inventory should be taken at the end of each quarter so that damaged items can be repaired and missing ones replaced quickly. If there is a good deal of catering business, there may be above-average loss resulting from damage and/or theft. In this case, a physical inventory should be taken more frequently.

Room Temperature

Attendees often complain about the temperature in the room during a function. Most newer facilitiess today have energy management systems that turn the air conditioner on automatically to precool the meeting room about an hour before the banquet or meeting begins.

Many facilities set the thermostat at 72° F, unless the planner requests a different temperature. Some planners have been known to request a 69° F temperature. The important thing is to know the group. If there are to be 90 percent men, keep the room cooler, as men wear more clothing than women. If it is an evening function and the women are wearing cocktail dresses, the temperature may have to be as high as 74° F.

Lectern or Podium?

There is some confusion over the terms *lectern* and *podium*. Some people say a lectern goes on a table, and a podium goes on the floor. Others say a podium is a base, and that you stand on a podium. To prevent this confusion, we recommend that you avoid the word *podium* and specify either a table lectern or a floor lectern.

Flag Placement

When the American flag is used at a function, it should always be placed to stage right (in the United States). The host country always has its flag to the far stage right.

Stage right is always determined by the right side of the speaker, facing the audience. Therefore, stage right is to the left side of the audience.

If a state flag is used, it is placed at stage left, with the lectern between the two flags. If the organization or association has its own flag, it is placed at far stage left, to the left side of the state flag.

When international flags are displayed (in the United States), the American flag is placed at the far stage right.

Rest Room Facilities

If the location has permanent rest room facilities, be sure they are unlocked, clean, and well lit. If your outdoor location is not equipped with rest room facilities, arrange for one portable toilet for every 100 guests. Deluxe portable sanitation facilities are available in mobile trailers and provide regular commodes, sinks, and lighting—rather than the portable single-stall portable potties seen on construction sites. Be sure there are directional signs.

Tents

Functions are often held in tents, which are usually rented. Many sporting events, such as golf tournaments and steeplechase races, may have a variety of corporate tents set up to host their best clients. These are off-premise events.

Some facilities short of function space may opt to increase saleable space with a tent. Or a resort with a golf course, beach front property, or other scenic amenity may wish to hold events on the property but away from the main building. If a tent is infeasible, you may want to expand your saleable area with awnings. An awning is a rooflike structural overhang that is attached to a permanent building, to be used in case of rain or for shade.

At one time all tents were made of canvas, which is cotton treated with mineral oil to make it waterproof. However, canvas has fallen out of favor because it is highly flammable. There are a number of other tenting materials now available.

Tents must be anchored, usually with stakes and sandbags. There are mechanical stake drivers and stake pullers, which make the job of erecting the tent considerably easier than in years past.

A clear span tent has a structure that allows it to function without internal poles for support. This is preferable to having to work around poles. Some tents are modular, in that several standardized sections function together as one system.

Many tents now have clear vinyl roofs, windows, and/or doors, to let light in and eliminate the claustrophobic feeling. It is not advisable to use vinyl in very cold climates. When the temperature falls below 0°F, vinyl often cracks.

Tents now come with a number of accessories:

○ Flooring and/or carpet
○ Dance floor
○ Heaters, air conditioners, fans
○ Power generator
○ Lighting
○ Hinged doors

When erecting a tent, make sure the ground is level. If the ground is not level and it rains, the inside of the tented area can get water runoff and become quite muddy.

Portable air conditioners or heaters are optional. When placing tents with clear vinyl on one side, be careful not to position the clear side toward the west if the party will be taking place during sunset hours.

Tents can be used solely for protecting the food area, or they may contain an entire party. It is common for one or more sides to be open to allow free movement in and out.

"Tent seating" is the number of people who can be accommodated under a tent. Following is the information needed to determine the size of tent you need:

A 16′ × 16′ tent will hold—

○ 45 people for a reception
○ 32 people for a buffet with seating
○ 24 people for a served dinner

A 20′ × 20′ tent will hold—

○ 65 people for a reception
○ 56 people for a buffet with seating
○ 40 people for a served dinner

A 20′ × 30′ tent will hold—

○ 100 people for a reception
○ 86 people for a buffet with seating
○ 60 people for a served dinner

A 30′ × 30′ tent will hold—

○ 180 people for a reception
○ 124 people for a buffet with seating
○ 100 people for a served dinner

A 40′ × 40′ tent will hold—

○ 350 people for a reception
○ 280 people for a buffet with seating
○ 240 people for a served dinner

Production and *Chapter* Service Planning 7

Production and service planning must be correlated with client needs to ensure smooth-running functions, satisfied guests, and fair profits. All factors must be evaluated so that the appropriate plans can be developed and implemented. Coordination is vital. Attention to detail is essential. And every detail is critical. You cannot take anything for granted. (See the Appendix for a sample Catering Function Checklist.)

 ## PRODUCTION PLANNING

A production plan lists the types and amounts of finished foods and beverages needed, when they must be ready, and when they should be produced. It also includes set-up timing and procedures. The chef and banquet manager must have copies of the banquet event orders (BEOs) so that they can incorporate them into the daily production and work schedules.

Quantity of Food Needed

The chef has to requisition foods from the storeroom. If a member of the kitchen staff needs something unusual that the catering operation does not normally carry in stock, he or she will have to prepare a purchase requisition a few days before the meal function and give it to the purchasing department. The purchasing agent will then have enough time to shop around for the product and get the best possible value.

The amount of food that must be requisitioned and produced depends primarily on the following:

○ Number of guests expected
○ Style of service
○ Expected edible yields

You should plan to prepare enough foods to handle the guaranteed guest count, plus a set percentage above that amount. Generally speaking, if the guarantee is 100 guests, plan for 10 percent more; if the guarantee ranges from 100 to 1,000 guests, plan for 5 percent more; and if the guarantee exceeds 1,000 guests, plan for 3 percent more.

If the guests are having a sit-down, preplated meal, it is less difficult to compute the food requisition amounts because you can control the portion sizes. For instance, if the main course is roast bottom round of beef, the serving size is 6 cooked ounces, and the expected edible yield percentage for the raw roast beef is 75 percent, you will need to requisition approximately 55 pounds of raw beef for a party of 100 guests. Fifty-five pounds will serve 110 guests, 100 plus an extra 10 guests. The calculations are as follows:

1 Divide serving size by edible yield percentage. This will tell you how much raw product you need per serving.

6 ounces/.75 = 8 ounces

2 Divide 16 ounces by the amount of raw product needed per serving. This will tell you the number of edible servings you can get from one raw pound of beef roast.

16 ounces/8 ounces = 2 servings

3 Divide the number of guests by the number of edible servings per raw pound. This will give you the amount of raw beef roast you must requisition.

110 servings/2 = 55 raw pounds

If you plan to use reception and/or buffet service for a meal function, it is more difficult to determine the amount of foods to requisition and to produce. There are some rules of thumb, however, that can help you make a reasonable estimate. For instance, at a reception where foods are displayed on buffet tables, guests will generally consume approximately seven hors d'oeuvres during the first hour of a reception, and fewer during the succeeding time.

Another rule of thumb suggests that guests will typically consume much less if there is a lot of mandatory "socializing," forcing them to visit and rub shoulders, thereby keeping them away from the food trays.

Another rule of thumb suggests that blue-collar persons will eat and drink more than white-collar and pink-collar employees.

Still another rule of thumb notes that if you crowd people into a room, they tend to eat and drink less than if they have more space to roam around. A crowded room makes it more difficult for guests to revisit the buffet tables.

As discussed earlier, the way you display your foods on a buffet table will encourage or discourage overconsumption. For instance, putting the less expensive items up front, the more expensive items farther back, and having chefs portion and serve some of the entrées can give you an extra margin of control.

In some cases, you may not be very concerned if you overproduce foods for a buffet. For instance, if you can get the client to agree to select the same menu items that are used in your other food outlets, overproduction is no problem because you can recycle any leftovers. If the menu items cannot be recycled, either you must be a good estimator or you will have to increase your competitive bid price for the catered meal function to take into account the additional food costs. This is even more stressful to accomplish if you have a policy that absolutely forbids any food stock-outs.

Unfortunately, it is very difficult to make an accurate determination of the amount of food to requisition and produce when you are dealing with self-service buffets and receptions unless you sell foods by the piece and clients agree to purchase a set amount. For that matter, even per-person pricing can be based on specific amounts and types of food items offered.

If there are no restrictions on a self-service function, however, you cannot compute reasonably accurate estimates unless there is a great deal of relevant historical data upon which to base them. Even if you do take a lot of time to estimate your needs, you have limited control over the serving sizes. As a result, you must always add a margin of safety to avoid food stock-outs.

Quantity of Beverage Needed

It is much easier to determine the amount of alcoholic beverages you will need than it is to forecast your food requirements. Unlike food, beverages are standardized, manufactured products. You do not have to worry about spoilage or quality and yield variations. Furthermore, as long as your liquor storeroom is well stocked, you will never run out of product. You cannot quickly prepare and serve an extra roast beef dinner if you are out of cooked roast beef, but as long as there are beverages in-house, you can make drinks.

Banquet and reception bars are usually set up with a par stock of beverages, ice, glassware, garnishes, and other necessary supplies about a half hour to an hour before the catered event is scheduled to begin.

The normal par stock used is influenced by the following factors:

○ Number of guests expected
○ The caterer's experience with similar events
○ Amount of storage space available at the bar

Joseph E. Seagram & Sons Inc. has developed rules of thumb that can be used to estimate the approximate amount of liquor needed for an average reception of 100 guests. For instance, if you have 100 guests, you would expect about half of them to consume about 3 glasses of wine apiece during the reception. Inasmuch as each 750-milliliter bottle of wine contains about 5 drinks, you will need about thirty 750-milliliter bottles. Consumption trends indicate that you will need about 25 bottles of white or sparkling wine and 5 bottles of red. (Generally, for every 2 bottles of red served, you should expect to serve 10 bottles of white or sparkling wine.)

Joseph E. Seagram & Sons Inc. also suggests that during the typical reception for 100 guests, 50 percent of them will consume 3 spirit drinks apiece. To accommodate the group adequately, consumption trends indicate that the basic portable bar should be stocked as follows:

Type of Spirit	No. of Liters
Blend	1
Canadian	1
Scotch	2
Bourbon	1
Gin	1
Vodka	3
Rum	2
Brandy/Cognac	1

Generally, you should expect liquor consumption to average at least 2½ drinks per guest during a one-hour reception, particularly if the event attracts a mixed-company crowd. Average consumption tends to drop at very large receptions, and it usually increases at male-only events. However, if you schedule enough help and stock enough inventory to handle 2½ drinks per hour, you should be able to accommodate any type of beverage function adequately.

If the beverage function's drink menu varies significantly from the type you normally serve, bartenders will have to change the types and amounts of beverages usually stocked at the portable bars. For instance, if a drink menu will offer only red and white table wines, gin, bourbon, vodka, Scotch, and an assortment of soft drinks, the bartender will have to adjust the typical par stock requisitioned from the liquor storeroom.

Usually you do not have to worry about stocking an exact amount of beverages at the banquet or reception bars because you can always depend on the bar back to replenish the supply quickly. You should, however, make an effort to forecast your needs as accurately as possible because this will help ensure a smoothly running event. In addition, if beverages have to be iced down, it behooves you to make sure that you have plenty of ice and beverages available; you cannot take a room-temperature item and chill it quickly unless you have the specialized equipment needed to do this.

In most instances, it makes no difference whether you overstock a banquet or reception bar because the merchandise can be used at other bars in your facility. However, if you need to purchase specific beverages for a function that will not be used in other bars, you will need to compute as accurately as possible the amount you should order.

For example, a meal function may require a unique dinner wine that must be special-ordered by the purchasing agent. If the expected guest count is 100, you will need to order enough wine to serve 110 persons. Usually you will estimate 2½ servings of wine per guest for the typical dinner banquet. In this instance, you will need to order enough wine to serve 275 glasses (110 × 2.5). Because the standard wineglass holds a 5-ounce portion (approximately 148 millileters [ml]), you will need to special order about fifty-five 750-ml bottles of wine. The calculation is as follows:

1   Divide the amount of liquor per 750-ml bottle by the serving size. This will tell you how many possible drinks you can obtain per container.

750 ml/148 ml = 5.07 possible drinks per bottle

2   Divide the number of servings needed by the number of possible drinks per container. This will tell you how many containers you will need to special order.

275 servings/5.07 = 54.24 750-ml bottles, rounded to
fifty-five 750 ml bottles needed

If you take into account overpouring, waste, and the fact that you usually cannot get all of the liquid out of a bottle (some of it will stick to the sides), you will need to increase your special-order size. For instance, if you assume that you will lose 1 ounce (approximately 30 ml) per 750-ml bottle, your special-order size will be about fifty-seven 750-ml bottles of wine. The calculation is as follows:

720 ml/148 ml = 4.86 possible drinks per bottle
275 servings/4.86 = 56.58 750-ml bottles, rounded to 57 750-ml bottles needed

Some suppliers may not allow you to special order anything in less than case-size lots. In our example, then, you may need to special order sixty 750-ml bottles (5 cases, 12 bottles per case) because the liquor distributor may not want to break a case for you. If you are faced with this situation, you may need to add a liquor surcharge to the client's final billing.

Alternately, you may charge the client for only the amount of wine consumed, keep the leftover product, and run it as a special for another event. Some unopened leftovers might also find their way into complimentary fruit baskets for favorite clients who generate a good deal of business for you.

If the catered event is held in a hotel or country club, opened and unopened wine can be sent to the client's hospitality suite or used for another function the client is planning. For instance, if the client has booked three meal functions, perhaps the leftover wine can be used for the next event.

The supplier may be willing to exchange unopened leftovers for something you normally use. Although the typical supplier may not want to take back in trade one or two bottles, he or she is usually quite willing to take back unopened cases in trade. If the client agrees, you can charge the client by the case, order extra from the supplier, keep the few leftover loose bottles, and return the unopened cases to the supplier.

Another alternative is to charge the client by the bottle or by the case and let him or her take home any leftover wine. Before you do this, however, check the local liquor code to see whether it is legal. For instance, your property may need to hold a package goods liquor license before you can let the client take home unopened liquor. And opened stock may have to be served solely for consumption on premises.

To avoid the leftover problem, you might special order, say, four cases of wine (forty-eight 750-ml bottles), put it all out on the dining tables, and when it runs out, back it up with another wine. However, make sure that you advise the client before doing this.

Quality of Food Needed

The quality of foods used is dictated by the product specifications and standardized recipes prepared by management. For instance, a catering operation that is part of a chain organization typically has a vice president of purchasing and a vice president of food and beverage operations on the corporate level, who usually have the final responsibility for making determinations about quality.

Before you requisition foods, you must examine the standardized recipes very carefully so that you know exactly what you need. For example, if the corporate recipe calls for Kraft cheese, you must requisition cheese of this brand name. You cannot requisition another brand of cheese because the recipe is specifically geared for Kraft. Other brands are not quite comparable, and the finished product will not be the same if you substitute another brand.

The same holds true for other product identification factors. You must requisition the correct product quality, size, color, package size, degree of preservation, type of processing, and so forth, if you expect to maintain quality control. Actual quality that differs from the standard, expected quality, no matter how slight, is unacceptable.

In addition to quality control, product specifications and standardized recipes help ensure cost control. When you cost out your standardized recipes, you will use purchase prices based on the types of ingredients noted in them. If you use a substitute and do not account for any difference in cost, your final accounting will show an actual food cost that is more or less than that for which you budgeted. If the actual cost exceeds the budgeted standard cost, the operation will suffer a loss. If the actual is less than the standard cost, clients will be cheated because they will have received foods that were inconsistent with the menu prices quoted.

Quality of Beverage Needed

As with food, the quality of beverages served will depend on the product specifications and standardized recipes used to prepare finished drinks. However, there is usually one more thing to consider with beverages: the client's desire to have certain brand names of liquor served at the catered event.

Some clients do not specify brand names. Because well brands usually cost less than call brands, some clients will be satisfied with them. Yet consumer preferences indicate that although people today are drinking less, they are drinking higher-quality products. Premium brands are in vogue, and more clients are asking the caterer to provide a choice of high-quality wines, spirits, and beers.

Brand names are the primary selection factors used in developing liquor product specifications, standardized recipes, drink menus, and stock requisitions. However, when requisitioning liquor from the liquor storeroom, there are a few additional factors that must be noted.

For instance, you will need to note the container sizes for each product needed. In general, for spirits, you will use 750 ml or 1 liter (l) bottles if you free-pour the drinks, and 1.5 l or 1.75 l bottles if you use an electronic dispensing unit to prepare drinks.

When requisitioning beers, more than likely you will want 12-ounce bottles or cans. If you have a portable draft beer dispensing unit, you would requisition the appropriate keg size that fits it.

Wines come in various container sizes. Generally, this flexibility allows the client more cost-saving opportunities. For instance, you can purchase wines in 750-ml and 1.5 l bottles. Less expensive products, such as well wines (i.e., house wines), can be purchased in larger bottles and in bag-in-the-box containers (i.e., a large plastic bag of wine inside a cardboard box that is designed to be used as a self-dispensing package).

As with food, your drink product specifications and standardized recipes help to ensure cost and quality control. Without these guidelines, it will be very difficult to forecast accurately the alcoholic beverage costs. In this case, price quotations offered to potential clients may not be as competitive as they should be.

Food Pre-preparation

Food pre-preparation (i.e., pre-prep) activities are generally performed a day or more before the meal function. They include all the food production steps that can be performed ahead of time that will not compromise the quality of finished menu items. For instance, if the menu calls for vegetables and dip, a pantry person can prepare these items the day before and refrigerate them. Or if the menu calls for an egg action station, a cook can pre-prep the egg mixes, dice the vegetables, and lay out the bacon on sheet pans the night before.

In general, the larger the function, the more pre-prep that must be done. For instance, a banquet of 5,000 prime rib dinners may require you to start pre-plating the meals several hours in advance and putting them in a hot cart. You would start out plating the rare portions, and end up plating the well-done portions. Alternately, you could plate the cooked meat cold the day before, hold under refrigeration, and heat, sauce, and garnish prior to serving.

Some caterers have adopted the *sous-vide* form of pre-preparation. This involves the production of finished or semifinished menu items about a week or more before they are needed. After they are produced, the foods are then vacuum packed and stored in the refrigerator until needed. Commercially prepared *sous-vide* products are also available.

Sous-vide production has expanded the number and types of menu items that can be pre-prepared. For instance, if you have a party next week and grilled salmon steaks will be on the menu, today you can sear, season, vacuum package, and then cook them in their plastic pouches. When done, the individually packaged steaks must be cooled rapidly and stored in the refrigerator. A few minutes before service, you reheat and plate them.

Sous-vide offers several culinary advantages. For instance, grilled salmon steaks can be cooked in their own juices and seasonings and several of them can be served at one time. Following normal cooking procedures, you would be unable to serve grilled salmon steaks to a large group of people while simultaneously maintaining quality control.

Unfortunately, *sous-vide* procedures can contribute to food-borne illness if they are not monitored closely. Sanitation is extremely important when food is vacuum packaged. If harmful bacteria are left in the package, some guests consuming the food may become ill.

The menu planner should try to include as many pre-prep items as possible. This makes it much easier to plan food production. It gives you more control over work schedules and allows you to utilize production labor more efficiently. It also ensures that the correct amount of foods will be available when it is time to prepare the finished products.

Bar Pre-preparation

Bar pre-prep is much easier than food pre-prep. Generally, it includes stocking the portable bars with all nonperishables whenever it is convenient to do so. Then, just prior to service, you pre-prep the nonliquor garnishes, requisition the liquor, load the ice bins, and ice down the wine bottles and bottles or cans of beer.

If the banquet bars are permanent or semipermanent fixtures, bar backs and/or bartenders can restock them after a catered event according to the specifications noted on the banquet event order (BEO) for the next function. For instance, when a party is over, the manager can take an ending inventory and determine the liquor usage for that function. The bar back and/or bartender can then replenish the bar with nonperishables so that the bar production workers the next day need only spend a few minutes pre-preping the perishables.

Food Preparation

Food preparation (i.e., prep) activities are performed just prior to the point of service. For example, your preparation schedule for hot foods should dovetail with your guest-service schedule. You would not want to produce these products too far in advance, or they will lose culinary quality. Nor would you want to produce them to customer order, as this will slow service.

A good food production schedule combines the pre-prep and prep activities. For instance, if you have a baked chicken item on the menu, you can do some pre-prep work the night before, such as washing the products, seasoning them, and laying them out on sheet pans. About an hour or so before service, you will prep them, that is, put them in the oven to cook.

Finish Cooking

Finish cooking involves cooking to guest order. For instance, the chef must wait for a guest to order a rare steak; he or she does not prep it in advance.

Finish cooking is the most difficult part of the food production plan. It is also the most labor-intensive. You must schedule a lot of worker hours, and the worker hours must be provided by highly skilled food handlers who can work under the demanding conditions that accompany most finish-cooking activities.

For instance, a chef working at an egg action station must be quick, efficient, and accurate. He or she will normally be producing two or three guest orders at a time and will need to remember them, as well as those that are coming in from other guests waiting in line.

Of course, some finish cooking is easier than others. For instance, with a roast beef item, you can pre-prep the roast the night before, prep it two or three hours before service, and finish cook it—carve and serve it—to customer order. In this case, the finish cooking involves a relatively easy task.

Bar Preparation

In most instances, bar prep is synonymous with bar service; that is, the same person who prepares the drink also serves it and, if applicable, collects cash or a drink ticket.

In those instances when a service bar is used, that is, a bar used by cocktail servers to obtain drinks for their guests, the prep and service activities are separated. The bartender preps drinks only when the servers order them. For cost-control purposes, a server must usually give a precheck ticket or some other record, such as a duplicate guest check or a computer-generated precheck, to the bartender before a drink can be prepared. In addition, the servers usually are also responsible for collecting cash or drink tickets.

Food Workstation Setup

Action stations, serving lines, and buffet tables must be set up prior to service. In some catering operations, the kitchen staff has this responsibility, whereas other facilities split the work between the kitchen and service staffs. For instance, cooks may be responsible for setting up the serving lines in the kitchen or in the service corridor and for setting up the action stations, and the kitchen and banquet setup crews together set up the buffet tables. In general, the kitchen handles the foods and the service staff handles the table setups.

Replenishing the Food Workstations

The kitchen is normally responsible for replenishing the food supplies on buffet tables, action stations, and serving lines. Usually a food runner is employed to handle this task. In some cases, however, the service staff may take on this duty. For instance, the kitchen crew may be responsible for stocking backup foods in hot carts and delivering them to a service corridor. A food server can then be assigned to replenish depleted food workstations with foods taken from these hot carts.

Employees assigned this responsibility typically must do more than merely refill serving containers. They must be able to anticipate customer needs, combine half-empty pans and make the combination appear as attractive as any other container, and react to the chef's last-minute instructions. They may also have to pitch in and help keep buffet tables and landing spaces clear of soiled tableware and trash.

Replenishing the Bars

Bar backs are responsible for replenishing liquor, ice, garnishes, glassware, and operating supplies such as coasters, swizzle sticks, and cocktail napkins. Most bartenders will also jump in and help restock merchandise in an emergency, such as when the bar back is helping out at another beverage function that is short-handed.

Cocktail servers may also help out in a pinch. For instance, if there are one or two special drink requests that cannot be prepared by the bartender because he or she does not have the stock available, a cocktail server may just go to another bar to fill them. Or if there are no other bars open in the catering operation, a cocktail server may go behind the bar temporarily and help the bartender to catch up.

Number of Food Production People Needed

Food production differs somewhat from food service in that food handlers usually have responsibility for food production throughout the catering operation. They may also be responsible for food production in other restaurants. For example, catering in a hotel or club may be part of the central kitchen's duties; handling the catered meal function may not be its only duty. Whereas the banquet service staff concentrates solely on the scheduled meal function to which it is assigned, the typical food handler must juggle many tasks.

It is therefore a bit more difficult to determine exactly how much food production labor is needed for a particular meal function. On one hand, the cooks on duty in a restaurant outlet may be able to handle the entire catered event along with their other responsibilities. On the other hand, a catered function may require a completely separate kitchen crew. For some meal functions, you may not have any additional variable labor costs; yet for others, the food production payroll will be a significant portion of total expenses.

In general, the number of food production work hours needed for a catered event will depend on the following:

○ *Number of guests.*
○ *Amount of time scheduled* for the catered event.
○ *Applicable union and company personnel policies.*
○ *Type of service style used.*   For instance, action stations require more production labor, whereas the typical buffet that offers only standardized menu items will need less.
○ *Amount of convenience foods used.*   Processed foods are less expensive to prep and serve. You need fewer labor hours to reconstitute them. You also avoid expensive labor expertise because the products require less skill to handle. However, their purchase prices are usually very high because of the built-in labor and energy costs that the manufacturer must capture.
○ *Amount of scratch production.*   This is the opposite of convenience food usage. The closer a food ingredient is to its natural state, the lower its purchase price. A significant amount of scratch production results in a low food cost. However, you will end up with a high labor cost inasmuch as you take on all of the pre-prep and prep burdens. If the local labor market is tight, the resulting labor cost incurred may be prohibitive.
○ *Amount of finish cooking needed.*   Too much finish cooking wreaks havoc with a food production labor budget. If the client wants a great deal of foods prepared this way, chances are that he or she must be willing to pay a handsome labor surcharge.
○ *Type of menu items offered.*   Some products take more time to pre-prep and prep. For instance, it takes more time to produce meat

loaf than roast beef, vegetable soup than onion soup, and gallan-
tine of capon than roast duckling.

○ *Number of last-minute requests.*   Flexibility is one of the hallmarks
of a successful catering operation. You must be flexible enough to
accommodate some unscheduled requests. For instance, you
should be ready to produce one or two vegetarian meals at a moment's notice. Ideally, clients will inform you well in advance
about special needs; however, chances are that there will be at
least one guest requesting an off-menu item at the last minute.

○ *Number of special diets.*   It can take almost as long to produce two
or three special diets as it does to take care of 50 standard guest
meals. If you know about these needs in advance, you can be
ready for them. Furthermore, once you start producing a different
menu item for each guest, you immediately lose the labor and
food cost advantages enjoyed by catering as opposed to regular
restaurant food production and service.

○ *Accuracy of mealtime estimates.*   It is not unusual for a meal function to start late and end late. This, unfortunately, may result in
overtime premium pay for some production staff. It also can require overtime premium pay in other departments, such as housekeeping and convention service in hotels, because their work
schedules may be thrown out of line.

When catered functions run behind schedule, you must expect to
incur a higher labor cost. It is also likely that the foods lose a good
deal of their culinary quality. Ironically, when this scenario occurs, the
guests can cause you to pay more for the privilege of hearing them
complain about the foods' marginal quality.

Some catering managers prepare staffing charts to help them determine the number of food production work hours needed, how many
persons to call in to work the function, and how these people should
be scheduled. Such charts usually relate the number of work hours
needed to the number of expected guests. For instance, if you expect
100 guests, you go down the column headed by 100 and in each cell
there will be a number of suggested work hours needed for each job
position.

Assume you are allowed 16 food production hours for 100 guests.
If the meal function will last four hours, you can divide the 16 work
hours into four 4-hour shifts and bring in four persons. You might also
schedule one 8-hour person and two 4-hour employees, or you can
plan any other acceptable combination.

How you apportion the allowable number of work hours will depend on many of the factors discussed earlier. For instance, if the menu requires a considerable amount of pre-prep, perhaps you should have an 8-hour person come in the day before. A great deal of finish cooking implies an opposite strategy.

Distributing work hours over a work schedule also depends on how many food production persons you want on board before, during, and after the meal function. Usually, you will have to stagger the work schedule in such a way that most of your production work hours are used when the lion's share of the production must be completed, with the remaining hours left over to cover the start-up and teardown periods.

Staffing charts work much better in the typical restaurant operation where the menu, production, and service are standardized and there is a consistent pattern of customer arrivals and departures, popularity of menu items, and amount of time it takes to turn the tables. They also work well in service planning because once you know the timing of the function, as well as the menu, number of guests, and style of service needed, you can usually lock into a standardized work schedule.

Kitchen staffing charts must be continually revised unless your catering business settles into some sort of predictable pattern. The director of catering will usually keep a close eye on the staffing chart and change it as needed. He or she will also be forever looking for that elusive pattern that can make it much easier to forecast food production payroll expenses and develop accurate food production work schedules.

Number of Bar Backs and Bartenders Needed

The number of bar backs needed for a catered function will depend primarily on the following:

○ Number of bars scheduled
○ Capacity of each bar to hold in-process inventories
○ Distance between the bars and the kitchen and storerooms
○ Degree of ease or difficulty associated with retrieving backup stock
○ Number of guests
○ Hours of operation
○ Variety of liquor stock, glassware, garnishes, and operating supplies needed at the bars
○ Applicable union and company personnel policies

Unless the catered event is very small, you will need at least one bar back. The typical banquet bar, especially a portable one, does not have a lot of storage capacity. It will usually need periodic replenishment.

If a small beverage function is scheduled, perhaps the bartender can do double duty and take on the bar back's responsibility. However, it can reduce service efficiency and cause guest dissatisfaction if the bartender is in the liquor storeroom and temporarily unavailable to prepare drinks.

The number of bartenders needed for a catered event will depend primarily on the following:

○ Number of bars scheduled
○ Types of drinks that must be prepared
○ Number of drinks that must be prepared
○ Number of guests
○ Hours of operation
○ Amount of bar back work that must be performed
○ Applicable union and company personnel policies

You will need at least one bartender for each bar location. For large beverage functions, you would usually schedule two bartenders for each bar plus any wine service personnel needed for the meal. Even for small beverage functions of, say, 50 to 60 guests, you may need two bartenders, or more, if the event is scheduled for only 45 minutes to an hour. In this case, speed is a high priority. With such a short time frame, guests will normally swamp the bar to make sure they get their desired number of drinks before it closes. One bartender may be unable to handle this onslaught.

For large beverage functions, such as a convention's opening night cocktail reception, a caterer generally tries to get by with one bartender for every 100 guests, whereas the typical professional meeting and convention planner prefers a ratio of one bartender for every 75 guests. The 1/75 ratio is usually the minimum necessary if you expect all guests to arrive at the same time. If you do not have enough bartenders when a crowd hits the door, some guests may have to wait for as much as an hour to get a drink.

If there are more than 1,000 guests, the ratio of one bartender to each 100 guests is appropriate. With a larger crowd, guests cannot move around as much. And with eight to ten bartenders, preparation and service tend to be quicker and more efficient because the bartenders can help each other and keep the lines moving.

The timing of a beverage function can also influence the number of bartenders needed. For instance, if 200 persons are leaving a business meeting at a large hotel or club and going directly to a cocktail reception, you many want to set a ratio of one bartender for each 50 guests so that they will be served quickly. If there is a break period between the end of the business meeting and the beginning of the cocktail reception, during which guests can take the time to go home or to their hotel rooms to freshen up, they will not arrive all at once. They will usually come in a few at a time. Consequently, you can use fewer bartenders to handle this group.

To alleviate pressure on the bartenders, you can schedule a few cocktail servers to pass glasses of champagne, still wines, bottled waters, and juices. This service also adds an extra touch of elegance to the event.

If the catered function calls for cocktail servers and/or a sommelier, perhaps you can reduce the number of bar backs and bartenders you would normally schedule. For instance, one cocktail server can be cross-trained (that is, to be a combination bartender and cocktail server) and scheduled as a floater (to fill in as a bartender or server as needed). Such flexibility can easily save a few labor hours over the long term.

By the same token, a food server, bus person, captain, or other member of the catering and kitchen staffs can be used to help out the bartenders and bar backs. For instance, it may be more economical to schedule one 6-hour bus person to handle busing and bar back duties than to schedule one 4-hour bar back and one 4-hour bus person.

If you decide to mix and match job positions and adopt these types of creative scheduling techniques, you will have to check the joint bargaining agreement, if applicable, and/or the company's personnel policies and procedures manual to see whether they are permissible. Furthermore, you must ensure that the relevant staff members have received the proper type and amount of cross-training.

Number of Cashiers Needed

If a cashier is needed to sell drink tickets, you will have to have at least one on duty. Normally, you will need only one cashier if the catered function is small or if it is a leisurely event where guests are not pressed for time. Larger functions, as well as those for which speed is essential, require more cashiers. Under these conditions, you generally will have to schedule one cashier for every two bartenders.

If you are using cashiers, you may want to schedule a plainclothes security guard to supervise and protect the cash-handling operations. A plainclothes guard is sometimes preferable to a uniformed guard because some guests may become a bit anxious if they see uniformed security.

If you have a security guard scheduled to supervise the liquor service, and if the group being serviced is not too large, he or she can also oversee the cash-handling operations. With a large group of guests, however, you should consider scheduling at least one security guard to supervise liquor preparation and service and one to oversee the cash-handling procedures.

Number of Ticket Takers Needed

If guests must use tickets to enter a function room, or if they need to use them to get into a meal or beverage function, you may or may not need to schedule a ticket taker to collect tickets. In most cases, clients will handle this chore personally; however, on some occasions you will be asked to provide such service.

Ideally, the client handles the collection of all entry tickets. You should avoid coming between the client and his or her guests in any kind of potential confrontation. You do not want to be put in a position where you must impose client-mandated sanctions on guests. Furthermore, some guests may not appreciate the caterer's assuming this position of control.

Drink tickets and similar tickets (such as entrée or concession tickets used by guests at meal functions) do not usually cause problems involving confrontation. Consequently, if guests are required to use them, there generally is no need to schedule separate ticket takers. In these cases, bartenders, servers, and chefs can collect the tickets.

Number of Banquet Setup Crew Members Needed

The number of persons needed to set up, tear down, and clean a function room will depend primarily on the following:

○ Amount of lead time available.
○ Size of the catered event.
○ Size of the room or other location.
○ Whether the room or other location is on your property or off-site.
○ Amount of time available between functions. For example, how much time do you have to tear down and clean up after a breakfast function and set up for an afternoon reception?

○ Whether you have to set up the entire room or just part of it. For instance, if you are catering off-site, the client may handle part of the setup. Or if you are catering a meal function at a local hall rented by the client, part of the rental fee may include room setup.

○ Applicable union and company personnel policies.

If you have a lot of time available, and/or if the function planned is for 50 guests or less, you can usually get by with only one crew member. For larger functions, or if time is precious, usually no fewer than two persons must be scheduled. Two or more crew members may also be needed if some tasks require the strength and agility of at least two persons to accomplish. For example, setting up a platform, rolling out and setting up a portable dance floor, or hanging signage or decorations often requires two persons working in tandem.

Usually, a caterer wants function rooms set up as soon as possible. All nonperishable items should be set out in advance so that staff members can concentrate on the last-minute details and not have to worry about doing things during "prime" times (i.e., times when guest service is a priority) that could have been done quite comfortably during slack times (i.e., downtimes when guests are not being served).

 # SERVICE PLANNING

Service planning is a much easier task than production planning. Once you know the timing of the function, the menu, the number of guests, and the style of service, you can usually develop an accurate estimate of the number of service work hours needed, the number and types of servers required, and the most efficient work schedule to be followed.

Types of Servers Needed

Depending on the type of catered event, the banquet manager will have to schedule one or more of the following types of service personnel:

○ Maître d' hôtel
○ Captain
○ Food server
○ Cocktail server

○ Sommelier
○ Food runner
○ Bus person

Service Duties

Service personnel are responsible for a wide array of duties. Unlike production staff members, servers are often called upon to jump in at a moment's notice and handle unscheduled requests and/or activities. For instance, although the typical client would not consider asking the chef to change the menu at the last minute, he or she may not be shy about asking the maître d' hôtel to set up an extra dining table, slow the service because the speaker is running a bit late, or push two tables together so that a larger group can create its own party atmosphere.

Service personnel must be very flexible. All of them should be trained to perform the following functions:

Napkin folding.

Table setting.

Placing table pads and tablecloths.

Presetting foods on dining tables.

Greeting/seating guests.

Taking food/beverage orders from guests (if applicable). This is done only if guests have a choice of entreés and/or beverages.

Serving food and beverages.

Submitting food/beverage guest orders to chefs and bartenders (if applicable). As with taking orders from guests, this would be done only if guests have a choice of entreés and/or beverages.

Opening wine bottles.

Pouring wine.

Hot beverage service.

Cold beverage service.

Crumbing tables.

Busing tables.

Carrying loaded cocktail, oval, and crescent-shaped trays.

Stacking trays.

Emptying trays.

Tableside preparation.

Using different service styles.

Handling last-minute requests for food, beverages, and/or service.

Handling complaints.

Directing guests to other facilities at the site. Although this can be done for on-site events, it is a bit more difficult to convey such information if the caterer does a lot of its business at off-premises locations.

Handling disruptions.

Dealing with intoxicated guests.

Refusing liquor service to minors.

Requisitioning tableware and linens.

Service Ratios

Service ratios, that is, the numbers of service personnel needed to handle given numbers of guests, are usually established by management. These ratios are the heart of the service staffing guide.

The number of service personnel needed depends on many factors, primary among which are the following:

○ *Number of guests.*
○ *Length of the catered function.*
○ *Style of service used.*
○ *Menu, especially its length and complexity.*
○ *Timing of the event.*   For instance, you may need more servers if there will be a considerable amount of time between courses and other activities, such as guests' listening to speakers, dancing, or watching stage shows. Similarly, if the group must be fed very quickly, you will need more service personnel; however, because you will not need them very long, you may be able to handle such an event adequately without exceeding your labor budget.
○ *Room setup.*   Is the layout and design conducive to quick, efficient service, or should bottlenecks be expected?
○ *Location of function room.*   How much distance is there between the kitchen and the function room? How easily can you go from the kitchen to the function room? Is there sufficient aisle space? Is the service corridor large enough? Are there enough service elevators?

○ *The probability that overtime must be scheduled.*   For instance, experience may suggest that a particular type of catered event, and/or a particular type of group, tends to run late. This eventuality may result in overtime premium pay for a few service personnel. However, if you can anticipate this problem, you should be able to schedule enough employees to handle the event properly without resorting to overtime.

○ *Number of head table guests.*   These guests require much more service attention than others.

○ *The number and type of extraordinary requests.*   For instance, a client may want extra labor to seat guests after they go through a buffet line. Some guests may request extra condiments, which will add to the service work load. And some clients, at the last minute, may want the room rearranged somewhat; the service personnel usually have to handle this type of last-minute request because the setup crew may be unavailable on short notice.

○ *Applicable union and company personnel policies.*   Unionized caterers may schedule only the minimum number of service personnel called for in the union contract. Nonunion facilities whose competitors are unionized may also follow these standard ratios.

The minimum number of servers, as well as the minimum number of each service job classification, that must be scheduled according to union regulations is usually insufficient to provide the level of service required by most catered events. You will generally need more servers if, for example, you have to serve a large luncheon very quickly or you must provide Banquet French service for a dinner function.

The union's joint bargaining agreement requirements typically provide enough servers to accommodate only small and/or easy-to-handle groups. These service minimums, however, at least give you something to work with when forecasting the number of servers needed.

Many caterers develop strict service ratios and do not vary from them even though a particular situation may call for an adjustment. For instance, some properties will budget one server for every 32 guests regardless of the style of service, the type of menu, or whether the servers are responsible for wine service.

If you adhere strictly to this 1:32 ratio, you may risk customer dissatisfaction. Some catered events can be handled adequately under this payroll-cost constraint. However, most functions will need more help, or else they cannot be serviced efficiently.

Irrespective of the quality of a catered function's food and beverages, room setup, and overall ambience, poor service reduces significantly the guests' appreciation and enjoyment of the event. National Restaurant Association (NRA) customer surveys consistently show that patrons rank the quality of service very high on their lists of desired restaurant attributes. They usually place it no lower than second on their lists, ranking it just slightly below the culinary quality of the food and beverages.

Poor service will overshadow any other favorable aspect of an event. Guests will never be pleased if the service is lacking. They will usually remember a bad experience much longer than a good one. The catering executive who tries to shave service costs to the bone will undoubtedly make a lot of clients and guests unhappy. He or she will also jeopardize repeat patronage.

If you are on a very tight labor budget, at times you will be between a rock and a hard place. You will be asked to maintain the budget, yet provide a level of service that will satisfy guests and encourage clients to return. You cannot risk coming in over budget. If the catered event's projected revenue will not cover the extra labor costs, the least you should do is ask the client to alter his or her menu or service requirements, or to agree to pay a modest labor surcharge so that you can schedule adequate staff.

The number of service personnel needed can vary from a low of about one staff member for every 8 guests to a high of approximately one staff member for every 40 guests.

The minimum service ratio for conventional sit-down meal functions with American-style service with some foods preset, is one server for every 20 guests. If you are using rounds of 10, you should schedule one server for every two dining tables. If you are using rounds of 8, two servers should be scheduled to handle five dining tables.

The minimum bus person ratio for this sit-down meal is one bus person for every three servers. If you are using rounds of 10, you should schedule one busperson for every six dining tables. If you are using rounds of 8, one bus person should be scheduled for every eight dining tables.

Some caterers schedule one bus person for every two servers. This is usually done for functions that include several VIPs or where extraordinary service is requested by the client. In general, however, you can make do with one bus person for every three servers because servers are normally expected to perform some busing work during a catered event.

If the conventional sit-down meal function includes Russian, Banquet French, or poured-wine service, you will normally need one server for every 16 guests. You should schedule one server for every two rounds of 8, or two servers for every three rounds of 10. One bus person for every six rounds of 10, or every eight rounds of 8, will usually suffice.

If the meal function includes Russian or Banquet French service, along with poured-wine service, you generally will need at least one server for each dining table and one bus person for every three dining tables. This ratio is appropriate whether you are using rounds of 8 or rounds of 10.

If the meal function is served buffet-style, servers and bus persons can usually handle significantly more guests. For instance, the minimum service ratio of one server for each 20 guests and one bus person for every three servers may very easily be increased to one server for every 40 guests and one busperson for every four servers.

In some cases you may want to maintain the ratio of one server for each 20 guests for a buffet-style meal function. For instance, if the kitchen schedules a small crew or if it has to handle several parties, it may be unable to refresh the buffet tables and help to serve guests. You might use the balance of your wait staff to focus on these tasks.

If the buffet requires considerable replenishment during a meal, you may need to schedule servers to handle the food-running chores. In this situation, normally one food runner (or other service employee) is needed for every 100 to 125 guests. You will need more runners if they are expected to accommodate several buffet stations spread throughout the function room. Conversely, if there are only a few buffet stations, other food servers who can share the workload, and/or a limited menu, you should be able to schedule fewer runners. Moreover, if the chef schedules the food runners, your scheduling task will be a bit easier.

Head tables usually receive the best service. If a catered function has head tables, plan to schedule at least one server for each head table. If a head table includes more than eight guests, you should assign two servers to accommodate them.

Ideally, the head table has its own bus person. If you cannot afford this, or do not need a separate bus person, you may assign the head table and one or two nearby dining tables to one bus person. If possible, you should not have head table servers handling both the serving and busing chores. They should devote their efforts to guest service.

Regardless of the style of service, you will usually have to schedule at least one floor supervisor. This supervisor may be a captain or a maître d' hôtel.

Generally, you should plan to schedule at least one captain for each catered event. For very large meal functions, plan to schedule one captain for every block of 250 guests (i.e., for every block of 25 rounds of 10). Alternately, you could schedule one captain for every ten to twelve servers.

The captain for a small catered event can supervise both the meal service and the reception service. For example, if there are only 100 guests, one floor supervisor is sufficient to handle both segments.

If you need to schedule more than one captain, assign one maître d' hôtel to coordinate their duties. For instance, if you have a meal function for 1,000 guests, you would typically assign one maître d' hôtel and four captains to supervise service. If there is a premeal reception, the maître d' hôtel should supervise both the meal service and the reception.

You should not try to serve a function without a sufficient number of floor supervisors. These men and women play an extremely important role in coordinating service and seeing to it that all guests are served efficiently. For instance, for a sit-down meal function, it is important to have each course served to all guests at approximately the same time. This will not happen by itself. It is a difficult feat to achieve and is almost impossible without adequate supervision and coordination.

If you need to staff a reception, you must schedule enough servers to supervise the food stations. In general, you should have one server responsible for every three food stations. If the stations are spread throughout the function room and there is considerable distance between each one, you will need more servers.

The servers responsible for overseeing the food stations can also perform some busing duties. For instance, they can help replenish the tableware, bus the landing space, and remove waste. Depending on the size and complexity of the reception, you may be able to get by with few or no bus persons.

You will need more servers if you intend to pass food trays butler-style during a reception. For a small catered event, one or two servers will suffice. As the function size increases, you normally need to schedule one server to handle one fourth of the function room, one eighth of the function room, and so forth. In general, you should plan to schedule at least two servers for every 75 guests. To conserve on the amount of food consumption, servers can be sent out in waves at timed intervals. Servers should be assigned to specific sections of the room to ensure that all guests have access to the food.

You also will need more bus persons if you have servers pass trays during the reception. The servers will usually be unable to pitch in and help with the busing duties because they will be too busy with guests. You should expect to schedule at least one bus person for every three to four servers.

Even if there is no food served during a reception, you still should schedule at least one or two bus persons to keep the landing space clear. Perhaps a dining room bus person or two can be brought in earlier than the others to cover the reception's busing needs; then, after the reception, they can help out during the meal function's rush period.

If you are using cocktail servers during a reception to pass trays of premade drinks, you will need at least one cocktail server for every two to three food servers. Usually, you need considerably fewer cocktail servers than food servers in this situation because guests tend to approach the food servers more frequently than they do the cocktail servers. For instance, a guest may take a glass of wine from a tray and nurse it all night, but that person will usually take more than one piece of food.

Very few catered events use cocktail servers to take guest drink orders, return to a service bar to fill them, and then go back on the floor to serve them. This type of service is infeasible for large-group functions. Generally, it is provided only for small functions, especially those that cater to VIPs. The typical kind of cocktail service used for standard catered events requires the guests to approach the portable bars, get their drinks, disappear into the crowd, and return when they want more drinks.

If you do use this type of cocktail service to take guest orders, however, your labor costs will increase significantly. In this situation, at best, a server can usually make only three or four passes per hour through his or her assigned floor area. During each pass, the server is usually able to carry, at most, only 12 to 16 drinks. In the best-case scenario, then, you would need one cocktail server to handle 48 to 64 drinks per hour. Furthermore, because this type of service is less efficient and requires more coordination and effort, you will need more bartenders to handle the work load.

Many receptions last only about one hour. Some last up to two hours. For a one-hour period, you normally expect each guest to consume at least 2½ drinks. For a two-hour period, you expect each guest to consume at least 3 drinks. If you have a one-hour cocktail reception for 100 persons, and the client wants cocktail servers to take drink orders from guests, you will need about three bartenders and five to six cocktail servers to handle the drink orders efficiently. If you have a two-hour reception, however, guests will not drink so quickly and some of them will tend to leave before the reception ends; consequently, you may be able to get by with fewer bartenders and cocktail servers. In this instance, unfortunately, most guests will do most of their drinking during the first hour, so you may be unable to reduce your service requirements significantly.

When clients are faced with the exorbitant labor cost associated with having cocktail servers take guests' orders, they generally decide against it. But even if a client is willing to pay the extra labor charges, you may still want to discourage such a labor-intensive style of service because there are too many opportunities for the catered event to bog down. For instance, at a predinner reception, if guests need to wait too long for their drinks, the reception, and ultimately the dinner, will probably run much longer than scheduled.

On the other hand, sometimes slower cocktail service can be a virtue. For instance, if there is a host bar at a cocktail reception, guests may be tempted to overindulge, whereas if they give their orders to a server, their consumption will probably be much less.

Work Scheduling

The banquet manager usually sets aside some time each week to prepare the service work schedules for the following week. Each week, he or she must prepare a fixed work schedule and a variable work schedule.

The fixed schedule represents the minimum number of persons and number of work hours needed to keep the catering operation open and active, regardless of the volume of business expected. For instance, if there is at least one catered function each day, you will need a handful of permanent full-time and/or permanent part-time persons scheduled to provide the level of service expected by guests.

If you do a great deal of catering business, these fixed employees can be scheduled solely for catered functions. If the catering business varies, with several peaks and valleys, you can still have permanent staff members assigned to catering, although you may have to share them with another department. For instance, in a country club you may have a 40-hour-per-week employee assigned to catering, with the understanding that if catering business is slow, he or she will work in the main dining room.

The more fixed employees you have, the easier it is to prepare your weekly work schedules. It is also more conducive to employee satisfaction. Fixed employees usually have steady, predictable work schedules. They appreciate the ability to plan their personal lives more accurately.

Variable labor is incremental labor. It will fluctuate with the volume of catering business. The caterer usually must schedule a large number of variable employees each week.

Unlike the typical restaurant operator, the banquet manager will have to prepare a variable work schedule each week. Catering business can be predictable, but the uniqueness of each catered function forces you to contact A-list and B-list employees every week in order to prepare a proper work schedule.

Work schedules are based primarily on the following factors:

○ Types of functions booked for the week
○ Expected length of each function
○ Number of guests anticipated
○ Styles of service required
○ Allowable labor costs
○ Employee availability
○ Degree of guest satisfaction required; that is, how much "pampering" do you have to provide?

Typically, you use this information, applicable union regulations, and the staffing guidelines set forth in the staffing charts to prepare the appropriate work schedules.

When preparing work schedules, you will have to allocate a sufficient number of work hours to cover the preopening and teardown periods. Stagger your servers so that some arrive and leave earlier than others. Aim to have the maximum number of workers available when the catered functions are in high gear, and fewer scheduled at function beginnings and endings.

Scheduling the appropriate number of work hours, and simultaneously adhering to your labor budget, is hard to accomplish in some situations. For instance, if you are working in a union facility, the union contract may require you to guarantee each employee you call in a minimum four-hour work schedule that day. If you need a few persons one day to cover three-hour shifts, you are free to schedule them for three hours apiece. However, you must pay them for four hours.

It was noted earlier in this chapter that the minimum number of servers required in the typical joint bargaining agreement usually does not cause problems for you because this minimum is normally insufficient to handle most types of catered events. However, the minimum number of guaranteed work hours can cause problems if you have several bookings that lend themselves to scheduling several service personnel for less than the minimum.

Even a nonunion facility may have a policy of paying a minimum number of work hours. For instance, it may wish to follow these standards in order to compete with unionized operations for workers. To say the least, this will make it more difficult to schedule economically some catered functions.

Timing of Service

The client and the catering sales representative normally discuss the timing of the service and relay their desires to the service staff. The banquet manager must note these desires and develop a plan that will provide maximum efficiency and a minimum number of bottlenecks.

Service will make or break a catered function. If half the guests are waiting for their entrees while the other half are eating dessert, there is a problem. If the head table, which usually receives the best service, is finished before other guests, the head table guests will have to wait for the others to finish or will have to begin the program while some guests are still being served or are still eating.

Timing problems can be minimized or avoided by scheduling extra servers. However, this accommodation may be cost-prohibitive.

An inexpensive way to minimize timing problems is to preset as much food and beverage on the dining tables as the client will allow. This is especially important if the client is in a hurry. For instance, if the group has only one hour for lunch, many food items, such as appetizers or salads, rolls, butter, relishes, and desserts, can be preset on the dining tables.

Some caterers can offer luncheons that are entirely preset. For instance, salad and/or sandwich luncheons can be preset in such a way that guests can sit down and eat quickly. In this case, servers would need to handle only beverage service and special requests.

To ensure proper timing, as well as smooth-running service, the captain normally calls the roll of all service personnel about an hour before the catered function is scheduled to begin. All employees are called by name to confirm attendance. Workstations are assigned. Servers are informed of any special diets, special service requests, and so forth, that will be needed. During the roll call, the captain will describe all menu items so that guests' inquiries can be answered without the need for servers to run back to the kitchen and check with the chef. Providing servers with a printed copy of the menu will make answering such questions easier.

For most receptions, there is generally a scheduled starting and ending time. At the beginning, it is usual for only a few guests to have arrived. Typically, by the time the reception is half over, all guests will be present. Toward the end of the reception you should begin to see guests leaving, a few at a time.

Some receptions will have all guests present when they open. For instance, a cocktail reception that begins immediately after a convention group's last business meeting of the day usually has maximum attendance when the doors open.

About 15 minutes before you want a meal service to start, you should begin calling the guests. You can start the music, dim the lights in the prefunction area, ring chimes, or make announcements to signal guests that it is time to enter the dining room for dinner. Servers should be standing ready at their stations when guests walk into the room, not against the wall talking with each other.

For most conventional meal functions, the salad course usually takes about 20 to 30 minutes, and the entrée about 30 to 50 minutes, from serving to removing of plates. Dessert can usually be handled in approximately 20 to 30 minutes. Normally, the entire banquet service will take about 1¼ hours for the typical luncheon and 2 hours for the typical dinner event.

More elaborate meal functions may take a bit more time to serve. Although the added diversions can enhance the dining experience, long meal functions tend to make guests a little anxious. Even if you are using elaborate service styles or similar attractions, guests will begin to think something is wrong with the catering operation if the meal lasts much longer than two hours. In addition, as mentioned earlier, some potential guests will be very reluctant to attend a catered event if they suspect it will run on too long.

Teardown Procedures

As the function winds down, servers can begin performing a bit of teardown work. For instance, prior to serving dessert, they can crumb tables and remove nonessentials (such as salt and pepper shakers and extra flatware). While the guests are enjoying their dessert, the servers can refill the condiment containers and put them away.

As guests begin to trickle out, the servers can see to it that all utensils and tableware requisitioned are cleaned and returned properly. They can inventory all service equipment. They can also see to it that any necessary paperwork, such as drink ticket and meal ticket accounting, is completed correctly.

Soon after all guests have left, all dining and buffet tables must be stripped. Soiled and leftover clean napery must be returned to housekeeping. Unless the tables must be set up for the next function, they will need to be broken down and put away by the banquet setup crew.

In properties such as hotels, the housekeeping or convention service staff members will have to come in and clean the floors, walls, hallways, mirrors, windows, and fixtures. In some facilities, servers help this crew; for instance, at the end of the function a server may run a vacuum cleaner over the heavy-traffic areas.

While housekeeping or convention service may be handling the cleaning chores, a server or two may be able to help set up for the next scheduled function. For instance, if you are tearing down after a luncheon and there is a dinner scheduled later, the banquet setup crew may want to get a head start by simultaneously tearing down and resetting the room. The crew would most likely appreciate any help service personnel can contribute. The kitchen staff may also need to recycle a few leftover foods. Sometimes these foods can be used for the next catered function, by a facility's restaurant outlets, or in the employee dining room.

If the leftover foods have lost some of their culinary quality, they should not be served again. For instance, foods that have been on a buffet table for an hour or more may be perfectly edible. However, they have probably deteriorated to the point where their appearance, taste, and texture are below your quality standards.

If the leftover foods are protein-rich, moist foods, they may have been contaminated during service. These potentially hazardous foods present excellent growing conditions for harmful bacteria. For instance, roast beef, cream-based soups, custards, and protein-rich salads made with mayonnaise or similar dressings should not be saved unless you are certain they are safe to eat. If there are any doubts, they should be discarded immediately before they have a chance to come in contact with wholesome foods and contaminate them.

Some clients may ask you to donate leftover foods they have paid for to a homeless shelter or a similar charitable organization. This is certainly a socially redeeming activity we can all support. However, if someone contracts a food-borne illness from these foods, the caterer may be liable for damages.

Some states have Good Samaritan laws that absolve you of liability as long as you used reasonable care when preparing, collecting, and delivering the leftover foods to a charitable organization. If you have not been negligent in handling these products and you sincerely believe they are safe to eat, you can donate them and not worry about being sued. However, if there is any question about the wholesomeness of the foods, you should discard them. Not only do you risk a lawsuit, you do no one a favor by distributing foods that could make people sick.

CATERING SAFETY AND SANITATION

Food and beverage production and service must be carried out in a safe and wholesome manner. Anyone handling foods and beverages must be trained to practice basic safety and sanitation procedures to ensure that employees and guests do not fall victims to accidents or food-borne illnesses.

All commercial foodservice operations must adhere to the sanitation standards set forth by their local health districts. These agencies periodically inspect food and beverage production and service personnel, equipment, and facilities to ensure that they comply with local rules and regulations.

Catering executives should consider following the sanitation guidelines developed by the Educational Foundation of the National Restaurant Association (NRA) when training employees. In fact, any employee who successfully completes the Educational Foundation's basic sanitation course will earn a certification that is viewed favorably by all local health districts. If an employee successfully completes an advanced course, he or she will earn the HACCP (Hazard Analysis Critical Control Points) certification.

Production and service equipment and facilities must meet pertinent standards of safety and sanitation. All commercial construction must meet building code guidelines. For instance, in most cities and counties in the United States, all food-contact equipment must display the familiar blue seal of the NSF (National Sanitation Foundation) International. Equipment that does not carry this seal usually cannot be used in commercial food and beverage operations.

The Underwriters Laboratory (UL) and the American Gas Association (AGA) inspect and certify equipment compliance with generally accepted safety standards. For instance, a gas oven displaying the AGA seal is safe to use in commercial production. Most local building codes usually require all equipment and permanent installations to meet or exceed safety standards promulgated by these types of independent inspectors.

The safe and sanitary food and beverage operation also meets standards set by other local government inspector-powered agencies. For instance, the fire marshal will inspect periodically for fire hazards, such as blocked exits, overcrowding, and discharged fire extinguisher systems.

The Department of Labor is also concerned with safety matters. For example, if you hire a few teenagers to work as bus persons or food runners, they will not be allowed to perform all types of work. Youngsters under 18 years of age usually cannot operate machinery such as slicers, food processors, and dough-cutting machines. Generally, they also cannot fill, refill, or light fuel containers, such as Sterno pots.

The local workers compensation agency is normally responsible for enforcing the mandates of the federal Occupational Safety and Health Administration (OSHA). The agency also insures employees for job-related injuries. Caterers can call upon the agency to help them develop effective employee safety-training guidelines. Furthermore, the agency can visit your property, point out areas of concern, and note what you can do to eliminate these hazards.

There are several safety and sanitation problems that must be controlled by the catering executive. The major risks are discussed in the following paragraphs.

Tableside and Action Station Cooking

Exhibition cooking poses many risks, even if it is performed by trained, professional chefs who have a great deal of experience with this type of work. Some parts of the country may prohibit exhibition cooking. Check the local fire code to see whether it is allowed in your area. And, if it is allowed, check further to see if there are any restrictions.

Action station cooking does not seem to be nearly as dangerous as tableside cooking. There is usually sufficient aisle space set up to minimize the threat of accidents.

Tableside cooking, especially the type involving flaming dishes, poses the most serious risk. For example, to enhance guest and employee safety, many companies have policies prohibiting this practice.

Rarely does tableside cooking result in a major fire. An accident would have to be very serious for any fire to combat the modern facility's sprinkler system. However, injury to guests is another matter.

Flaming dishes are an attractive addition to a catered event. They provide an exciting and entertaining change of pace. Clients and guests are always pleased with presentations of this type. Unfortunately, the curious guest who gets a little too close to the action is liable to inhale hazardous gas and/or come into contact with a spark or flame.

The inhalation of gases tends to be a greater risk than the fire itself. Usually, whenever you flame a dish, an extra server is stationed nearby to watch the spectacle and react to any emergency. This minimizes the fire hazard. However, you may not be able to control gases because you ordinarily are not aware of their leaking until some harm occurs.

You must be very careful when using Sterno, butane, propane, or other types of cooking fuels. Propane is especially troublesome and risky. It does not matter how much training a chef has had. A leaking propane tank is not obvious. Furthermore, lighting the burners can present some anxious moments if too much gas is allowed to enter the burners before you light them.

Propane is a dangerous fuel. It is recommended that it be used only outdoors. It is so combustible that, depending on temperature, humidity, and the amount of air space between the tanks and the grills, there is a good chance that the equipment will malfunction and cause a serious accident.

Most tableside cooking units use butane fuel, which is usually the best fuel to use. It is much safer than propane. It also is preferable to Sterno because you can control the temperature and size of the flame much better with butane than you can with Sterno.

Tableside cooking should be limited to a single sauté or wok station that is no closer to guests than the diameter of a 60-inch round dining table. The work area must be well ventilated. You should not allow exhibition cooking in a low-ceilinged room or in a room that does not have proper ventilation.

If a client prefers the excitement and attraction of tableside cooking, you can indulge this request safely by providing a flaming display on an elevated platform situated away from the dining areas on one side of the function room. The display can be used to prepare a few portions, with the bulk of production performed in the kitchen.

Another compromise is to have a flaming parade around the perimeter of the function room with the lights dimmed. For instance, food servers can carry a few flaming baked Alaska desserts or a few flaming kabobs from the kitchen to a dining room service area. Once there, servers can douse the fires, plate the foods, and serve a few guests. As with the flaming display, the remaining production and pre-plating can be done in the kitchen.

Burns

Even if you do not provide flaming tableside cooking, guests are still subject to accidental burns. For instance, if you have unprotected candle flames on each dining table, napery can be set afire should the candles tip over. Or guests may accidentally burn themselves or their clothing if they reach over a flame without realizing how hot it is. If you want to put candles on each table, use the votive-type containers, such as chimneys, as these setups can prevent accidental burns or fires.

Buffet service also presents several potential hazards that can cause burns. For instance, hot chafing dishes can be very dangerous to the unsuspecting guest. Handles and utensils can get very hot. And the steam created by the typical chafing-dish setup can build up and escape, thereby seriously burning someone standing nearby.

If Sterno or a similar fuel is used to keep the contents of chafing dishes hot, the fuel can "flame out"; that is, if the lid on the Sterno container is left open too wide, you may suddenly have a flame surrounding the bottom of the pan and possibly even enveloping the whole chafing dish.

If you use Sterno, do not allow anyone to refuel the little pots while they are in use. Sometimes you cannot see the slight flame emitted by the fuel. If you try to refuel while the pot is still burning, you may burn yourself badly. In fact, many years ago a young chef in a local Las Vegas hotel lost his life when his chef's jacket caught fire while he was trying to refuel Sterno pots on a buffet table.

Even though we in the industry tend to refer to Sterno as a generic product, it is in fact, a brand of fuel. There are other less expensive fuels you can use. However, according to Anthony Marshall, president of the Educational Institute of the American Hotel & Motel Association (AH&MA) and a well-known attorney, we should use only the Sterno brand. He warns that, unlike the Sterno brand, other brands may be poisonous. Look for a skull and crossbones on the label. If such fuels are left unlighted on a buffet table, guests may think they are a kind of dip, consume some, and die. In fact, Marshall notes a specific incident in which a woman died after consuming an off-brand fuel at a luau, thinking it was guava jelly, and the facility was held responsible for her death.

Hot carts positioned throughout the function room pose another burn hazard. Portable steam tables can also be a problem, as can hot-beverage setups.

To prevent these types of accidental burns, you must see to it that any exposed hot surface is clearly marked. For safety purposes, most manufacturers mark hot surfaces at the factory when the equipment is being manufactured. In fact, your local government may require this type of marking before such equipment can be used in local commercial foodservice operations.

Falls

Guests are always subject to falls. Most of them are unfamiliar with the function room. Some of them are not careful when roaming around the room, thereby bumping into other guests and servers. And many of them may not immediately recognize portable electrical and/or sound drop cords laced throughout the area.

To minimize the possibility of guests falling, you should never allow any loose item to be placed on the floor. For instance, if a drop cord must be used, it should be secured and marked conspicuously.

Similarly, if there is a slope in the floor, it should be marked clearly. Furthermore, all tables, carts, tray stands, and other equipment must be placed in the correct locations and secured properly.

Broken Glass

Broken and chipped tableware is another hazard that seems to be more prevalent at catered events than in regular restaurant service. The time pressures associated with most catered functions increase the risk that guests will inadvertently encounter damaged items.

Chipped plateware can usually be found and removed from service before it ends up in front of guests. However, the same cannot always be said about broken glassware. Indeed, the possibility of a guest finding a piece of broken glass is always present whenever employees are rushing to serve a group of people.

Hurried bartenders, bus persons, and other employees who clear tables and landing spaces may also increase the number of broken glasses and the possibility of a guest's getting a piece of glass in his or her food or beverage.

Bus persons should be taught to dump ice out of glasses before placing them in bus trays. The ice overloads the trays; it also causes glasses to slip around and bang into each other. Either way, the potential for chipped and broken glassware increases, along with the increased possibility that glass chips will get into the food and beverage supply.

Likewise, glasses should not be stacked in bus trays. Flatware should never be put into glasses, and plates should not be mixed with glasses. All of these practices increase the possibility of broken glass getting into a guest's drink or meal.

Ice or cold water should never be put into hot glasses. The glasses may crack and split. This is not troublesome if a glass breaks completely before it is served to a guest. There is a serious problem, however, if the glass merely sprouts a hairline crack; when the guest sees this, he or she will be leery of all other food and beverage offerings. Worse yet, if a guest actually drinks from this glass, he or she may receive a cut lip.

Glasses should never be used to dip ice out of an ice bin. If the glass breaks, you will have to empty the bin and clean it thoroughly. Use plastic scoops to dip ice and put it into glasses; metal scoops should not be used because they can chip the glasses. One of the last things you want is a guest receiving a piece of glass in his or her drink.

Food-Borne Illness

One of the caterer's worst nightmares is to cause an outbreak of food-borne illness. Imagine the agony and negative publicity you would suffer if guests became ill after consuming contaminated food at one of your events.

Food-borne illness can be traced to many origins. The products may be contaminated when purchased. They may become contaminated during production and service. Or they can become contaminated if stored under improper conditions.

Improper storage conditions, used for an excessive period of time, is generally the greatest problem faced by the typical catering operation. The "time/temperature" dilemma rears its head whenever potentially hazardous foods must be held for long periods of time on a buffet table.

Potentially hazardous foods must be stored at 40° F or below, or at 140° F or above. The 40° F to 140° F range is the danger zone. If potentially hazardous foods must go through the danger zone (such as when they are cooked), they must go through it as quickly as possible, because at these temperatures harmful bacteria will thrive.

Foods on a buffet table are especially vulnerable to the time/temperature problem. For instance, if you offer a meat loaf entrée, a chafing dish may be unable to maintain the temperature required. If a guest or employee contaminates this cooked food, and the food is not served for a while, harmful bacteria can multiply and, eventually, someone may become ill.

If you are serving cold potentially hazardous foods on a buffet table, they must be kept at or below 40° F. For instance, a cold potato salad made with protein-rich ingredients should never be allowed to sit unrefrigerated for more than a few minutes. It should be displayed on a cold table.

To prevent these time/temperature problems, you must ensure that the service equipment can hold foods at the proper temperatures, see to it that foods are not kept on the buffet table any longer than necessary, and eliminate the possibility of contamination by guests by installing sneeze guards in front of the foods.

You can also minimize problems of this type if you are willing to forgo the use of some of the more troublesome foods. For instance, if eggs are to be used in a menu item that will not be cooked, such as hollandaise sauce, you can use pasteurized frozen eggs instead of fresh shell eggs. You can also refuse to serve items with raw eggs such as Caesar salad, items with raw meat such as steak tartare, or raw seafood.

Intermediaries and Suppliers | Chapter 8

Some catered events require much more than food and beverage service. In addition to food and drink, some clients will need unique audio, visual, and/or lighting services. Some will require specialized dining table and buffet table presentations. And others may need something extra special to ensure that guests come away from their functions with many happy memories.

Clients who are planning several meal and beverage functions, such as meeting and convention clients, may also ask for something more than food and beverage service if only to relieve monotony. They may want something unusual to recharge the guests' batteries so that they have an extra store of energy to draw on when tackling the remaining business sessions.

Unique attractions are also used by clients to highlight celebratory catered events. Awards dinners, weddings, new product introductions, and the like, are made more exclusive and memorable if clients provide a smorgasbord of food, beverages, and other services specifically designed to maximize their impact on the guests.

Caterers can sometimes be conflicted when dealing with clients who want special services. After all, if clients spend a lot of money for these things, how much will they have left over for food and beverages? You certainly do not want to speak ill of clients' ideas, but it is your responsibility to point out that they should strike a proper balance between decor and food and beverage. In the long run, we know that guests are most impressed with the quality and value of the food and beverage received and that other services cannot compensate for mediocre products. You must be cautious, however, when discussing these points; at no time should you attempt to feather your nest at the expense of the client's needs and desires.

The catering executive must be prepared to entertain a variety of requests for special services. Usually, only the small, refueling type of catered meal functions are built solely around food and beverage service.

Most events require some sort of additional service. These extras can range from the mundane (such as a videotape player, a TV monitor, an overhead projector, or a screen) to the spectacular (such as a skydiving stunt).

A caterer must often coordinate many special requests. He or she will have to help plan, organize, and implement an assortment of unusual and unique requirements. He or she may also have to advise clients of the most effective and economical combination of special services needed to ensure success. Like a band leader, the caterer must see to it that all food, beverage, and special services are playing from the same sheet of music.

PROVIDING OTHER CLIENT SERVICES

Caterers specialize in providing food and beverage service. Although some are capable of providing additional services, others prefer to leave these to outside experts.

A caterer cannot be all things to all people. He or she realistically must draw the line somewhere. Cost considerations render it virtually impossible to store all of the specialties that clients may potentially desire.

When dealing with services other than food and beverage, the caterer is usually faced with five options. The caterer can (1) provide as many of these services as possible itself, (2) steer clients to outside service contractors, (3) expect clients to find their own outside service contractors, (4) authorize concessions—that is, provide in-house space for outside service contractors to set up shop, or (5) use some combination of these four possibilities.

Other Client Services Provided by the Facility

A facility usually will provide its own special services only if it is economically feasible to do so, or if there are no outside contractors that can be trusted to do the work correctly and efficiently.

Some facilities are even starting their own in-house destination management departments. In this case, the caterer does not have the added responsibility of dealing with things that may be beyond his or her experience, and yet the facility retains 100 percent of the business and guest satisfaction. This arrangement provides "one-stop" shopping.

Some special services can be very profitable, particularly if they are not labor-intensive. For instance, providing a few pieces of audio-visual (AV) equipment and one technician to a group does not usually involve a lot of variable costs. Consequently, its contribution margin can add considerably to overall profits.

Unfortunately, however, some special services are very capital-intensive. For instance, most lighting equipment is quite expensive. To make matters worse, it tends to become obsolete quickly, thereby requiring you to replace it periodically with even more expensive items. It is cost prohibitive to let this equipment sit idle. Unless the facility uses it often, you may not earn an adequate return on your investment.

Providing a full range of AV services can be another expensive undertaking. AV technology changes so rapidly that it is difficult to keep pace. A complete in-house AV system is a major investment, but one that is required in conference centers, exhibition halls, and resorts located in rural areas where outside service contractors are not readily available.

In some instances, a facility may be happy to break even with such services as lighting and sound if it means that clients will spend freely on food and beverage services. In this case, it may be good business to offer the client a loss leader if it helps to secure other profitable business for the facility.

Outside Service Contractors

Clients occasionally require services the facility is unable to provide. If outside service contractors must be used, the facility may have an approved supplier list for the client's convenience. If not, it is up to the client to secure the necessary services and coordinate them with the catering executive.

The following are the types of outside service contractors most commonly used by clients:

○ Decorator
○ Designer
○ Audiovisual
○ Photographer
○ Transportation
○ Media coverage
○ Specialized security
○ Printer
○ Host/hostess
○ Talent bookers
○ Florist
○ Specialized food, e.g., subcontracting a sushi bar from a local Japanese restaurant
○ Furniture
○ Exhibit equipment, e.g., pipe and drape, pop-up booths, etc.

Some caterers have a list of approved outside service contractors that they recommend to potential clients whenever special services are needed. These contractors are those they feel are capable of doing the job properly. Before adding a contractor to the approved list, the caterer normally requires appropriate references and proof of adequate insurance. A caterer does not want to risk recommending someone whose ineptness will cause client and guest dissatisfaction and ruin the chances of repeat patronage.

Service contractors range from full-service to single-service operations. Full-service general service contractors, such as The Freeman Companies or GES Exposition Services, rent pipe and drape, dance floors, risers, temporary carpeting, furniture, AV equipment, exhibits, and a variety of other items. Single-service contractors include florists, photographers, limousine companies, and the like.

Some caterers may not want to recommend outside service contractors because such a recommendation may represent a possible conflict of interest. They fear that someone may accuse them of taking kickbacks. They also run the risk of clients complaining that they were steered to inadequate, costly outsiders whose inability should have been well known to the catering executives.

Sometimes a client may want to use an outside service contractor that the caterer would like to avoid. Generally, however, you must be willing and able to work with any outside service contractors selected by clients.

Many potential clients, especially large conventions that hold events throughout the country, have long-term contracts with several outside service providers. This is an effective cost-saving procedure, because a service contractor will normally offer clients a generous volume discount if they purchase a large amount of services. A caterer will have to work with these outsiders if it wants to book the catering business.

If you book a very large catered function, subcontracting may be the logical way to handle the event. For instance, if a caterer has to feed 50,000 people at a large convention, different parts of the meal might be subcontracted with other caterers.

In some cases, especially with subcontracted food or beverages, the caterer will add a profit markup of about 20 percent to the subcontractor's charge.

In-House Concessionaires

Large hotels, convention centers, and conference centers that do not want to provide their own special services, yet do not want to inconvenience potential clients, may grant a few outside service contractors concession status. These contractors, then, will automatically receive a client's business unless he or she wants to make other arrangements with another service contractor. The facility usually allocates the concessionaire some storage space within the property so that necessary equipment and materials can be kept on-site. The concessionaire will also need a bit of space to house employee work areas. A concessionaire usually has its own backup warehouse facilities off-site. By having on-site space, however, the concessionaire can service clients quickly and efficiently. Furthermore, emergencies or last-minute requests can be handled immediately when employees and equipment are readily available at a moment's notice.

Facilities usually charge a commission to in-house vendors. It is important to understand that these costs must be passed on to the end user, and with high commissions, your mutual clients may end up paying $60 to $80 for a simple slide projector.

Some facilities charge outside vendors a surcharge for the right to work in the venue. This is done to discourage the client from using a favorite vendor. Instead, the client must use the in-house vendor. This ensures that the caterer will not lose its commission.

Combination of In-House and Outside Services

Occasionally, a facility may provide some services itself while the client is expected to secure others. For instance, if a convention needs specialized sound and lighting services, you may be able to provide microphones and speakers, but the client may have to use an outside service contractor to provide the necessary lighting.

A facility can usually provide a few of the most commonly needed client services. For instance, it is the rare facility that cannot provide basic AV equipment, such as overhead projectors, screens, microphones, speakers, slide projectors, TV monitors, videotape players, and film projectors. If the facility is new, it may have several of these items built in. If nothing else, it can rent a few of these items and relieve the client of this chore.

Occasionally, a facility may want to offer a few complimentary client services in order to secure a large catering contract. For example, if a client needs a microphone for a luncheon speaker, the facility may provide it free of charge. This type of service is relatively inexpensive to provide because you can often tap into a house sound system (i.e., PA (public address) system) very easily. The client will appreciate the additional consideration and remember it when it is time to plan the next catered function.

Outside Services and Rental Procedures

Compile a list of vendors that you can recommend to clients for music, floral arrangements, photography, paper goods, limo services, bakery goods, and so on. Include price ranges for their products and services. It is common to use vendors to deliver the kind of products we sell. It is also a source of revenue that goes straight to the bottom line.

Guidelines for using vendors may vary regionally; however, certain rules may apply:

After making price comparisons, select one or two primary suppliers for each service when possible.

○ *Benefit:* You develop and maintain a working relationship that results in better service and in-house discounts.

○ *Example:* Using the same booking agency for all entertainment may result in a free band for the employee holiday party.

Agree up front, and in writing, on the discount the vendor will provide. Discounts normally range from 10 to 20 percent. The agreement should not in any way imply that you will do business with only that vendor.

○ *Benefit:* The guest is charged the published price, so you are not adding to the cost. The discount comes directly to the caterer.
○ *Example:* When the invoice from a baker comes, it may state:

Wedding cake

1 cake for 150 persons	*$250*
Less discount	*25*
Total due	*$225*

You have collected $250 from the client. The $25 goes straight to the bottom line.

This is a source of income that is often overlooked and that requires little time and effort. The following paragraphs include guidelines to help you select and work effectively with your vendors.

Flowers.   Contact a reliable local florist and show him or her your banquet and meeting space so that floral arrangements can be balanced with the colors in these areas. Ask the florist to provide you photographs of several arrangements in different styles and price ranges. Provide clients with a list of prices for centerpieces and corsages that include the prearranged mark-up for your facility.

Bakeries.   Establish a working relationship with a good bakery in your area that can provide the facility with a wide assortment of breads, decorated cakes, and unusual pastries. Collect photographs of birthday, wedding, and other special occasion cakes as sales aids, along with a price list for clients.

Rental Agencies.   Create and maintain a list of names, numbers, and pertinent information about the rental agencies in your area, so that you can respond readily to special requests. Clients may need all kinds of equipment and extras, from silver punch bowls to tuxedos or costumes.

Printing.   A printer can provide everything from invitations to banquet menus, place cards, and signs.

Photographs.   Professional photographers are in demand for many types of functions, from weddings to awards banquets. When comparing prices, be aware that some photographers charge separately for time, film, proofs, and pictures.

Music.   Include bands and other musical entertainment as part of your banquet package. Know which rooms accommodate a dance floor or stage. Know where the electrical outlets are located and the power capacity of the facility. Be aware of union regulations for musicians in your area.

AUDIOVISUAL SERVICES

Audiovisual (AV) services are probably the most common type of additional services needed by catering clients. You must be able to counsel your clients regarding the best options and help them to match their particular needs with the most effective and efficient AV systems.

The main purpose of an AV system is to communicate. Presentations are made to sell, train, inform, and entertain. The most effective and memorable presentations use AV equipment to "show and tell." Without such capability, presentations are apt to lack the "punch and power" needed to make a lasting impression on guests.

Types of AV Services

Clients can usually find the AV services they need very easily because there are several types and varieties available for today's electronic meetings (see Figure 8.1). The general types of AV services and equipment clients can order are described in the following paragraphs.

Microphone.   The most commonly used types of microphones are (1) lectern, (2) table, (3) floor, (4) lavaliere (also called a necklace or lapel

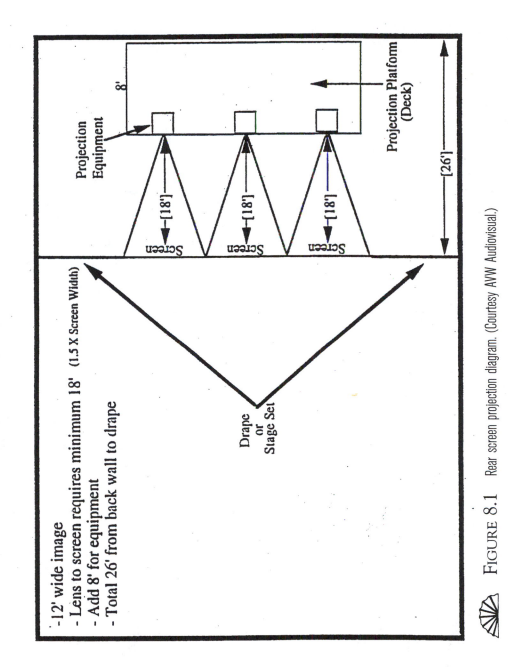

FIGURE 8.1   Rear screen projection diagram. (Courtesy AVW Audiovisual.)

295

microphone), (5) halo (also called a suspended or boom microphone), and (6) hand-held. Most are available corded or cordless. A cordless microphone, although more expensive, allows greater freedom and flexibility for the speaker. Be aware that cordless microphones use a radio transmission and can be picked up by outside ham radio operators.

The use of more than one microphone usually requires a mixer. Standard mixers have four channels and can handle four microphones. A sound technician should be engaged when larger mixers are used.

Screen.   There are two basic types of projection screens: those for front-screen projection and those for rear-screen projection. The appropriate screen size must also be used to ensure comfortable viewing for all audience members. Function room size and layout are important factors, but the recommended screen size generally depends primarily on the audience size.

Tripod screens are available up to 8′ × 8′ and are for front projection only. Suggested audience sizes for tripod screens are as follows:

60″ × 60″	For audiences up to 50
70″ × 70″	For audiences of 50 to 75
84″ × 84″	For audiences of 75 to 100
96″ × 96″	For audiences of 100 to 150

Fast-fold screens snap to a rigid aluminum frame and can be used for front or rear projection, either supported by adjustable legs or "flown" (hung from the ceiling). With front-screen projection, the media projector is located within or behind the audience. Suggested audience sizes for fast-fold screens are as follows:

Rectangular	Square	
6′ × 8′	8′ × 8′	For audiences up to 150
7½′ × 10′	9′ × 9′	For audiences of 150 to 200
9′ × 12′	10′ × 10′	For audiences of 200 to 300
10½′ × 14′	12′ × 12′	For audiences of 300 to 500
12′ × 16′	14′ × 14′	For audiences of 500 to 750
15′ × 20′	16′ × 16′	For audiences of 750 to 1,500

Images are projected onto one of the following screen surfaces:

○ Matte white—the most common screen surface. It diffuses the available light evenly over a wide area; especially useful in large, wide rooms.

○ Glass-beaded—the surface contains chemically coated glass beads. This produces superior image brightness (about three times that of the matte white). However, the optimal viewing angle is much narrower.

○ Lenticular—this type of surface is similar to a lens, in that it controls light and sends it to a predetermined area. It is most often used in stereo projection, for which viewers must wear 3-D glasses. These screens are normally not very large. The biggest one available measures approximately 6 feet by 6 feet.

With rear-screen projection, the media projector is placed behind the screen and images are projected through a translucent screen surface (see Figure 8.1). The screen surfaces are made of glass, acrylic, or vinyl. They attach only to fast-fold frames.

As compared with front-screen projection (see Figure 8.2), the primary advantages of rear-screen projection are as follows:

1 No interference with projection beam of light.
2 No tripping over drop cords or other equipment.
3 No need to dim the lights, which permits attendees to take notes easily.

The following are its major disadvantages:

1 It takes up a lot of space (see Figure 8.3). Depending on the screen size and type of lens used, you will usually need about 15 to 30 feet behind the screen.
2 The area behind the screen must be completely dark.

The size and type of screen required are related to the audience needs, room size, and room dimensions. To determine the maximum screen size, subtract 4 feet from the minimum ceiling height. If you use the maximum height, guests seated in the back row will be able to see the screen unobstructed by heads in the front rows.

Examples Of
Front Projection Placement

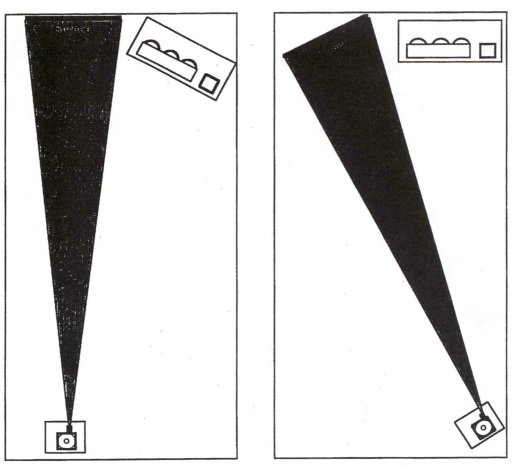

Center Set

Corner Set

FRONT PROJECTION

All front projection screens are reflective surfaces that "bounce" the projected image back to the audience.

- Advantage: Good quality image, evenly distributed.

- Disadvantage: Ambient light can be a problem, room lights should be lowered.

 FIGURE 8.2   Examples of front projection placement. (Courtesy AVW Audiovisual.)

DETERMINING SPACE FOR REAR SCREEN PROJECTION

1. Determine tallest screen usable based on "clear" ceiling height of room.

   • In large rooms, bottom of screen should be 5' from the floor.
   • Subtract 5' from clear ceiling height and this is the tallest screen usable.

Example:

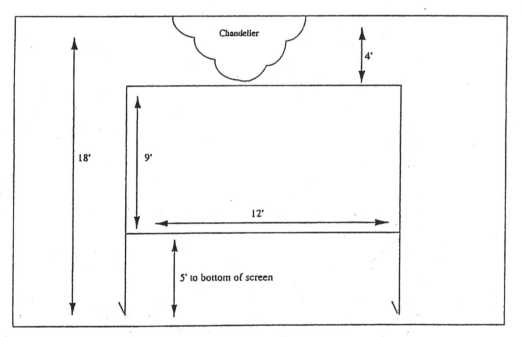

("Clear" ceiling height is 14' from floor to bottom of chandelier.)

2. Multiply width of screen by 1.5 and this will give you "lens to screen" distance. Add 6' - 8' for walk-space behind equipment.

(See next page for diagram)

FIGURE 8.3   Determining space for rear screen projection. (Courtesy AVW Audiovisual.)

Overhead Projector.   This equipment bounces an image off a 45-degree mirror onto a lens placed above the object. The object is either a transparency or an acetate sheet that can be written on with a special marking pen by a speaker during his or her presentation. Overhead projectors can be used in a lighted room, although subdued lighting is best.

The standard projector accommodates transparencies measuring 8½″ × 11″. Audience size should be limited to 150 for best results. This piece of equipment cannot be remote controlled.

Keystoning, whereby the image is smaller at the bottom of the screen than at the top, is a common problem with overhead projectors. It is easily corrected by positioning the screen as illustrated in Figure 8.4.

Sound.   A good presentation depends on the quality of the equipment used to convey it. Without a good sound system, the most carefully planned presentation will flop.

There are two general types of sound systems: distributed and clustered. The distributed system is preferred when human voices must be projected. Loudspeakers are placed strategically along the ceiling so that all of the audience is equidistant from the signal (i.e., sound) source. The clustered system is used primarily for music. In this case, loudspeakers are usually placed about 15 to 30 feet above and around the stage.

A sound system includes four major components:

1   Signal sources—The most common sources are microphone, audiotape, videotape, laser disk and filmstrip with audio track.
2   Audio mixer—This equipment combines several signal sources and sends mono or stereo signals to the amplifier and, ultimately, to the speakers. The mixing system is usually an audio "box" that accepts multiple microphone, sound projector, or tape player hookups and allows these inputs to be "mixed" through a sound system with the help of an amplifier. Mixers automatically adjust for volume, sound level between speakers, feedback, and equalization, thereby minimizing labor costs.
3   Amplifier—This equipment takes the signal from the audio mixer and boosts it to the level required by the speakers.
4   Speaker—There are various types and sizes of speakers. They must be arranged in the room in such a way that they can fill it completely and evenly with sound.

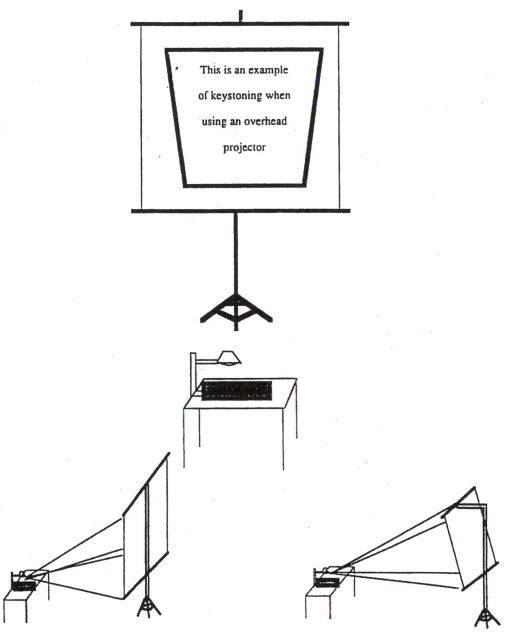

KEYSTONE CORRECTION

This is an example
of keystoning when
using an overhead
projector

Side View without Keystone Correction   **Side View with Keystone Correction**

FIGURE 8.4   Keystone correction. (Courtesy AVW Audiovisual.)

Many facilities have built-in house sound systems. These systems usually are adequate for public addresses and background music. However, they usually are not designed to project musical instruments or live singing.

AV Technician.   For elaborate AV presentations, the client will usually need to hire at least one technician. For instance, if you are using four or more sound sources in a function room, it is recommended that you schedule one AV technician for that room to coordinate and supervise the production.

Audio Recorder.   The two basic types are reel-to-reel and cassette tape recorders. Several sizes are available.

Video Recorder.   Video cameras are often used to record events or parts of events.

Carousel Slide Projector.   This equipment can be used for front or rear screen projection from horizontal and vertical slides on a screen. The slides are placed in front of a single light source one at a time. There are similar slide projectors that do not use a carousel to hold the slides. Stronger lenses and "extra bright" bulbs are recommended for larger rooms, but they are more costly. A stronger bulb can provide sufficient brightness to a 14-foot-wide screen for an audience of up to 600 people. Carousel slide trays are 80-slot or 140-slot, and at least one tray is usually included in the price of the projector.

Messager Slide Projector.   This equipment is much smaller than the typical carousel projector. Instead of using a carousel to hold the slides, a magazine is used to stack the slides, which are then gravity fed in front of two light sources. Two light sources allow the images to blend (i.e., "fade") into each other, thereby eliminating dark spots and ensuring smooth transitions.

This projector is more convenient to use than a carousel slide projector. For instance, the user does not have to insert slides into a carousel; he or she merely needs to stack them in the magazine. Moreover, the user knows exactly which slide is projected on the screen because each slide's number can be displayed on a digital readout attachment.

Xenon Slide Projector.   This equipment is typically used in large function rooms for large groups. In a large room, the projected images must be big enough for everyone to see. The images projected by the typical carousel slide projector begin to lose clarity and focus if they are enlarged too much. However, the Xenon slide projector projects a much sharper, crisper large picture that can be seen easily from afar.

This projector is more complicated and usually must be adjusted to accommodate each slide's unique features. Generally, an AV technician must be employed to run it.

TV Monitor. A TV monitor is similar to a regular TV screen; the major difference is that the monitor produces a much higher picture quality. Monitor screen types include the following:

○ *CRT (cathode ray tube).* This monitor is made from a vacuum tube, is limited in size, very heavy, and subject to magnetic field distortions.

○ *LCD (liquid crystal display) panel.* This is an electronic device that sits on top of an overhead projector in lieu of a standard transparency. It is sometimes referred to as an *electronic transparency.* It is designed to project computer-generated data onto the screen. Some models have built-in electronic storage and random-access retrieval capability, which enable the presenter to use some data while storing the rest of it for a later discussion.

○ *Plasma.* This monitor is very thin and lightweight, with an unlimited screen size.

○ *Receivers.* These have tuners that allow reception of broadcast or cable signals. They have internal speakers; sound and video are received on one cable.

○ *Monitors.* Standard monitors have no tuners, but have multiple inputs and a higher resolution than receivers.

○ *Combination VHS/receiver (combo unit).* An internally mounted VHS player that works well in confined spaces. No cables are needed for playback of videos.

○ *Multiscan Monitors.* These are designed primarily for high-resolution computer use.

If a client wants to show a video, he or she can usually select one of three types of video systems:

1 Uses a regular TV set wired to accept video.
2 Uses a TV monitor wired to accept video.
3 Uses a video projection system wired to accept video. This system uses a video projector, a special projection screen (that can be up to

30 feet wide), a video playback unit, and a patch into the facility's in-house sound system.

As a general rule of thumb, when viewing videotapes, you should:

- Use a 19-inch TV monitor for 10 people or fewer.
- Use a 25-inch TV monitor for 11 to 25 people.
- Use a 35- to 46-inch TV monitor for 26 to 50 people.
- Use a big-screen TV for groups of more than 50 people.

You can also use a combination of these four options. For instance, in a room with 20 to 40 people, you can use two TV monitors with a common, portable sound speaker.

Video Tape Player.   Sometimes referred to as a VCP (videocassette player). It is designed specifically to play prerecorded videotapes to be shown on a TV monitor. A VCR (videocassette recorder) can also be used to show prerecorded videotapes.

Audio Tape Player.   This equipment is designed to play prerecorded audio-tapes. Some types of equipment used to record audio presentations can also be used to play prerecorded tapes.

Camera.   There are three basic types: film, digital, and video cameras.

Film Projector.   This equipment is used to project prerecorded motion picture film images on a projection screen. There are usually four types available: 35 mm, 16 mm, Super-8, and 8 mm. Most projectors have built-in sound speakers, which are adequate for small groups. To accommodate large audiences, most projectors can be patched into the in-house sound system.

Opaque Projector.   This equipment is similar to an overhead projector; the major difference is that its light is reflected from above instead of from beneath. It can be used to show solid materials, such as book pages, photographs, or small three-dimensional objects. Unlike the overhead projector, however, this equipment requires that the room be dark in order for people to see the images projected on the screen.

Slide/Sound Synchronizer.   This is a combination slide and audiotape presentation. For instance, a carousel slide projector can be advanced automatically by inaudible pulses on one stereo channel, while the other channel presents audio messages, such as music or voice-over narration.

Dissolve Unit.   This equipment allows two or three carousel slide projectors focused on the same screen to create a smooth transition from one slide to another. As the slides advance, they will fade into each other.

Simultaneous Translation.   With this service a translator sits in a booth and listens to a speaker. As the speaker talks, the translator immediately translates his or her remarks and delivers the translation into a microphone that feeds into headsets worn by audience members.

There are two basic types of simultaneous translation systems: cabled and wireless. The wireless system is more expensive, but is more convenient to use. It allows maximum mobility.

Some systems allow audience members maximum control over the headset volume. Although these are more expensive than systems without this option, again, they are more convenient to use. They also are preferred by audience members who wish to listen selectively to a speaker's remarks.

Most systems allow audience members to interact with the speaker and each other. For instance, an attendee may want to ask the speaker a question. The question can be easily translated back to the speaker and his or her translated responses communicated to the audience just as quickly. You can use several translators to accommodate a number of languages.

If you receive requests for this type of service and you wish to provide it yourself, check with local embassies, consulates, colleges, or universities for bilingual persons. Be certain, however, that anyone hired to do this type of work has had formal simultaneous-translation training and/or work experience.

Closed-Circuit TV (CCTV).   Typically, only major conference centers have this type of capability. The video camera and TV monitors are generally used by groups to set up interactive training sessions. However, the system can also be used for other purposes, such as providing security for exhibition areas, VIPs, and cash bars.

Projection Table.   Standard projection tables vary in height, weight, and size. They are designed to hold projection equipment. They usually have detachable, adjustable legs that can be manipulated for height and storage, as well as locking casters, heavy-duty cords, and several plug outlets.

Some projection tables are more elaborate, designed to interact with other projection equipment. For instance, some have electronic pointers that can be used to enhance a slide presentation.

Slide.   Most slides used are 35 mm color film and measure 2 inches square (including the mounting). To ensure consistent focus, use only glass-mounted slides.

Motion Picture Film.   Most educational and industrial films today are either 16 mm or Super-8. Occasionally, you will find an 8 mm film. The soundtrack is usually dubbed onto the film during the printing or processing stage. For best results, the soundtrack should be patched into a facility's in-house sound system.

Videotape.   The following are the most commonly used videotape formats:

o   VHS (a 1/2-inch format)
o   Betacam (a broadcast quality, 1/2 inch format)
o   1-inch (a broadcast-quality format)

If a client will be using two different formats, he or she will need two separate video tape players. None of these videotape formats are compatible with the others' equipment.

Multimedia System.   This is a complete sight/sound environment. It combines audio, video, and special-effects equipment (such as lasers, computers, and smoke-making machines).

Video Projector.   This is an expensive piece of equipment that allows presenters to show videos on a big screen or to hook up a computer to use a Power Point presentation or connect to the Internet.

Optional Accessories.   Laser pointers, wireless remotes, acetate sheets, and markers are among the optional accessories available.

Electrical Service.   Audio, lighting, and video equipment should have separate circuits to help prevent hums and buzzes. Separate outlets do not necessarily mean separate circuits. There can be four wall outlets all connected to the same circuit. Lighting equipment has the greatest power requirements. Because the average current per breakered electrical circuit is 20 amps, and the average voltage for an outlet is 110 volts, four 1,000-watt lights (a typical lighting tree configuration), which equals 40 amps, requires two separate circuits to use all of these lights without tripping a circuit breaker. Large setups require separate "power drops," that is, additional power brought in. The provision of 24-hour power in a convention center is a special-order item.

Recording

When a client wishes to audio record an event, generally the best results are obtained by patching into an in-house sound system. This results in a much better quality sound than if tape recorders are placed strategically on the lectern or throughout the function room.

When video recording, the client may want to use "speaker enhancement" video screens and/or a computer-controlled video wall. This allows a good view for guests who are not close enough to see the action firsthand. With such equipment, action is seen as it happens, including the speaker's face, audience reactions, and audience members asking questions. If an instant replay is desired, it can easily be presented.

When designing the function room layout with video recording in mind, make sure the cameras are located so that they can "see" everything you want to record. They should also be located outside the traffic lanes. Another important factor is lighting. To ensure a clear, sharp picture, all subjects must be well lit.

Another important part of any recording is the recording microphone. The placement of microphones is critical. If the audience is to ask questions, you will need microphones placed strategically throughout the room. Otherwise, there will be blank spots on the tape. Furthermore, the speaker may have to repeat the questions.

A speaker using an overhead projector or similar equipment may want to use a lavaliere microphone so that his or her hands are free to manipulate the equipment. This type of microphone will also ensure that the sound will not fade while the presenter is moving about the stage.

Someone should test the recording system before the client and guests enter the room.

Selecting an AV Service Contractor

When a client needs to use an outside AV service, you may be asked to recommend one. If so, you should investigate those available in your local area and develop a list of approved suppliers.

Before adding a firm to your approved supplier list, you must verify that it is able to perform adequately. There are a number of characteristics that you should evaluate before deciding whether a service contractor can handle clients' needs.

○ A proven reputation. Ask AV professionals for references. Call the references and ask:

How capable technically were the AV representatives?

Did the firm have all necessary equipment?

How responsive was the firm to last-minute requests?

Was the final bill equal to the original competitive bid?

○ Certification of communication technology specialists by the International Communication Industries Association. An AV firm with these specialists on staff is committed to continuing education within this highly technical and ever changing industry.

○ The proximity of the AV firm to the facility.

○ The availability of deliveries and installations after normal business hours.

○ The number of field representatives.

○ The number of delivery vehicles.

○ Do all field representatives and drivers carry beepers or cellular phones so that they can be contacted quickly?

○ Rental charges for equipment. Make sure that you learn the total charge for delivery, setup, and postproduction.

○ Charge (if any) for backup emergency equipment.

○ Deposits required.

○ Refund policies. For instance, if an equipment order is canceled at the last minute, will part of the deposit be returned? Inquire also about the procedures used to reconcile disputed charges.

○ Setup time needed.

○ Rehearsal time needed.

○ Staging area(s) required.

○ Client assistance provided. Many clients will need assistance in planning their AV needs. The approved AV service contractor should be able to provide sufficient input and assistance in developing these plans. A client may also need some help in computing his or her budget for AV production, equipment, labor, delivery, installation, and postproduction costs.

○ Labor charges. Labor can be the largest part of a client's AV budget.

However, armed with the correct information about the catered event, the AV firm should be able to develop a detailed labor schedule that complies with union contracts and gives the client a realistic expectation of actual labor costs.

Unfortunately, actual labor charges tend to exceed budgeted costs because the client and the AV service contractor cannot anticipate all contingencies. For instance, there may be a problem in getting into the facility to set up sound equipment because another catered function is running late. Delayed access to function rooms, as well as tight turn-around times, last-minute on-site changes, and incomplete agendas are the most common reasons for labor cost variances.

Furthermore, such cost variances may increase if union labor must be scheduled. Many facilities and AV companies have contractual agreements requiring union labor for AV services. With complex, elaborate setups, more than one union may be involved. Because most labor contracts include hourly minimums, meal penalties, overtime rates, and show calls (i.e., employees required to come in; they will be paid even if there is no work for them to do), the actual labor charge can be significantly greater than the budgeted cost.

The more your AV service contractor knows about the catered function, the easier it will be to predict accurately the final, actual labor cost. Moreover, the event's show coordinator will then be able to select and schedule a crew capable of handling the event properly.

○ The firm's ability to coordinate with other service contractors. For instance, if a separate lighting service contractor is required, the two firms will have to work together smoothly to avoid glitches that can add to final costs and cause guest dissatisfaction.

○ Other services that can be provided by the AV firm. Some clients appreciate a one-stop shopping opportunity. It is good practice to be able to recommend to them AV firms that can perform related services. For instance, some AV service contractors offer a wide variety of services, such as theme parties, laser and pyrotechnics shows, videoconferencing, personalized slide presentations, and simultaneous translation.

Accommodating a Client's AV Needs

If a client is using AV services, the catered function must be held in a room where sound is transmitted effectively. The walls should have absorbent panels and be at least 1 inch thick. If air walls (i.e., moving partitions) are used, they should be 2 to 4 inches thick. The seals and gaskets must be intact and tightly secured to prevent sound leaks.

Wool or thick-pile rugs are excellent floor coverings. These will absorb unwanted sounds, such as those created by footsteps and the moving of equipment.

The function room's ceiling should not be too high, or sound can reverberate. If the local building codes require very high ceilings, you will need to have an acoustical material installed to reduce this effect or, if the client allows, you can position the speakers appropriately so that this problem is minimized. Usually, if there is any potential for sound reverberation, you can quickly overcome it by installing temporary fabrics, tiles, baffles, or other acoustical material.

If a client is using an outside AV service contractor, be certain that the firm is apprised of the facility's logistics. For instance, the firm must be aware of accessibility, freight elevators, height and width of the doorways, and so forth, in order to plan and implement the project correctly. The firm should also be informed of other events in the facility that may possibly interfere with installation and teardown procedures.

Finally, make certain the client realizes that all outside services will be billed at the actual cost, which may or may not be the same as the competitive bids submitted.

ENTERTAINMENT

Many catered events offer some type of entertainment. The offerings run the gamut from the mundane to the spectacular. For instance, at one end of the spectrum is the strolling violinist, and at the opposite end are internationally famous singers headlining major show productions.

As with any outside service contractor, the facility can develop an approved supplier list for potential clients to use. This can be relatively easy for those facilities that offer entertainment in their restaurant and bar outlets or have a corporate entertainment director.

If a client requires entertainment, the responsibility for booking, scheduling, and coordinating it usually falls to the client. The caterer's major involvement in the entertainment decision is to take it into account when planning the catered event. For instance, if a dance band is scheduled, everything from banquet setup to work scheduling will be influenced. Considering the major impact that entertainment will have on the event, the catering executive cannot work effectively unless he or she is privy to this information.

The caterer must also know whether there are any additional services that must be provided. The entertainment contract will indicate what these services are and who is responsible for securing them. Require the client to show you the entertainment contract before the client signs it. There may be conditions that you cannot meet or that will require you to add extra charges.

Generally speaking, the key variables the caterer must consider are the following:

- *Lighting requirements.* Will the entertainment provide its own lighting? Will there be a separate outside lighting service contractor? Will the facility's permanent system suffice?
- *Number of dressing rooms needed.* Also note where they must be located.
- *Sound systems.* Many entertainers have their own systems and technicians. Your responsibility is to provide sufficient space and electrical power. Policy may require you to charge the client for this extra space and electrical power.
- *Rehearsal time and facilities needed.* If you must hold the function room space for a day or two before the event so that rehearsals can be held, you will probably have to charge the client extra for this accommodation.
- *Setup time.* In lieu of rehearsal time, or in addition to it, you may have to hold a function room for an extra day or two so that the entertainment production can be set up properly.
- *Security.* Some entertainers have their own security guards. Others may depend on the facility for all security or for additional security to supplement their own.
- *Staging requirements.* In addition to setting up a stage and runway, you must know whether you need to dovetail with the lighting and AV service contractors.
- *Dance floor.* You should also know whether one or more dance floors are needed.
- *Buffer area.* This is the space between the entertainers and the audience. Some big-name acts want quite a distance between them and their fans, primarily for security purposes.
- *Liability.* A glance at the contract will tell you whether there is any potential liability concern. For instance, some magicians use un-

usual and potentially dangerous props that may expose the facility to a lawsuit if guests are injured. You also need to know whether the facility will be responsible for the entertainer's personal property. If so, you must control the handling of these items.

○ *Complimentary food, beverage, and/or sleeping rooms.*   You may want to offer entertainers the hospitality of the house as a goodwill gesture. Alternately, the client may agree to pay their tabs.

○ *Operational logistics.*   Some entertainers may have demands that can affect the facility. For instance, a singer may require a larger dressing room, or an entertainer may request special foods and beverages. Ask to see the entertainment contract "rider" that outlines special requirements.

LIGHTING

Lighting is most commonly used to provide safety and security. It is primarily used to illuminate public and work areas properly so that they meet local building code requirements and to create a relaxed atmosphere.

Lighting, however, can be much more than this. In can be used to overcome a plain, pedestrian environment, highlight persons, products, and specific function room decors, illuminate platform speakers and other entertainers, focus attention on a particular spot, create a more exciting and dramatic dance floor, frame an area, follow awardees from their seats to the stage, and provide other decorative touches.

Lighting can also be used to tell a story. For instance, you can use laser equipment to project company logos, pictures of awards recipients, names of VIPs, and so forth, on a wall so that guests can view them as they enter the facility.

Depending on the client's needs, he or she can use the facility's permanent lighting system or employ a qualified outside lighting service contractor.

Facility Lighting System

The typical facility does not own specialized lighting equipment that can be used to create light shows or any other type of unusual production. Normally, it can provide spotlights and similar equipment. However, it is not set up to accommodate unusual requests and will require an outside service contractor. In some cases, sufficient electrical power, space, overhead beams, and so forth, are included in the original building design in anticipation of these needs.

Conference centers, resorts, and hotels in rural areas may have sufficient lighting equipment and resources to handle most special requests. These facilities may feel obliged to provide such services because clients expect such convenience, and when they are located in an out-of-the-way area, there may not be nearby service contractors.

If a client requires only enough lighting to illuminate the function room, then no additional lighting service is required. But if lighting will be used as a form of decoration, few facilities can provide a complete service package.

INTERMEDIARIES

At times the caterer will not work directly with a client. Instead, he or she will be dealing with an intermediary hired by the client to arrange a catered function.

Clients such as corporations or associations often outsource all or parts of an event to intermediaries. For instance, if there will be several meal and beverage functions, two or more facilities involved, and many outside service contractors, a potential client may be more comfortable employing a seasoned professional experienced in producing these types of detailed affairs.

Intermediaries are often used for civic and political fund-raising events when it is necessary for them to solicit financial support and to sell tickets. For instance, fund-raising fashion shows, theme parties, charity auctions, and art shows are typically planned and implemented by professional intermediaries.

The catering executive typically has mixed feelings about intermediaries. Their professionalism is certainly welcome. They know what they are doing. Unlike some clients, they do not have to be educated about every detail. Furthermore, the client is paying for their work.

On the other hand, intermediaries are generally more astute shoppers than typical catering clients. They tend to drive harder bargains. They sometimes want more control over events than the typical catering executive is willing to surrender. And there may be some uneasy moments if, in addition to getting a fee from the client, an intermediary solicits a commission from the facility for including its property in the event. As some facilities will not pay this type of commission, a client may not be aware of all potential facilities capable of handling his or her needs.

Independent Meeting Planner

Professional meeting planners, sometimes referred to as "contract planners" or "multimanagement companies," are probably the most common type of intermediary used by clients. Clients can hire them to plan and implement entire functions. Or they can be engaged to perform specific services, such as site selection, negotiations, or registration of convention attendees.

Independent meeting planners specialize in producing convention programs, business meetings, training programs, and similar events. They are capable of coordinating all necessary business functions, meal functions, beverage functions, and outside service contractors. They usually meet the needs of small and medium-sized companies that require professional assistance but do not have the resources to hire in-house planners. Most government clients also engage intermediaries of this type.

Special-Events Planner

Special-events planner intermediaries are sometimes engaged by corporations to plan and implement company parties and similar affairs. They usually have a select clientele list that are served on a periodic, predictable basis. For instance, a special-events producer may plan a particular company's annual picnic every year. Clients tend to prefer this type of long-term arrangement because it ensures continuity and variety.

Professional sports teams typically use special-events planners to coordinate after-game parties, half-time events, parades, and so forth.

Major events, such as the Olympics, corporate centennial celebrations, major openings, presidential inaugurations, and so forth, usually use several planners. For instance, the Coca-Cola Company's 100th birthday celebration in Atlanta required the services of several special-events specialists, with each one responsible for one specific part of the celebration.

If several special-events planners are used, one of them may be responsible for overseeing and coordinating everyone's efforts. He or she may also need to develop a master plan for the overall event and decide how each planner will be used.

Independent Party Planner

An independent party planner is an intermediary similar to a special-events planner. The primary difference is that he or she tends to work more often with noncorporate clients. For instance, a small group of persons wishing to organize a 20-year high school reunion tends to use this type of intermediary to help publicize, plan, and implement the function.

High school reunions are the most common type of reunion function. However, other reunions, such as college, family, military, company alumni, and so forth, are quickly becoming commonplace as clients realize how easy it is to accomplish what was once thought to be an impossible task.

Independent party planners usually take over all aspects of the function. They book the site, handle mailings, book entertainment, prepare a memory book, and so forth. Many of them also "lend" clients the deposits required by caterers, thereby allowing clients, who are volunteering to help out, to avoid paying out-of-pocket for up-front expenses; they can wait until their guests pay them before they have to pay the planners.

Many independent party planners are brokers who subcontract most or all portions of a function. For instance, if a group wants to hold a prom function, it may contact this type of intermediary, who will then select the caterer, help plan the menu, hire a decorator, and engage the appropriate entertainment.

Ground Transportation

Some ground transportation firms specialize in providing limousine service for guests. They can pick up and drop off guests and can be on call for personal needs during conventions. Shuttle or bus service is often employed because it is more efficient, and in most cases, a low-cost alternative to using taxicabs.

A few ground transportation companies specialize primarily in entertainment. For instance, some trips, such as charter boat cruises and trail rides, are planned strictly for their entertainment value.

Some ground transportation firms specialize in transporting a client's personal property. For instance, a local transport operator may pick up air-freighted or rail-freighted convention materials, such as equipment and product samples, and deliver them to an exposition hall. The same firm can also retrieve leftover merchandise and return it to the airport or railway yard.

Travel Agency

A travel agent's typical responsibilities are to sell individual or package tours, rental cars, sleeping rooms, and transportation tickets. Some agencies, however, have expanded their role to include meeting-planning services. For instance, if a client uses a travel agent to secure airline and sleeping-room reservations, it is fairly easy to use that agent to book a meeting room and catered luncheon for a client who wants to deal with only one person for all services. With the increase of travel purchases over the Internet, travel agents are eager to generate other sources of revenue. However, some caterers are not comfortable in working with travel agents, who expect commissions on all bookings, including catered events.

Travel agents are usually uncomfortable with guarantees. They are used to making "breakage." Recall that breakage is the cushion of money tour operators make when they include the cost of an item in a package and that item is not used. For example, if a tour group is given coupons for a breakfast buffet and half of the group's members decide to sleep in instead of eating, they do not turn these coupons in to the facility. The facility, then, does not have the coupon to submit to the tour operator for payment. Because the cost of the buffet was factored into the cost of the package, the tour operator gets to keep that money. Contrast this arrangement with having to give a caterer a guarantee and having to pay for the guaranteed number whether the people show up or not.

Combined Travel Agency and Independent Meeting Planner

Sometimes a travel agency and an independent meeting planner, two specialized intermediaries, are merged. The travel agency has the transportation expertise, and the planner has convention and meeting management abilities. Together they provide an attractive option for clients. In fact, in many instances, this combination gives even the smallest client a one-stop shopping opportunity.

Destination Management Company

A destination management company (DMC) provides a liaison between an out-of-town client and all of the services of a destination that the host property does not offer. DMCs range from those that provide very specialized services to full-service firms capable of handling all logistics. For instance, some companies provide only ground transportation (such as buses, limos, and vans), whereas others can handle personally, or can subcontract, everything a client needs. For instance, full-service firms can book entertainment, plan theme parties, coordinate tours and spouse programs, and handle off-site events (including catering) at museums and other local attractions.

Full-service firms can also provide personnel. For instance, exhibitors may want to hire local models to work exhibit booths. Trained registration personnel can also be hired. And "moving decor," such as costumed models, caricature artists, and celebrity look-alikes, can be used to help carry out the theme of an event. Generally, it is much cheaper for out-of-town corporate and association clients to hire these persons locally than to pay transportation and per-diem maintenance for company employees.

Destination management companies are often used to secure props for theme parties. For instance, a destination management company can see to it that a 1960s party has a vintage Mustang or Corvette on display. Appropriate balloon art and pyrotechnics displays can also be coordinated by this intermediary.

Many out-of-town clients are willing to pay a local destination management company to provide guidance in an unfamiliar area. It is very difficult for a client to judge the quality of services available if he or she has never visited the area. The intermediary can relieve the client of this burden. Furthermore, it can handle negotiations and oversee every detail, thereby ensuring a successful event.

Clients whose events are held in a different area every year prefer working with destination management companies. These intermediaries have made it easy for clients to indulge this preference by locating themselves in major convention cities. In fact, some national firms, such as USA Hosts, have local offices in several major convention cities that provide large corporate clients one-stop service as well as favorable quantity-discount prices for this service.

Of course, there are independent destination management companies that work in only one part of the country. Because of their specialized approach, clients may find them to be the best option. The Association for Destination Management Executives (ADME) can be visited at *http://www.adme.org.*

Convention and Visitors Bureau

The local convention and visitors bureau (CVB) is an attractive option for the out-of-town client who wants to book an event in a particular area but is unfamiliar with it. The CVB can provide useful information about the area, such as family attractions, transportation, hotels, and amount of available exhibit hall space, that can be used by a client to evaluate its suitability for an event.

The CVB can be an extremely valuable one-stop-shopping source for clients. For instance, if a client wants to plan a convention, he or she can send the CVB a Request for Proposal (RFP), that is, a list of requirements for meeting and sleeping accommodations and meal and beverage services. The CVB will distribute the "leads" to local hotels and outside service contractors, thereby relieving the client of the tedious task of shopping around. Many CVBs now accept RFPs online.

The CVB's most tangible benefit for clients is the time saved. In addition to providing suitable alternative selections for clients, it can also provide considerable logistical support at the local level.

Because the typical CVB is funded by "room" taxes paid by local hotel properties, a client can usually use its services inexpensively or free of charge. The CVB can also offer promotional material to clients free of charge. For instance, clients can often get free name tag holders, brochure shells, small mementos, the services of registration personnel, and similar support. Most bureaus will use their advertising budgets to absorb such costs.

Government Agencies

You may need to work closely with government agencies when planning a special event. For example, you may have to inform the fire department if you are putting on an outdoor pyrotechnics display. You will also have to make sure that the pyrotechnic company producing the display acquires the appropriate liability insurance, typically $1 million.

The fire department may also have to oversee and inspect any portable electrical power setup to ensure it is grounded properly and safe to use in a public area. In some jurisdictions, a fire marshal must approve banquet room setups to make sure that guests will be able to evacuate safely in the event of a fire.

The local health district typically must approve portable, temporary tents, cooking lines, serving lines, and so forth, to be certain that you are not violating health guidelines.

You may need special parking permits for buses, parade permits, or a temporary off-site liquor license.

If a client has a public official, such as a city mayor or state governor, speaking at a meeting, you may be dealing with bodyguards, or in the case of the President of the United States, the Secret Service.

Cooperating with Other Facilities

Some catered events are so large that two or more caterers must co-operate in servicing them. Attendees are often shuttled from one area to another. If you are involved in this sort of "co-op" venture, someone will have to coordinate and direct it. The client usually handles a great deal of the organization needed, but the individual caterers must go beyond this. Without communication, guests may not receive enough menu variety.

Rental Companies

Many caterers do not wish to own and store equipment that is not used often. It is too expensive and inconvenient to do this. Generally, when specialized equipment is required, it is more economical to rent it, as off-premise caterers usually do. The cost is, of course, passed on to the client either through separate, itemized billing or by inclusion in the per-person charge.

Caterers typically rent the following types of equipment:

○ Audiovisual
○ Refrigerated storage
○ Freezer storage
○ Generators
○ Transportation
○ Tables and chairs
○ Tableware (flatware, china, etc.)
○ Service utensils (chafing dishes, ladles, etc.)
○ Linens (clients often want colors or patterns the facility does not own)
○ Centerpieces (clients often rent or bring in their own centerpieces)
○ Lighting
○ Tents

Staffing | Chapter 9

The importance of staffing in the service industry cannot be overestimated. The catering department's reputation rests on its ability to prepare and serve a consistent quality of food and beverages. Without the proper amount and type of personnel, a caterer cannot hope to develop or maintain a sterling reputation.

What motivates a client to book business with a particular caterer? What is the difference between one caterer and another? Certainly, each caterer lays claim to some sort of unique benefit that it alone can provide to clients. However, if you scratch the surface of any caterer's reputation, chances are you will find that its perceived level of service is one of its most important features.

Conceivably, a client could rent a hall and perform all the shopping, cooking, serving, and cleaning chores. And he or she could probably do it at less than half the cost of hiring a caterer. Why, then, would that client agree to book a catering function knowing full well that it will not be cheap?

The obvious answer is that such clients, like all customers, are willing to pay for someone else to do the work. Yet, more than that, they are willing to pay a premium for someone to do the work in a timely and efficient manner, and certainly better than they can do it themselves.

One of the best things that can happen to you is for clients to say yes, they did spend a great deal, but they got their money's worth. In other words, they received value for their dollars.

Conversely, one of the worst things that can occur is for clients to perceive that they did not get a good value. No matter how low the price is, if a client does not perceive value, it is too high.

Staffing is critical. It is an organization's lifeblood. Experience shows that customer satisfaction and repeat patronage are influenced primarily by food and beverage quality, service, and sanitation and cleanliness. An inadequate, undermanned, undertrained staff is incompatible with the successful catering operation.

EMPLOYEE RECRUITMENT

Even if you are in a large departmentalized property, you should not rely solely on the facility's human resources department to secure adequate staffing. You cannot merely pick up the phone and call the employment manager whenever you have a job opening. Rather, it is very important to adopt a proactive approach in order to satisfy your staffing needs.

Staffing is an ongoing activity, primarily because the typical catering department's staffing requirements fluctuate widely. This is especially true for the group of employees who work part-time and/or on very unpredictable schedules.

There is a critical core of permanent, fixed-cost, full-time and part-time managerial and hourly staff members. Many of these people are career oriented and/or satisfied with their current positions. Consequently, they are apt to remain with you. This does not mean, however, that this core will never change; it is subject to change at a moment's notice. For instance, a permanent part-time head bartender may suddenly leave you to take a full-time bartending job with a competing caterer.

Many staff members are variable-cost employees who tend to work for more than one caterer. Although most of them prefer part-time status, some are looking for full-time employment. If they secure something permanent, chances are they will leave you on short notice.

Many variable-cost employees may be busy when you need them. For instance, some may be working at their regular jobs and cannot break away to help you, and others may be working at another catered function that day.

Variable-cost employees also tend to move in and out of the industry. It is not unusual for food and cocktail servers and bus persons to qualify for employment in other segments of the service industry. For instance, the people skills and customer-contact skills that food servers develop are the major prerequisites for many job positions in department stores, supermarkets, and boutiques.

An unfortunate fact of life in the service industry is the labor shortage that frustrates your efforts to build and maintain an adequate staff. Not only must you compete with other caterers for a diminishing labor pool, you must also fight other retailers.

To say the least, maintaining an adequate number of qualified employees is no easy task. No one likes to encounter severe employee turnover. However, the fluctuating demands for staff members in the catering industry have resulted in a certain amount of "structural" (i.e., unavoidable) turnover that you must combat daily.

The caterer must be willing to constantly cultivate potential employees. This is especially important for your hourly staff. Your A-lists and B-lists can never be too long. You do not want to get to the end of them and find that you still do not have enough people to staff the upcoming catering events.

You also need to cultivate and develop your fixed-cost employees. Because the typical way of doing this is to promote people from the variable-cost employee group, it is even more important to spend as much time as possible recruiting entry-level employees.

Job Specifications

For management positions, candidates must have technical work experience along with the requisite human skills. For many hourly positions, you also prefer job candidates with a reasonable amount of catering work experience. However, you may conceivably hire persons for many positions who have minimal or no work experience in our industry.

If a person has a willingness to do the work and possesses customer-contact skills and a positive attitude toward the catering industry, he or she can be trained to perform capably. For instance, with patience and understanding you can turn energetic people into excellent food and cocktail servers.

A lack of technical skills can place an additional burden on you and the rest of your staff because of the extra training that must be done. Generally, managers in the foodservice industry are accustomed to hiring and training neophytes. In fact, many of them prefer to do this rather than retrain new hires and break old habits. They believe that it may be much easier to start with a blank slate.

It is one thing to hire someone without catering work experience, but quite another to hire a person who has no work experience in customer-contact positions. There is generally no way to predict how someone will react when put into a high-pressure situation in which guests are blowing off steam. The various personality tests available do not adequately predict a newcomer's initial reactions.

The same holds true if you contemplate hiring someone who has never worked a paid job outside the home. If you hire such a person, you encounter all the problems associated with hiring someone with no catering work experience plus those that crop up whenever someone is introduced to the realities of the workplace. Not only must you teach novices how to perform their jobs, you also must teach them the protocols of working for a living.

When recruiting job candidates, you must also see to it that they possess the appropriate credentials. For instance, some positions may have to be staffed solely with union members. A few may require college degrees or similar training. Secretaries should be knowledgeable in word processing, e-mail, catering software, record keeping, and related tasks. Other positions may require persons who have current alcohol server awareness training certificates. And some employees may need current health cards issued by the local health district.

Minimum age is another job specification for workers who prepare, sell, and/or serve alcoholic beverages. In most parts of the United States, these persons must be at least 21 years old. As a general rule, facilities hire minors for kitchen pre-prep, food runner, and similar jobs. However, the catering department usually does not hire minors, because it is almost impossible to see that they are not involved in alcoholic beverage service.

Job Description

It is imperative to maintain up-to-date, current job descriptions so that job candidates know exactly what to expect if they come to work for you. You do not want to be put into the position of relating inaccurate information, as it can cause undue grief, job dissatisfaction, and unnecessary employee turnover.

Job descriptions must paint accurate pictures of all job duties that must be performed. Candidates may misinterpret job parameters because the job descriptions are too vague. The recruiter may exacerbate this problem by failing to address the specific job needs during the interview process.

Recruits' misinterpretation of their jobs may be one of the key variables responsible for excessive employee turnover. In general, if you can keep an hourly person for 30 days, or a management person for one year, chances are that he or she is satisfied with the job and the company and is likely to remain for a while. If you paint a realistic picture up front, and then see to it that reality does not vary significantly from this description, your employee turnover will probably be much less than the industry average.

Labor Pool

The catering executive should work closely with the human resources department to develop an adequate labor pool. He or she should inform human resources of potentially fruitful areas in which to seek job candidates so that its efforts are not wasted. For instance, if you think that the local college can generate adequate job candidates, encourage the human resources department to recruit on campus.

The catering department should not hesitate to adopt a proactive approach. It should have a long-term staffing plan that notes expected terminations and resignations, as well as anticipated total staffing needs. It should also take the lead whenever possible and seek out job candidates and send them to human resources for interviewing and possible hiring.

The labor pool sources that can yield capable job candidates are discussed in the following paragraphs.

Promotion from Within.   Employees like promotion-from-within policies because this gives them an opportunity to move up in the company. Career ladders may attract potential employees who would otherwise not perceive your facility as a good place to work.

Job Referral.   Current catering employees may have friends or relatives who may wish to apply for job openings. This could be a win-win situation, in that the current employee may receive some type of bonus and the catering department gets another good employee who knows what to expect. Unfortunately, problems resulting from conflicts of interest or nepotism may arise in such situations. Because of these problems, some employers severely restrict this hiring practice.

Use Employees from Other Departments.   A part-time employee in another department may be a good addition to your A-list or B-list. This can be another win-win situation, assuming it does not violate company policy. You must be careful when engaging a person from another department part-time, because jealousy and hard feelings can develop. For instance, it may be rather ticklish if a part-time coffee shop employee finds your department more inviting and requests a transfer.

Using other department employees can also cause overtime problems. For instance, if in one week an employee works five full days in the restaurant dining room and one full day for you, he or she would have to be paid overtime premium pay for the sixth day. Federal regulations mandate that an employee must be compensated 1½ times his or her regular rate of pay for all hours worked in excess of 40 per week. Furthermore, in some states an employee may be entitled to overtime premium pay for all hours worked in excess of 8 per day (if the normal workweek is 5 days, 8 hours per day) or 10 per day (if the normal workweek is 4 days, 10 hours per day).

Union Hiring Hall.   A unionized facility may have to use the union hiring hall for permanent and temporary hires if the job positions are unionized. In some cases, the union may sponsor internships and apprenticeships that can provide you with a steady, albeit ever changing, supply of young, enthusiastic workers.

Culinary Schools.   Culinary schools are a good source of permanent, full-time employees. They also represent a good pool of part-time workers who need to earn work-experience hours to complete their degree requirements. Moreover, the instructors may be interested in working part-time, or they may be willing to work for you during their summer vacations.

Colleges and Universities.   Concentrate your recruiting efforts on the many universities and two-year colleges offering hospitality management training. You may be able to attract graduates for full-time positions. And because most college programs require students to earn a minimum number of work hours in the hospitality field, try to set up a system whereby your part-time staff is continually replenished with underclassmen.

Many other college majors may be willing to work part-time. Our industry is flexible enough to work around most school schedules. Students are usually favorably disposed to part-time catering work because of its ability to accommodate almost anyone's personal schedules. Call the schools' placement offices and ask them to post your job openings.

Homemakers.   Homemakers constitute one of the best sources for A-list or B-list people. You may need to be extra flexible with these workers because they will not work if your needs conflict with their personal family responsibilities.

Seniors.   Many retired persons want to remain active in the workaday world. They are increasingly included in many retailers' part-time labor pools. Several types of foodservice operations are eager to hire seniors on a part-time basis. They usually bring a favorable combination of work experience, enthusiasm, patience, personableness, and dedication that makes them extremely valuable employees.

Avoid trying to convert part-time employees, especially seniors, into full-time employees. Because this is usually an unattractive option for such workers, it is best to avoid this temptation lest you lose valuable part-time personnel.

Private Industry Councils.   Many business persons support institutes and similar organizations that can be good sources of full-time and part-time labor. These groups are quite active in sponsoring job fairs, apprenticeship programs, and job training opportunities that can dovetail nicely with your employment efforts.

Employment Agencies.   Public and private employment agencies may yield full-time job candidates. Public agencies operated by state unemployment compensation departments can be good sources of hourly wage earners. They may be preferable to private employment agencies because they do not charge fees for their services. Because of the fees involved, employers tend to use outside private "head hunters" only when it is necessary to hire middle- and top-management personnel.

Government Job-Training Agencies.   In your area there may be one or more local government agencies sponsoring job-training programs on their own or with the cooperation of the federal government. For instance, the local workers compensation insurance program may sponsor several rehabilitative training programs for injured employees who cannot go back to their old jobs. You may be part of these training efforts by providing jobs for the trainees. In some cases your cooperation can result in payroll savings, because some programs grant tax credits and/or pay part or all of the wages during the training periods. Moreover, a successful trainee may eventually take a full-time, permanent position with your facility.

Day-Labor Operations.   Day-labor organizations are similar to public and private employment agencies. The major difference is that they usually "lease" people to you on a daily basis. For instance, if you need a few extra hands to set up an outdoor tent, a call to the local "manpower" agency may yield the exact amount of labor required. You get only the amount of help needed. And it is more convenient to pay one price for it rather than putting everyone through the normal, expensive, hiring procedure.

Day-labor operations may hire street people, which may tend to turn off the typical employer. However, if you assign workers only those jobs they are capable of doing, you should obtain favorable results.

Other Caterers.   Although it is not neighborly to steal employees from your competitors, you should not let this stop you from spreading the word about job opportunities at your property. Furthermore, because all caterers use part-time persons, there is ample opportunity to offer someone one or two workdays at your facility while allowing him or her to keep another job.

Usually, some of your employees are working for several caterers anyway. For example, a few of them may be on the B-list of every major property in town. You might as well take the initiative and maximize the potential of this labor source by publicizing, always using good taste, your job opportunities.

Professional Associations.   Among the most fruitful sources of sales and management personnel are professional associations. Many hospitality managers belong to one or more professional associations. For instance, many catering professionals belong to the National Association of Catering Executives (NACE).

One of the benefits association members enjoy is being kept apprised of current career opportunities available in their fields of expertise and interest. Use these built-in grapevines to advertise current job vacancies.

Volunteer Groups/Charitable Organizations. It is becoming quite common to use members of groups and organizations such as churches, synagogues, booster clubs, band parents, and so forth, in concession stands/retail operations in large facilities such as stadiums, arenas, and resorts. The members work for a percentage of the revenue, which goes to the group or charitable organization. These people are also used in some nonskilled positions, such as bus persons, buffet servers, and food runners, when it makes sense for the catered event. In this case, the members are paid the going hourly rate, with the earnings going to the group or charitable organization.

A downside of this labor source is that the members donating their time can be more vocal about what they are willing to do. They are not threatened with the loss of a job, so they have to be "managed" more delicately. Another potential problem is that one or two members may end up watching the event, or participating in it, instead of working; this is especially likely if they are working a big event or if they know several of the guests.

Reduction of Employee Turnover. The seeds of employee turnover or employee retention are planted when a job candidate is interviewed, and take root when the new hire gets a chance to experience reality and compare it with your promises. Turnover and retention are also directly related to the type and amount of job training and development provided to employees. Studies by the National Restaurant Association (NRA) show that lack of training and development is one of the main reasons people leave their jobs.

The costs of hiring, orienting, training, putting up with lower productivity for a while, and so forth, can add up very quickly. If you can reduce turnover, the potential payroll savings are handsome. Moreover, a reduction in employee turnover relieves the pressure for you to cultivate other labor sources.

Job Application

The job application is the most common instrument used for the initial screening of potential employees. Applications are usually filled out in the human resources department by walk-ins—persons who respond to classified ads or who merely stop by to see whether you need help.

The job application can be an excellent prescreening device. The employment manager can use it to weed out unqualified job candidates, those who do not possess the requisite experience, education, and other pertinent characteristics.

If you find someone to fill a job position, you still need him or her to complete a job application and go through the rest of the candidate-processing procedure.

Job Interview

A walk-in seeking a job is usually given a prescreening interview if the job application reveals some promising information. Typically, the prescreening interview involves a discussion of some basic questions, such as, When can the person report for work? What is the depth of his or her work experience? Will the person be comfortable working under your property's particular rules and regulations? and so forth.

A prescreening interview is also an excellent opportunity to determine whether a job candidate is likely to succeed at your facility. Some facilities use a prescreening process to determine whether a job candidate has the proper attitudes, skills, and work habits needed to perform effectively.

If a candidate passes the prescreening interview, the interviewer should take time to check references before moving him or her along in the candidate-processing procedure. Telephone calls should be made to verify information indicated on the application and during the prescreening interview.

A facility may also include some testing procedures. For instance, your facility may have a policy of giving all job applicants a tray test (to see whether they can successfully balance a tray full of plates or glasses), an integrity test, a physical exam, and so forth, before they can qualify for the next step in the employment process. Many facilities also require a pre-employment drug test.

If the reference check yields favorable information, the job candidate is usually then formally interviewed by you or someone on your staff. In some cases, he or she may be interviewed by you and other management personnel in the catering department. This is especially likely if the person is applying for an entry-level sales or management position.

After this interview, it is generally up to you to determine whether the facility should offer the position to the applicant. If you want to hire the person, human resources will then extend the job offer formally, complete the employment process, and schedule the new hire's first workday.

ORIENTATION

In a large facility, the human resources department is responsible for orienting all new hires. This procedure normally takes the better part of one workday. Smaller facilities should also complete some or all of the following steps.

Orientation usually involves providing new hires with non-job-related information. For instance, new hires are usually

- Introduced to the company's philosophy
- Fitted for uniforms
- Given an employee handbook and explanation of the information it contains
- Given a welcoming by the general manager and other major department heads
- Exposed to general lectures dealing with property security procedures, company history, career opportunities, and so forth
- Given a tour of the property
- Assigned locker room space, parking places, name tags, and so forth
- Introduced to their supervisors and co-workers.

TRAINING

The human resources department and the catering department ordinarily share the training efforts. For instance, human resources may provide general training in life safety, customer courtesy, complaint handling, telephone procedures, drug and alcohol awareness, and so forth, with catering taking responsibility for the initial and ongoing specific job-related training.

The Food & Beverage Committee of the Hotel Sales & Marketing Association International developed training guidelines that can be used to familiarize a catering department's new hire with all pertinent operating and nonoperating activities. Although these guidelines were developed for management positions in hotels, any new hire, depending on his or her position, should be familiarized with the following areas:

1   Banquet Sales Manual.   All catering sales representatives should be familiar with your catering policies and procedures. New entry-level salespersons who are unfamiliar with the general sales systems used in catering should pay particular attention to the following:

    a. Catering files and filing procedures
    b. Tracing procedures
    c. Solicitation procedures
    d. Catering sales analysis
    e. Booking procedures
    f. Procedures used to prepare banquet event orders (BEO), pre-function sheets, and convention resumes
    g. Dates and space reservation procedures
    h. Confirmation procedures
    i. Cancellation procedures
    j. Specific job responsibilities
    k. Sales techniques
    l. Credit procedures
    m. Guarantee procedures

2   Food and Beverage Department.   If relevant, the new hire should be exposed to some or all of the following food and beverage operating procedures:

    a. Food and beverage controller's office
        (1)   General banquet food and beverage cost requirements
        (2)   Exposure to banquet food and beverage cost calculations
        (3)   General food and beverage accounting procedures
        (4)   Food controls
        (5)   Beverage controls
        (6)   Guarantee and attendance calculations
        (7)   Variance analysis
        (8)   Profit-and-loss statement analysis
        (9)   Computing total banquet costs
       (10)   Percentage analysis
       (11)   Payroll cost analysis
       (12)   Profit ratios

    b. Kitchen
        (1)   Executive chef's responsibilities
        (2)   Banquet chef's responsibilities
        (3)   Banquet menus
        (4)   Banquet change orders
        (5)   Staffing

      (6)   Stock requisitions
      (7)   Food pre-prep
      (8)   Food prep
      (9)   Banquet dish-up
      (10) Evaluating potential menu items
      (11) Month-end inventories
      (12) Portion control

c. Steward
      (1)   Payroll forecasts
      (2)   Review of banquet menus
      (3)   Staffing
      (4)   Stock requisitions
      (5)   Equipment preparation
      (6)   Equipment inspection
      (7)   Equipment storage
      (8)   Coordination with kitchen and service
      (9)   Salvage procedures
      (10) Sanitation procedures
      (11) Refrigeration
      (12) Equipment par stocks
      (13) Equipment inventories
      (14) Supplies storage
      (15) Equipment and supplies purchasing

d. Banquet manager
      (1)   General service procedures
      (2)   Coordination with kitchen and steward
      (3)   General supervisory procedures
      (4)   Banquet rooms
      (5)   Function room setups
      (6)   Pre-meal-service meetings
      (7)   Seating charts
      (8)   Function room maintenance
      (9)   Menu meetings
      (10) Preconvention meetings
      (11) Coordination of tableware and napery
      (12) Payroll forecasts
      (13) Forecasted repair and maintenance needs
      (14) Work scheduling
      (15) Housekeeping work sheets
      (16) Styles of service

e. Beverage

       (1)   Banquet menus
       (2)   Coordination with steward and banquet manager
       (3)   Stock requisitions
       (4)   Change orders
       (5)   Guarantees
       (6)   Sales and cost data
       (7)   Prefunction meetings—roll call and briefing
       (8)   Stocking banquet bars
       (9)   Bar teardown
     (10)   Beginning and ending bar inventories
     (11)   Cash reconciliation
     (12)   Drink ticket reconciliation
     (13)   Month-end inventories
     (14)   Work scheduling

  f.   Room service
       (1)   Hospitality suites
       (2)   Liquor control
       (3)   Room-service checks
       (4)   Coordination with room setup
       (5)   Amenity service packages available

  g.   Food and beverage manager
       (1)   Daily revenue and payroll report
       (2)   Filing system
       (3)   Restaurant outlets
       (4)   Bar outlets
       (5)   Forecasting
       (6)   Payroll analysis
       (7)   Menu analysis
       (8)   Coordination with the district or regional director of food and beverage (if applicable)
       (9)   Coordination with the corporate vice president of food and beverage (if applicable)

3   Purchasing
  a.   Product availability
  b.   Seasonal variations
  c.   Special items not commonly used
  d.   Banquet menu reviews
  e.   Banquet order sheets
  f.   Order sizes
  g.   Ordering procedures

    h. Purchase price trends
    i. Plant visits
4 Convention Service
    a. Review of function room setup checklists
    b. Banquet room assignments
    c. Banquet room capabilities and limitations
    d. Hospitality suites
    e. Clearing space for catering functions
    f. Preconvention meetings
5 Tour and Travel
    a. Travel agents
    b. Tour wholesalers
    c. General sales procedures
    d. Meal coupons
    e. Other coupons
    f. Product and service prices
6 Front Office
    a. Reservations
    b. Front desk procedures and software
        (1) Check in
        (2) Check out
        (3) Baggage handling
    c. Coordination with sales department
    d. Room and suite tours (if applicable)
    e. Bell desk
    f. Concierge
7 Credit/Accounting
    a. Credit procedures
    b. Deposit requirements
    c. Collections
        (1) Procedures
        (2) Problems
        (3) Outside collection agencies
        (4) Types of accounts
8 Human Resources
    a. General personnel procedures
    b. Coordination with hotel departments
    c. Compensation packages
9 Engineering
    a. Sound

    b. Lighting

    c. Utilities available in function rooms

    d. Charges for utilities, labor, and equipment

10 Public Relations and Advertising

    a. Food and beverage promotions

    b. Newspaper clippings

    c. Outside calls

    d. Aware of functions at other hotels

    e. Contact individuals responsible for buying catered functions

    f. Familiarization with competing hotel catering departments' offerings

11 Safety

    a. Recognizing safety hazards

    b. Slippery floor procedures

    c. Customer safety

    d. Proper utilities hookups

    e. Setting up crosswalk areas

    f. Fire codes

    g. Health codes

    h. Evacuation routes

12 Laundry and Valet

    a. Napery controls

    b. Stock requisitions

    c. Soiled napery storing procedures

    d. Usage charges

    e. Uniforms and costumes

The department head should use these suggested guidelines to develop an appropriate training program for each new hire. The new hire's progress should then be monitored, with the department head submitting a training report to the director of catering at the conclusion of the training period.

The training report should be reviewed with the trainee before a final draft is prepared. For instance, each time an entry is made in the report, the trainer and trainee should visit together for a few moments to discuss the entry and determine whether any changes must be made in the program. This is also a good time to discuss the trainee's progress and clear up any problems.

In the case of some new hires, it can be useful to have them prepare a personal report at the end of their training period. For instance, if you are training a new catering sales representative, you may want to ask him or her to submit a written report detailing what was learned after visiting and working in all other departments. This report can give you a valuable insight into the trainee's communications skills. It can reveal whether additional training is needed, and it can tell you whether future training programs should be modified.

COMPENSATION

Typical compensation packages include a combination of at least some of the following: salaries, wages, gratuities, commissions, bonuses, tips, required employee benefits, and discretionary employee benefits. In large facilities, compensation packages are developed and coordinated by the human resources department. You should know specifically the types and amounts of compensation allowed for each position so that potential candidates will not be misled while you are cultivating them.

Management positions normally receive predetermined salaries unrelated to the amount of time worked. Some managers, however, may receive performance bonuses and/or commissions. For instance, a catering sales representative may receive a modest fixed salary plus a percentage of all business booked.

Nonmanagement, wage-earner positions are usually compensated on an hourly basis. Some of them may also receive a preset split of the gratuities collected for each catered event. If a client leaves a tip, the wage earners typically share it as well.

Required employee benefits are usually referred to as payroll taxes. They include primarily the employer's contribution to the federal government's Social Security, Medicare, and unemployment benefit tax programs. Some states also require employers to contribute monies to their unemployment benefit programs and the state-operated workers compensation programs.

As a general rule, the minimum cost of required employee benefits is equal to about 15 to 18 percent of your total payroll expense. For instance, if you pay a server $10.00 per hour, the employer's hourly out-of-pocket expense for this employee is about $11.50 to $11.80 per hour after factoring in these payroll taxes.

In some parts of the country, the total payroll tax expense is much higher because the tax percentages will be applied to the payroll expense plus the amount of gratuities and declared tips. For instance, if a $10.00-per-hour server averages an additional $5.00 per hour gratuity and tip income, the hourly payroll tax expense for this employee will be about $2.25 to $2.70 (15 to 18 percent of $15.00). The employer's hourly out-of-pocket expense for this employee, then, is about $12.25 to $12.70.

Typical discretionary benefits are health, dental, optical, and life insurance paid for by the company or offered to employees at a reduced rate. Some companies also provide stock option plans, profit-sharing plans, 401(k) plans, free meals, matching contributions to selected charities, paid vacation time, paid sick days, insurance coverage for dependents, formal training, career opportunities (such as promotion from within), reimbursement of educational expenses, flexible work scheduling, uniform allowances, and reduced-cost meals, beverages, and sleeping rooms at other company-owned or operated properties.

Generally, only full-time employees qualify for the full range of discretionary benefits. Some facilities may offer a limited number of discretionary benefits to part-time employees who work at least 20 hours per week. Employees working 19 hours or less per week usually do not qualify for discretionary benefits.

Some facilities, especially unionized properties, have generous overtime pay policies that exceed those mandated by federal and state labor regulations. They may also have very generous holiday pay policies. For instance, union and/or company policy may require you to pay double time instead of time and a half for all overtime worked, straight time for all state and federal holidays not worked, and double time for all state and federal holidays worked.

Financial Controls and Reports

Control procedures must be used to ensure that actual performance is in line with planned performance. The control cycle begins when a potential client considers booking business at your property, and it does not end until the catered function is completed to everyone's satisfaction.

Before a control system can be implemented, you must set standards of performance. For instance, if you book a beverage function and you expect each bottle of liquor to yield approximately 15 drinks, the actual number of drinks served per container must be consistent with this standard. If your bartenders pour more or less than 15 drinks per container, you may have a control problem. If they pour too many drinks per container, the customers are usually receiving a reduced portion size. If they pour too few drinks per container, chances are that there is excessive waste or customers are receiving excessive portion sizes.

It is management's duty to set the required standards and policies by which all catered events will be run. All operational procedures—from booking the business, to purchasing, receiving, storing, issuing, producing, and serving the finished products, to function room selection and setup, to final bill tabulation and collection—must be standardized. If all employees follow the standard operating procedures, chances are that you will reach your cost-control and quality-control goals with minimal difficulty.

One of management's primary responsibilities is to see to it that actual results are in line with the standards. To do this, management must develop data-gathering and data-analysis procedures that can be used to compute actual results and compare them with the standards. If there are variances between the standards and the actual results, management must move to identify and solve the underlying problem(s). This correction phase of control is the most difficult one, because it is not always easy to diagnose what went wrong. If you cannot get at the root of the problem, it is impossible to solve it.

For example, if your bartenders are consistently pouring more drinks per container than you expect, there are many potential causes for this variance. Underpouring of each drink is the most logical cause, although mechanical problems with the liquor-dispensing machinery, inadequate record keeping, and failure to account properly for those guests who ask for short pours are also possible reasons.

Another difficult aspect of the control process is the potential to overcontrol everything. It does not make sense to cost-control yourself out of business. You cannot spend a dollar to control a dime. There comes a point at which some controls are not cost-effective. For instance, computerized automatic liquor-dispensing units will increase your ability to control drink service. Unfortunately, the expensive investment in these systems may never be recovered in a reasonable period of time.

Overcontrol can also put a manager in the position of concentrating solely on inanimate objects and ignoring clients and guests. You cannot dwell so much on cost-related matters that you begin to lose sight of the customer. You must satisfy your clients and guests. However, if you are spending too much time gathering, processing, and analyzing data, you may be neglecting your customers.

It is very difficult to strike just the right balance between effective control and customer service. If you take good care of the guest, your expenses and profits usually will fall into line. But if you concentrate solely on every penny, eventually you will not have to worry about control because you will have no business left to control.

Michael Hurst, past president of the National Restaurant Association (NRA) summed it up best when he remarked that you can achieve maximum control by closing your business; this is the only way to avoid control problems. If you want to stay in business and build it into a profitable enterprise, Hurst suggests that you manage from the front door, not the back door. Taking care of the clients and guests and providing consistent value is the best recipe for success in the food and beverage industry.

This chapter discusses the generally accepted control procedures used in the on-premise catering industry. By adopting these procedures, the director of catering takes a giant step toward minimizing variances and maximizing client and guest satisfaction.

CONTROL DOCUMENTS

Banquet Event Order

The banquet event order (BEO), sometimes referred to as the function sheet, is the basis of a facility's internal communication system between departments. It is also the basic building block upon which the catering department's accounting and record-keeping systems are constructed (see Figure 10.1).

A BEO is prepared for each meal and beverage function, and copies are sent to the departments that will be directly or indirectly involved with the event.

Usually, all departments receive a copy of each BEO a week or more before the catered function is held. This ensures that all department heads have enough time to schedule and complete their necessary activities that support the event.

BEOs are generally numbered sequentially for easy reference. It is important to assign an identifying number to each BEO so that department heads can resolve any discrepancy easily and quickly. For instance, if banquet setup is unclear about a particular event's requirements, it can call the catering office for additional information regarding BEO 175. This is certainly easier and more accurate than using clients' names or other forms of identification, all of which can be garbled and misinterpreted after two or three phone calls.

The typical BEO contains the following information:

○ BEO number
○ Function day(s) and date(s)
○ Type of function

BANQUET EVENT ORDER

Distribution

General Manager
Accounts Receivable
Front Office Cashier
Valet Parking
Inventory Control
Sales
Food & Beverage Director
Chef
Executive Steward
Bar Manager
Catering Director
Banquet Manager
Audiovisual
Banquet Housemen
File

Date: _____

Name: _____

Address: _____

In Charge: _____

Booked by: _____

Food	Beverage

Special Attention:

Food and Beverage Prices:

Master Account Number:

Approved by: _____

Date: _____

FIGURE 10.1. Example banquet event order (BEO).

- Client name with signature line
- Client address
- Client contact person, or person in charge
- Person who booked the event, and authorized signature(s)
- Name of function room
- Beginning time of function
- Expected ending time of function
- Number of guests expected
- Number of guests to prepare for
- Menus
- Style of service
- Function room setup
- Special instructions (such as in regard to centerpieces, parking details, miscellaneous labor charges, sleeping room blocks, napery, table sets, bar arrangements, props, entertainment, electrical/engineering needs, unique underliners, VIPs, and special amenities)
- Prices charged
- Master billing account number
- Billing instructions
- Reference to other BEOs or other relevant records
- Date BEO was completed
- Signature of person preparing (or approving) the BEO
- List of departments receiving a copy of the BEO

Prefunction Sheet

Some catering companies want to warn all departments well in advance of future catering activity. For instance, management may want everyone to have a good idea of the amount and types of catering business booked for the next month. This can be done by preparing a monthly prefunction sheet that briefly notes the types of groups and number of guests expected during the following month.

The prefunction sheet serves many purposes. Its major advantage is that it allows each department head to preplan his or her staffing needs for the long term. Other advantages are as follows: kitchen and purchasing can use this information to plan tentative ordering, pre-preparation, and preparation schedules; the storeroom can plan its inventory-management procedures more effectively; the convention service and steward departments will have plenty of time to secure additional furniture, equipment, and tableware if needed; and housekeeping can plan its heavy-cleaning routines more easily if it knows what to expect.

Change Order

Clients usually have opportunities to make alterations in their booked functions. For instance, they may be able to order changes in the menu one week before the event is scheduled, switch from table service to buffet service three days before, and decide to add extra bars 24 hours in advance.

At times, several changes must be made at the last minute. For example, if a function that initially expected 400 guests suddenly expands to 600 guests, the facility may need to move the buffet line into the prefunction space in order to accommodate additional seating.

Sometimes a change may be suggested by the caterer. For instance, if the purchasing agent has a problem getting a particular wine, the catering sales representative will have to meet with the client and discuss alternate brands that can be served for the same price.

Such alterations must be communicated to all departments involved with the catered event. The most efficient way to do this is to prepare an addendum to the original BEO.

A BEO addendum is usually referred to as a banquet change order or banquet change sheet. It contains the original BEO's identification number as well as other pertinent identifying factors. It also includes, very specifically, the changes that must be made. The department head must clearly note what must be eliminated and what must be added to the scheduled catered event.

To avoid confusion, the catering facility should use a simple color-coded system to ensure that changes are recorded accurately. For instance, a facility may use a three-color system: white—original BEO; canary—revisions; pink—guarantees. In this case, if a change must be communicated, all relevant departments will receive them on canary or pink paper, update their original BEOs, and reduce the paper flow so that only one copy is retained. A similar system that is computerized can further reduce the paper flow.

Resume

A resume is a summary of function room uses for a particular convention or meeting. It is normally used whenever a client books two or more catered events to be held consecutively (see Figure 10.2).

A convention resume may more appropriately be referred to as a function room resume, because this report emphasizes function room use for a particular client. It usually includes the major highlights, while deferring to the pertinent BEOs for specific details. For instance,

CONVENTION RESUME

Distribution
General Manager
Accounts Receivable
Front Office Cashier
Valet Parking
Inventory Control
Sales
Food & Beverage Director
Chef
Executive Steward
Bar Manager
Catering Director
Banquet Manager
Audiovisual
Banquet Housemen
File

Date: _____

Name: _____

Address: _____

In Charge: _____

Booked by: _____

Date	Hours	Function	Room	Guest Count

Room, Equipment, Labor Charges:

Room Setups:

Equipment Setups:

Special Attention:

Billing Instructions:

Master Account Number:

Approved by: _____

Date: _____

FIGURE 10.2. Example convention resume.

if you book a one-week convention and there are 15 meal, beverage, and business meeting functions, the convention resume will highlight each function, when the function rooms will be booked, and when they will be dark. This document generally includes the following information:

○   Function day(s) and date(s)
○   Types of functions
○   Client name
○   Client address
○   Client contact person, or person in charge
○   Person who booked the events, along with authorized signature(s)
○   Beginning times of functions
○   Expected ending times of functions
○   Number of guests expected
○   Furniture and equipment needs
○   Function room names
○   Room setups
○   Special instructions
○   Room charges
○   Labor charges
○   Equipment charges
○   Master billing account number
○   Billing instructions
○   Reference to other relevant records
○   Date convention resume was completed
○   Signature of person preparing (or approving) the resume
○   List of departments receiving a copy of the resume

Catering Contract

Caterers typically require clients to sign formal catering contracts before the events are scheduled to take place. This is especially true in dealing with large functions.

Sometimes a facility will forgo the use of formal contracts and instead rely on signed BEOs or signed letters of agreement. These documents may be every bit as legally enforceable as formal contracts. Usually, however, they do not include the typical boilerplate language (i.e., standardized legalese) found in most formal contracts. Signing an agreement is much less threatening to most people than signing a contract.

You should never book or confirm a catered event without a signed agreement. Usually, an unwritten contract cannot be legally enforced in a court of law unless you are dealing with an agreement worth $500 or less. But even for small parties, it is good business practice to detail in writing both your and the client's responsibilities and obligations.

If you have standardized contract or agreement forms, you can give a copy to a potential client to read and study before progressing any further. This gives the client enough time to examine the terms and conditions and to ask questions about anything that is unclear.

You are not in business to intentionally fool clients. But you must realize that, for example, some of them may see the notation "buffet service with entrée tickets" and jump to the conclusion that guests can take and eat all they want. If you suspect that they do not know that the term "entrée ticket" indicates that guests will receive an entrée only if they present a ticket, but that they can help themselves to everything else, it is up to you to explain it thoroughly and head off any potential trouble. The last thing you want is an unhappy group of guests.

Many facilities develop standardized contracts that contain a considerable amount of boilerplate clauses with enough blank space available to write in specific details as needed. For typical functions, the standard boilerplate contract will usually suffice. But if there is anything unusual that must be addressed, the caterer's legal counsel, or other representative, must add it.

If a convention client requires atypical services, the facility's and the client's legal representatives may work together to develop a mutually agreeable contract. They must negotiate and ultimately reduce their agreement to writing. This agreement can then be added to the standard boilerplate contract, or it can stand alone.

Some catering departments do not have to get involved with contract preparations. For instance, if your catering department is part of a hotel sales department, the director of sales may handle all contract negotiations. He or she may take care of adding clauses, explaining policies, detailing the property's responsibilities and obligations, and so forth. Only occasionally would you need to participate in these developments.

The basic catering contract usually includes the following details:

1 Contract date
2 Function day(s) and date(s)
3 Function time(s)

4   Appropriate client and facility signatures
5   Function room(s) tentatively assigned
6   Menus
7   Style(s) of service
8   Function room setup(s)
9   Other client services, such as:
  a.   Audiovisual
  b.   Lighting
  c.   Sleeping rooms
  d.   Transportation
  e.   Security
10   Head-count guarantees (and/or dollar amount guarantees)
11   Estimated cost summary
  a.   Food and beverage charges
  b.   Consumption taxes
  c.   Gratuities
  d.   Labor charges
  e.   Room charges
  f.   Cancellation penalty
  g.   Deposits
  h.   Other charges
12   Billing procedures
13   Procedures that must be used if changes are necessary
14   All catering policies (see Chapter 1)
15   Client's responsibilities and obligations
16   Other standard contract language, such as:
  a.   *Person signing contract represents he or she has full authority to legally bind the client.*
  b.   *The contract shall be binding upon the parties, as well as their heirs, administrators, executors, successors, and assigns.*
  c.   *Client has read the contract and completely understands its contents.*
  d.   *Client stipulates that he or she is not signing the contract under duress.*

CREDIT MANAGEMENT

If a client is eligible for credit, the caterer's credit manager will evaluate the client's credit rating and, if credit is approved, set up a master account number. He or she will then detail the property's deposit requirements and billing procedures.

Very few clients are eligible for credit. As a general rule, clients are expected to pay in advance. This is especially true for clients who may not generate repeat business, such as those booking one-time political fund-raising events. It is also typical in the catering industry to require advance payments from the shallow market segment (see Chapter 2).

Probably the major reason caterers are reluctant to advance credit is that the services provided are completely consumed. You can re-possess a car or other tangible asset if a customer reneges, but this op-tion does not exist for the seller of catering services.

Credit terms, however, can be a major selling tool. For instance, all other things being equal, a client may select your property because it offers generous credit terms. The more generous the credit terms, in effect, the lower the price will be for the catered event, because the client can hang onto his or her money for a while longer and leave it in the bank to draw interest income.

Offering credit also tends to increase sales revenue. Although some of the added sales may result in bad debts, a judicious use of credit will more than offset them. The rationale for offering credit is to increase sales, suffer a bit of bad debt expense, but generate incre-mental net profits to more than offset the bad debts. In the long run, if you offer credit, you may be able to earn significantly more profit than if you operate on a cash-only basis.

There is a trend in the catering industry to allow clients to use their personal or company credit cards to pay for catering services. This procedure virtually eliminates credit risk. It also makes the caterer's job a lot easier, because the credit card company handles all the credit verification chores and billing procedures. Unfortunately, this service may be very costly; depending on the type of card used, you can pay as much as 5 or 6 percent of credit card charges to the credit card company. On the other hand, there are Internet providers who will let someone use a credit card to pay with no charge to you. These services take the money from your customer and put it in your account. There is no charge because the services make money selling advertising on their web sites. These services are very popular with folks who buy and sell on ebay.

Most hotels and conference centers offering catering services op-erate their own credit departments (sometimes referred to as a hotel's "city ledger"). Many catered functions exceed several thousand dollars, and bank cards and travel and entertainment credit cards cannot be used to pay for them because their credit limits may be too low. The typical hotel usually takes a credit card payment for only small functions. For example, if you are serving a business luncheon for 25 guests in a private dining room, you may be willing to treat this affair as if it were a normal restaurant transaction.

Deposit

Repeat clients eligible for credit may not need to put up a deposit. However, they are generally expected to put up about 25 to 80 percent of the estimated final bill, depending on the size of the catered function and the client's credit rating.

The deposit must usually be made at least 30 days prior to service. If a contract is signed several months in advance, you may extract a minimal earnest-money deposit, of perhaps 5 percent, at that time. You may then require the client to increase this deposit to, say, 25 percent 30 days before the booking date.

When taking a deposit, the credit manager will issue a receipt to the client. For instance, the deposit will be recorded in the client's file, a copy of a check-received memorandum will be issued to the client, and a copy of this receipt will also be placed in the client's file.

Billing Procedures

When dealing with clients eligible for credit, the credit manager bills them according to the terms and conditions noted in the catering contract. The final accountings are prepared immediately after the catered events. Some clients are billed for the total amount due, while others are given a credit period during which they are required to follow a specific payment schedule.

In a few cases, creditworthy clients do not have to pay immediately after the event. The facility usually sets up a billing cycle that is mutually agreeable to both parties. Moreover, tradition and competition sometimes enter the picture, whereby specific credit periods are granted to certain clients as a matter of standard operating procedure. For instance, some corporate clients are accustomed to seven-day to two-month billing cycles for all their purchases. Government clients are also accustomed to these billing cycles. You may need to offer these credit terms in order to be competitive with other caterers soliciting these clients.

Collection Procedures

If a client fails to make a scheduled payment, the credit manager can set in motion preplanned collection procedures.

If a client is late, the credit manager usually calls the client immediately to discuss the problem and possible solutions. If this effort fails to produce results, sterner measures are instituted. For instance, a registered letter may be sent or the bill may be faxed. These procedures remove the opportunity for the client to say that the bill was lost in the mail.

If all these efforts yield nothing, then the manager may turn the problem over to the facility's corporate credit department. This office usually employs more sophisticated collection procedures. It will also take the drastic step of turning over the account to an independent bill collection agency.

Other Credit Procedures

The credit department may have to be involved with other credit-related issues. The credit manager, either alone or in conjunction with the catering executive, may be faced with the following considerations:

1   Tax-free clients must demonstrate this status by providing evidence of tax-free numbers and any other related documentation.

2   If clients are promised complimentary products and/or services, the final billings must be adjusted accordingly.

3   Some caterers pay referral fees or other types of commissions. If so, the credit manager may need to provide data necessary to compute them correctly.

4   A property may want to offer clients cash discounts if they pay their bills before the due dates. If so, the credit manager will have to adjust the final billings or see to it that cash rebates are mailed to clients.

5   If a client cancels a catered event after the cancellation grace period expires, the credit manager must determine whether he or she forfeits the entire deposit, or whether part of it can be refunded. In some cases, particularly when a client cancels at the last minute, perhaps the deposit is insufficient consideration. If so, the credit manager will have to compute the appropriate charges and institute collection procedures.

6   Some clients may have refunds due. For instance, you may want a client to put up a refundable deposit for audiovisual (AV) equipment. When the equipment is returned on time and in acceptable condition, the credit manager may credit the deposit to the final billing, or he or she may process a separate refund check.

Another form of refund is buying back drink tickets from guests who did not use all of them. Usually, a caterer will not buy back those that were purchased by the client and given to the guests. However, if a guest purchases extra drink tickets and does not use them all, the property may have a policy of repurchasing them.

7 Returns and allowances may have to be factored into the final billing. For example, if you had to make a last-minute menu substitution that was less expensive than the original selection, the credit manager may have to adjust the final billing. Conversely, if the chef had to use a more expensive substitute, the manager may not wish to pursue the matter because it was not the client's fault that the original item could not be procured. However, the client and the catering executive may discuss the matter and perhaps split the difference. If so, the credit manager may have to take this into account when processing the final billing.

POSTEVENT EVALUATION

It is important to review each event in terms of profitability, challenges, and desirability of rebooking. There are two types of evaluation: internal (departmental evaluation) and external (client evaluation). You need both in order to improve operations. Clients may not see the effect of operational challenges on their events. Yet although a client may think that an event was great, there may be internal changes necessary in order to streamline future events. A sample postevent critique form and show recap form are available in the appendix.

FOOD AND BEVERAGE–COST CONTROL

Effective control of product costs is based on standard operating procedures. To ensure consistent, predictable results for its business, top management must establish budgetary standards, quality standards, labor standards, layout and design standards—the list goes on.

If there is one major, overriding problem afflicting many businesses in the food and beverage industry, it is the lack of standards. This is understandable, owing to the fact that such standards are difficult to establish, implement, monitor, and revise. The poorly trained manager has only so much time. When rushed, he or she may neglect company standards and permit unacceptable practices.

Even those establishments that have complete sets of standards can fall prey to the inability or unwillingness of managers to apply them consistently. The best control procedures are worthless if they are not used correctly.

Management must develop and implement a consistent cycle of control. Moreover, it must monitor the control system continuously so that needed changes can be made quickly and efficiently.

The food and beverage operation's cycle of control begins with the purchasing function. It continues through receiving, storing, issuing, production, and service. Checks and balances are inserted throughout the cycle to pinpoint responsibility and reveal any problems.

The main purpose of product-cost control, or any other expense control, is to ensure that actual costs parallel standard (i.e., budgeted) costs. Unlike the typical restaurant business, catering is in a better position to minimize variances between standard and actual costs. After all, as a manager, you know what to expect and when to expect it. Consequently, it is easier to forecast your needs and prepare for them accordingly.

However, catering's advantage over the typical restaurant operation is not as great as it may initially appear. For instance, even though you know what to expect, guests are notorious for arriving late, leaving late, and/or requesting special attention at the last minute.

As a general rule, the potential to minimize variances between actual and standard costs is a bit easier for the typical catering department. Yet although this may be true, the system is not error-free. It can be as close as possible to being error-free, however, if you pay careful attention to every major operating activity.

Purchasing

The food and beverage cycle of control begins in the purchasing agent's office. This person is responsible for selecting and procuring the needed products at the most economical prices. Values obtained by the purchasing department initially establish the ultimate costs of doing business.

Probably the most critical cost-control tool used by the purchasing agent is the product specification (see Figure 10.3). Food and beverage costs, as well as the quality of finished menu items, cannot be predicted accurately unless you are using standardized, consistent product specifications. You must use the same ingredients time after time, or the finished products' costs and culinary qualities will vary unpredictably.

Intended Use	Packaging Procedure
Exact Name	Degree of Ripeness
Brand Name	Product Form
U.S. Grade	Color
Product Size	Trade Association Standards
Expected Yield	Chemical Standards
Package Size	Inspection Procedures
Type of Packaging	Instructions to Suppliers
Preservation Method	Quantity Limits
Point of Origin	Cost Limits

FIGURE 10.3.   Typical information included on food, beverage, and nonfood supplies specifications.

Another major cost-control technique is to identify appropriate suppliers, who can handle your needs adequately, and include them on an approved supplier list. When ordering, only these approved suppliers should be used. Exceptions must be authorized by top management.

The purchasing agent also contributes to cost and quality control by calculating the optimal order sizes for each ingredient purchased. If you underorder, you risk stock-outs and unhappy guests. If you overorder, you risk spoilage and excessive inventory carrying charges.

Catering lends itself nicely to computing optimal order sizes because, unlike typical restaurant service, most catered events are quite predictable. If, for instance, you expect 100 dinner guests, and you normally prepare for 105, you then order enough merchandise to prepare and serve 105 meals. In most cases, you do not have to anticipate customer demands because you know about them well in advance. Furthermore, if the ingredients used for catered events are also used in other restaurant outlets in your facility, you can even order a little additional stock to be safe and not worry about its going bad in storage.

Receiving

Unlike the typical restaurant operation, hotels and other large properties usually do a very good job in receiving their shipments. They usually assign at least one full-time receiving agent to ensure that deliveries are consistent with purchase orders and product specifications.

Large caterers usually follow the invoice receiving technique. This system requires the receiving agent to do the following:

1   Compare the delivery slip (i.e., invoice) with the purchase order. You must be certain that the shipment is the correct one and that it contains all the items originally ordered.

2   Compare the products delivered with the invoice and the purchase order. All three must match.

3   Inspect the quality of each item. The shipment must meet the product specifications. If not, it should not be accepted unless a superior authorizes receipt.

4   Inspect the quantity of each item. Weights, volume, counts, and so forth, must be accurate.

5   Arrange for credit from the supplier, if applicable. If there is any problem with product quality or quantity, the receiving agent must get a credit slip from the driver. If the driver is an independent trucker, you will have to send a request-for-credit memorandum to the supplier's credit department. Before your accounting department's accounts payable division pays the bill, it must account properly for any and all credits.

6   Sign the invoice, retain a copy to send to accounting, and arrange to store the shipment.

Storage and Issuing

The major purpose of storage is to protect the merchandise from theft and spoilage. Theft is minimized by keeping everything under lock and key, restricting access to the storeroom facilities, and using a standardized issuing system whereby anyone wanting merchandise from the storeroom must complete and sign an authorized stock requisition and take responsibility for the products (see Figure 10.4).

Spoilage is minimized by maintaining appropriate sanitation standards and rotating the stock correctly. Products must also be stored in the appropriate temperature and humidity environment.

Canned goods and other dry storage groceries should be stored at about 70°F (50°F is ideal), with approximately 50 percent relative humidity.

Frozen foods should be stored at 0°F or less. Refrigerated meats, seafood, and poultry should be stored at the coldest temperature possible without freezing; dairy products at about 34° to 38°F; and produce at about 36° to 40°F. Each of these refrigerated product categories

				No. XXXXX	
		FOOD REQUISITION			
Dept.: _____			Date: _____		19 ___

Quantity	Unit	Description	Issued	Unit Price	Amount

Ordered by: _____	Distribution
Issued by: _____	White Copy: Controller _____
	Yellow Copy: Storeroom _____
Received by: _____	Pink Copy: Chef _____

FIGURE 10.4.   Example food requisition form.

requires approximately 85 percent relative humidity. Ideally, you will have at least three separate walk-in refrigerators so that the recommended temperature and humidity can be maintained.

Products in the typical food service operation's storage facilities normally do not spoil to the point where they are inedible. They may lose just enough culinary quality to render them unfit for service. For instance, flaccid lettuce can be eaten without risking food-borne illness; however, you cannot expect customers to pay for it. The challenge of maintaining culinary quality is a little more daunting in the food and beverage industry than it is perhaps in a homemaker's kitchen.

Production

Pre-prep and prep procedures offer several opportunities for cost overruns. To combat this tendency, the catering executive should work with the chef and/or food and beverage director to develop adequate production controls. The following are the major production controls to emphasize:

1 *Always use standardized recipes.*   Standardized recipes are just as important as product specifications. It is useless to purchase the same quality merchandise every time if you do not use consistent pre-prep and prep procedures (see Figure 10.5).

2 *Develop a standardized production plan.*   The timing of pre-prep and prep activities is another crucial factor affecting product costs. This is particularly true for foods; if you produce foods too far in advance, chances are that you will have a lot of finished items past their peak of culinary quality that cannot be served.

Because you have a good idea of how much to produce and when the finished items will be served, you can usually develop a very accurate production plan. It is this knowledge that gives you a cost-control advantage over the typical restaurant operation; predictability minimizes cost variances.

3 *Supervise portioning procedures.*   There is a tendency to over-portion foods. Guests who help themselves may be likely to take more than they can eat. And employees have a tendency to put a little more on the guest's plate, especially if the guest is witnessing the dish-up process.

It is also true that we have a tendency to create excess scrap, that is, waste, during the production process. This is especially likely if we are rushed. Because you usually have sufficient lead time and know what to expect, chances are that correct production planning can virtually eliminate this problem.

Many foodservice experts believe that if you use standardized product specifications and recipes, if you make a conscious effort to reduce avoidable waste, and if you maintain portion control, the odds are excellent that your actual costs will be in line with your standard costs. Minimizing or eliminating cost variances should be one of the food production manager's major goals.

STANDARD RECIPE FORM		

Product Name:

Equipment Needed:

Yield:

Serving Size:

Preparation Time:

Temperature(s):

Ingredients	Quantities	Method

FIGURE 10.5. Example standard recipe form.

Service

If you have enough servers, you will probably not encounter any significant service problems that could cause cost and quality variances. However, good service does not just happen. Someone must supervise and monitor the service function to ensure that cost and quality standards are met and all guests are satisfied.

The most critical aspects of service control are the following:

1   *Dish-up should be done as close as possible to service time.* Culinary quality suffers if finished items have to sit any longer than necessary. Products past their peak of quality cannot be served; they usually end up in the garbage, with your product costs increasing accordingly. Service costs may also increase if you need to plate and serve quite a bit of food to replace products that cannot be served.

2   *An expeditor should be used to coordinate production and service.* This person usually sees to it that servers' needs are communicated properly to production people and that guest orders are delivered from the kitchen and served to the guests in a timely manner. A supervisor or manager usually fills this critical role as part of his or her overall responsibilities.

3   *A food checker should be used to inspect the quality of finished menu items.* He or she should also be responsible for ensuring that only the correct amounts of meals and beverages are served. For instance, as meals are carried from the kitchen to the banquet room, the food checker will keep a running tally of them and compare the total served to the expected number of guests noted on the banquet event order (BEO). Like the expeditor position, this role may be filled by an existing supervisor or manager.

In some cases the expeditor may also perform the food checker's duties. For small catered events, he or she might keep the tally as well as maintain coordination between production and service.

Food and Beverage—Cost Control Record-Keeping System

Your cost-control efforts are incomplete if you do not have a way of gathering and analyzing cost data. You will need an effective data-gathering and analysis procedure for at least two reasons: first, you must have some means of calculating standard and actual product usage, and second, these data may be needed to calculate a client's final billing.

If you are primarily interested in calculating standard and actual costs, use the "standard-cost" record-keeping system.

The standard-cost system is a rather long, arduous procedure that is not usually performed in the typical foodservice operation unless it is fully computerized. It is usually too difficult and time-consuming to operate this system by hand.

The system requires you to calculate the standard cost for each menu item. You must precost each menu item; that is, you must determine the exact standard cost for each one. This requires you to cost out each recipe and calculate the expected (or potential) product cost per serving (see Figure 10.6).

Once you have the potential product cost for each serving, you then multiply it by the number of servings used. This gives you the total standard cost.

To compute the actual cost, you must take a physical inventory of all foods and beverages left at the end of the catered function and cost it out. This ending inventory is then inserted into the following formula to compute the total actual cost:

Beginning inventory (the previous ending inventory)
plus: issues from the storeroom
plus: direct purchases (i.e., deliveries that bypass the storeroom and go directly to production)
<u>minus: ending inventory</u>
equals: total actual cost

The total standard cost is compared with the total actual cost. If there is a significant variance, you need to go back through the cycle of control and see whether you can spot the problem(s). That is, you must examine your purchasing, receiving, storing, issuing, pre-prep, prep, and service procedures to see what needs to be corrected. You then make the necessary correction(s) so that future catered events do not suffer the same fate.

If there is a significant cost variance, the problem is typically due to one of four reasons:

1   There may be errors in the record-keeping system. This is often the primary reason. It is always best to check this first because, just as a piece of equipment's failure to work can easily be the result of neglecting to plug it in, small arithmetic errors can cause huge variances.

PRODUCT COST ANALYSIS			
Product: _____			
Ingredients	Unit Price	Amount Used	Ingredient Cost

Total Product Cost: _____

Number of Servings: _____

Cost per Serving: _____

Target Cost Percentage: _____

Menu Price: _____

 FIGURE 10.6.   Example product cost work sheet.

2 Check your purchasing and receiving procedures. Sometimes the products ordered are not consistent with the specifications; for instance, you may be ordering a more expensive product without realizing it. Or you may be receiving an incorrect product, one that either costs too much or does not work properly in your recipes.

3 Review your standard recipe costs. Sometimes these data are out-of-date and cannot give you an accurate analysis.

4 Be alert to overproduction and/or overportioning. If the first three reasons do not explain the problem, you will usually discover that excessive leftovers and/or portion sizes are the culprits.

Some foodservice managers cost out recipes only once in a while, whereas others cost out each event's BEO. When submitting a competitive bid to a client, the catering executive should always calculate current recipe costs. Likewise, you may need the current standard costs if you book an event that will be priced according to the amount of food and beverage consumed.

Another way of gathering and analyzing cost-related data is to use the product-analysis record-keeping system. This system (sometimes referred to as the critical-item inventory system) concentrates on food and beverage usage, rather than on their costs.

This system is not as accurate as the standard-cost system, but it is much easier to use. However, although it exchanges a bit of accuracy for time saving, the information it yields is sufficient to control product costs. It is a common type of product-cost record-keeping system used in the foodservice industry.

In a nutshell, this system involves a comparison of banquet room counts to production counts. For instance, if the kitchen plates 125 steak dinners, the banquet records should reveal that 125 guests were served. The kitchen usage should compare favorably with head counts, plate counts, meal tickets, or any other service records used. Any variance must be investigated and the underlying problem(s) corrected.

The products counted are usually only the critical, i.e., expensive, items. For example, if you book a party for 100 T-bone steaks, you tend to concentrate your food cost control efforts solely on the meat. You should take time to compare kitchen counts with banquet room counts. In addition, you should match these data with the stock requisition records and check for consistency. If everything works out correctly, there will be 100 T-bone steaks noted on the stock requisition and/or direct purchase invoice, 100 prepared, and 100 served.

Some foodservice experts are critical of this system primarily because it neglects other product costs. However, the product costs it neglects are not nearly as expensive as those that are monitored. As a result, although not infallible, the system does provide a reasonable measure of product cost control. Furthermore, this system provides enough information to calculate the final billings of those catered functions that are priced according to the amount of guest consumption.

Other foodservice experts also criticize this system because if you rely on it exclusively, you will ignore raw product purchase prices and edible portion costs. If this happens, you may not have sufficient data on which to base menu prices. Nor do you know whether your month-end actual cost calculations reflect reality, because you have no standard cost with which to compare it.

It appears that the product-analysis system will be with us for some time inasmuch as the standard-cost system cannot effectively be used unless the food and beverage facility is fully computerized or a large central accounting staff is maintained. The cost of an integrated facility computer system is expensive and may not be cost-effective for the typical food and beverage operation. However, without a computer system, it is difficult and time-consuming to maintain accurate, current recipe costs.

A form of product analysis that is used exclusively for beverages is sometimes referred to as the ounce system of control. With this procedure, the manager establishes a standard number of drinks that should be poured from each container, and the actual number of drinks served should be consistent with the standard.

For instance, if you use 1 liter containers of vodka, and the average drink size is 1.5 ounces, the potential number of drinks per bottle is 22.5 (33.8 ounces/1.5 ounces = 22.5 drinks). At the end of a beverage function, if you note that 2.7 bottles of vodka were used, the sales records for vodka should reflect approximately 60 drinks served (2.7 bottles × 22.5 drinks = 60.75 drinks). In this instance, after taking an ending inventory and calculating the expected number of drinks served, you should have approximately 60 drink tickets in the ticket lockbox. You expect 60 drinks to be served (standard usage), so you should collect about 60 drink tickets (actual usage).

At the end of the beverage function, the manager calculates the usage of each brand of liquor and determines the total number of potential drinks served. This total serves as your basis of comparison, the standard to which is compared the actual number of drink tickets collected.

In general, you expect the actual number of drinks served to be a bit less than the standard. For instance, if the bartenders do not use a liquor-dispensing machine and have to free pour, chances are there will be some overpouring. Furthermore, with free pouring, you cannot get all the liquor out of a bottle; some of it will remain on the sides of the bottle because you usually do not have time to wait for every drop to drip out.

Faced with this situation, you may need to adjust your standards. For instance, you may plan to lose, say, a half ounce of liquor per container and revise your standards downward. For instance, in the aforementioned vodka example, you might expect 22 drinks per container instead of 22.5.

For complete control, you will need to relay the beverage-usage data to the head cashier so that he or she can audit the performance of the cashier assigned to the beverage function. The basic comparison here is between the number of drink tickets sold, the number collected by bartenders, and the amount of cash collected. The cash collected and the number of drink tickets sold should match exactly. However, you expect the number of drink tickets collected to be a little less than the number sold and the cash collected, because a few guests may not use each drink ticket purchased.

If the bartenders collect cash from guests, you may want to use the standard-sales record-keeping system for beverage functions. This system (sometimes referred to as the potential-sales system or the reverse audit) is quite similar to the ounce system, in that it concentrates on usage and not on product costs. The major difference is that it allows you to control cash as well as product usage.

To use this system, you need to calculate a bottle value for each container of liquor stocked in inventory. The bottle value represents the amount of sales revenue a container of liquor should generate. For instance, if the 1.5-ounce serving of vodka noted in the preceding example sells for $5.75 per drink , the bottle value of a liter of vodka is approximately $129.38 (33.8 ounces/1.5 ounces = 22.5 drinks; 22.5 drinks × $5.75 = $129.38). If you note at the end of the function that 1.7 liters of vodka were used, the cash collected should be approximately $219.95 (1.7 bottles × $129.38 = $219.95).

At the end of every beverage function, you must calculate usage rate for each brand of liquor. Each brand's usage rate must then be converted to its standard sales revenue. After each brand's standard sales revenue is calculated, a grand total of standard sales revenue must be determined. This grand total serves as your overall standard sales figure, which is then compared with actual sales revenue—that is, total cash collected. The comparison should show very little variance.

A variation of using the standard-sales record-keeping system is to keep track of disposable glassware usage. For instance, if you use

9-ounce plastic cups for mixed drinks that are sold for $5.00 apiece, and there are 100 cups missing at the end of the event, the cash collected should equal $500 and the beverage inventory should be consistent with the preparation and service of 100 mixed drinks.

Controlling Product Costs for Buffets, Receptions, and Open Bars

If guests are able to serve themselves, or can order drinks without using drink tickets or other forms of documentation, your cost-control procedures must be adjusted to take into account average usage figures. Because you do not control portions or guest usage rates, your purchasing, production, and service strategies must be based on historical averages. This requires you to analyze previous catered events periodically in order to keep up-to-date on average customer usage in your facility.

Another key area that will need revision is the record-keeping system used. If you use the product-analysis system, you must be sure to use relevant averages or else you will have no control over the critical items. For instance, if you are serving veal cutlets on an all-you-can-eat buffet line for 100 guests, and in reviewing past events you note that each guest takes, on average, 1½ servings, at the end of the event the kitchen and banquet-room counts should balance at about 150 servings.

Unfortunately, in working with averages, there is a greater opportunity for "inventory shrinkage." For instance, in the aforementioned veal cutlet example, you have no way of knowing whether 5 of the 150 servings were pilfered by employees unless you use additional, more subtle, cost-control procedures designed specifically to thwart such activity. This discrepancy is particularly troublesome if the client's final billing is based on guest consumption.

Unfortunately, in our industry there are many opportunities for undetected pilferage and shoplifting if you must work with average cost data. Deploying mystery shoppers, providing extra supervision in the function room and kitchen, and similar techniques must often be used to minimize them.

Product-Cost-Reduction Techniques

Although cost reduction technically is not the same as cost control, many persons see no difference between them. The typical food and beverage operation spends about a third of its sales revenue on product costs. Any little decrease, therefore, will have a major favorable impact on net profits.

The following product-cost-reduction techniques are commonly used in the foodservice industry:

1 *Seek long-term competitive bids from suppliers.*   This allows you to maximize your purchasing power. Suppliers may be willing to offer price concessions if they can count on your business.

2 *Qualify for purchase-price discounts.*   For instance, many suppliers will grant quantity discounts if you purchase a huge amount of one type of item. Before agreeing to a huge purchase, however, make sure that you have enough storage space and cash or trade credit available to handle it.

If you submit large purchase orders, you may qualify for a volume discount. This type of discount is offered if you purchase a large dollar amount of several types of items.

Some suppliers offer promotional discounts, whereby they may reduce the purchase price if you agree to promote their products in your operation. For instance, if you allow them to put tent advertisements on your dining room tables, you may receive a 1 or 2 percent price reduction.

Cash discounts can also be lucrative alternatives. These are granted by some suppliers if you pay your bill before the due date. Purchasing agents routinely ask suppliers if they offer any type of discount for prompt payment.

3 *Investigate other purchasing opportunities.*   Suppliers occasionally offer other cost-reduction opportunities the caterer may find attractive. For instance, you may be willing to take advantage of

○ New products: These usually carry some sort of temporary introductory price that is much lower than normal. You might stock up on some of these items and use them to accommodate a few catering functions. For instance, a new frozen chicken entrée may come on the market. You may be able to get two free cases for every one you purchase at the regular price. If you have the storage room and the money, you might stock up on this product and offer it as a low-cost alternative to some of your clients who are on tight budgets.

○ Stock-discontinuation sales: Like new products sold at introductory prices, discontinued stock at sale prices can save money, thereby increasing your net profits or allowing you to be more competitive when soliciting cost-conscious clients.

○   Trading for products instead of paying cash. Many businesses have trade-out arrangements with certain suppliers. For instance, instead of paying cash for your canned groceries, you may find a supplier who is willing to accept payment in kind. Although trading is not commonly done for food commodities (it is more common with services, such as outdoor advertising), it is worth pursuing because bartering can save a good deal of money. It is cheaper to pay a $100 invoice with $100 worth of sleeping rooms and menu items, because your out-of-pocket costs are much less than the $100. And if you allow these trade credits to be used only during your slow periods, there will be no extra pressure on your production and service staffs.

4   *Use more raw food ingredients.*   Raw foods are much cheaper than pre-prepared convenience items. Unfortunately, they usually require you to spend more for labor and energy inasmuch as you will need to do most, if not all, of the pre-prep and prep work. However, except for restaurant operations, the typical on-premise caterer has sufficient production space and labor on hand to make the use of raw ingredients an economical option.

PAYROLL-COST CONTROL

There are two main lines of defense against payroll-cost variances: Maximize the sales revenue, and use effective work scheduling techniques.

As with most cost control problems, your troubles seem to vanish whenever you have a great deal of business. For example, an extra server's salary does not seem important when you are busy every day. It is usually so small in comparison with the heavy volume of business that it probably would not show up in a cost analysis. Excessive sales revenue cures many ills.

The manager's second line of defense against payroll-cost variances is effective use of the work schedule. Your work-scheduling skills will have a major impact on your ability to minimize variances between the standard and actual payroll costs.

The work schedule represents the standard payroll cost. It is based on the facility's staffing guide, and the staffing guide is based primarily on the number of guests expected. As the guest count increases, the number of payroll hours and number of staff members needed also increase.

Unfortunately, the relationship between number of guests and number of work hours and staff members needed is not easily predictable. For instance, there is no neat formula that tells you how many work hours you need for each guest, nor is there a calculus that reveals the additional number of work hours that should be scheduled if five more guests show up. Furthermore, you cannot always predict whether you will need more staff members to handle a few more guests; for example, if one server can handle 14 guests, he or she may be able to handle 16 with no additional trouble.

The optimal payroll cost is an illusive figure in the foodservice business. Unlike food and beverage costs, payroll costs are not completely variable. They have been tagged with several descriptions, such as semivariable costs, semifixed costs, and stepwise variable costs. The fact remains, however, that if you plot payroll costs against sales revenue on a graph, you will not get a straight line.

Factors Affecting Payroll Cost

The optimal payroll cost is unpredictable because there are so many factors affecting it. Although some factors are controllable, many of them are not. And the degree of control that can be exercised can vary considerably among catering operations. Indeed, if you manage a particular property and have mastered its payroll cost control vagaries, you may find that a transfer to another property will cause you to regress temporarily in your expertise, inasmuch as some techniques you used at the previous facility cannot be effectively used at the new one.

The following are the key factors that affect the amount and cost of payroll needed:

- Menu
- Style of service
- Guest count
- Guest arrival patterns
- Facility layout and design
- Type of equipment
- Employee tenure
- Employee turnover
- Local labor market conditions
- Hours of operation

- ○ Union regulations
- ○ Federal and state labor department regulations
  - **a.** Minimum wage
  - **b.** Tip credit
  - **c.** Meal credit
  - **d.** Child labor restrictions
  - **e.** Overtime premium pay
- ○ Amount of payroll taxes
  - **a.** Social Security
  - **b.** Medicare
  - **c.** Unemployment insurance
  - **d.** Workers compensation insurance
- ○ Amount of other employee benefits (e.g., health insurance, holiday pay, etc.)

Payroll-Cost-Control Record-Keeping System

As with any type of cost-control record-keeping system, the primary objectives are to compute standard and actual costs, compare them, and evaluate and correct any unacceptable variances.

The standard payroll cost is computed by costing out the work schedule and tacking on the cost of payroll taxes and other employee benefits. If you are lucky, a healthy part of the work schedule will be fixed. But if the bulk of your work schedule is variable, you may have to calculate standard costs daily.

You must expect the typical catering work schedule to lean heavily in the direction of variable-cost employees, because many catered functions booked in your facility may need completely different crews. Furthermore, if the client is paying separately for labor, you will need to cost out the entire work schedule.

You cannot avoid calculating standard payroll costs. Competitive bids rely on accurate cost estimates. Because payroll is a considerable chunk of the total cost needed to prepare for and serve a catered event, chances are that the catering sales representatives will continually calculate current payroll cost estimates.

Actual payroll costs are computed by costing out the time records and adding the appropriate amount of payroll taxes and other employee benefits. Some time records are fixed; for example, secretaries', supervisors', and managers' salaries may not vary. However, variable-cost employees normally use a time clock and/or sign a time sheet.

The fixed costs and variable work hours are converted to a total actual payroll cost. This actual cost is then compared with the standard. As always, if there is a significant variance, the problem(s) must be uncovered and corrective action taken.

If there is a significant variance, chances are that you can trim your labor force a bit without compromising guest service. Usually, however, you cannot eliminate smaller variances unless you increase your sales revenue. This is why up$elling is so critical. The added revenue allows you greater flexibility, which in turn enhances service and pleases clients and guests. Long after the catered events are over, clients will be talking about the food, beverage, and service they received. Rarely will they even remember the prices paid.

Payroll-Cost-Reduction Techniques

The typical food and beverage operation spends, at the very least, approximately 25 percent of each sales revenue dollar for payroll, and about another 5 percent or more for employee benefits. In some cases payroll, employee benefits, and payroll-related administrative costs can exceed 40 percent of a foodservice operation's sales revenue. As a result, no payroll-cost-control procedure is considered complete unless it includes one or more cost-reduction techniques.

Among the payroll-cost-reduction techniques used in the hospitality industry are the following:

1 *Employee leasing.* Instead of hiring employees, you can lease the entire staff from a leasing company. In some cases this can save money because the leasing company consolidates and handles all the human-resources administrative details, thereby relieving the caterer of this costly burden. The leasing company can also consolidate several small employers' employee benefits needs, qualify for large-employer discounts, and pass on some of the savings to its clients. Clients can typically save between 2 to 4 percent of their current labor costs by using employee leasing.

2 *Hiring "rehab" employees.* In some instances, if you agree to participate in rehabilitative efforts by hiring physically or mentally disabled persons, allowing the local workers compensation agency to place trainees in your facility, or hiring individuals in certain targeted social or economic groups, you may receive a monetary reward. For instance, a workers compensation agency may pay part of a trainee's wages for a few weeks. Or you may qualify for an income tax credit if you hire a person in a targeted group.

3 *Use independent contractors in lieu of employees.* For some tasks you may be able to employ independent contractors instead of hiring employees to do the work. For instance, instead of hiring cloak-

room or valet parking attendants, you may want to hire an independent service. This can be more convenient in the long run inasmuch as you do not have to maintain extensive personnel files, process payroll checks, or handle all other relevant administrative details for these workers. You merely send a check once a month to the service and use the time saved to pursue more profitable activities.

4 *Use part-time employees in lieu of full-time employees.* Part-time employees working 19 hours or less per week do not usually receive discretionary employee benefits, such as health insurance. They also permit a great deal of flexibility in scheduling. The downside, however, is that you have more persons on the payroll, which can significantly increase your costs for uniforms, employee meals, and other personnel-related items.

5 *Use more pre-prepared convenience foods.* When using convenience foods, you do not need as many employees, nor do you need very many highly skilled (hence, costly) employees. The drawback is increased food costs.

Food purchase prices are much higher for convenience products because they include the costs of food, production labor, and the energy needed to produce them. Generally, however, frozen-food entrées can be used to maximize the productivity of current production labor, as it allows food handlers to increase significantly the numbers of guests that can be served during the day.

6 *Institute more self-service options.* This measure reduces payroll at the expense of food and beverage costs. The hope is that the extra foods and beverages guests will take when left on their own will not entirely wipe out the payroll-cost savings. Unfortunately, when guests help themselves, they take more time to go through the lines, the event tends to drag on, and some guests may be displeased with the slow pace.

7 *Eliminate overtime premium pay.* The labor laws, as well as union regulations, require you to pay overtime premium pay under certain circumstances. For instance, an employee may have to be compensated 1½ times the regular rate of pay for any hours worked in excess of 8 per day.

At times you may encounter this problem, as some catered events are bound to run longer than expected and you will need to keep some persons on board to take care of the stragglers. If such overruns are common, you will be much better off scheduling one or two persons to come in later during the event. They can stay to take care of closing down. And instead of being stuck with overtime premium pay, you will be able to pay the more economical straight-time wage.

Another way to prevent overtime premium pay is to negotiate with clients and ask them to agree in advance that if the events run longer than anticipated, they will be responsible for paying the additional labor charges.

Alternately, you might schedule a supervisor or manager to handle any last-minute overruns. Management employees usually do not have to be compensated at overtime premium rates. They normally receive straight salaries that do not vary with the amount of hours worked.

8   *Reduce costly employee turnover.*   Proper employee selection, orientation, and training should help to reduce employee turnover and the subsequent costs of hiring replacement personnel.

9   *Use labor saving equipment.*   Under some circumstances, you may be able to reduce your payroll costs by investing in labor saving devices. For instance, a computerized automatic bar may increase worker productivity enough for you to reduce the number of bartenders needed. It can also enhance your quality control efforts.

The expensive investments that usually must be made in this type of equipment, however, may not be recovered easily. Chances are that you will not see a payroll-cost reduction sufficient to justify any major investments. However, if an investment can pay for itself in about three years or less, it is generally considered a good choice.

Be careful, however, when estimating the cost savings that supposedly accompany labor saving equipment. Our industry has been unable to take full advantage of many labor saving technological advances because, after all, we are in the personal service business. It can be easy to overestimate cost savings, particularly if we rely on enthusiastic equipment salespersons for these estimates.

10   *Institute a profit-sharing plan.*   Profit sharing and similar forms of employee-motivation techniques can reduce employee turnover as well as increase employee productivity. In the long run, the extra pay and benefits given to long-term employees usually pale in comparison with the increased sales revenue and profits generated by experienced staff members.

CONTROL OF OTHER EXPENSES

The catering executive usually concentrates on controlling product and payroll costs primarily, because they represent a very large chunk of the sales revenue dollar. This "prime cost" (i.e., product cost plus payroll cost) is about 50 to 55 percent of the typical foodservice operation's sales revenue. Consequently, it is understandable that a manager's cost-control efforts will be aimed in this direction.

But there are some other controllable expenses that deserve your attention. In general, these include operating expenses (such as for napery, tableware, soaps, chemicals, and paper products), costs of utilities, repairs, and maintenance, and administrative and general expenses (such as for telephone, postage, and office supplies).

The key to controlling these expenses is to be on the lookout for waste, pilferage, and incorrect use of equipment.

Waste is a typical problem in using paper products, production equipment, soaps, chemicals, and similar items. For instance, it is not uncommon for employees to use too much of a chemical in the rinse water, be over generous with the use of paper napkins and doilies, turn the oven on long before it is needed, and neglect to sort soiled napery correctly. Although these actions do not necessarily cause significant decreases in net profit, they will add up quickly if you do not monitor them.

Office supplies and telephone use are subject to employee pilferage as well as to waste. Personal use of the company's e-mail and Internet connections can also eat into profits. Subtle controls, such as taking inventories of office supplies and restricting long-distance telephone use, should be applied to minimize these problems.

Employees must be trained adequately in the use of equipment before they are allowed to operate it. If they do not know how to use equipment correctly, they may injure themselves and the equipment. Incorrect equipment use is a major cause of increased repair and maintenance expenses, as well as higher workers compensation costs. Moreover, incorrect use of equipment will drastically reduce the equipment's useful life. One of the paradoxes of the food and beverage business is that we would never allow someone to drive a car without a driver's license, yet we may be willing to let someone operate a $50,000 dish machine without proper training.

COMPUTERIZED CONTROL PROCEDURES

A caterer can gain many benefits by computerizing its operations and information systems. However, because computerization is an expensive undertaking, to justify its investment, a computer system must offer substantial benefits to the facility and to its guests, such as the following:

- ○ Improved guest service
- ○ Streamlined handling of paperwork and data
- ○ Improved control over day-to-day operations
- ○ Generation of complete, timely reports
- ○ Reduced cost of paper supplies
- ○ Increased sales revenue
- ○ Increased employee productivity
- ○ Reduction of clerical staff
- ○ Job enrichment, resulting from the reduction of repetitive tasks
- ○ Ability to keep current sales and expense data on file

Selecting a Computer System

It is important to take your time and consider carefully all available options before making a decision to invest in a computer system. Consider some of the following rules before making your decision:

1   Never be the first user of a particular computer system. The first user usually is placed in a high-risk position.

2   Avoid purchasing or leasing a computer system from a firm that has many large clients, unless you are one of them. The largest users will receive priority service from the computer firm.

3   Before buying a system, always observe someone else using a similar system at a similar property. Interview the users and seek their opinions.

4   Decide specifically what you want the system to do for you. This tells you the type of software you will need to purchase or rent.

5   Once the software is selected, look for the appropriate hardware. Be certain that the hardware is compatible with other computer systems used at your property. If possible, do not select hardware that requires you to take data from one machine, reformulate it, and enter it into another machine. Data reentry significantly reduces the benefits of computerization and increases the potential for error.

6   Select an adequate computer service firm. The firm should provide sufficient training and technical backup. The company should have a "help hotline." Furthermore, the firm must be able to adapt the standard software to coincide with your property's overall system.

A good backup service is important even if the caterer has computer people on staff. Many on-site computer people are front-office or back-office oriented and may find food and beverage service perplexing.

Computer Uses

All catering offices should be computerized. The savings in labor and time more than justify the expense. Today's computers are more user friendly and need not be intimidating for the novice user. All that is needed is a little time, patience, and some basic instruction. Software is constantly being upgraded and new programs developed. There is software on the market that can do just about anything a catering office would need.

○ Desktop publishing for menus, brochures, and similar promotional materials
○ Sales analysis
○ Bookings analysis
○ Cancellation report
○ Group-booking log
○ Daily tracer-list printout of current and previous clients
○ Sales-call report
○ Group-profile sheet
○ Banquet event order (BEO)
○ Function resume
○ Lost-business report
○ Prefunction sheet
○ Catering contract
○ Daily event schedule
○ Forecast
○ Daily function room schedule
○ Work schedule
○ Graphic room layout
○ Space management
○ Link to outside suppliers and service contractors
○ Payroll processing
○ Recipe costing
○ Menu pricing
○ Inventory management
○ Recipe-nutrition analysis
○ Invoice control
○ Product-cost analysis
○ Payroll-cost analysis
○ Equipment scheduling
○ Word processing

- ○ Time clock
- ○ Production schedule
- ○ Break-even analysis
- ○ Menu planning
- ○ Tip reporting
- ○ Tip allocation
- ○ Server analysis
- ○ Stock requisition
- ○ Department-by-department comparison
- ○ Open-guest-check report
- ○ Cashier analysis
- ○ Communication with other departments
- ○ Link with corporate headquarters
- ○ Billing
- ○ Inventory reorder
- ○ Yield management
- ○ E-commerce opportunities

See the companion web site for this book at (http://www.wiley.com/college/shock). This site is updated regularly and includes links to many computer services useful to the catering industry.

Working with Other Departments

The catering department in a large facility does not operate in a vacuum. Although it is often the only one visible to the client, it depends on many other departments for its success.

The catering department cannot do it all. It cannot perform all the necessary tasks. It must have the cooperation of other departments. One could think of the catering department as the orchestra leader: It assembles the players, develops the music, and supervises the performance. A successful catering event, like a pleasing musical performance, occurs when all people involved play their roles well.

This chapter discusses the other departments that contribute to the catering department's success and the major relationships that exist between them and the catering staff.

KITCHEN

It is extremely important to have a good working relationship with the chef and his or her staff. These food experts are perhaps the most important players in the catering orchestra. At times, they will be your salvation.

The chef must know as soon as possible the menu, the number of guests, the timing, and all other relevant aspects of a booked function. He or she must ensure that the proper amount and type of foods are ordered, production is scheduled properly, and an adequate and appropriate work force is retained for each event.

The chef must also be privy to any and all budgetary constraints. He or she gives the last word in costing the menu. If, for example, the catering sales representative is preparing a competitive bid for a corporate meeting planner, the chef's food cost estimates must be obtained.

The chef can work with you in combating budgetary constraints, planning heart-healthy meals, outlining theme parties, and developing other pertinent customer-pleasing suggestions. He or she usually knows what will be in season, menu trends, typical customer likes and dislikes, cost trends, quality trends, and product availability. Chefs usually love the opportunity to contribute. Many of them enjoy being creative.

In most facilities, the catering staff participates with the chef in developing standardized catering menus. Usually, the food and beverage director and the purchasing agent are also part of the menu planning team. The menus prepared by this group become one of the major tools in the catering sales representative's sales kit.

It is essential to check with the chef before committing to any off-the-menu selections. Many clients want something special and disdain the standardized menus. Although you may want to accommodate them, you cannot do so without checking with the chef or the sous chef in charge of banquet functions.

Some off-the-menu selections may be infeasible because they cannot be prepared in bulk. For instance, it is usually futile to ask the chef to prepare individual chocolate soufflés for 1,000 guests, club sandwiches for 750, or Maine lobsters for a group of 500. These food items usually are impossible to produce correctly for large groups.

Some menu items may also be impossible to produce and serve because the facility does not own the necessary equipment. For instance, is there enough broiler and oven space to prepare 2,000 New York steak dinners? Are there enough slow-cook ovens to cook and hold roast sirloin for 1,500 guests? Can the kitchen prepare and hold 1,000 chef salads with the available refrigeration space?

A menu item may not be feasible because the property does not have the appropriate labor to do the work. There may be an insufficient supply of labor, or there may be a lack of personnel with the skills needed to prepare a specific recipe. For instance, is there a sufficient quantity and quality of labor to produce an ice carving, a five-tiered wedding cake, or fancy carved vegetable garnishes?

According to catering executive John Steinmetz, to get along well with the chef, you should adhere to the following rules:

1   Always consult with the chef before promising a special menu or any changes to a standardized menu.
2   Ensure that the chef receives the menus well in advance of the events. You should notify the chef at least ten days in advance.
3   Ensure that the chef receives timely updates of guarantee changes, special needs, and other major alterations. Do not wait until the last minute.
4   Do not spring any surprises on the chef.
5   Do not make it difficult, or impossible, for the chef to achieve his or her budgeted food, payroll, and other operating costs.

BEVERAGE

Large hotels, clubs, and conference centers employ a separate beverage manager. His or her job description is similar to the chef's in that they both administer departments that produce finished menu products and serve them to guests.

The beverage manager usually oversees the facility's main bars, service bars, special events bars (i.e., banquet bars), room-service beverage deliveries, hospitality suite bars, and individual-access bars (i.e., locked bar cabinets located in sleeping rooms).

Catering typically works with the beverage manager when developing beverage functions, planning beverage menus, and evaluating product and service options. The beverage manager may also help catering managers schedule the appropriate number of bartenders, bar backs, cocktail servers, and bus persons.

PURCHASING

Most large facilities employ a full-time purchasing agent. His or her primary responsibilities are to prepare product specifications for all foods, beverages, and supplies, select appropriate suppliers, maintain adequate inventories, obtain the best possible purchase values, and ensure that product quality meets the property's standards.

The purchasing agent normally works very closely with the kitchen and beverage departments. He or she must be made aware of all catering events booked in order to purchase the necessary stock.

On a day-to-day basis, the purchasing agent orders sufficient merchandise to satisfy the property's normal business needs. Catering, however, is additional business and must be handled separately. For instance, if 2,500 chicken breasts are needed for a scheduled party, the purchasing agent must order enough to satisfy the restaurant outlets' needs for chicken breasts as well as the additional 2,500 needed for the party.

Standard catering menu items are usually readily available from local purveyors. In fact, a menu item may be standardized primarily because it is easy to obtain. If a catering sales representative is negotiating for off-the-menu item selections, however, the purchasing agent should be consulted to see whether the products are available, what they cost, and how long it will take for them to be delivered to the facility.

If the catering executive is considering a menu revision, he or she will also need to check with the purchasing agent to see whether the planned changes are feasible. Cost and availability trends must be evaluated very carefully in order to avoid mistakes in menu planning.

RECEIVING AND STOREROOM

All but the smallest properties have a central warehouse storeroom (sometimes referred to as the commissary) where all food, beverage, and supplies are kept under lock and key. Only authorized persons are allowed to enter the storage areas and/or obtain products from the storeroom manager.

Storeroom personnel work closely with the receiving department. In some operations, both functions are housed in one department. Receiving agents check in deliveries, and storeroom clerks help them move shipments from the receiving dock to the warehouse. The merchandise remains in the storage areas until department heads requisition them.

To obtain these products, a department head must fill out a stock requisition and hand it to a storeroom clerk. The requisition establishes the fact that the department head is now responsible for these items. Once the requisition is processed, the department head can pick up the products or have them delivered by a storeroom attendant.

Production and service departments that are handling a catered event requisition most of the products needed to service the event. For instance, the kitchen will requisition food and the beverage department will requisition beverages. The catering staff, however, will also need to requisition some things, such as paper products, decorations, and office supplies.

 HOUSEKEEPING

A hotel or conference center housekeeping department's primary responsibilities are to clean sleeping rooms, function rooms, and all public areas. It also works with maintenance to ensure that the property is kept in good repair.

In some facilities, housekeeping is responsible for selecting replacement carpeting, upholstery, and fabrics. If you are involved with these decisions, be sure to avoid light colors and materials that do not have a pattern. Stains and spills show up quickly on light-colored materials, and cigarette burns are quite obvious in unpatterned carpets. Incidentally, repeating patterns on carpeting are excellent guides for setting out tables and chairs symmetrically.

The housekeeping department, especially the linen room, is the source of table napery, tablecloths, skirting, employee uniforms and costumes, laundry and dry cleaning, and valet services. The catering staff must see to it that the linen room manager has sufficient lead time to ensure that all necessary supplies are available.

In many facilities, housekeeping is responsible for precleaning function rooms and other public areas as outlined in the catering department's instructions or in the convention service department's directives. It also is involved with cleaning up after functions are completed. Housekeeping must be apprised of special functions well in advance so that the necessary work can be scheduled and carried out properly.

Function rooms must be cleaned in plenty of time to avoid any embarrassing situations. For example, you do not want last-minute furniture moving to mar an otherwise successful event.

Function rooms must be torn down and cleaned immediately after guests depart. If you wait too long to do this, stains have time to set in upholstery or carpets and vermin will be attracted to the debris.

Immediately after an event or meeting, the catering or convention service staff strip the tables; housekeeping should come in and clean the walls, carpets, and furniture. Any items needing repair should be reported to the maintenance department. Rooms cleaned immediately after a function will "show" much better to prospective clients. A dirty room does not make an easy sell.

Lobbies around function rooms (sometimes referred to as prefunction space if receptions are held there before the main event) require continuous attention from housekeeping. Attendees will leave soiled ashtrays, cups, newspapers, and so forth, lying about, and these should be removed as quickly and unobtrusively as possible. Routine dusting, polishing, trash removal, and vacuuming should be done when guests are not around. Special attention should be paid to items slipped into planters.

Public rest rooms are especially in need of constant attention. Many persons abhor a dirty rest room and are quick to lose respect for management if one is encountered.

At the very minimum, rest rooms must be cleaned thoroughly twice a day. They must be checked constantly for quick cleanups and restocking of tissue, seat covers, towels, and toiletries. Attendants must also check periodically for equipment failure and, if finding any, must report the problem to the maintenance department.

To reduce confusion and increase efficiency, some facilities assign several, or perhaps all, function room housekeeping chores to the convention service department. This is particularly true for very large hotels that specialize in convention business.

A few properties sometimes use an outside contract cleaning service to handle certain housekeeping tasks. For instance, if you do not have the proper equipment and/or employee talent, you may not want to try cleaning large chandeliers, outside windows, or copper façades. Night cleaning is often handled by contract labor.

Convention Service

Some hotels and conference centers have a convention service department to handle banquet setup and banquet service. The banquet setup division is responsible primarily for setting up function rooms, tearing them down, and putting away the furniture and equipment.

Banquet setup works hand in glove with banquet service. The banquet service division is responsible primarily for providing meal service. It may also be responsible for providing beverage service.

In lieu of a convention service department, there may be an arrangement whereby banquet setup and banquet service activities are performed by the catering staff, or by the catering staff in cooperation with other departments. For instance, catering may share this work with the kitchen and housekeeping staffs.

Smaller operations do not usually have separate convention service departments. Their small size usually requires them to allocate the necessary duties to other departments.

Convention service activities can be housed in various departments and can be designated by many terms. Banquet setup, banquet service, convention porters, and housemen are just a few of the titles used to describe these important activities and personnel.

Convention service is the backbone of the catering and convention departments. Function room setup and teardown, room maintenance and cleaning, transporting furniture and equipment throughout the function room areas, and other related duties must be performed quickly and efficiently. All catered functions depend on the swift completion of these critical activities.

The major activity of convention service is function room setup. This involves many aspects, the most critical of which is the need for all furniture and equipment to be in place by a certain time. Of foremost importance in function room setup is receiving the proper information from the catering/convention coordinator. He or she must have a good working knowledge of the type, amount, and capabilities of the furniture, equipment, staff, and facilities so that client requests can be handled correctly.

Function room setup begins with information obtained from the client. This information must be complete and conform to the property's physical constraints. Table sizes, exhibit booths, registration needs, and so forth, require physical setups. Someone has to obtain the proper furniture and equipment, transport it to the correct location, and install it properly. Before this can be done, convention service employees must know and understand the client's needs.

There are usually three types of banquet setup employees. The first are the regular or full-time employees. These employees are scheduled for a full workweek or are the first persons called when a function room must be set up.

The second type of employee is the steady extra. Such persons are on call, but are considered permanent employees. Although these employees do not receive full employee benefits, they usually receive prorated benefits based on the number of hours worked. The primary advantages that steady extra employees provide to the employer is that they can be used only when they are needed, but when they are called to work, they are as productive as full-time employees because they are familiar with the job, property, furniture, and equipment.

The third type of employee is the one-time recruit hired temporarily to help set up an unusually large function, or to assist regular employees temporarily overburdened with large and/or several back-to-back catered functions that require quick turnarounds. Employees of this type usually receive limited training and are not around long enough to become familiar with the property. Consequently, they are used primarily to move furniture and equipment and perform similar manual labor.

Convention service requires an adequate storage facility to house all necessary furniture and equipment. The storage of these items, however, involves more than just the housing of tables, chairs, portable dance floors, risers, meeting equipment, and convention materials when not in use. The storage area must be large enough, as well as sufficiently convenient to the function rooms, to facilitate the constant movement of furniture and equipment in and out of the function rooms. Unfortunately, adequate storage in the convention service department is sometimes overlooked when hotels, conference centers, and clubs are designed and constructed. This lack can cause continuing problems and frustration.

A proper storage area allows you to store all furniture and equipment as well as transport equipment needed to move these items. For instance, you need enough room to store table and chair carts, which are used to transport several tables and chairs at one time, thereby allowing quick and efficient movement to and from function rooms.

The storage area should be large enough to house and organize an inventory of spare parts. For instance, if a houseman loses a piece of portable dance floor trim and cannot find another one in storage, there is an increased risk of someone tripping on an improperly installed dance floor. If you lose a section of a portable dance floor, it decreases the size of the floor and increases the risk of guest dissatisfaction. Adequate storage space and proper storage procedures can prevent problems associated with missing, lost, or stolen pieces.

The storage area must also allow you to store furniture and equipment as close as possible to the function rooms. For instance, a portable dance floor should be stored near the function rooms because it is too heavy to transport easily.

The ability to move a dance floor is a major concern. Heavy-duty carts are typically used to transport the 3' × 3' squares of wood and metal. Each full cart can weigh more than 500 pounds. Damage can occur to walls, doors, and employees by improper movement and handling. The probability of damage increases if this heavy load must be transported a great distance.

Where applicable, the storage area must be able to accommodate meeting equipment such as blackboards, easels, podiums, water pitchers, glasses, ashtrays, pads, and pencils. It may also have to house audiovisual (AV), computer, and lighting equipment. In some facilities, some or all of this equipment is stored in other departments. Convenience, however, quickly overrides departmental lines, and convention service typically finds it necessary to store many items that were originally intended to be stored elsewhere. Properly stored equipment is not damaged as easily as items left in hallways.

The storage area must also be able to accommodate the temporary storage and movement of clients' convention materials. Some clients send convention materials, such as registration packets, machinery, and sample products, to the property via independent carrier services. These materials are extremely important to clients and their attendees. A lost or misplaced package can be devastating for a meeting planner.

Convention service is responsible for the safe delivery of convention materials to the function rooms. Although receiving convention materials may be the responsibility of other departments, such as the receiving or storeroom department, convention service accepts responsibility when taking the goods out of the storage area.

Generally, receiving and storeroom departments do not want to store convention materials. The primary reason is that their facilities are not designed to hold the varying types and amounts of materials that arrive for different groups. Owing to the nature of the receiving activity, however, it is logical that these departments are the ones to maintain an accurate accounting of all packages sent to the facility.

All delivered convention materials must be signed in, counted, and inspected for damage at the point of transfer from the independent freight company. Properties assume a liability in the form of a bailment when they take possession of items they do not own, so it behooves them to ensure that all shipments meet client standards.

It is essential to maintain clear records of all client shipments. Clients must ensure that their instructions are communicated to the property. This is very important, because receiving clerks are not usually allowed to accept a client's shipment unless they know in advance when it will be delivered and the inspection procedures they must follow. If clerks refuse to accept shipments, they can create tremendous difficulties for the unsuspecting clients.

A clear audit trail must exist in order to track any client property delivered to the facility. The facility that denies receiving a client's shipment loses that client's respect when the independent carrier service can show a copy of the packing slip signed by an employee who received and took possession of the shipment. Liability exposure increases if the convention materials are misplaced internally and this misplacement causes the client embarrassment and/or monetary losses. You risk losing future business if potential clients suspect your facility will mishandle their convention materials.

Housemen or convention porters must sign for convention materials when they obtain them from the receiving or storeroom department. The materials must then be taken directly to the appropriate function room areas.

A secure and central location must be provided in the function room areas to store convention materials. Employees must then ensure that the materials are delivered to the appropriate person at the right time and place. In addition, they must have the client, or client's representative, sign for the delivery so that the facility is relieved of responsibility for lost materials.

When the function is completed, convention service is usually involved with shipping unused convention materials back to the client's home or place of business. When shipping materials, you must be apprised of the client's shipping and payment instructions. Nothing can be shipped without this information.

The facility will usually comply with the client's shipping and payment instructions, with the exception of cash-on-delivery (COD) shipments. Most properties do not want to ship anything COD. If for any reason the addressee refuses a COD shipment, it will be returned to you and you will be billed by the independent carrier service for the shipping costs. It may then be very difficult, or impossible, to get reimbursed by the client.

Banquet setup and banquet service are two of the most visible activities, in that almost all of their work is witnessed firsthand by clients and their guests. These departments are responsible for the staffing, service, and successful completion of each catered event. They are usually only second to the kitchen and beverage departments in terms of their influence on client and guest satisfaction.

MAINTENANCE

The maintenance department is in charge of all property maintenance and repairs. Its employees perform routine maintenance, such as calibrating oven thermostats, oiling motors, and changing filters. They also are responsible for repairs, such as fixing broken water pipes, changing burnt-out light bulbs, and reconditioning worn equipment.

If the catering department has a repair need, it must fill out a repair requisition and send it to the maintenance department supervisor. The supervisor then prioritizes these requisitions and prepares work orders for maintenance employees. The employees work their way through the prioritized stack of work orders. If you are under a time constraint and need work done quickly, you will need to note URGENT! on your requisition. This will move you up on the priority list, but top management may have a policy of charging a department's budget a little extra for express service because it will usually disrupt the normal work schedule and may require some employees to work overtime.

ENGINEERING

The engineer generally is responsible for all major property systems, such as heating, ventilation, and air-conditioning (HVAC), refrigeration, electrical, plumbing, and sewer. He or she also supervises the property's energy management systems. Furthermore, the department usually works hand in glove with maintenance to ensure complete, co-ordinated control of the physical plant.

The catering staff must see to it that the engineer is contacted whenever a booked function requires sound systems, such as microphone, computer, recorder, and speaker hookups. Although the audio-visual (AV) department normally handles the delivery and setup of this equipment, the engineering staff is typically responsible for hooking it up and unhooking it.

The engineering department will have to know each function's energy requirements so that it can accommodate them. For instance, if a banquet requires several buffet stations, it may be necessary to install several electrical drop cords when the room is being set up by the banquet setup crew. In addition, if there are any special lighting needs, the engineer must see to it that the appropriate power is available and that the systems are set up and torn down properly.

Engineering must also be aware of each function's beginning and ending times, as well as the expected number of guests, so that the proper amount of heating or cooling can be directed to the meeting and banquet rooms. When function rooms are closed they are usually not heated or cooled during these periods. The engineer must have advance notice as to when they will be used, because it takes about 20 minutes to an hour to adjust a room's temperature.

When determining room temperature needs, the engineer will take into account the size of the room, number of attendees, time of day, the "solar load" (i.e., the heat the building absorbs from the sun), the type of HVAC system, ceiling height, the amount of heat given off by appliances, amount of insulation, outside weather conditions, the amount of body heat given off by employees and guests, and type of function. For instance, a large room requires more heating or cooling. And a large group of people will quickly raise the temperature of a room.

PROPERTY MANAGER

The property manager is responsible for all outside areas of a facility. Normally, he or she supervises landscaping, snow removal, pool and spa maintenance, and parking lot and sidewalk maintenance.

In some large facilities, there may be a separate property management department working independently and reporting directly to the general manager. In others, and in smaller properties, property management functions are usually housed in the engineering or maintenance departments.

In some small facilities, an independent service contractor may handle part or all of the outside grounds keeping. For instance, maintenance may handle the pool maintenance and cleaning chores, and an independent gardener may stop by once or twice a week to take care of landscaping needs.

Occasionally, a catering sales representative will book a function to be held on the grounds. For instance, many weddings are held outdoors, including the ceremony, reception, dinner, and entertainment. To service these events properly, the catering staff will have to coordinate its efforts with the grounds crew to ensure that any needed tents are erected, sprinkler systems shut off, parking lots roped off, portable heaters installed, portable lights erected, and so forth.

STEWARD

The typical hotel, conference center, or club employs an executive steward whose major responsibilities include supervising kitchen sanitation and the china, glass, and silver stockroom. He or she provides one of the key links connecting the kitchen and other food and beverage production areas to the point of guest service.

The catering staff must work with the executive steward to ensure that a sufficient number of employees are scheduled to clean the dirty dishes, pots, pans, silverware, and utensils generated by catered events. Adequate work hours must be scheduled to perform the necessary kitchen, bar, and pantry cleanup after the functions end. If special china, glass, and/or silver is needed, the catering staff usually must requisition it from the executive steward.

Some properties employ kitchen stewards. Their responsibilities are similar to those of executive stewards, except that they also have food purchasing duties. Normally, smaller properties use kitchen stewards to oversee the kitchen sanitation crew, handle the chef's and bar manager's food and beverage purchases, check in shipments, and monitor all storeroom facilities. Being relatively small, these properties do not have separate purchasing agents, receiving supervisors, or storeroom supervisors. In this case, it may be easier to coordinate your efforts with only one person instead of several.

Print Shop

Many large operations have a central copying center to handle their most common printing needs and a contract with an outside printer to handle all special requirements and jobs that cannot be done in-house. For instance, the central copying center may have computerized desktop publishing capabilities to print standardized menus, but its equipment may be insufficient to produce four-color, glossy convention programs.

A few large operations do all of their printing in-house, which allows them to maximize quality control. It also gives them maximum flexibility, inasmuch as they do not have to accept an outside printer's scheduling requirements. Furthermore, an on-site print shop may be the most economical option.

The typical catering department uses a lot of printed materials. Many catered functions call for printed programs, menus, name badges, place cards, personalized matchbooks, signage, and accounting records. Although clients can opt to select their own printers, the convenience of an on-site print shop is a much appreciated benefit.

When the catering staff has a printing need, it usually must fill out a work requisition form and give it to the print shop or central copying center manager. He or she then prioritizes the work and assigns it to the appropriate employee(s), or if necessary, subcontracts the order to an outside printer.

ROOM SERVICE

A hotel or conference center room service department usually handles all guest room food and beverage service. It is responsible for delivering food and beverage menu items, and for retrieving leftovers, soiled tableware and napery, tables, and equipment.

Generally, catering does not get involved with guest room functions. However, the catering staff may occasionally need to coordinate with the room service crew to handle hospitality suites or small, intimate meal and beverage functions held in a guest suite. For instance, a major corporate convention may have several VIPs who require extensive room service. It may host several hospitality suites during the cocktail hours. Or it may decide to hold a board of directors luncheon in the president's suite instead of in a function room.

The borrowing of equipment between room service and catering is an area in which each side must work well with the other.

HUMAN RESOURCES

The primary responsibility of the human resources department is the recruiting, developing, and maintaining of an effective employee staff. It is also responsible for administering many personnel-related matters. For instance, it must process all relevant government paperwork, handle grievances, work with union representatives, and manage employee compensation packages.

The director of catering will work with human resources whenever there are job openings in the catering department that must be filled. The human resources department in a large facility has an employment manager whose main activities include helping department supervisors to develop job specifications and job descriptions, and developing and implementing recruiting programs, job application procedures, interviewing procedures, and methods used to process new hires.

When the catering department needs a new employee, the director of catering may have to fill out a job opening form listing the position, work hours, skills required, and other pertinent information.

For entry-level, nonmanagement catering jobs, the employment manager conducts prescreening interviews of job applicants, develops a list of one or more qualified candidates, and sends it to the catering department. The catering manager then makes the final hiring decision, usually after personally interviewing qualified applicants.

For supervisory and management catering positions, the director of catering often finds a qualified candidate and sends him or her to the human resources department for processing. For instance, a catering executive may find an appropriate supervisory candidate through his or her membership in the National Association of Catering Executives (NACE). In fact, this professional organization publishes employment openings in the job bank section of its magazine, *The Professional Caterer*, and on its web site *(http://www.nace.net)*.

The director of catering may also uncover viable managerial job candidates through his or her membership in other professional organizations and other contacts in the foodservice and food supply industries. For example, a few telephone calls to respected food suppliers in your local area can quickly reveal qualified people who desire to make a career move.

Occasionally, the catering executive may find a potential job candidate to fill an hourly position. For instance, a current staff member may recommend a friend to fill a job opening. In this case, the catering executive would send this person to the human resources department so that all necessary processing can be performed. As a general rule, however, hourly job candidates are generated solely by the human resources department.

Once a person is hired, he or she is processed by the employment manager. This process generally involves an employee orientation, uniform fitting (if applicable), ID preparation, and assignment of a payroll authorization number, parking place, and employee locker.

The employment process may be shortened a bit for part-time catering employees. For instance, employees on the A-list and the B-list may be scheduled temporarily at the discretion of the catering director. However, the employment manager must process them initially before they can be included on these lists.

The employment manager may also provide some training to new employees. A large human resources department often employs a director of training who shoulders this responsibility. The director of training typically provides some basic training as part of the orientation process. Job-related training, however, is usually an effort shared by the training director and the catering director.

The director of catering will also be involved with human resources whenever employee problems arise. A large human resources department typically employs an employee relations manager to handle situations of this type. However, if, for example, there is a problem with a catering employee's paycheck, the catering director must be part of the solution. This is also true if there is an employee benefits dispute, disciplinary problem, union contract dispute, or employee grievance.

 CONTROLLER

The controller is responsible for securing all company assets. He or she normally supervises all cost-control activities, credit applications, payroll processing, accounts payable, accounts receivable, data processing, night audit, and cashiering.

The catering department's major relationships with the controller involve report preparation, cashiering, and accounts receivable.

All departments prepare reports, many of which are generally coordinated and printed by the controller's office. For instance, budgets, profit and loss statements, and activity reports are usually prepared in final format by the controller's management information system (MIS) data-processing center, based on information provided by the departments.

Many catered events have cash bars. The controller's office assigns cashiers to sell drink tickets to the guests. Guests then exchange these tickets for beverages. At the end of the function, the cash collection is compared with the ticket count and the amount of missing beverage inventory. If everything goes according to plan, these three totals will be consistent with each other.

For open bars and some meal functions, drink and meal tickets may be purchased in advance by the client and distributed to the guests. Guests then exchange them for food and beverages. The controller's office will ensure that used tickets are consistent with the amount of missing food and beverage inventory.

At times a client will be billed at the end of the function for all food and beverages consumed by guests. For instance, an open bar at a wedding may be set up in such a way that cashiers or bartenders keep track of each drink served. When the final billing is prepared, the number of drinks served is multiplied by the agreed-upon selling price. This total is then added to the other bill charges.

When a potential client is shopping for catering services, he or she may need to put up a modest deposit to hold space. The catering sales representative then enters a tentative booking in the master catering book and, after obtaining the potential client's permission, asks the credit manager to run a credit check on the client. It is important to obtain this permission in advance, because many clients will not agree to a credit check until after the functions are booked and billing is requested.

If credit is denied, usually the catering sales representative contacts the client and tries to resolve the problem and salvage the event. In this situation, the client will have to prepay unless the credit manager is willing to change his or her mind and make other arrangements.

As noted earlier, most caterers are not in the habit of granting clients long-term, favorable credit terms and conditions. For instance, political functions and social events, such as weddings, are seldom granted the luxury of postevent billing.

If credit is approved, or if the client has indicated that prepayment will not be a problem, the sales representative will contact him or her to confirm the event and outline billing arrangements. When confirmed, the event is changed from a tentative booking to a permanent one after the client has signed the agreement.

The controller's office prepares final billings and sends invoice statements to the clients. It handles collections and processes payments. If there are any problems, such as invoice disputes, late payments, or bounced checks, the catering department may have to help the credit manager resolve them.

SECURITY

Security is often a facility's least visible department, but by far not the least important. You know it is doing an effective job when guests do not recognize its presence.

Catered events present unique security challenges. Large groups may need someone to control foot traffic. Some groups may have considerable personal property that must be protected. Some of them may include VIPs who require additional attention. Other groups may attract disruptive protestors. And still others carry the seeds of potential disruption; for instance, proms and fraternity parties must have security guards to prevent underage drinking and rowdy behavior.

The catering department must keep the security department apprised of all special functions, because there may be some potential security problems it can spot that can go unrecognized by the catering sales representative and client. If such a situation is detected, the chief of security will have an opportunity to reconcile it beforehand.

The chief of security usually receives copies of all banquet event orders (BEO) in advance. This allows him or her to schedule the appropriate amount and type of security. It also gives the security chief sufficient lead time to process special needs, such as hiring temporary security guards, renting special equipment, and/or setting up perimeter barriers.

SALES

In most hotels and conference centers, the sales director is responsible for selling, advertising, promotion, public relations, marketing research, and other relevant marketing efforts. The sales department usually handles all local business on its own, but if the property is part of a chain organization, it is backed up by a corporate sales and marketing staff that solicits and coordinates regional and national business.

As mentioned earlier, in some properties the catering department is part of the sales staff. In this situation, catering sales and service employees report to the sales director, and kitchen and bar staffs report to a banquet manager employed by the food and beverage director. In this type of organizational structure, a convention service staff housed in the sales department may provide some or all catering services.

Catering must work hand in glove with the sales staff. At times their efforts may overlap. For example, a convention sales representative may be trying to sell sleeping rooms, function space, and meal functions to a meeting planner, and at the same time the meeting planner may be working with a catering sales representative to schedule a trial event, such as a small luncheon or reception. To say the least, there must be a great deal of coordination and cooperation in order to avoid any duplication of efforts and to ensure that the more profitable business is booked first, thereby maximizing function room space utilization and sales revenue.

The best option is to have catering involved with the selling process so that clients view the facility's staff as being a team.

 FRONT OFFICE

The front office is considered to be the heart of a hotel or conference center. It is the hub of activity. It is usually the second contact (reservations being the first) guests make with the property. And it tends to be the place that influences customers' first, and most lasting, impressions of the facility.

The front office normally includes the reservations, PBX (Public Branch Exchange), registration, cashier, and guest services sections.

The catering department will need to work closely with reservations whenever conventions are booked. Reservations will keep a running tally of sleeping rooms blocked and sleeping rooms booked. The catering staff will use this information to forecast attendance at the various catering events scheduled by convention clients.

PBX is the property's communications hub. Catering will cross paths with this front office section whenever telephone calls are routed to its department, messages are taken and delivered, and clients request special communications service.

A catered event may require extraordinary communications service or equipment. If so, PBX may be part of the team handling these needs. If, for example, a large convention requires several phones in the reception areas, PBX may deliver and retrieve them, engineering may hook them up and tear them down, and PBX may provide an operator or two to monitor incoming and outgoing calls.

The registration desk is the source of sleeping room occupancy statistics. If, for example, a large convention is checking into the property, the catering director will want to be kept up-to-date on the number of registrants so that accurate guest-count estimates can be computed for each catered event.

The front desk cashier handles guest checkout. Normally this involves guests paying sleeping room, room service, gift shop, restaurant, lounge, and incidental charges. At times, however, the costs of catered events may be part of a departing guest's final accounting. If so, the catering staff must ensure that accurate data are made available to the front desk clerks and cashiers so that guest folios can be posted correctly and the proper accounting prepared within the time required.

The guest services components includes the bell desk, valet parking attendants, door attendants, concierge, and property hosts.

Bell desk employees are trained to promote the property's amenities, especially the restaurant and lounge outlets. They can also put in a good word for the catering staff.

At times, bell desk personnel may be involved more directly with catered functions. For instance, some of them may serve as ushers, tour leaders, or airport shuttle drivers for convention attendees. At some hotels, the bell staff handles packages going to and from function rooms. These duties include shipping.

Many properties provide valet parking services. These services are usually under the direction of a parking supervisor (or garage manager).

The typical guest must pay for reserved parking lot space and valet-attendant services. An extra daily charge is normally added to the guest's folio, as the standard sleeping room rate does not normally include this amenity.

If a guest is part of a catered event, he or she may not have to pay separately for parking; it may be part of the total package price quoted by the catering sales representative for the entire function.

Parking charges may be waived by the catering sales representative if the event booked generates considerable other income for the property. If parking charges are very high, you may not be allowed to waive them; however, you can usually discount them for large groups.

If the parking facility is operated by an outside parking concession, the parking charges ordinarily cannot be waived. In some cases, however, the concession agreement may grant the property some discount privileges that can be passed on to catering clients and their guests. Absent such an agreement, either the client or the catering department must pay the concessionaire.

The concierge is an important part of the guest services team. This person specializes in providing information to guests about on-property activities, amenities, and off-property attractions, such as where the best shopping, restaurants, and tourist attractions are located. Some catering clients and their guests undoubtedly will be influenced by this person's advice.

A few properties employ property hosts to service their high-spending clients. For instance, in Las Vegas, most facilities employ casino hosts to cultivate high rollers.

To some extent, catering sales and service representatives are similar to property hosts in that they try to cultivate long-term relationships with profitable clients. For instance, a professional association may be so pleased with a particular catering executive that the group is liable to stick with this person even if he or she moves to a competing property. These relationships add to the value of the catering executive.

AUDIOVISUAL

Some large hotels, and almost all conference centers, have audiovisual (AV) departments that are responsible for maintaining an inventory of AV equipment. In-house AV departments are also commonly found in large, rural resorts that do a considerable amount of convention business.

The AV department may own the equipment or rent it from an outside service as needed to accommodate an event. It may also be involved with delivering the equipment to function rooms and retrieving it when it is no longer required. In addition, it may be responsible for providing AV technicians.

Many properties do not want to operate an AV department. The equipment inventory needed is very expensive. Repair and maintenance are also quite costly. Moreover, the equipment can quickly become obsolete and have to be replaced well before its useful life expires.

Although properties are reluctant to operate their own AV departments, they do want to make this convenience available to the guests. This is absolutely necessary if you want to offer clients one-stop shopping opportunities.

One way to provide in-house AV services economically is to grant an outside AV company an exclusive concession inside the property. Ideally, the concessionaire will have adequate in-house storage space so that services can be provided quickly and efficiently.

Catering clients can opt to use their own outside AV services. For instance, a major convention client may have a long-term contract with a large national firm that provides a wide array of meeting and convention services. In this case, the client will save money because of the quantity discounts available with national contracts. An added benefit is that over time, the national firm will learn and understand the group's unique needs and personalities and tailor its services accordingly.

Most catering clients will not use off-premises AV companies unless the property's AV equipment is priced exorbitantly. They prefer the convenience of an on-site department. For instance, when the department is located in the facility, a client can see the equipment beforehand, backup equipment can be retrieved quickly, and qualified technicians are on-site and can respond immediately if problems arise.

Catering must see to it that the AV manager is kept apprised of all client AV needs. The equipment, its delivery and pick up, and any necessary technicians must be scheduled well in advance. Sometimes the facility is so busy that the AV manager must use and reuse a particular piece of equipment several times during the day, for several functions. During the high season, close communications are necessary in order to pull off these scheduling miracles.

RECREATION

Many properties offer several types of recreation activities for guests. Some facilities have swimming pools, health clubs, and spas, and some have additional recreation amenities, such as golfing, tennis, beaches, trail riding, and boating.

Salespersons tend to use a property's recreation offerings as a loss leader when trying to influence a meeting planner's selection of a facility. For instance, a meeting planner may be offered free use of a spa for all convention attendees. If this complimentary amenity is used to secure a booking, it is imperative that the spa manager knows about it well in advance so that he or she can be ready to serve the extra guests properly.

Providing complimentary recreation amenities sounds as though this may be an expensive giveaway, but in reality it costs the property very little. For example, many attendees will not use the spa facilities; however, they will be favorably impressed with the perceived value offered. Nor does a property incur an out-of-pocket cost by promising clients preferred tee times or tennis court times. The only time this type of loss leader has a significant impact on the bottom line is when a guest recreation activity (such as golfing) is provided by a nearby outside source. In this case, the outside contractor will typically expect a minimum payment regardless of the number of guests taking advantage of the amenity.

ENTERTAINMENT

A few properties employ entertainment directors. These executives are responsible for dealing with agents and booking entertainment acts. They also are responsible for dealing with entertainment licensing authorities. For instance, the American Society of Composers, Authors, and Publishers (ASCAP) and Broadcast Music Incorporated (BMI) collect fees from businesses that provide musical entertainment to their guests for profit-making purposes.

If a catered event requires some sort of entertainment, the entertainment director may be involved with the decision. If a client books his or her own entertainment, the entertainment director may still be involved; for example, he or she may provide a list of available acts to the meeting planner, help the meeting planner contact a speakers bureau, or help to schedule the events.

The entertainment director must always be made aware of any catering activity in the facility because this can influence his or her selection of acts. For instance, if a Western-wear association convention is booked, the entertainment director may want to arrange to have a country-and-western act performing in the lounge.

BUSINESS SERVICES

Business services are clerical, secretarial, and Internet services provided by a hotel or conference center to its guests. Facilities that accommodate business travelers and the meetings and conventions business typically make such services available to all guests for an additional charge.

Many catered events require some business services. For instance, a convention may need copying and typing services. It may need someone to take minutes, collate reports, or handle incoming and outgoing fax or telex messages. Some clients may need slides or photographs coordinated for a presentation. And some may need a "computer doctor" to help them prepare or revise a power-point presentation.

As with guest recreation activities, a few properties may provide a modest amount of complimentary business services to clients who book a large amount of catering business.

The business services manager must know as soon as possible the types and amounts of business services clients will need. This is very important, because most employees working in this department are on-call, temporary employees who usually have full-time jobs elsewhere. They will need advance notice so that they can adjust their schedules accordingly.

Glossary

ACF   American Culinary Federation

ACOM   Association for Convention Operations Management

action station   Found at receptions and buffet meals. Chefs prepare foods to order and serve them to guests. Sometimes referred to as performance or exhibition cooking. Common items include omelets, pasta stations, sushi bars, etc.

agneau   Lamb.

AH & MA   American Hotel & Motel Association

air wall   Portable divider used to partition a large function room into smaller rooms.

AIWF   American Institute of Wine and Food

à la broche   Cooked on a skewer.

à la carte   Individual items from a menu that are prepared and served to order and priced separately, as opposed to *table d' hôte* or *prix fixe* (all inclusive).

à la king   Cooked in white cream sauce with vegetables, usually chicken.

à la mode   (1) In the style of; (2) ice cream on pie; (3) mashed potatoes on beef.

à la Newberg   Sauce of butter, cream, egg yolk, and (sometimes) sherry, usually lobster.

à l' anglaise   English style.

à la Provençale   Cooked with garlic and olive oil.

à la vapeur   Steamed.

à l' etuvée   Stewed.

à l' huile d'olive   In olive oil.

A-list   Includes the catering department's steady extra employees. They are the first ones called to work when temporary help is needed.

American service   Another name for *plated service*. The most common style of table service in the United States. Food is plated in the kitchen.

ananas   Pineapple.

angels on horseback   Baked bacon-wrapped oysters.

antipasto   Italian appetizer; usually includes olives, peppers, salami, marinated vegetable salads, sliced cold meats, and similar foods.

appetizer   First course of a meal, such as a soup or fruit cup.

arachide   Peanut.

artichaut   Artichoke.

asperges   Asparagus tips.

aspic   Calves' foot jelly. The product comes in powder form or in sheet-gelatin form. It is melted in a saucepan and used to coat and protect buffet foods or foods that will be shown in competition.

au gratin   Foods sprinkled with bread crumbs and/or cheese crumbs and baked until browned.

au jus   Served with natural juices.

au lait   With milk.

au naturel   Plainly cooked.

au champignons   Cooked with mushrooms.

AV   Audiovisual.

bababes   Banana.

baby spots   Small spotlights in the ceiling that are often aimed at table centerpieces for highlights.

baguette   Long French bread; crunchy crust.

baked Alaska   Cake base with ice cream, covered with meringue, and then browned just before service.

ball   Formal social gathering for dancing. Dinner is usually served. Dancing is often done between courses and after dinner.

banquet   Formal, often ceremonial, dinner for a select group of people.

banquet event order (BEO)   Lists menu and details for a catered event. Sometimes called a *function sheet*, or an *event order*.

Banquet French service   Platters of food are composed in the kitchen. Each food item is then served by a server from platters to individual plates.

base plate   Large empty plate set in the center of each place setting and used as a base for several courses. Usually removed prior to entrée course.

béarnaise sauce   A derivative of the hollandaise mother sauce. It is prepared by adding a tarragon reduction to hollandaise. Béarnaise must be kept on or near heat or it will separate and break down. Usually served on filet mignon.

béchamel   Sauce of flour, butter, milk, diced onions and carrots, and veal or chicken stock.

beef Strogonoff   A Russian dish of sautéed tenderloin tips served in a sour cream sauce over noodles.

beignet   (1) A French doughnut, square-shaped, minus the hole, lavishly sprinkled with powdered sugar; (2) foods dipped in batter and deep fried.

beurre   Butter.

bien cuit   Well done, as in "steak cooked well done."

bisque   Soup thickened with vegetable puree; usually a shellfish soup.

blanchi   Blanched.

blanquette   White meat in cream sauce.

bleu or blue cheese   White cheese, marbled with blue-green mold. Spicy flavor.

blintz   A thin pancake stuffed with a cream cheese mixture, fruit, or meat.

B-list   Includes a catering department's casual laborers. They are called to work if sufficient temporary employees are not available on the A-list.

block   A number of sleeping rooms reserved for a large group.

boeuf à la bourguignonne   Traditional beef stew with vegetables in Burgundy wine sauce.

bombe   Molded dessert of ice cream, whipped cream, and fruit.

bonbon   Any sweet candy.

book   To secure a piece of business, sell a catered event.

bordelaise   Prepared with Bordeaux wine.

borscht   Russian beet soup; served chilled.

bottled water   Defined by the U.S. Food and Drug Administration as "water that is sealed in bottles or other containers and intended for human consumption." Common types sold include:

carbonated (sparkling) water   "Naturally carbonated" refers to water whose carbon dioxide content is from the same source as the water; "carbonated water" refers to water to which carbon dioxide has been added.

drinking water   Water from a government-approved source. It must undergo some type of processing, such as filtration or disinfection.

natural water   Water from protected underground sources, such as springs or wells. It cannot be processed, but it may be filtered or purified.

seltzer   Filtered tap water that has been artificially carbonated and has been flavored with mineral salts.

spring water   Water from a deep underground source that flows naturally to the surface. If it is unprocessed, it may be labeled "natural."

bouillabaisse   Wine-flavored mixed seafood stew.

bouilli   Boiled.

boula boula   Blend of green turtle and green pea soups with unsweetened, browned, whipped cream on top.

bouquetiere   Mix of vegetables in season.

bourgeoise   Plain, family-style.

boxed   Draped with a tablecloth that is folded, creased at corners, and pinned.

box lunch   Light lunch in a box packed to take out.

braise   Moist heat cooking method used to tenderize and flavor meats.

break-out session   A session during which small groups, formed from a large group meeting, discuss specific details introduced during the general, large group meeting.

Brie cheese   Cheese with an edible white crust and a creamy yellow-white interior. Mellow flavor.

brioche   A buttery, egg-rich, yeast dough bread, usually ball-shaped with a smaller ball pressed on top.

brouille   Scrambled.

brunch   Midmorning meal. Usually includes breakfast and luncheon food selections.

buffet service   Presentation of food, offered on a table from trays, chafing dishes, and similar equipment.

by the bottle   Liquor served and charged for by the full bottle. Usually, all bottles that have been opened must be paid for by clients.

by the drink   Liquor served and charged for by the number of drinks prepared and served.

by the piece   Food served and charged for by the piece. Typical pricing method used for a reception.

cafeteria service   Similar to buffet service, except guests do not serve themselves; they are served by counter attendants and often use trays to carry selections.

call brand   Client specifies particular liquor label (i.e., brand). Opposite of *house brand* or *well brand*.

Camembert cheese   Cheese with edible white crust and creamy yellow interior. Mild to pungent flavor.

canapé   Hot or cold appetizer with bread or cracker base.

canard   Duck.

candelabra   Ornamental branched holder for more than one candle.

canopy   Drapery, awning, or other rooflike covering.

caper   Pickled green bud of a Mediterranean bush.

capon   Castrated young chicken; tender, plump, and juicy.

captain   Person who oversees servers in a room or section of a room at meal functions.

cart service   A type of French service whereby foods are prepared at tableside. Servers then compose individual plates for guests.

carver   In-room attendant who carves and serves meats during a reception or buffet.

cash bar   Private room bar setup whereby guests pay for drinks. Opposite of *open bar*.

caterer   Person or company providing food, beverages, equipment, and other services. May be on-premise or off-premise.

cater out   Term used when an on-premise caterer does off-premise catering.

caviar   Sturgeon roe (eggs); lightly salted. The lighter the color, the better quality.

centerpiece   Decorations and/or flowers placed in the center of a banquet, conference, or buffet table.

charger   A large plate, often used as a platter.

chateaubriand   Thick tenderloin steak cut from the center, or "barrel," of the tenderloin.

chaud   Hot.

chef's choice   Selection of food items (such as types of vegetables) determined by a chef to accompany an entrée.

chemise   With skins, as in "boiled potatoes with skins on."

chiffonade   Foods served with shredded vegetables.

chocolat   Chocolate.

chop suey   Chinese stew.

chou-fleur   Cauliflower.

CHRIE   Council on Hotel, Restaurant & Institutional Education.

chroucroute   Sauerkraut.

CMAA   Club Managers Association of America.

coeur   Heart.

collete   A buffet showpiece coating sauce made with mayonnaise and gelatin.

compote   Stewed fruit; usually served in a glass.

con carne   With meat.

concession   The privilege of maintaining a subsidiary business within a facility.

confiture   Jam.

conserves   Preserves with nuts.

consommé   Clear soup, served hot or chilled.

continental breakfast   Light morning meal usually consisting of rolls, pastries, butter, jam or marmalade, chilled juices, and hot beverages.

convention   Traditional annual meeting. Attendees come together for meetings, general sessions, and so forth, to further a common purpose.

convention resume   A summary of function room use for a convention or meeting; includes room setup instructions and banquet event orders.

coquilles St. Jacques   Scallops prepared with butter; served in a scallop shell.

cordial   A liqueur usually served after dinner.

corkage   A charge placed on liquor purchased by a client outside the hotel and brought into the property. The charge usually includes the cost of labor, ice, glassware, and mixers.

coupe   Ice cream dessert.

court bouillon   (1) Fish stock; (2) a rich, spicy soup or stew, made with fish fillets, tomatoes, onions, and sometimes mixed vegetables.

cover   Place setting for one person. Another name for *place setting*.

covers   Actual number of meals served at a catered meal function or in a foodservice facility.

crepe   A thin pancake.

croissant   A crescent-shaped puff pastry roll.

cru   Raw, uncooked.

cutoff date   Time when client must release tentatively reserved function room space or commit to its purchase.

dais   Raised platform. Head tables and some action stations are usually situated on a dais.

damask   Woven silk or linen fabric used for napery.

demi   Half.

demitasse   Small cup of coffee.

diable   Deviled.

dinde   Turkey.

dinner   Evening meal for a group.

double cloth   Use of two tablecloths on a banquet table for decorative purposes. Usually two different colors are used. Also called an overlay.

drapery   Decoratively arranged tablecloths or skirting on the front of head tables and around reception and buffet tables.

dry snacks   Finger foods, such as peanuts, pretzels, potato chips, and corn chips, usually served at receptions.

dualing menus   Serving a split entrée, such as Surf & Turf.

duchesse   Mashed potatoes mixed with eggs; forced through a pastry tube.

du jour   Of the day.

eau   Water.

éclair   Pastry filled with custard or whipped cream.

eggs Benedict   Poached eggs on English muffin with Canadian bacon (or ham) and hollandaise sauce. Holds well when preplated and held in hot boxes.

en casserole   Food served in the same dish in which it was baked.

en coquille   In a shell or shell-shaped ramekin.

energy break Refreshment break at which nutritious foods and beverages are served. May also include stretching or other forms of exercise.

English service Another name for *family-style service*.

entrée Main meal course. (In Europe, the term is used to describe the appetizer.)

épice Highly spiced.

epinards en feuilles Leaf spinach.

escargots Snails cooked in broth.

étouffée Succulent, tangy, tomato-based sauce.

family-style service Platters and bowls of foods are set on the dining tables, from which guests serve themselves. Usually involves guests passing the containers to each other.

farci Stuffed.

filet mignon Most expensive cut of the beef tenderloin.

fines herbes Herb mixture.

finger bowl A small bowl of hot water, sometimes scented, served with fresh napery to a guest after a meal so that the hands can be rinsed.

finnan haddie Smoked haddock.

flambé Meat dish or dessert item flamed with spirits.

floor-length linen Covers table across the top and down to the floor.

Florentine Served with spinach.

foie Liver.

foie gras Seasoned goose liver.

fond Bottom.

fournée Baked.

free pour Alcoholic beverages poured by hand without the use of shot glasses or other measuring devices.

frit Fried.

fraises Strawberries.

framboises Raspberries.

froid Cold.

fromage Cheese.

fumé Smoked.

function A catered meal or beverage event.

function sheet Another name for *banquet event order* (BEO).

galantine Boned meat pressed into a symmetrical shape. Usually includes truffles. When the loaf is sliced, a decorative pattern is revealed. Served cold.

ganging menus When two or more groups in facility have the same menu.

garni Garnished.

garnish Food decoration, usually edible, that adds color and form to a food presentation.

gâteau Cake.

glacé (1) Ice; (2) ice cream; (3) iced.

goblet   Glass with stem and foot.

gobo   Small spotlight used to highlight decor. Templates can form light images on ceilings and walls.

goulash   Hungarian meat dish seasoned with paprika.

granité   A coarse-textured sorbet.

gras   Fat.

gratuity   Mandatory charge added to food and beverage prices. Usually equal to 17 percent of food and beverage prices.

grille   Grilled or broiled.

Gruyère cheese   The best Fondue cheese; pale yellow, firm textured, with or without holes.

guarantee   The minimum number of servings to be paid for by a client, even if some are not consumed. A caterer usually requires the guarantee to be solidified 48 hours in advance.

gumbo   Cajun soup.

hache   Finely chopped or sliced.

hand service   One server is assigned for each two guests. Servers wear white gloves. When serving, they stand behind their guests, holding two composed plates. When the signal is given, all guests are served at the same time.

haricots verts   Thin (French-cut) green beans.

head count   Actual number of people attending a catered function.

head table   Table used to seat VIPs, speakers, and other dignitaries, often elevated.

hollandaise sauce   Sauce of egg yolks, clarified butter, lemon juice, and spices.

homard   Lobster.

hors d'oeuvres   Small appetizers.

hospitality suite   Room or suite of rooms used to entertain guests.

host bar   Another name for *open bar*.

house brand   Brand poured when client does not specify particular liquor label (i.e., brand). Another name for *well brand*. Opposite of *call brand*.

houseman   Service-staff member who handles function room setup and teardown.

house wine   Wine recommended by the catering sales representative. Usually offered to clients at a reasonable price. It is the property's wine *well brand*.

HSMAI   Hotel Sales & Marketing Association International.

huile   Oil.

HVAC   Heating, ventilation, and air-conditioning.

ice carving   Decorative carving from large block(s) of ice, used to enhance a buffet or reception table.

IFSEA   International Food Service Executives Association.

incentive event   Celebratory event intended to showcase persons who meet or exceed sales or production goals.

incentive travel   A reward given by companies to employees who meet or exceed sales or production goals.

inclusive price   Price charged clients that includes all applicable gratuities and consumption taxes.

in-house service   Service provided directly and entirely within a facility.

intermezzo   The break in dinner just prior to the entrée. A sorbet is usually served. A short period of dancing may also be included.

Irish stew   Lamb stew with dumplings.

ISES   International Special Events Society.

jambon   Ham.

jardiniére   Diced, mixed vegetables.

jigger spout   Adapter on a liquor bottle, used to eject a premeasured amount.

job description   List of duties that make up a particular job position.

job specification   List of qualities (such as work experience and education) a job applicant must have in order to be considered for a particular job.

keg   Container holding bulk quantities of beer, wine, soda pop, or soda pop syrup.

lapin   Rabbit.

letter of agreement   Document used in lieu of a formal contract; lists services, foods, beverages, and so forth. It becomes binding when signed by the facility and the client.

linen   Another name for *napery*.

liqueur cart   Rolling cart that includes a selection of cordials. Usually passed after dinner.

liter   Metric unit of measurement used to package spirits and wines. Equal to approximately 33.8 ounces.

loss leader   Item offered by a retailer at cost or less than cost to attract customers. Also referred to as a price leader.

lyonnaise   Cooked with onions.

macedoine   Mixture of vegetables or fruits.

maître d' hôtel   Floor manager. Responsible for all aspects of meal service.

Manhattan clam chowder   Clam soup made with tomatoes.

manpower agency   Firm specializing in providing day-labor workers.

medallion   Small, round piece of meat.

meeting planner   Person hired by large companies, professional associations, and trade associations to plan, organize, implement, and control meetings, conventions, and similar activities.

minestrone   Italian vegetable soup.

minimum   Smallest number of covers and/or beverages served at a catered event. A surcharge may be added to the client's bill if the minimum is not reached.

mock béarnaise sauce   Made by adding a tarragon reduction to mayonnaise, which is more stable than hollandaise and therefore will not break (separate). In off-premises catering, if sauce cannot be prepared on-site, mock béarnaise must be used because the real product will not travel without breaking.

Mornay sauce   Cream sauce thickened with eggs and grated cheese.

mousse   (1) Light, airy dessert dish made with beaten egg whites and whipped cream; (2) finely ground meat, seafood, or poultry served in a mold.

mousseline   Hollandaise sauce (or mayonnaise) with whipped cream.

moutarde   French mustard.

MPI   Meeting Planners International.

NACE   National Association of Catering Executives.

napery   Tablecloths, napkins, and other fabric table coverings.

napkin fold   A decorative way of folding napkins.

napolean   Flaky, iced French pastry with cream or custard filling.

New England clam chowder   Clam soup made with milk and potatoes.

noir   Black.

noix   Walnuts.

nouille   Noodle.

NRA   National Restaurant Association.

NSF   National Sanitation Foundation.

O'Brien   Sautéed with onions and green peppers.

oeuf   Egg.

off-premise catering   Catering for a function whereby foods are prepared in a central kitchen and transported for service to an off-site location.

oignon   Onion.

oiseaux   Edible birds.

open bar   Private room bar setup in which drinks are paid for by the client. Opposite of *cash bar*.

OSHA   Occupational Safety and Health Administration.

over-set   Number of covers set surpassing the guarantee. Paid for by the client only if actually consumed.

PA system   A facility's in-house public address system.

pain   Bread.

pain grille   Toast.

panache   Mixed vegetables (usually two vegetables).

pane   Prepared with bread crumbs.

parmentier   Served with potatoes.

party planner   Similar to corporate-event producer. Works with noncorporate clients to design and implement private parties.

pastry cart   Selection of desserts on a rolling serving cart.

pâté   A combination of finely ground meats and spices forming a loaf. Some pâtés are spreadable, some are sliced. Classical meats used include goose liver, duck liver, chicken liver, and veal. Usually served as an appetizer.

PCMA   Professional Convention Management Association.

peach melba   Ice cream served on a peach half, topped with raspberry syrup and whipped cream.

pêche Peach.

pele Peeled.

per diem Per day; for example, some meeting attendees, such as government employees, have a limited amount of money they can spend per day on food and other expenses.

per person A method of pricing food and/or beverages according to the number of guests expected to attend a catered event.

petite marmite French soup with small pieces of beef and vegetables, served in small covered pots with toast floats.

piccalilli Pickled relish of chopped cucumber, green tomato, and onion.

pièce de résistance Main dish (entrée).

pigs in blankets Indicate method of preparation. For example: (1) franks baked in pie crust or mashed potatoes; (2) baked oysters wrapped in bacon; (3) sausage wrapped in a pancake.

pipe and drape Lightweight tubing and drapery used to separate exhibit booths, staging areas, or similar locations.

piquant Spicy; highly seasoned.

place setting Another name for *cover*.

plated buffet Selection of preplated foods and entrées set on a buffet table. Can also be set on a roll-in cart.

plated service Foods arranged on individual plates in the kitchen and then served to guests.

plus, plus Addition of gratuities and consumption taxes to the standard prices charged for food and beverages. Designated on a catering contract and a BEO by the notation "+ +."

podium Raised platform where a speaker stands when delivering his or her remarks.

poire Pear.

pois Peas.

pomme Apple.

pommes de terre Potatoes

pommes au four Potatoes baked in their skins.

pommes nouvelle New potatoes.

pommes pont neuf Long pieces of fried potatoes.

pommes purées Mashed potatoes.

pony glass A small stemmed glass used for cordial service.

porc Pork.

potage Soup.

poule Hen.

poulet Young chicken.

pre-event (function) meeting Meeting between client and caterer to review upcoming function and make last-minute adjustments. Also called *precon meeting*.

premium beer High-priced beer. Has a higher alcoholic content than light beer and regular beer.

premium brand   Most expensive liquor brand offered by the facility. Sometimes referred to as a *call brand*.

prep area   Space used for food production not visible to guests.

preset service   Placing plated foods on banquet tables prior to seating guests.

professional association   Group of persons who practice a particular professional activity.

proposal   Communication sent by a facility to a potential client detailing the facility's offerings and asking prices.

purée   Mashed.

quenelle   Dumpling.

quiche Lorraine   A custard pie of onion, bacon, and mushrooms.

ragout   Stew with rich gravy.

ramekin   Dish used for both baking and serving.

reception   Stand-up social function at which beverages and light foods are served. Foods may be presented on small buffet tables or passed by servers. May precede a meal function.

réchauffé   Reheated; warmed over.

reduction   The base from which the flavor of a sauce is derived. The volume of liquid in the saucepan diminishes as the liquid evaporates, thereby concentrating the flavor.

refresh   To clean a function room after a meeting, or during a meeting's break periods. Usually includes refilling water pitchers, removing soiled articles, changing glassware, and performing other light housekeeping chores.

refreshment break   Time between meeting sessions. May include coffee, soft drinks, and/or food items. Some breaks are planned around a theme.

refroidi   Chilled.

riser   Platform used to build a stage or stairs.

roll-in   Foods and/or beverages preset on rolling tables and moved into a function room at a designated time.

room turnover   Amount of time needed to tear down and reset a function room.

roti   Roast.

roulade   Rolled.

rouleau   Roll of.

roux   Mixture of butter and flour used to thicken sauces and soups.

Russian service   Foods are cooked at tableside. Servers put them on platters and present platters to guests seated at dining tables. Guests serve themselves.

sans arete   Boneless.

sans peau   Skinless.

sauce au beurre   Butter sauce.

sauce Robert   Brown gravy with lemon juice, minced onions, dry mustard, and white wine.

sauerbraten   Beef seasoned with onions, vinegar, and brown sauce.

sauté   To fry lightly in a little fat.

seminar   A group receiving instruction and direction from an expert in a particular subject matter.

service bar   Bar located outside a function room or restaurant outlet in a service area not visible to guests.

service charge   Charge added to standard food and beverage prices. Usually used to defray the cost of labor, such as housemen, servers, technicians, and other personnel. May be in addition to or in lieu of a gratuity.

service contractor   Outside company used by clients to provide specific products or services, such as dance floors or flags.

set plate   Another name for *base plate*.

sherbet glass   Short glass container with foot and stem.

shish kabob   Lamb pieces and other foods cooked on a skewer.

shot   Single-serving measurement of spirits.

shoulder   Period of slow business. Time between a caterer's peak and low seasons.

show plate   Decorative plate preset at each place setting and removed before service begins.

shucker   Person who opens fresh clams and oysters at a food station in view of guests.

signature item   Product or service for which a facility is well known. The facility specializes in providing this item.

silver service   Another name for *Russian service*.

skirting   Pleated or ruffled table draping used on buffet, reception, and head tables.

SMERF market   Social, military, education, religious, and fraternal market.

snifter   A large short-stemmed goblet used for cordials.

sommelier   A wine steward.

sorbet   A frozen product having a mushy consistency. Designed to be a palate cleanser. Served just prior to the entrée. It has a tart flavor, never sweet, and usually a wine or champagne base.

soufflé   A baked, fluffy dessert or main dish of milk, egg yolks, stiffly beaten egg whites, and seasonings.

sponsored bar   Another name for *open bar*.

station   A server's assigned area. Also refers to the individual buffet tables located throughout a reception area, with each table offering one food item or representing one theme.

steady   A server employed full-time by a facility.

steak tartare   Raw, ground filet mignon; highly seasoned.

supper   Light evening meal. Usually served after 9:00 P.M.

supreme   Sauce cooked with a browned roux, thinned with chicken stock, and seasoned with lemon juice and parsley.

table d'hôte   Full-course, fixed-price meal.

table wine   Class of wine naturally fermented to about 12 percent alcohol. Typically used as a house wine.

tallow carving   Display piece carved from lamb's fat and wax. Usually all white, but can be tinted.

tap   Device used for starting or stopping the flow of beverage from a container.

tent   Portable shelter. Usually used to house outdoor functions.

terrine   Similar to a pâté. It is baked in an earthenware dish from which it is served.

theme party   Party at which all foods, beverages, decorations, and entertainment relate to a single theme.

ticket exchange   Banquet-control procedure whereby guests exchange an event coupon from their registration packet for an actual event ticket and seat assignment. Increases control; also tends to reduce the number of no-shows.

tip   Voluntary gift clients give to employees for extra-special service.

trade association   Group of persons employed in a particular trade.

truss   A framework suspended from the ceiling to hold stage lighting.

underliner   A plate used under a bowl, a glass, condiments, and so forth.

union call   Additional servers obtained from a labor source shared by several facilities. A facility hires servers as needed from this common labor source to work individual catered functions.

veau   Veal.

velouté   White sauce. Used as a base for other sauces.

vert   Green.

vichyssoise   Potato/chicken-broth soup. Served chilled.

vol-au-vent   A puff-pastry shell, or cup, usually filled with a creamed meat entrée or a fruit/custard dessert.

Waldorf salad   Dish of diced apples, celery, chopped walnuts, mayonnaise, and whipped cream.

water station   Table or side stand with pitchers of water and glassware. Intended to be a self-service station.

well brand   Another name for *house brand*.

workshop   Persons meeting together to gain new techniques, skills, knowledge, and so forth. Usually involves participants training each other.

Appendix

ACTION STATIONS

Pasta Station

Fettucini with Alfredo Sauce

Spinach Tortellini filled with Ricotta Cheese

and served with

Marinara Sauce made from Fresh Plum Tomatoes

Medley of Italian Green Vegetables

including

Spinach, Zucchini, and Lima Beans with Garlic Olive Oil

Displayed with Bread Sticks and Freshly Grated Romano Cheese

$ 6.50 per person

Oriental Stir Fry Station

Chicken Stir Fry with Bamboo Shoots

Shrimp Stir Fry with Water Chestnuts

Steamed Rice

Displayed with Fortune Cookies and Chopsticks

$ 5.50 per person

Carving Station

Tender Steamship Round of Beef to serve 200 guests.....$ 400.00

Roast Tenderloin of Beef to serve 30 guests ....$ 250.00

Roasted Turkey to serve 50 guests....$ 275.00

Honey Glazed Ham to serve 50 guests....$ 225.00

Each station requires an attendant at $50.00 each for a one-hour function. Add $35.00 for each additional hour. All food and beverage prices are subject to a 15 percent service charge, to cover the cost of setting up and service for your function. Prices will be quoted inclusive of the service charge upon request. (January 2001)

CATERING FUNCTION CHECKLIST

The following list shows important items that should be discussed or explained to the client:

A. GENERAL INFORMATION

1. Name of Client/Group _____

   Type of Function _____

   Address _____

   Date of Function _____

   Person in Charge _____

   Phone Number _____

   Fax Number _____

   E-Mail Address _____

_____ 2. Person(s) authorized to sign the check

_____ 3. How and where will meeting be posted?

_____ 4. Billing address, if different from confirmation address

_____ 5. Attendance (explain guarantee and overset policy)

_____ 6. Will registration or course materials be delivered to the facility?

_____ 7. How are messages to be handled?

_____ 8. Ticket control (Do servers pick up tickets? does this include the head table?)

_____ 9. Will there be an invocation? anthem? opening remarks?

_____ 10. Starting and ending times (be specific for all functions)

_____ 11. Review labor and service charges with client

B. ROOM SETUP

_____ 12. Type of setup—seating arrangements (banquet rounds, rectangular tables, classroom, etc.)

_____ 13. Head table size (number to be seated, elevated on a platform, etc.)

_____ 14. Staging requirements (get specific height)

_____ 15. Will a materials table be needed?

_____ 16. Will a registration table be needed?

_____ 17. Legal pads and pens/pencils—up$ell

_____ 18. Mineral water—up$ell

_____ 19. Candy—up$ell

_____ 20. Will banners need to be hung?

_____ 21. Lighting requirements

_____ 22. Special linen requirements

_____ 23. All major functions to have a floor plan

_____ 24. American or state flag needed?

_____ 25. Piano?

C. AUDIOVISUAL REQUIREMENTS

_____ 26. Number of podiums needed

_____ 27. Amplification and number of microphones

_____ 28. Number of easels

_____ 29. Blackboards

_____ 30. Electrical requirements

_____ 31. Specific AV needs (e.g., electric pointer, overhead projector, video player, size of screen, etc.)

D. DECORATIONS AND MUSIC

_____ 32. Up$ell music requirements (background dinner music, pianist, harp, flute, strolling strings, dance band, music for theme coffee breaks, etc.)

_____ 33. Up$ell table centerpieces (e.g., fresh arrangement, silk flowers, candles, etc.)

_____ 34. Up$ell decorations (theme props, trees, backdrops, etc.)

_____ 35. Up$ell special table settings

_____ 36. Up$ell special printed menus

_____ 37. Up$ell special lighting

E. BREAKFAST

_____ 38. Up$ell virtues of a group breakfast versus premeeting coffee break

_____ 39. Up$ell new menu ideas

_____ 40. Up$ell upgraded buffets or brunch

_____ 41. Up$ell champagne or "eye-openers" (mimosas, screwdrivers, bloody Marys, etc.)

F. REFRESHMENT BREAKS

_____ 42. Up$ell a premeeting continental breakfast if a full group breakfast is not planned

_____ 43. Up$ell distinctive (theme) midmorning and midafternoon breaks

_____ 44. Up$ell flavored coffees

G. LUNCHEON

_____ 45. Up$ell an appetizer selection

_____ 46. Up$ell upgraded salad (Caesar, Nicoise, Roquefort dressing, etc.)

_____ 47. Up$ell new entrée ideas

_____ 48. Up$ell premium vegetable sides (artichokes, snow peas, etc.)

_____ 49. Up$ell specialty desserts (crepes, peach Melba, Haagen Daz ice cream, etc.)

_____ 50. What type of wine would the client prefer? (Up$ell a champagne toast for awards or retirement luncheons)

_____ 51. Offer a selection of ethnic menus for variety

H. RECEPTIONS

_____ 52. Bar arrangements (host or cash)

_____ 53. Explain bartender charge

_____ 54. Up$ell theme menus

_____ 55. Up$ell action stations (pasta, gyros, etc.)

_____ 56. Up$ell in-room meat carving stations

_____ 57. Up$ell passed hors d'oeuvres

_____ 58. Up$ell an additional reception to follow dinner

I. DINNER

_____ 59. Up$ell upgraded appetizer (shrimp cocktail, crab legs, etc.)

_____ 60. Up$ell soup course (French onion, clam chowder, etc.)

_____ 61. Up$ell upgraded salad (Caesar tossed tableside or individual salads dressed by servers)

_____ 62. Up$ell champagne, dessert wine, or cordials

_____ 63. Up$ell special blend or flavored coffees and liqueur station

_____ 64. Up$ell specialty dessert (waiter parade of baked Alaska or flaming cherries jubilee prepared tableside, etc.)

THE WEDDING CHECKLIST

Client's Name: _____

Address: _____

_____

Phone Number Home: _____ Fax: _____

Phone at Work: _____ Fax: _____

Name of Bride: _____ Name of Groom: _____

Future Name of Bride: _____

Contact Address: _____ Phone Number: _____

Location of the Wedding Reception: _____

_____

Minimum Number of Guests Expected: _____

Day and Date of the Wedding: _____

Location of the Ceremony: _____

_____

Ceremony Start Time: _____ End Time: _____

Transportation: _____ Type: _____ Company: _____

Driver's Name: _____ Phone Number: _____

Reception Start Time: _____ End Time: _____

Location Planning

Receiving Line/Introductions _____ Time: _____

Gift Table: _____

Guest Book Table: _____

Escort Table: _____

Bridal Table: _____

Equipment Requirements: _____

Tables for Guests (number and size) _____

Type of Chairs _____

Chair Covers: _____

Napkins: Color _____   Size _____   Quantity _____
                    Color _____   Size _____   Quantity _____

Linens: Color _____   Size _____   Quantity _____
                    Color _____   Size _____   Quantity _____
                    Color _____   Size _____   Quantity _____
                    Color _____   Size _____   Quantity _____

Banquet Cloths: Color _____   Quantity _____

Skirting: Color _____   Total Footage _____

China Color and Pattern: _____

Glassware Type: _____

Silverware: _____

Ancillary Services

Support Staff: _____   Number _____   Location _____

Responsibilities: _____

Music: Name _____   Phone: _____

    Start Time: _____   End Time: _____

    Hourly Play Time: _____

Family Tables: _____

Proposed Menu: _____

Hors d'Oeuvres: _____

Type of Bar: _____

Champagne Toast: _____   Time _____

Cake Cutting: _____   Time _____

Meal: Buffet _____   Served _____   Sit Down _____   Cocktail _____

Proposed Food Items: _____

Hors d'Oeuvres: _____

Passed: _____

Stationary: _____

Appetizer: _____

Soup: _____

Salad: _____

Intermezzo: _____

Entrée: _____

Dessert: _____

Wines: _____

Floral Requirements

Tables: Number _____ Size _____ Type _____

Buffets: Type _____ Quantity _____

Type _____ Quantity _____

Bride: _____

Groom: _____

Bridesmaids: _____

Wedding Party: _____

Best Man: _____

Cake: _____

Photographer: Name _____ Phone _____

Time of Attendance _____

Videographer: Name _____ Phone _____

Time of Shooting _____

Cake: Bakery _____ Phone _____

Type _____ Spec. Requirements _____

Delivery Time: _____ Refrigerate: ____ Yes   No ____

Cake Knife and Server: _____

Bride and Groom Glasses: _____

Cocktail Napkins: Color _____ Quantity _____

Inscription _____

Printer _____ Phone _____

Date Promised _____

Matches: Color _____ Quantity _____

Inscription _____

Printer _____ Phone _____

Date Promised _____

Floor Plan: _____

POST EVENT CRITIQUE

Event Name _____

Event Date(s) _____

Client profile: _____

Attendee profile: _____

Profitability: _____

Challenges in sales process, execution, or planning: _____

Overall success (client, attendees): _____

Food and beverage (special diets, special products, unusual setups, theme parties, etc.): _____

_____

What portion of the budget was spent on décor? _____

Room rental charge? _____

Was anything provided as complimentary? At a discounted price? If so, what? _____

_____

Feasibility of repeat bookings? _____

Additional comments, recommendations: _____

_____

| (signed) | (title) | (date) |

SHOW RECAP FORM

Show: _____

Date(s): _____

Date: _____

Department: _____

Dept. Head/Manager: _____

Sales Executive: _____

Event Coordinator: _____

Overview:

A. Staffing (Concerns, Problems—Service Problems, Delays, etc.—Comments) _____

_____

_____

_____

_____

_____

_____

B. Culinary/Bakery _____

_____

_____

_____

C. Stewarding (Equipment, Follow-Up, etc.) _____

_____

_____

_____

D. Catering Sales _____

_____

_____

_____

_____

E. Commissary _____

_____

_____

F. Georgia World Congress Center (GWCC) Operations (Set-Up, Housekeeping, Engineering, etc.) _____

_____

_____

_____

Linen and Table Compatibility Chart

Linen Sizes:	72" Round	60" Round	54" Round	48" Round	36" Round	8' Banquet	6' Banquet	8' Lecture	6' Lecture
132" Round	To the Floor								
120" Round	24" Drop	To the Floor							
108" Round	18" Drop	24" Drop	27" Drop				Decorative Top Cloth		
90" Round	9" Drop	15" Drop	18" Drop	21" Drop	27" Drop	Decorative Top Cloth	Decorative Top Cloth	Decorative Top Cloth	Decorative Top Cloth
72" Square	Decorative Top to Edge	Decorative Top 6" Drop	Decorative Top 9" Drop	Decorative Top 12" Drop	Top Cloth 18" Drop	Decorative Top Cloth	Decorative Top Cloth	Decorative Top Cloth	Decorative Top Cloth
60" Square	Decorative Top Table Center Only	Decorative Top 3" Drop	Decorative Top 6" Drop	Decorative Top 12" Drop	Decorative Top Cloth	Decorative Top Cloth	Decorative Top Cloth	Decorative Top Cloth	Decorative Top Cloth
Banquet Rectangle with Round Corners						To the Floor on All Sides	To the Floor on All Sides	To the Floor on All Sides	To the Floor on All Sides
60" × 120" Banquet Top with Square Corners						Front and Back 15" Drop	Front and Back 15" Drop	Front and Back 20" Drop	Front and Back 20" Drop
21' Table Skirt	Full Table with 2' Overlap					Full Table All Sides			
17' Table Skirt		Full Table with 1' Overlap	Full Table with 2' Overlap	Full Table with 4' Overlap		Three Sides	Full Table All Sides	Three Sides	Full Table All Sides 2' Overlap
10" Wide Runners 8 feet long	Decorative Strip	Decorative Strip	Decorative Strip	Decorative Strip	Decorative Strip	Decorative Strip	Decorative Strip	Decorative Strip	Decorative Strip

Note:
1. Standard table height is 30".
2. All drop measurements are calculated from table edge down.
3. Skirting can be done with velcro clips and pins.

SPECIAL MEAL REQUEST FORM

Following this form are the menus for the entire conference. As caterers, we realize that not all guests prefer the same foods. Some individuals have specific dietetic requirements, and some have specific dislikes (such as seafood, game meats, etc.). Please take a moment to look over the menus. If a menu features an entrée that you cannot eat, fill out the following information and return it to the NACE Registration Desk. Please make sure that your Special Meal Requests are turned in by 10:30 A.M. on Saturday morning to allow time for the kitchen to accommodate the request.

Name _____

Meal Function Requiring Change _____

_____

Meal Requested _____

Name _____

Meal Function Requiring Change _____

_____

Meal Requested _____

Name _____

Meal Function Requiring Change _____

_____

Meal Requested _____

Name _____

Meal Function Requiring Change _____

_____

Meal Requested _____

Name _____

Meal Function Requiring Change _____

_____

Meal Requested _____

Index

Accounts:
  payable, 392
  receivable, 392
Accuracy in Menus, 158
Acetate sheet, 306
Action station, 121, 147, 148, 153, 155,
     159, 166, 172, 173, 174,
     218–219, 233, 257, 259, 260,
     261, 281–283, 401, 416
Advertising, 44, 45, 336, 394
  word-of-mouth, 79, 96, 98, 99
Air wall, 310, 401
Aisle (cross-aisle), 214, 218, 221, 281
Alcohol-awareness training, 206–207,
     324
Alcohol Beverage Commission (ABC),
     204, 205
A-list, 24, 25, 163, 207, 276, 323, 326,
     391, 402. *See also* Steady extra
Ambience, 104
Ambient light, 212
American Business Information, Inc., 75
American Business Lists, Inc., 75
American Culinary Federation (ACF),
     31, 401
American Gas Association (AGA), 281
American Hotel & Motel Association
     (AH & MA), 207, 283, 401
  Educational Institute, 283
American Institute of Wine & Food
     (AIWF), 37, 401
American Medical Association (AMA),
     31
American Society of Association
     Executives (ASAE), 31–32, 39
American Society of Composers,
     Authors, and Publishers
     (ASCAP), 398
Amplifier, 300

Anniversary, 33, 35, 74
Antitrust law, 51
Apprenticeship, 326, 327
Approved supplier (list), 290, 307, 308,
     310, 354
ARAMARK, 5
Artificial intelligence, 64
Association, 31, 38, 39, 74, 86, 110, 154,
     220, 313, 317
  for Convention Operations
     Management (ACOM), 401
  for Destination Management
     Executives (ADME), 317
  professional, 31, 65, 328, 396, 412
  trade, 31, 414
Attendant, 18
Audience separation, 221
Audio:
  mixer, 300
  recorder, 302
  tape (player), 300, 304
Audiovisual (AV) (department), 59,
     225–226, 294–310, 387,
     397–398, 402
  accommodating a client's needs,
     309–310
  selecting an outside service contractor,
     307–309, 397
  technician, 302, 303, 397
  types of services, 294–307
Audit trail, 385
Average:
  check, 45, 51
  contribution margin, 45. *See also*
     Contribution margin
  guest count per function, 45
  revenue per function, 45
AVW Audiovisual, 223, 295, 298, 299,
     301

Awning, 247

Baby spot, 402
Bacteria, 286
Bad debt, 349
Bag-in-the-box container, 257
Bailment, 385
Bakeries, 293
Baldridge, Letitia, 100
Ball, 402
Band stand, 215
Bank maze, 216
Banquet, 402
  assistant manager, 17
  cloth, *see* Napery
  event order (BEO), 18, 240, 242, 250,
     257, 341–343, 344, 346, 359,
     362, 402, 407
  manager, 17
  -room count, 362, 365
  sales manual, 332
  service, 382
  setup, 382
    number of crew members needed,
     266–267
  setup manager, 17
Baptism, 36
Bar back, 18
  number needed, 263–265
Bar Code program, 207
Bar layout, 229–231. *See also* Layout and
     design
Bar Mitzvah, 36, 142
Bartender, 18
  charge, 187
  number needed, 263–265
Bartering, *see* Trade, -out arrangement
Base plate, 403
Bat Mitzvah, 36, 142

Beer, 184
Bell desk, 395, 396
Beverage:
    charges, 186–189
        flat rate, 189–190
        per bottle, 188–189, 404
        per drink, 187–188, 404
        per hour, 189
        per person, 189
        sliding scale, 189
    cost, *see* Control, cost, food and
        beverage
    department, 379
    function, 64, 214
        purpose, 181–183
        type, 194–200
    neutral, 184
    package plan, 193
    preparation, 259. *See also* Production
    prepreparation, 258
    quality needed, 256–257
    quantity needed, 252–255
    replenishing workstation, 260
    station, 218
    workstation setup, 258, 260
Beyond Cuisine, 78, 120, 179
Bill-collection agency, *see* Collection,
    agency
Billing, 363
    cycle, 350
    procedures, 348, 349, 350
Birthday, 37
Black Angus Beef, 51
B-list, 24, 25, 163, 207, 276, 323, 326,
    328, 391, 403. *See also* Casual
    labor
Blood alcohol concentration (BAC), 201
Blue laws, 203
Body language, 89, 91
Bonus, 337
Booking, 403
    confirmed, 108
    pace, 42
    tentative, 108, 393
Bottle value, 364
Bowling-alley effect, 210
Branding, 51
Break a case, 254
Breakage, 40, 316
Breakeven analysis, 58
Breakeven point, 58
Breakfast, 166–167
    continental, 167
    English-style, 166–167
Break-out session, 404
Bridal:
    coordinator, 40
    shower, 78
Bride's, 35

Broadcast Music Incorporated (BMI), 398
Brochure, *see* Catering, brochure
Broken glass, 284–285
Broker, 315
Budget, 112
Buffer area, 311
Buffet layout, 231–236. *See also* Layout
    and design; Service, type
    (style), buffet
Building:
    code, *see* License (permit; code),
        building
    opening, 32
Burns, 283–284
Bus cart, 218
Business:
    cycle, 84
    license, *see* License (permit; code),
        business
    services (department), 399
Busperson, 18
Butane, 282

Cabaret tax, *see* Tax, cabaret
Caesars Palace, 210
Callaway Gardens, 117
Call brand, 185, 188, 190, 256, 404
Camelback Inn, 5
Camera, 304
Cancellation fee (charge), 63
Canvassing, 50, 86
Capital intensive, 289
Captain, 18, 405
Case-size lot, 254
Cash:
    bar, 18, 186, 187, 188, 190, 191, 192,
        230, 392, 405
    collected, 364, 365
    discount, *see* Discount, cash
    rebate, 351
Cashier, 18, 191, 219, 392, 395
    number needed, 265–266
Cash-on-delivery (COD), 386
Casino host, 396
Casual labor, 25, 58. *See also* B-list
Caterer, 405
    types, 3–5
Catering:
    assistant director, 17
    book, 393
    brochure, 52, 57, 66–74, 75, 77, 84,
        85, 90, 98, 100, 102, 103. *See
        also* Wedding, brochure
    business, 3
    contract, 346–348, 350, 393, 409
    corporate, 3
    department:
        functions, 6
        objectives, 6–7

        organization, 7–14
    director (DOC), 17
    Function Checklist, 249, 417–419
    major challenges, 23–26
    manager, 17
    mobile, 5
    off-premise, 3, 176–179, 410
    on-premise, 1, 2
    policies, 19–23, 42, 66
    Research Institute, 35
    safety and sanitation, *see* Safety;
        Sanitation
    sales manager, 17
    sales representative, 17
    social, 3
    staff positions, 14–15
    types, 3–5
Cater-out, 1, 3, 139, 405
CaterSource, 7
CaterSource, Inc., 41, 86
Ceiling treatment, 242
Cellar temperature, 198
Centerpiece, 241, 405
Center plate, 240
Chaine des Rotisseurs, 37
Chair, 228
Chamber of commerce, 74
Change order, 344
Charger, 405
Charitable organization, 74, 329
Chef, 378, 379
City ledger, 349
Clerk, 18
Client:
    contact, 87–88
    decision maker, 38–41, 48, 50
    evaluation, 352
    inquiry, 80–84
    meeting with, 88–92
    objections, *see* Objections
    other services, 288–294
        combination of in-house and outside
            services, 292
        provided by the facility, 289
        provided by in-house
            concessionaires, 291–292
        provided by outside service
            contractor, 290–291, 292–294
    relations, 98–99
    solicitation, 84. *See also* Soliciting
        business (at a current event)
Closed circuit TV (CCTV), 305
Closing:
    the sale, 93
    statement, 95
Club Managers Association of America
    (CMAA), 405
Coca Cola (Coke), 33, 38, 51, 159, 160,
    314

Cocktail reception, *see* Reception
Cocktail server, *see* Server, cocktail
Coffee station, 231
Cold call, 84, 85, 89
Collection:
    agency, 351
    procedures, 350–351
College, 326–327
Combination (cash and open) bar, 186
COMDEX, 33
Comfortably crowded, 217
Commissary, *see* Storage (storeroom)
Commission, 40, 44, 66, 291, 313, 316,
        337, 351
Common law, 207–208
Compensation, 337–338, 390
Competitor profile, 65
Complimentary food, beverage, and/or
        sleeping rooms, 312, 351
Computer:
    hardware, 374
    selection factors, 374
    -service firm, 374
    software, 374, 375
    uses, 375–376
Conceptual skill, 16
Concession (Concessionaire), 289,
        291–292, 396, 405
    ticket, 18, 266
Concierge, 395, 396
Confirmation (notice), 36, 77
Consumer Price Index (CPI), 63
Contemporary Hotel, 111
Contract, 77, 87, 95, 108, 312
    food service, 5
    national, 397
    outside, *see* Service, contractor
    planner, *see* Meeting planner
Contribution margin, 53, 56, 58, 62. *See
        also* Average, contribution
        margin
Control (controlling), 6, 341, 362, 363,
        365
    computerized, 360, 373–376
    correction phase, 340, 360, 362, 369,
        370
    cost, 230, 232, 256, 257, 259, 340,
        357, 392
        food and beverage, 144–145, 230,
            259, 352–367
        other expenses, 372–373
        payroll, 367–372
    cycle, 339, 353, 360
    documents, 341–348
    over, 340
    portion, 357
    quality, 256, 257, 258, 340, 354, 372,
        389
    record-keeping system, 359–365

ounce, 363–364
payroll, 369–370
product-analysis, 362–363, 365
standard-cost, 360–362
standard-sales, 364–365
service, *see* Service, control
state, 205
Controller, 392–393
Convenience food, *see* Food,
        convenience
Convention, 31, 406
    conference/service manager, 17
    materials, 219, 315
    porter, *see* Houseman
    resume, 344–346, 406
    service, 335, 382–386
    and Visitors Bureau (CVB), 317–318
Cooperating with other facilities, 319
Copy center, *see* Print shop (printing)
Corkage, *see* Cost, corkage
Cost:
    actual, 256, 309, 353, 360, 363, 369
    budgeted (expected; potential;
            standard), 256, 360, 363, 367,
            369
    control, *see* Control (controlling),
            cost
    controllable, 373
    corkage, 21, 187, 192, 193, 203, 406
    edible-portion, 363
    effective, 340, 363
    fixed, 53, 58, 59, 60, 369
    food, *see* Control (controlling), cost,
            food and beverage
    inventory carrying, 354
    labor (payroll), 152, 190–193, 261,
            262, 308, 309, 367, 368, 369,
            370
        bar backs, 190–191
        bartenders, 190
        cashiers, 191
        cocktail servers, 191
        factors affecting, 368–369
        margin analysis, 58
        security, 192
    opportunity, 64
    overrun, 357
    prime, 56, 63, 372–373
    recipe, 65, 363
    reduction techniques, 365–367,
            370–372
    semifixed, 368
    semivariable, 53, 368
    shipping, 386
    variable, 53, 58, 59, 60, 261, 368, 369
        step-wise, 368
    variance, 44, 309, 340, 341, 357, 359,
            360, 362, 367, 369, 370
    work sheet, 361

Council on Hotel, Restaurant &
        Institutional Education
        (CHRIE), 405
Cover, 105, 216, 236, 239, 240, 406, 411
    charge, 23
    naked, 236
Craze, *see* Fad
Credit:
    application, 86, 392
    card, 349
    check, 86, 393
    department, 335
    history, 48
    management, 66, 348–352
    manager, 348, 393
    period, 350
    rating, 348, 350
    reference, 86
    slip, 355
    terms (policy), 21, 64, 349, 350, 393
    trade, 366
    verification, 86, 349
Credit Bureau/Equifax, 86
Critical-item inventory system, *see*
        Control (controlling), record-
        keeping system, product analysis
Cross-training, *see* Training, cross-
CRT (cathode ray tube), 303
Culinary school, 326
Customer:
    appreciation party, 37, 65
    base, 54
    -contact skill, 323, 324
Custom Menu/Item Cost Sheet, 61
Cutoff date, 406

Daily event, *see* Event (show), daily
Dance floor, 215, 311, 384–385
Danger (temperature) zone, 285
Data:
    processing, 392
    reentry, 374
Day-labor operation, 328, 409
Dead space (area), 212, 245
Decor, 116, 222, 225
    moving, 112, 243, 317
Deep pockets, 207, 208
Del Coronado Hotel, 35
Delivery:
    sales, 5
    slip, *see* Invoice
Demand, 64, 65
    elasticity of, 58
Demographics, 109, 145, 184
Departmental evaluation, 352
Department of Labor, 281
Deposit, 19, 49, 59, 63, 106, 108, 308,
        315, 348, 350, 351, 393
Designated-driver program, 202

Desktop publishing, 68, 97, 375, 389
Destination management company, 289, 316
Detail meeting, *see* Pre-event (pre-function) meeting
Diary, *see* Function, book
Diary clerk, *see* Scheduler
Diet restrictions, 145, 242, 262
Differentiation, 51
Dining-room layout, 226–229. *See also* Layout and design
Dinner, 74, 174–176, 182, 406
    awards, 74, 175
Directing, 6
Directional sign, 246
Direct mail, 74–75, 84, 85, 97
Director of training, *see* Training, director
Discount, 93, 102, 103, 124, 125, 292, 293, 366, 370, 396
    cash, 351, 366
    promotional, 366
    quantity, 317, 366, 397
    volume, 291, 366
Disney (World), 111, 113
Display:
    area, 219–220
    restriction, 22
Dissolve unit, 305
Double cloth, 406
Downtime, *see* Slack time
Dramshop law, 207, 208
Dressing room, 311
Drink:
    potential number per container, 363
    ticket, 18, 186, 191, 219, 230, 259, 265, 266, 279, 352, 363, 364, 365, 392
Drug test, 330
Dun & Bradstreet, 86

Earnest money, *see* Deposit
Economic development authority, 74
Edible yield, *see* Yield, edible
Eisen, Ricky, 112
Electrical service, 306–307
Electronic pointer, 306
E-mail, 82, 373
Employee:
    benefits, 337, 370, 383, 392
        discretionary, 337, 338, 371
        required, 337
    blue collar, 251
    fixed (cost), 276, 322, 323
    full-time, 371
    handbook, 331
    leasing, 328, 370
    motivation, 372
    on-call, 399
    one-time recruit, 384

    orientation, 331, 391
    part-time, 371
    pink collar, 251
    productivity, *see* Productivity (labor)
    recruitment, 322–331, 390
    rehab, 370
    relations-manager, 392
    retention, 329
    steady, 413
    turnover, 323, 325, 329, 372
    uniform (costume), 243
    variable (cost), 276, 322, 323
    white collar, 251
Employment:
    agency, 327
    manager, 322, 330, 390, 391
Encyclopedia of Associations, 39
Energy (management system), 106, 245
Energy break, 407
Engineer, 18
Engineering (department), 335–336, 387–388
Entertainment, 59, 125, 215, 294, 310–312
    contract, 312
    department, 398–399
    tax, *see* Tax, consumption
Entrance, 112
Entry:
    confirmed, 108
    prospective, 107
    tentative, 107
    ticket, 266
Environment, 106
Epergne, 241
Equalization, 300
Equipment:
    inventory, 245
    limitations, 152
    usage, 373
Ethics, 24
Event (show):
    daily, 34
    fund-raising, 37
    manager (coordinator), 40
    special, *see* Market, special events
    ticket, 219
    timing, 224
Event Solutions, 25, 112
Exercise break, 169
Exhibition cooking, *see* Action station
Exhibitor directory, 33
Expeditor, 359

Fad, 154
Falls, 284
Fax, 80, 81
Features, 92
Feedback, 300

Filmstrip, 300
Fine Host, 5
Finish cooking, 259, 261, 263
Fire code, *see* License (permit; code), fire
Fire department (marshal), 318
Flag (placement), 246
Flatware, *see* Tableware
Floater, 265
Flowers, 293
Flyer, 97, 98
Font, 68
Food:
    and beverage department, 332–334
    and beverage manager, 334
    -borne illness, 258, 279, 285–286, 356
    checker, 359
    complimentary, 312
    convenience, 152, 261, 371
    cost, *see* Control (controlling), cost, food and beverage
    and Drug Administration (FDA), 159
    easy-to-produce, 149–150
    entertainment value, 153–154
    finger, 174
    fun, 117
    handler, 18
    hard-to-produce, 147–148
    made from scratch (raw), 261, 367
    market availability, 150–151
    mood, 168
    paired with wine, 153, 197
    potentially hazardous, 279, 285, 286
    preparation, 258–259. *See also* Production
    prepreparation, 257–258
    production staff needed, 260–263
    quality needed, 255–256
    quantity needed, 250–252
    replenishing workstation, 260
    runner, 260, 272, 281
    seasonal, 149
    server, *see* Server, food
    sink-to-the-bottom, 170
    steward, *see* Food, handler
    walk-away, 167
    workstation setup, 259–260
Food & Wine, 26
Food Arts, 26, 198
Franchise (fee), 44, 50, 65
Fraternal organization, 28, 74
Freeman Companies, The, 290
Free pour, 187, 363, 407
Front office, 335, 395–396
Function:
    book, 48, 107–108
    room:
        appearance, 209–212
        cleaning and maintaining, 243–244
        communication in, 244–245

beeper method, 244
callback method, 244
cell phone method, 245
walkie-talkie method, 244–245
layout and design, 224–225. *See also*
Layout and design
location, 212
rental rate (charge), 20–21, 53, 58,
59, 60, 64
resume, *see* Convention, resume
selection, 209
setup (seating), 222–248
conference-room, 221, 227
difficulty, 224
hollow-square, 221, 227
picnic, 227
planning, 222–248
premovement, 225
schoolroom (classroom), 214, 221,
224
sit-down dinner, 224
theater (auditorium), 214, 220,
221, 224
U-shaped, 221, 227
sheet, *see* Banquet, event order
(BEO)
space requirements, 213–222
status, 224
teardown, 225, 278–280
temperature, 245–246
turnover (turnaround), 93, 105, 309,
384, 412
utilities, 212–213
Fund-raising event, *see* Event (show),
fund-raising
Funeral roses, 241
Fun food, *see* Food, fun

Garage manager, 396
Gayle Research, 39
George Washington University, 34, 109
Georgia World Congress Center, 426
GES Exposition Services, 290
Gift, 43, 165
Glassware, *see* Tableware
Gobo light, 408
Goldblatt, Joe, 34, 109
Good Samaritan law, 280
Goodwill, 57, 312
Gourmet club, 37
Government agencies, 318, 327–328
Graduation, 36–37
Gratuity, 19, 53, 63, 162–165, 187, 337
Grievance, 390, 392
Ground transportation, 315
Group-history file, 47, 50, 65
Guarantee, 19–20, 59, 63, 408
guest (count), 148, 250, 316
meal, 40, 170

price, 59
Gueridon, 156, 157
Guest:
background, 145–146
check (duplicate), 259
count, 213–214
services, 395, 396
Guide to Executive Manners, 100
Gunther, Peter E., viii, x

HACCP, 280
Handicapped seating, 221
Head:
count, 362, 408
hunter, *see* Employment, agency
table, *see* Table, head
Health:
card, 324
care, 106
district, *see* License (permit; code),
health
Heating, ventilation, and air
conditioning (HVAC), 387,
408
Help hotline, 374
High roller, 396
Holiday pay, 338
Homemaker, 327
Honesty and integrity, 16
Hospitality Suite, 171, 188, 195, 205,
255, 390, 408
Host bar, *see* Open (sponsored), bar
Hotel Sales & Marketing Association
International (HSMAI), 331,
408
House brand (liquor; wine), 257, 408. *See
also* Well brand
Housekeeping (department), 381–382
Houseman, 18, 383, 408
*How to Manage a Successful Catering
Business*, 126
Human resources (department), 322, 325,
329, 330, 331, 335, 337,
390–392
Human (interpersonal) skill, 16, 323
Hurst, Michael, 341

Ice-breaker party, 171
Ice Magic, 241
Ice Occasions, 241
ICW (In conjunction with), 33
Incentive:
event, 32, 408, 409
travel, 30, 32
Indemnification, 22
Independent contractor, 370–371
Indirect (other) income, 42
Individual access bar, 379
Industry council, 327

Infrastructure, 105
In-house sound system, *see* Sound
(system), in-house
Insecticide, 140
Insert, 98
Insurance (rider), 177, 242, 290. *See also*
Liability, insurance
Integrity test, 330
Interest income, 349
Intermediary, 313–314. *See also* Service,
contractor
International Communication Industries
Association, 308
International Food Service Executives
Association (IFSEA), 408
International Special Events Society
(ISES), 409
Internet Movie Data Base, 113
Internship, 326
Introductory-price offer, 366
Inventory:
beginning, 360
carrying charge, *see* Cost, inventory
carrying
ending, 258, 360, 363
physical, 245, 360
shrinkage, 365
Invoice, 355, 393
dispute, 355
statement, 393
Issuing, 355–357, 360

Jaeger, Jane, x
JELL-O, 159
Job:
application, 329–330, 390
description, 16–19, 324–325, 390, 409
enrichment, 374
fair, 327
interview, 330–331, 390
opening, 390
referral, 325–326
specification, 15, 323–324, 390, 409
training, *see* Training
Joseph E. Seagram & Sons Inc., 252

Ketterer, Manfred, 126
Keystoning, 300, 301
Kickback, 16, 291
Kitchen, 378–379
count, 365
Kiwanis, 28
Korbel Champagne Cellars, 199
Kosher preparation, *see* Service, type
(style), kosher; Diet restrictions
Kraft, 255

Labor, 152–153
cost (charge), *see* Cost, labor (payroll)

Labor (*Continued*)
  incremental, 276
  intensive, 152, 259, 275, 289
  pool, 325–329
  productivity, *see* Productivity (labor)
  -saving equipment, 372
  shortage, 323
Lacto-ovo vegetarians, 145. *See also*
        Vegetarianism
Landing space, 220, 260, 273, 274
Laser:
  disk, 300
  pointer, 306
Laundry, 336
Lawry's Seasoned Salt, 117
Lawsuit, *see* Litigation
Layout and design, 152
LCD (liquid crystal display) panel, 303
Lead, 318
  time, 266
Lectern, 246
Leftovers, 362
Letter of agreement (catering), *see*
        Catering, contract
Levy Corporation, 5
Liability, 181, 186, 196, 280, 311–312,
        385, 386
  absolute, 207
  insurance, 21, 177, 318
  third-party, 207–208
License (permit; code):
  admission, 23
  building, 210, 211, 280, 281, 312
  business, 21, 178, 191
  fire, 116, 211, 213, 214, 242, 281
  health, 21, 178, 192, 206, 280, 318
  liquor, 21, 139, 177, 178, 188,
        203–204, 230, 255, 318
    off sale, 204
    on sale, 204
    potential violations, 188, 204–206
    tavern, 203
    temporary, 204
    wine and beer, 203
  private-club, 203
Lighting, 59, 111–112, 219, 225–226,
        306–307, 312–313, 387
  hotel lighting system, 311, 312–313
  party, 172
  service contractor, 309, 311. *See also*
        Service, contractor
Light tree, 111, 307
Limited consumption bar, 186
Line-item budget, 44
Linen room, 238
Linen and Table Compatibility Chart,
        238, 427
Lions, 28
Liquor:

cage, 231
illegal sales, 200–204
laws, 200–208
license, *see* License (permit; code),
        liquor
Litigation, 201, 215
Lockbox, 230, 363
Logistics, 310, 312, 316
Loss leader, *see* Menu, pricing, loss leader
        method
Lost-business file, 47, 48–49
Luncheon, 169–171
  nonworking, 170
  working, 170
Luxury tax, *see* Tax, luxury

Mailing list, 74, 75, 85
Maintenance (department), 386–387
Maitre d'hotel, 18, 273, 409
Management information system, 392
Manpower agency, *see* Day-labor
        operation
Marginal revenue, 58
Market, 50, 96
  availability, *see* Food, market
        availability
  business, 28–30, 42
    deep, 30, 42, 66
    events, 30–34
    mid-level, 30
    shallow, 28–30, 349
  and competition analysis (survey), 46,
        47, 50–51
  education, 29
  military, 29
  niche, 117
  segment. 49, 66, 76
  share, 54
  social, 34–38, 40
  social, military, education, religious,
        and fraternal (SMERF), 28, 413
  special events, 34–38, 40, 109,
        199–200
    planner, 314
Marketing, 23
  budget, 44–47
  the four P's, 51–79
    place, 51–52
    price, 19, 52–65, 409. *See also* Menu,
        pricing; Net price; Yield,
        management
    products and services, 52
    promotion, 44, 65–79, 394
  plan, 41–44, 47, 49, 50, 51, 52, 78, 99
  relationship, 48, 99–100
  research, 47–51, 394
  telephone, 100–102
  tools, 96–98
Mark-up (factor), 58, 293

Marriott Corporation, 150
Marriott Hotel, viii, x
Marshall, Anthony, 283
Mashgiach, 142
Master account number, 348
Master bill, 164
Meal, 143, 212, 214
  coupon, 40
  function, 64, 194, 196
    purpose, 144
    type, 165–176
  heart-healthy, 378
  penalty, 309
  ticket (entrée), 18, 219, 232, 266, 279,
        347, 362, 392
  working, 155
Meeting, 148–149, 220–221
Meeting planner, 38, 52, 150, 154, 164,
        169, 314, 409
Meeting Planners International, 410
Meetings and Conventions, 196
Mega-events, 38
Menu, 66, 70, 77, 217
  a la carte, 73
  balance, 151–152
  bingo, 71
  card, 240
  commemorative, 74
  customized, 70, 74, 90, 95, 96, 120,
        144
  dualing, 150, 406
  ganging, 407
  misrepresentation of:
    brand name, 159–160
    dietary or nutritional claims, 162
    means of preparation, 161
    means of preservation, 161
    merchandising terms, 160
    point of origin, 160
    price, 159
    product identification, 160
    quality, 159
    quantity, 158–159
    verbal and visual presentations,
        161–162
  mix, 57
  planning, 144–158, 183–185
    beverage, 183–185
    food, 144–158
  precosting, 60, 360, 378
  price plus, plus, 165, 411
  pricing, 51, 145, 162, 186–194
    a la carte, 73
    beverage, *see* Beverage, charges
    by the piece, 404
    component method, 60, 61
    food cost method, 55–56
    highest method, 55
    intuitive method, 55

level method, 62
loss leader method, 55, 63, 289, 398, 409
management guidance/policies, 55
objectives, 54
percentage method, 56
per person, 411
prime cost method, 56
reasonable method, 55
range method, 62, 63
table d' hote, 413
trial and error method, 55
souvenir, 74
standardized (offerings), 148
substitution, 22
trends, 154
Mercedes Benz, 38
Microphone, 294–296, 307
lavaliere, 307
Microsoft, 33
Minimum, 409
Mixer (system), 296
Monitor, 303
multiscan, 303
standard, 303
TV, 303
Motion picture film, 306
Multimanagement contract company, 39
Multimanagement company, *see* Meeting planner
Multi-media show (system), 306
Music, 294
Mystery shopper, 365

Napery, 237, 238, 239, 279, 283, 410
Napkin fold, 236, 238, 410
National Academy of Motion Picture Arts and Sciences, 33
National Association of Catering Executives (NACE), viii, x, 3, 25, 35, 39, 115, 328, 391, 410
Educational Foundation, viii
National Restaurant Association (NRA), 2, 50, 158, 207, 270, 280, 329, 341, 410
Educational Foundation, 207, 280
National Sanitation Foundation (NSF) International, 280, 410
Nepotism, 326
Net price, 162, 163
Networking, 100, 144, 171, 173, 182, 195
New product introduction, 32, 366
NFL, 38
Night audit, 392
No-host bar, *see* Cash, bar
Noise pollution, 212
Nonsmoking section, 221
No-tipping policy, 19
Nutrition, 70–71, 146–147, 149

Objections, 93–96
Occupational Safety and Health Administration (OSHA), 281, 410
Off-the-street business, *see* Walk-in business
Omni Hotel, 117
One-stop shopping, 52, 104, 120, 124–125, 289, 309, 316, 317, 318, 397
Open (sponsored) bar, 186, 187, 188, 189, 275, 365, 392, 408, 410, 413
Order size, 250–255, 354
Organizing, 6
Oscar parties, 33
Other income, *see* Indirect (other) income
Outdoor party, 138–142
Outside contractor, *see* Service, contractor
Outsource, *see* Service, contractor
Over:
portioning, 362
pouring, 187, 230, 363
production, 362
-set, 410
time premium pay, 262, 270 309, 326, 338, 371, 372, 387. *See also* Cost, labor (payroll)
Overhead, 60, 63
Overlay, 237, 238

Packing slip, 386
Parade (permit), 318
Parking permit, 318
Par stock, 252, 253
Party planner, 315, 410
Payroll processing, 392
PBX (Public Branch Exchange), 395
Pedersen, Shelley, 78, 120, 179
Per diem, 411
Performance station, *see* Action station
Personal (outside) food and beverage, 21
Personnel policies, 261, 263, 264, 265, 267, 270
Photo, 78
Physical exam, 330
Pilferage, 365, 373
Pin spots, 236
Pipe and drape, 219, 235, 411
Place. *See also* Marketing, the four P's, place
card, 240
setting, *see* Cover
Planning, 6
Plants, 222
Plate count, 362
Plateware, *see* Tableware

Platform, *see* Riser
Plus, plus, *see* Menu, price plus, plus
Podium, 246, 411
Popularity (index), 58
Porter, *see* Houseman
Portion control, *see* Control (controlling), portion
Posi Pour, 187, 230
Poster, 97
Post-event (post-function) critique (evaluation), 43, 352, 424
Potential-sales system, *see* Control (controlling), record-keeping system, standard-sales
Power drop, 307
Precheck ticket (machine), 187, 230, 259
Precosting, *see* Menu, precosting
Pre-event (pre-function) meeting, 411
Prefunction:
sheet, 343
space, 278, 382
Premium brand, 185, 188, 189, 190, 256, 411, 412. *See also* Call brand
Prescreening, 330
Presentatioin, 98
Power Point, 306
Press release, 97
Price, *see* Marketing, the four P's, price
Prime:
cost, *see* Cost, prime
time, 267
Print shop (printing), 59, 294, 389–390
Private industry council, 327
Privilege tax, *see* Tax, privilege
Product:
identification factors, 256
life cycle, 41
specification, 255, 256, 257, 353, 354, 355, 357, 361, 379
usage, 188, 258, 359, 364
actual, 359, 363
average, 365
standard (potential; expected), 359, 363
Production, 249, 357
planning, 249–267, 357
schedule, 250, 258
Productivity (labor), 45, 224, 225, 226, 244, 371, 372, 384
Products and services, *see* Marketing, the four P's, products and services
Professional Convention Management Association (PCMA), 410
Profit center, 58
Profit-sharing plan, 372
Projection table, 305–306
Projector:
film, 304
opaque, 304

Projector (*Continued*)
  overhead, 300
Prom, 36–37
Promotion, *see* Marketing, the four P's, promotion
Promotional discount, *see* Discount, promotional
Promotion-from-within policy, 325
Proof, 205
Propane, 282
Property:
  host, 395, 396
  manager, 388
  tour, 90
Proposal, 53, 66, 76–78, 80, 86, 87, 88, 100, 104, 107, 109, 119, 144, 412
Props, 116, 222
Provimi Veal, 51
Psychographics, 145
Public:
  address (PA) system, *see* Sound (system), in-house
  relations, 44, 63, 65, 336, 394
Purchase:
  direct, 360
  minimum, 20
  order, 354, 355
  requisition, 250
Purchasing (department), 255, 334–335, 353, 379–380

Q factor, 60
Qualify (sales leads), 86
Quantity discount, *see* Discount, quantity

Reader board, 51
Receiver, 303
Receiving (department), 354–355, 380–381
  invoice technique, 355
Reception, 155, 171–174, 182, 184, 185, 194, 198, 211, 214, 216, 220, 229, 251, 264, 273, 274, 275, 278, 365, 412
Rechaud, 156, 157
Recipe:
  cost, *see* Cost, recipe
  standardized, 255, 256, 257, 357, 358
Recognition event, 32
Recording, 307
Recreation (department), 398
Reference (check), 86, 330
Referral:
  business, 37, 43, 44, 46, 48, 79, 80, 84, 86
  fee, 65, 351
  group, 65
  list, 94

Refreshment break (center), 167–169, 195–196, 231, 237, 412
  permanent, 169
Refund (policy), 19, 63, 308, 351
Registration (information) desk, 220
Rehearsal:
  facilities, 311
  set, 225–226
  time, 308, 311
Rental company, 292, 294, 319
  charges, 308
Repair requisition, *see* Work (repair), requisition
Repeat (return) business (patronage), 37, 43, 44, 46, 48, 57, 84, 85, 98, 99, 143, 271, 290, 322, 349
Request-for-credit-memorandum, *see* Credit, slip
Request for Proposal (RFP), 318
Reservations, 395
Rest room, 246, 382
Resume, *see* Convention, resume
Return on investment, 54, 289
Returns and allowances, 352
Reunion, 35–36, 315
  planner, 35, 36
Reverse audit, *see* Control (controlling), record-keeping system, standard sales
Riser, 215, 216, 412
Ritz Carlton, 239
Roll-in (cart), 155, 221, 412
Roman, Michael, 41, 43, 86
Room block, 20
Room-rental rate (charge), *see* Function, room, rental rate (charge)
Room service (department), 195, 390
Room Size Calculator, 222
Room turnover, *see* Function, room, turnover (turnaround)
Rotary, 28
Royalty (fee), 44
Ry-Krisp, 159

Safety, 177, 280–286, 336
Sales:
  actual revenue, 364
  analysis, 45–46
  benefits, 92–93
  budgeted (expected; potential; standard) revenue, 364
  blitz, 84, 85
  department, 394
  procedures, 79–96
  tax, *see* Tax, consumption
Sanitation, 177, 258, 280–286
Sanka, 159
Scheduler, 17
Screen, 296–299

fast fold, 296, 297
front (projection), 296, 297
plasma, 303
rear (projection), 295, 297, 299
speaker enhancement, 307
surface, 297
types, 303
Seasonality, *see* Food, seasonal
Seating:
  cabaret-style, 173
  mix, 222
Secret Service, 318
Security (department), 22–23, 59, 60, 230–231, 266, 305, 311, 393–394. *See also* Cost, labor (payroll), security
Seminar, 33, 413
Senior (citizen), 327
Seroptomist, 28
Server, 18
  cocktail, 18, 191
  food, 18
  types needed, 267–268
Service, 359
  bar, 259, 274, 413
  charge, 19, 53, 162, 163, 164, 165, 413
  in concert, *see* Service, type (style), hand
  contractor, 22, 23, 24, 88, 226, 229, 290–291, 292, 313, 314, 318, 382, 388, 397, 398, 413. *See also* Intermediary
  control, 359
  corridor, 219, 220, 234, 260, 269
  duties, 268–269
  elevator, 269
  level, 50
  minimums, 270
  planning, 267–280
  ratios, 269–275
  schedule, 258
  timing, 277–278
  type (style), 121, 122, 154, 158, 171, 217, 221, 240, 250, 261, 267, 270, 273, 276, 278
  action station, *see* Action station
  American (plated), 71, 156, 270, 402, 411
  Banquet French, 156, 270, 272, 403
  buffet, 155, 166, 171, 175, 221, 239, 251, 261, 272, 283, 365, 404
  butler, 155, 156, 173, 174, 273
  cafeteria, 155, 233, 404
  family-style (English), 156, 407
  French (cart), 72, 121, 140, 156–157, 175, 221, 405
  hand, 157, 408
  kosher, 36, 142, 145
  plated buffet, 155, 411

poured-wine, 188, 196–199, 230, 272
preset, 156, 167, 171, 175, 277, 412
reception, *see* Reception
Russian (silver), 121, 156, 175, 221, 272, 412, 413
self, 21, 174, 205, 221, 251, 252, 371
wave, 157
Serving Alcohol with Care course, 207
Set plate, 413
Set-up charge, 20, 21
drink, 193, 203, 204
Shelf life, 150
Shoplifting, 365
Short pour, 340
Shoulder (period), 29, 84, 413
Show:
call, 309
plate, 413
recap form, 425–426
Side stand, 218
Signal (source), 300
Signature (item), 7, 117, 239, 413
Simultaneous translation, 305, 309
Site visit, 80
Skelton, Gayle, 173
Skirting, *see* Table, skirting
Slack time, 224, 267
Slide, 306
projector:
carousel, 302
Messager, 302
Xenon, 302–303
sound synchronizer, 304–305
Smoking section, 221, 242
Sneeze guard, 286
Social-host law, 207, 208
Socializing, 251
Solar load, 388
Soliciting business (at a current event), 79. *See also* Client, solicitation
Sommelier, 18, 196, 230, 265
Sound (system), 219, 300, 311, 387
clustered, 300
distributed, 300
in-house, 292, 302, 304, 307, 410
leaks, 310
reverberation, 310
technician, 296
Soundscape, 111
Sourcing, *see* Canvassing
Sous vide, 257, 258
Space:
availability, 51
requirements, *see* Function, room, space requirements
utilization (percentage), 46, 104–106
Speakers, 300

Special diet (meal), *see* Diet restrictions
Special events, *see* Market, special events
Special Events: The Art & Science of Celebration, 34
Special Event, 25
Special Meal Request Form, 428
Special needs, *see* Diet restrictions
Spillage, 230
Spirits, 183–184
Spoilage, 354, 355
Staffing, 321
chart (guide), 262, 263, 269, 276, 367
plan, 325
Stage right (left), 246
Staging (area), 219, 308, 311
Standard of identity, 160
Standards Of Business Practices, 158
Statler, Ellsworth, 16
Steady extra, 24, 383. *See also* A-list
Steinmetz, John, 111, 379
Sterno (pot), 281, 282, 283
flame out, 283
Steward, 19
executive, 388–389
kitchen, 389
Stock:
-discontinuation sale, 366–367
requisition (storeroom), 250, 255, 256, 355, 356, 362, 380
rotation, 355
Stockout, 148, 172, 251, 252, 354
Storage (storeroom), 355–357, 380–381
restricted access, 355
temperatures and humidities, 355–356
Street people, *see* Day-labor operation
Subcontractor, 291, 315, 317, 390
Substitution, *see* Menu, substitution
Suggestive selling, 103
Surcharge, 153, 254, 261, 271, 292
Synchronizer (sight/sound), 304–305

Table, 217, 226–228
Captain's, 240
head, 122, 170, 216, 228, 240, 270, 272, 277, 408
setting, *see* Cover
-side cooking, 281–283. *See also* Action station
skirting, 235, 413
liner, 235
stage (platform), 235
tent, 98
type, 214
60-inch round, 226
66-inch round, 226
72-inch round, 226
banquet, 6, 8, 226
cocktail, 227
half-moon, 227

oval, 227
quarter-moon, 227
schoolroom (classroom), 227
serpentine, 227
tuxedo, 227
Tablescape (tabletop), 236–242
Tableware, 239, 240
Take-out sales, 2, 5
TAM (Techniques of Alcohol Management) course, 207
Tax:
cabaret, 162
consumption, 19, 53, 162, 163, 187
credit, 328, 370
entertainment, 19, 162
exempt client, 5, 19, 351
exemption certificate, 19
-free number, 351
luxury, 162, 192
Medicare, 337
payroll, *see* Employee, benefits, required
privilege, 192
room, 318
sales, 19, 162
Social Security, 165, 337
Teardown procedures, *see* Function, room, teardown
Technical skill, 15–16, 324
Technology, 106
Telephone:
recording, 97
solicitation, 84, 85
Tent, 140, 179, 246, 247
clear span, 247
modular, 247
seating, 248
Testimonial (letter), 48, 69, 78, 82, 83, 94
Theft, 355
Theme:
party, 104, 110–119, 176, 414
refreshment break, 117–119
The Professional Caterer, 391
The Wall Street Journal, 167
Third-party liability, *see* Liability, third-party
Ticket:
exchange, 414
taker, 19
number needed, 266
Tickler file, *see* Tracer file
Time records, 369
Time/temperature problem, 285, 286
Timing, *see* Event, timing
Tip, 19, 162–165, 337, 414
pooling, 164, 165
Tobasco Sauce, 159
Tour:
property, *see* Property, tour

Tour (*Continued*)
  and travel, 335
Tracer file, 47, 49–50, 65, 85
Trade:
  -out arrangement, 367
  puffery, 159, 160
Trading area, 47
  primary, 47
  secondary, 47
Training, 99, 281, 327–328, 329,
     331–337, 391
  cross-, 265
  director, 391
  report, 336
  session, 33
Transparency, 300
  electronic, 303
Transportation, *see* Ground transportation
TransUnion, 86
Travel agency, 39, 316
  combined with meeting planner, 316
Traveling exhibition, 34
Tray:
  jack, 218, 220, 239
  test, 330
Truss, 414
Truth-in-menu guidelines, 158–162
TRW, 86
Twin entrée, *see* Menu, dualing
Typeface, *see* Font

Uncontrollable act, 22
Underliner, 414
Underwriter's Laboratory (UL), 281
Unemployment compensation, 327, 337
Union:
  call, 414

hiring hall, 326
minimums, 270, 276–277
regulations (contract), 3, 25, 64, 177,
     261, 263, 264, 265, 267, 270,
     276, 277, 294, 309, 324, 338,
     371, 392
USA Hosts, 317
U.S.A. Today, 167
United States Department of Agriculture
    (USDA), 159
U.S. Open Championship, 40
University, 326–327
University of Nevada, Las Vegas, 76
Upgrade, 57, 103, 104
Up$elling, 42, 57, 82, 88, 100, 103–104,
     111, 116, 120, 121, 124, 169,
     370

Vacuum-packed, 257
Valet, 336, 396
Value, 27, 31, 41, 54, 55, 57, 91, 94, 95,
     102–103, 322, 341, 353, 380,
     396, 398
Variance, *see* Cost, variance
Vegan, 145. *See also* Vegetarianism
Vegetarianism, 145
Vendor, 292
VHS player, 303
Video:
  conference, 309
  playback unit, 304
  projection system, 303–304
  projector, 306
  tape, 78, 98, 300, 306
  tape player, 304
  tape recorder, 302
  wall, 307

Voice mail, 81, 97
Volume discount, *see* Discount, volume
Volunteer group, 329
Votive container, 283

Walk-in business, 80, 84, 86, 105
Walk and talks, 171
Wall treatment, 242
Waste, 373
Web site, 75–77, 78, 376
Wedding, 34–35, 42, 74, 78, 119–138
  brochure, 122–123
  checklist, 133–138, 420–423
  consultant, 124, 125
  package (plan), 124, 127–132
  planner, 35
Well brand, 185, 188, 256, 257,
    414
Whispering Peak, 198
Wine, 184, 198
  list, 153
  paired with food, 153, 197
  steward, *see* Sommelier
Wireless remote, 306
Work (repair):
  order, 387
  requisition, 387, 390
  schedule, 263, 267, 275–277, 367
    fixed, 275, 369
    variable, 275, 369
  shop, 414
Workers compensation, 281, 328, 337,
    370, 373

Yield:
  edible, 250
  management, 64